The Complete Scrapbook

GENERAL HOSPITAL

The Complete Scrapbook

BY GARY WARNER

GPG

GENERAL PUBLISHING GROUP
Los Angeles

Publisher: W. Quay Hays
Editor: Peter Hoffman
Contributing Editor: Murray Fisher
Art Director: Nadeen Torio
Assistant Art Director: Wesla Weller
Color and Pre-Press Director: Gaston Moraga
Production Assistants: Tom Archibeque, Alan Peak, Michael Lira, Lindsay Murai

Co-Writers: Melissa McNeill, Phil Seldis
Research Coordinator (NY): Donna Hornak
Research Coordinator (LA): David Sperber
Research Consultant: Robert L. Schork
Very special thanks to Dawna Kaufman
Jacket design: The Spier Group

For information:
General Publishing Group, Inc.
2701 Ocean Park Boulevard
Santa Monica, CA 90405

Library of Congress Cataloging-in-Publication Data

Warner, Gary, 1957–
    General Hospital : the complete scrapbook / by Gary Warner.
        p.   cm.
    Includes index.
    ISBN 1-881649-40-7
    1. General Hospital (Television program)   I. Title.
    PN1992.77.G462W37   1995
    791.45'72–dc20   95-45771
                                                                              CIP

Printed in the USA
10 9 8 7 6 5 4 3 2 1

General Publishing Group

TABLE OF CONTENTS

INTRODUCTION

*V*ery few television viewers in the year 1963 could have predicted that a daytime serial entitled *General Hospital* would become the tremendous success it has been during the past thirty-three years.

After all, the ABC Network had been struggling for years to develop and televise a daytime soap, one which the viewing public could have a love affair with and cling to year after year after year.

That struggle finally ended when the highly respected and talented writing couple, Frank and Doris Hursley, delivered a pilot script to ABC second to none. It was the sort of script that when submitted to me to test for the role of Dr. Steve Hardy, sent my pulse racing. I, myself, had always been a soap fan, and now came the opportunity to star in one!

It was not one of my accustomed roles. It was not the part of a gangster, not the part of a cop, not the part of a cowboy; it was a part close to my heart, the part of a down-to-earth doctor who cared deeply, not only for his patients, but for his fellowman as well.

Whomsoever had the opportunity to view that initial *General Hospital* episode on April 1, 1963, will most certainly attest to how well-produced it was, how well-performed it was and how well-received it was.

The magic that captured my heart way back then went on to capture the hearts of three generations of viewers. And today, 8,560 episodes later, amidst new faces, new producers, new writers and a whole new legion of fans, the magic continues.

—John Beradino

JOHN BERADINO

ACKNOWLEDGMENTS

*H*ow is it possible to capture 8300 episodes of superb daytime drama in 200+ pages? With a lot of help, that's how! I salute the multitude of professionals who contributed their time and talent to this monumental project, not the least my co-writers Melissa McNeill and Phil Seldis, and my researchers, Donna Hornak, David Sperber and Robert L. Schork. They toiled under incredible pressure to make this book a reality. I am forever indebted to these talented colleagues.

I must record my admiration for Executive Producer Wendy Riche's entire production staff at *General Hospital,* especially Associate Producer Marty Vagts and Coordinating Producer Jerry Balme. Writers Assistant Davis Goldschmid and Script Continuity person Elizabeth Korte were incredible resources for me. (Who else but Davis knows—or cares—that Grant Putnam was patient #402?) George Doty IV, Fritz Curtis, Susan Brandes, Nate Fissell, Marc Dabrusin, Debbi Genovese, Dania Guthrie, Brooke Eaton, Hilda Recio, Chris Magarian, Kathy Wetherell, Chris Mullen, Michelle Val Jean, Mark Teschner, Lisa Snedeker, Gwen Hillier all contributed immeasurably to the making of this tome. Wendy, your fifth-floor ensemble is an incredibly gifted group.

A 21-gun salute to ABC's sharp-shooting Photography Department, led by Peter Murray and Jill Yager. Thanks must also go to Craig Sjodin, Ann Ferrell, Maria Melin and freelancer Jim Warren. I could never have completed this project without Ann Limongello's unflagging assistance in organizing the thousands of photographs that have been snapped on the set of GH over the past 32 years.

I wish to recognize the ABC Daytime brass—Pat Fili-Krushel, Cody Dalton, Regina DiMartino, Barbara Bloom, Nina Silvestri and Angela Shapiro for their key roles in the creation of this book. Special mention is due to Senior Vice-President Maxine Levinson for her guidance and enthusiastic encouragement over the past eight years. I offer kudos for the contributions of Esther Swan, Jane Elliot, Stuart Damon, Joanne Berg, Marilyn Orrico, Timothy Lund, Sallie Schoneboom, Sheryl Fuchs, Galen Gary, Jennifer Rosen, Jon Merdin, Mickey Dwyer-Dobbin, Stacy Balter and GH's extremely knowledgeable publicist Scott Barton.

Thanks to General Publishing Group, led by Quay Hays, for masterminding the assembly of my pages with taste and skill. Editors Peter Hoffman and Murray Fisher, as well as Dana Stibor, Sharon Lynn Hays and Joni Solomon deserve a wealth of praise.

On a personal note, thanks to my brother, Dr. D. Michael Warner, for turning me on to his favorite soap thirty years ago. And to the late Emily McLaughlin, whose tender portrayal of Nurse Jessie Brewer captured a nine-year-old boy's heart.

Finally, on behalf of the millions of GH viewers, I express my gratitude to the innovative team of the late writers Frank and Doris Hursley, and Executive Producer Selig J. Seligman for having the courage and insight to bring GH to life back in 1963. And to Wendy Riche for keeping the tradition of excellence alive today.

General Hospital's original opening title sequence.

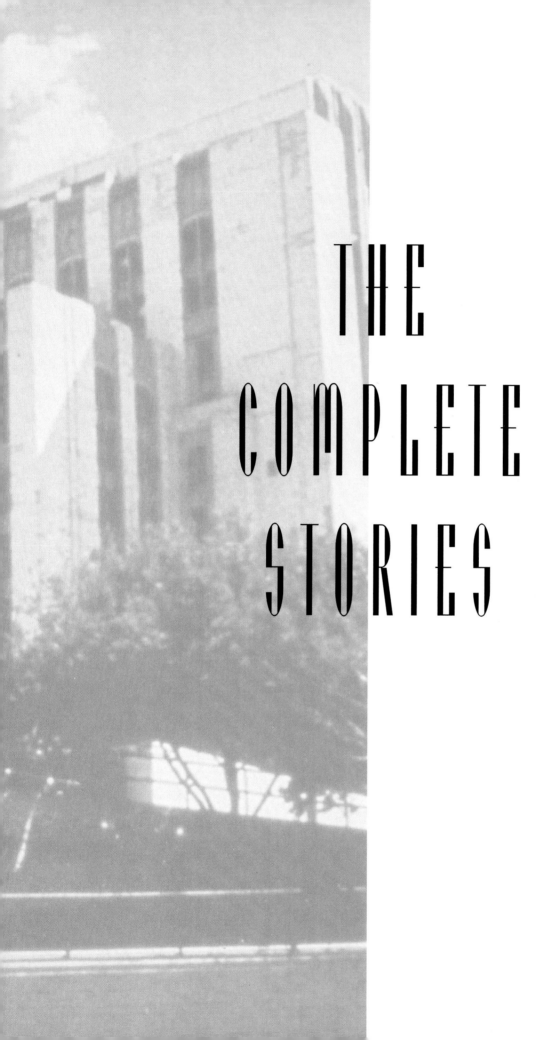

THE
COMPLETE
STORIES

Anyone who knew Dr. Steve Hardy was convinced that dedication was his middle name. Dr. Hardy spent his days, nights and even weekends on the seventh floor of General Hospital. When he wasn't making rounds, Steve Hardy tended to his administrative duties as Chief of the hospital's Internal Medicine Department. Late into the night, he would bury himself in the mounds of paperwork that piled up on his desk in Room 714, the cubbyhole of an office located just to the right of the seventh floor nurses' station. Busy as he was, Steve would often steal a moment out of his busy schedule to grab a cup of coffee in the medicine room with his friend and confidante, nurse Jessie Brewer, but rarely did he spend any time at home in his tiny, bare apartment. Steve spent even less time with his fiancée, Peggy Mercer, who was growing increasingly impatient with her man.

"Steve, why is it always you?" she demanded to know after yet another last minute cancellation because of a sick patient who needed attention.

"Peg, it's my job. I prescribed the treatment and if it's not working out, I have to find out what the reason is."

"Can't someone else find out?"

"I'm sorry Peg. Look, things will be a lot different after we're married."

"Your patients will always come first, won't they?" answered Peg, who came to realize what everyone at General Hospital already knew—Dr. Steve Hardy was married to medicine.

Born to missionary parents—both doctors—Steven Hardy was raised in China. From the time he first put his parents' stethoscopes to his ears, Steve knew he wanted to follow in their footsteps and dedicate his life to the practice of medicine.

That decision cost Steve his relationship with Peggy in the fall of 1963, when she left him for a "more exciting" man, writer Roy Lansing. A subsequent romance with socialite Priscilla Longworth ended abruptly in 1964. Caught up in his work,

As Chief of the Internal Medicine Department, Dr. Steve Hardy devoted his every waking moment to healing the ills of the patients on General Hospital's seventh floor. With him every step of the way was nurse Jessie Brewer. Steve and Jessie were colleagues, confidantes, and dear friends for decades.

When *General Hospital* began, Steve was engaged to Peggy Mercer. Their relationship suffered when a frustrated Peggy came to realize that Steve was far more devoted to his job than he was to her.

Steve barely took notice of his lagging love life. He placed greater importance on his friendships, especially the close personal bond he shared with nurse Jessie Brewer, whose turbulent marriage to intern Phil Brewer gave them both plenty to talk about. The beautiful and soulful nurse had been pursued by nearly every man in town. And it came as quite a shock to her suitors—and her fellow staff members—when Jessie married the bold and brash Dr. Brewer, who was seven years her junior.

Young and eager to practice medicine, Dr. Phil Brewer got into hot water in the spring of 1963 when he performed a lifesaving hysterectomy on a General Hospital patient, Janet Fleming. The surgery went smoothly; however, in his haste, Dr. Brewer had failed to obtain written consent from the patient or her husband, Fred Fleming. His carelessness quickly came back to haunt him when Mr. and Mrs. Fleming filed malpractice charges against Phil, who faced the end of his medical career. A serious rift developed in the Brewer marriage when Jessie sympathized with Janet Fleming's plight. Like Janet, Jessie Brewer had a strong maternal instinct. She desperately wanted children, but had chosen to wait until Phil had completed his internship and residency. As Phil waited for the medical board to decide his fate, the gap widened in the Brewer marriage. Finally, the tension between the Brewers exploded in a hail of painful accusations.

"In a good marriage, a husband and a wife are supposed to pull together in bad times," Jessie told her husband. "We always pull in opposite directions."

"Why can't you stop being a mother and let me fight my own battles?" Phil shouted back. The argument ensued, and an age-old problem resurfaced.

"I'm sorry I'm not as young and pretty as Cynthia," cried Jessie.

Jessie had good reason to be jealous of Phil's "friendship" with Cynthia Allison. She was indeed pretty—and much younger than Jessie. Phil had developed an easy rapport with Cynthia, an old college friend who was now a teacher at a nearby nursery school. The Brewers often double-dated with Cynthia and her fiancé, Dr. Ken Martin, who worked at General Hospital. Throughout Phil's crisis with the medical board, he turned to Cynthia, not Jessie, for compassion and comfort. Occasionally, the two "friends" would steal away

Time and again, Jessie forgave her much-younger and always philandering husband, Phil Brewer. Often, Jessie ignored the obvious and tried to see the good in Phil, whose flirtatious ways and affairs were the talk of the seventh floor.

for afternoons at the beach. Just to talk, at first. Eventually, Phil and Cynthia began a torrid affair.

Jessie was finally able to use her considerable influence with Janet Fleming to get her to drop the charges against Phil. Thanks to his dutiful wife, Phil's medical future was secure. Still, their marital squabbles continued as Jessie applied subtle pressures upon Phil to work harder to fulfill his dream of becoming Chief Resident at General Hospital. As the months passed, Phil's secret affair with Cynthia heated up. Realizing she loved Phil, a tormented Cynthia broke her engagement to Ken and convinced Phil to break up with Jessie.

Jessie prepared for the worst when Phil, on rounds at the hospital, asked to speak with her privately later that night at home. When Phil arrived at their tiny apartment, he wasted no time in informing Jessie that their marriage was over.

"The fact is, I love Cynthia and she loves me."

"This isn't some kind of bad joke, is it Phil?"

"No, Jess. I know I sound like an ungrateful skunk after all the things you've done for me, but I can't deny my feelings any longer. I love Cynthia."

A despondent Jessie filed for divorce, then discovered a shocking truth of her own. She was pregnant with Phil's child! Leaning on her dear friend, Steve Hardy, Jessie insisted that she did not want Phil to know of her delicate condition.

"I don't want him back out of a sense of duty," she confided in Steve, who promised not to tell Phil. But eavesdropping nurse Lucille March never made such a pledge! As subtle as a truck, Lucille blabbed Jessie's secret to Phil, who promptly had a change of heart. With a child on the way, he wanted to save his marriage and quickly took action to halt the divorce proceedings. He broke the news to a heartbroken Cynthia, who, on the rebound, married the man she had dumped months earlier, Dr. Ken Martin.

For "the baby's sake," Phil tried to convince Jessie to take him back. All he had to do was flash that endearing smile, and Jessie was hooked. Despite Phil's foibles, Jessie couldn't deny the love she felt for this handsome young man.

Jessie and Phil's tentative marriage didn't last long. The union shattered on July 24, 1964, when Jessie miscarried their baby.

"The only reason for my marriage is gone," Jessie cried to Steve, who tried in vain to persuade her not to give up the hope of having another child. Clearly, Jessie knew her husband better than Steve did. When Phil soon returned to his philandering ways, Jessie went through with her original plan to divorce. The Brewer marriage was over.

As the painful memories of her marriage to Phil subsided, Jessie began to go out on tentative dates with her lawyer, Lee Baldwin. A lifelong bachelor and recovering alcoholic, Lee was a fixture on the seventh floor of General Hospital, where he volunteered as an addiction counselor. It was apparent to everyone that he had deep feelings for Jessie Brewer. But Lee realized that they had to take things slowly, because Jessie needed time to get Phil out of her system. And that would prove difficult because, despite the dissolution of their marriage, there was no way that Jessie could avoid seeing her estranged husband. Phil and Jessie's paths continued to cross on a daily basis on the seventh floor of General Hospital. They were not through with each other—not by a long shot!

Patients came and went from General Hospital's seventh floor, but few had more impact on Steve and Jessie than teenager Angie Costello, a victim of a terrible car accident. The daughter of a widowed grocer, sweet Angie had everything to live for—until the night she went for a late night drive with her boyfriend, Eddie Weeks. It was a fateful mistake. Eddie had been drinking. When his car crashed, Angie's head struck the windshield. She was in bad shape. Skillful surgeons worked hours in the OR to stitch Angie's angelic face back together. Now, wrapped in a mummy-like mask of bandages, she faced an uncertain future. Despondent, Angie contemplated suicide.

"I don't want anybody to see my face. I don't even want to see it myself. Why don't you just leave the bandages on it?" she cried to her doctor, Steve Hardy.

"Angie, you can't hide behind these bandages forever. You'll have to get used to your face, however it looks. Come back into the world again, live again."

"Who wants to be alive with a face like this, Dr. Hardy? I wish I were dead!"

Jessie and Steve gently doled out much more than just professional care to their new patient. Jessie Brewer spent her off-hours sitting by Angie's bedside, reassuring her in her time of need. In many ways, Jessie served as the mother

GREAT MOMENTS

"Look at me! I wish I was dead! What would Eddie want from a girl like me?" Distraught and suicidal, teenager Angie Costello became General Hospital's very first patient when her face was severely lacerated in an auto accident caused by her boyfriend Eddie's drunken driving.

that Angie never had. With Jessie and Steve's calming influence, and months of skin grafts, Angie made a full recovery. Still, the pained girl faced another crisis when she was called to testify at the drunk driving trial of her boyfriend, Eddie.

"You've got to lie for me," Eddie pleaded. "You're my only hope, Angie."

Angie refused to look at him. She knew that Eddie had been guzzling beer and "hard liquor" on that wild and carefree night that ended in tragedy. Angie's father Mike, an honorable man, urged her to tell the truth in court. Eddie's crusty dad, Al Weeks, begged the girl not to betray his son. On the stand, the District Attorney cornered Angie on the crucial question as to whether Eddie had been drinking before they got into the car. Her evasions were desperate and ingenious, but the futility of her quest to protect Eddie became ever more evident as the D.A. hammered away. Finally, Angie cracked, as much from the pressure of the D.A.'s questions as the pleading, accusing eyes of her father who had repeatedly urged her to tell the truth.

"All right, yes! Eddie was drinking. But he just had a few beers!" Angie's collapse was not a complete confession, but it was enough to damage Eddie's case and wreck their relationship. Sentenced to probation, Eddie bitterly rejected his young love. During the summer of 1964, they tried to pick up the pieces of their shattered love, but despite their efforts to bring back the magic, Eddie and Angie were through.

Angie was overcome with emotion when she discovered that Eddie had "pinned" his new girlfriend, Dorothy Bradley.

"Will you get married?" Angie nervously asked Eddie upon his surprise visit to the "Isle of Capri," Mike Costello's newly opened pizzeria.

"Oh, that's a long way in the future," he brazenly responded. Jessie Brewer couldn't help but notice Angie's distress over what Eddie had told her. Jessie suspected that Angie was harboring a secret and asked her a point blank question.

"Are you going to have a baby, Angie?"

"I don't know, Jessie. But Eddie and I did sleep together."

Jessie arranged for her to be examined by GH's resident gynecologist, Dr. John Prentice. The results were as expected: Angie was pregnant. Throughout this trying time, Jessie calmed and comforted the distraught teenager, privately wish-

"Oh, Audrey, when will you wake up?" Lucille March constantly badgered her younger sister Audrey to mend her wild ways and settle down with Steve Hardy.

ing that it was she who was having the baby instead of Angie. Jessie stayed right by Angie's side, abiding by her decision to give the baby boy up for adoption to Janet Fleming, the same woman who had nearly destroyed Phil Brewer's career after he had performed a hysterectomy on her.

Two years after their tragic auto accident, Angie and Eddie found their way back to each other. Marrying at a Justice of the Peace, the kids decided that they wanted their baby back. When Janet Fleming refused to give up "her child," Angie and Eddie resorted to drastic measures—and kidnaped the baby! On the run, the desperate young parents settled into a dingy, one-room apartment in Chicago, and enjoyed several weeks of familial bliss before being apprehended. Ably defended by attorney Lee Baldwin, Angie and Eddie were placed on probation and forced to return their baby to the Flemings. Thanks to the concerned efforts of caring professionals like Steve, Jessie and Lee, the young married couple looked forward to a bright and promising future—together at last.

Full of eagerness and a zest for life, Audrey March arrived at General Hospital on February 21, 1964 to visit her much-older sister Lucille, senior nurse on the seventh floor. Dr. Hardy happened to be passing by the nurse's station when he caught sight of the pretty blonde stewardess, still dressed in her perfectly pressed blue uniform. The chemistry was instant and unmistakable.

As a high-flying stewardess, Audrey had jetted around the world. It was the perfect job for the fun-loving young woman. She often exasperated Lucille, who frowned upon her sister's wild ways. In the early days of transcontinental jet travel, airlines staffed their flights with nurses—and, like her older sister, Audrey was a registered nurse.

But much to Lucille's chagrin, Audrey became a flight attendant on the day she received her nurses' cap.

Intrigued by the handsome Dr. Hardy, Audrey opted to stay in town for a while and when the opportunity to serve as a private duty nurse came up, she grabbed it. Her first patient was Randy Washburn, a well-known junior executive engineer suffering from malaria. At the same time, the blond beauty began seeing Dr. Hardy, who was eager and less restrained around Audrey than he had ever been with any of his many "dates."

In 1964, Audrey March became private duty nurse for hotshot junior executive Randy Washburn, who was being treated by Dr. Phil Brewer for malaria. Audrey found Randy "exciting" and nearly married him. Instead, she chose Dr. Steve Hardy.

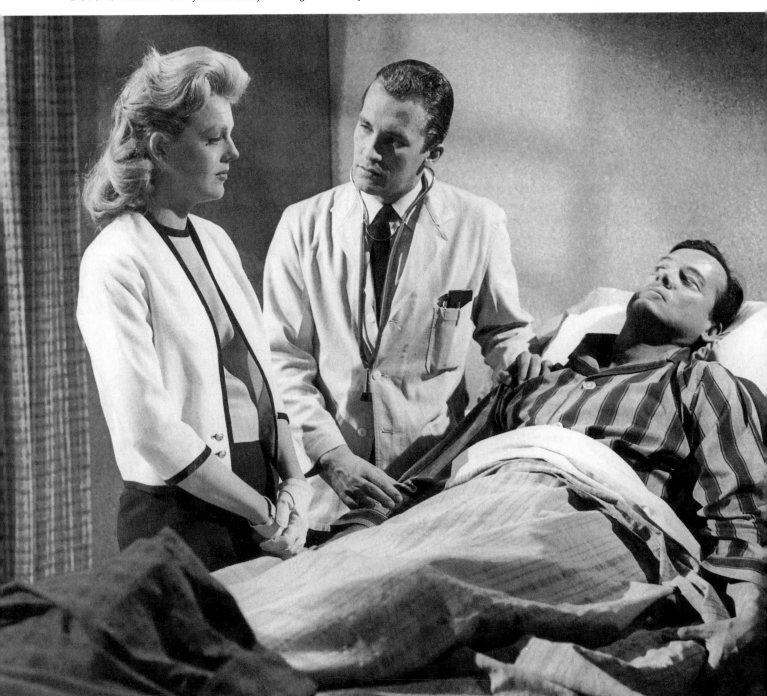

Still, Randy—not Steve—was the kind of man Audrey March usually found exciting. He was worldly and fun—just like her. As he recovered from his illness, Randy took a liking to Audrey, but she found herself increasingly drawn to Steve. After years of fun and frolicking, Audrey yearned for a husband and a child. She was intrigued by the strong, silent Dr. Hardy.

"Here you are, an attractive man, and you've never been married. You spend your whole life working in a hospital," Audrey told Steve over martinis during their first date.

"I'm just a darn square, is that it?"

"Oh, I don't know. I can't believe you are just a square, Dr. Hardy. I bet behind that stern exterior and all those professional attitudes, there is a real, living, exciting human being—a man, not just a doctor."

"Audrey, you make me feel like I'm missing out on something. I've never met anyone like you before."

Audrey had shaken up the staid Steve Hardy. They fell in love and cautiously planned to marry, but when it came to setting the wedding date, Steve dragged his feet. Audrey became convinced that Steve loved his job much more than he loved her. She convinced herself that she could never be the kind of woman Steve wanted and needed. Meanwhile, Randy Washburn tantalized Audrey with jewelry, exotic vacations—and a tempting

Like his brother Lee, cardiologist Tom Baldwin lost his heart to Jessie, who was engaged to marry Dr. John Prentice. When Prentice died under mysterious circumstances, Tom and Jessie were accused of his murder.

offer to become his wife. Audrey was caught in the middle—should she marry the man with the exciting lifestyle or the doctor who was infinitely dedicated to his job?

"I don't consider myself good enough for you, Steve," Audrey told her fiancé, believing she was letting him off the hook. "The kind of woman you ought to marry is someone like Jessie. I've seen the two of you together and I think she would be absolutely the ideal woman for you."

Steve was stunned when Audrey went on to break their engagement. Then, he was doubly astonished when she accepted Randy's enticing offer to marry him in the Philippines. However, just before departing, Audrey collapsed. The diagnosis was grim. Audrey was suffering from lymphoma. Fortunately, radiation treatment arrested the spread of the disease. Steve stood by Audrey's side throughout the ordeal while Randy was…. nowhere to be found!

Nearly losing Audrey convinced Steve that he couldn't bear to be apart from the woman he loved. At Jessie and Lucille's urging, Steve summoned up the courage to once again ask Audrey to marry him. Overwhelmed with joy, Audrey accepted his proposal. In early 1965, Steve and Audrey became man and wife. After years of partying, Audrey couldn't wait to settle down and have children. However, after two years of trying, she was still unable to conceive a child. Believing Steve to be sterile, Audrey took action. Not wanting to hurt his feelings, she resorted to lies and deceit to solve her problems. Telling her husband she was going to attend a reunion of stewardesses in San Francisco, Audrey secretly prepared to undergo a procedure of artificial insemination. Her plan ran aground temporarily when she learned that she must first have the written consent of her husband. Determined to go through with the procedure, Audrey forged Steve's signature and underwent the insemination. It worked. She became pregnant. But guilt-ridden by her elaborate deception, she finally told Steve what she had done. Betrayed and bitter, he moved out.

"I feel like a failure as a man," he confided in Jessie. Soon, tests revealed that Steve was not sterile after all! That meant that Audrey's unborn baby might be his! The Hardys reconciled and celebrated with a second honeymoon in Hot Springs. However, on their way home, tragedy struck when

WHODUNIT

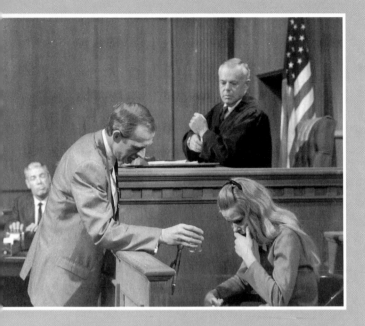

Who killed Jessie Brewer's husband, Dr. John Prentice? Was it foul play or suicide? Three weeks after marrying Jessie, Dr. Prentice died suddenly from a lethal mixture of drugs. Jessie and Dr. Tom Baldwin were charged with the crime, based on the allegations of Dr. Prentice's jealous daughter Polly who did everything in her power to fuel District Attorney Chase Murdoch's suspicion that they conspired to kill her father. In a stunning turn of events, Polly finally broke down on the stand and confessed that she had given her father the pills which he took to end his own life.

they were involved in a horrifying car crash—just a few miles from General Hospital. Steve emerged from the accident unscathed, but Audrey was brought to the hospital in an ambulance. She survived, but her unborn baby was not so fortunate.

"Our baby is dead," Steve informed Audrey when she awoke in her hospital room. Ever the doctor trained in proper bedside manner, Steve carefully sidestepped the rest of the facts: Audrey may never be able to have another child. Devastated by her loss, Audrey filed for divorce from Steve and left for Vietnam to aid orphaned children. Once again, Steve Hardy was alone. In

typical fashion, he poured every ounce of his energies into his duties at General Hospital. But he would never forget Audrey. Not ever.

Phil Brewer tried to make Jessie forget his indiscretions, but the pain she felt over Phil's illicit romance with Cynthia was too deep. When Jessie filed for divorce, he drowned his sorrows with liquor, then wildly headed straight to Jessie's apartment to win her back—the only way he knew how.

"Don't do this, Phil," cried Jessie, tears gathering in her eyes.

"You love me, Jess. I know you do. Let me prove it to you," he murmured, physically overwhelming her.

Later that night, Phil realized the enormity of what he had done to Jessie. After writing her a letter of apology, he quickly left town. Jessie became pregnant, and once again kept her delicate condition a secret from Phil. She confided in Steve, Lucille and Lee Baldwin, whose long-lingering love for Jessie surfaced soon after Phil's departure. Ever gallant, Lee offered to marry Jessie in order to give the baby a name. First they had to wait for Jessie and Phil's divorce decree to become final. On that day, Jessie Brewer would become Mrs. Lee Baldwin. As the big day approached, Lee and a very pregnant Jessie planned their wedding. However, their plans changed drastically when nosy nurse Lucille March spilled the beans about Jessie's pregnancy to Phil, who rushed back to town.

"I will never let Lee Baldwin marry you and raise my baby," said Phil to Jessie, pleading for her to wait one month to prove his renewed devotion. Despite her vow not to let Phil get to her, it was apparent to Jessie's closest friends that she still had a great residue of loving feelings for Phil that she had to face. Shaken by Phil's return, Jessie worried that if she broke up with Lee, his devastation would be so great that he would begin drinking again. She just couldn't do that to such a nice man! She vowed to go through with the marriage. But on the eve of their wedding, Jessie unexpectedly went into labor. Phil was delighted—after all, Jessie's divorce was not yet final. The baby would be born with his name! Lee was miserable—but strong. His carefully laid plans collapsed because he had not married Jessie in time to legitimize her child.

Jessie gave birth to a beautiful daughter, Nancy Brewer. Though Lee loved Jessie, he gallantly released her from the "burden" of their engagement.

A crisis intervened before Jessie could make a decision about her marital future. Something was terribly wrong with baby Nancy! Doctors broke the news to Jessie and Phil that their baby suffered from a life-threatening heart ailment. Phil, a skilled cardiologist, was anguished by the realization that he could do nothing to save the life of his precious child. Nancy Brewer died on July 27, 1966 leaving Jessie and Phil—and their hopes for reconciliation—shattered. Finally, after years of misery, Jessie realized that she had to get Phil Brewer out of her life once and for all! When she divorced him, Phil left town in shame, taking a new job in San Francisco.

Lee Baldwin was heartened by the arrival of a new nurse at GH in the summer of 1966. She was Meg Bentley, a widow with a young son Scotty and a teenage stepdaughter Brooke at home. Scotty was a darling child. But Brooke deeply resented Meg, believing that Meg had "stolen" the affections of her late father. Now, at 17, she had grown hostile, making Meg's life miserable at every turn. No doubt—Brooke Bentley was a wild child!

"We speak the same language," Lee happily informed Steve Hardy about his growing fondness for Meg. They became great friends and confidantes, but Meg and Lee's relationship was strictly platonic because she was engaged to another man—Dr. Noel Clinton. The trusty nurse was in for a huge shock, however, on the eve of her wedding, when Noel made a stunning announcement.

"I'm deeply sorry to have to tell you this, Meg, but I can't marry you. I'm in love with Brooke," admitted Noel. Meg absorbed the startling news that her fiancé was having an affair with her stepdaughter. Yes, she had suspected all along that Brooke had a crush on Noel, but not for a moment did Meg surmise that Noel had returned Brooke's feelings. The morning after his confession, Noel left town with young Brooke—and they soon became man and wife.

In her grief, Meg turned to Lee, who was ready to help her through this terrible life crisis. This was also a difficult period of adjustment for young

Dr. Steve Hardy asked kidney specialist Dr. Tracy Adams to join his staff in 1968. When the hospital's executive committee proposed to veto his recommendation to appoint the black female doctor, Steve threatened to resign. He got his way when the board backed down. Dr. Adams became a valued member of the G H staff.

In General Hospital's first sensational murder trial, Lee Baldwin defended Jessie against charges that she killed her husband, Dr. John Prentice. Lee lost the case and Jessie was sent to jail, but an eleventh hour confession by her step-daughter Polly set her free.

Scotty Bentley. Overnight, he had lost his sister and the man he had hoped would become his father. Fortunately, Lee Baldwin became a surrogate father to the boy. Meg smiled with deep satisfaction every time she saw Scotty and Lee together. Late in 1966 she married Lee, who happily adopted Scotty. The Baldwins were a family!

After her divorce from Phil, Jessie resisted Audrey and Lucille's efforts to set her up on dates with a host of General Hospital's most eligible doctors. Instead, Jessie's affections were aroused by Dr. John Prentice, her longtime hospital colleague. Dr. Prentice, an obstetrician, had fallen critically ill early in 1967. Despite herculean efforts by his fellow doctors, the prognosis for John Prentice was

grim—his heart was giving out. And Jessie was right by his side throughout every phase of his illness. After years of putting up with Phil Brewer's shenanigans, Jessie found John Prentice a welcome relief. He doted on her. He made her feel like a beautiful woman worthy of the love of a good man. John Prentice was a good man. But he was a dying man.

Dr. Prentice's twenty-year-old daughter, Polly, resented her father's affection for Jessie. After all, she had always been "daddy's girl" and now there was someone else usurping her number one position. Her anger reached a pinnacle when John married Jessie, then informed Polly that he had made out a new will, giving everything to his new wife.

"Daddy, how could you?," cried Polly upon hearing the news. Dr. Prentice had carefully thought out his reasons for giving Jessie control of his entire estate.

"I love you, my dear Polly. However, I trust Jessie implicitly to take care of your needs."

Polly was appalled—not to mention bitter and vengeful! Just days later, John Prentice was dead. At first, doctors believed that he passed away from natural causes. However, Steve Hardy and the newly arrived Dr. Tom Baldwin (Lee's younger brother) soon learned from the pathologist's report that Dr. Prentice died from "the ingestion of quantities of barbiturates combined with alkaloids." Was it suicide or perhaps foul play? Polly Prentice did everything in her power to fuel District Attorney Chase Murdoch's suspicion that Jessie had killed her father. Polly also provided them with a possible reason for Jessie committing the heinous crime when she intimated that Jessie and Tom Baldwin (who had dumped Polly) were having an affair in the weeks before her father's untimely passing! After Lt. Todd, the chief investigator, determined that Jessie Prentice's fingerprints were on the bottle of the medication (Alkaloid X34) that killed her husband, she was charged with murder! Weeks later, Tom Baldwin was also charged as an accessory to the murder. Thanks to the deceitful Polly Prentice, two of General Hospital's most esteemed staff members were behind bars.

In court, Polly's damaging testimony sealed Jessie and Tom's fate. On April 8, 1968, the defendants stared into the blank faces of the jurors and

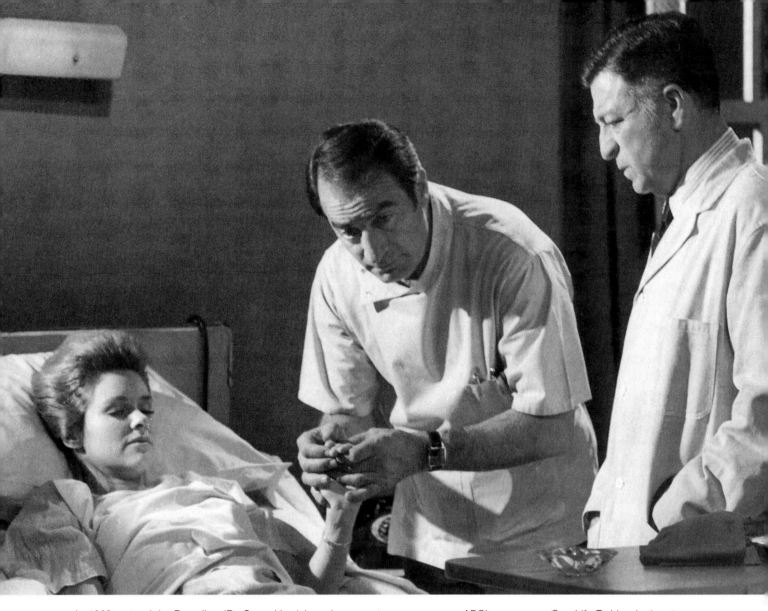

In 1969, actor John Beradino (Dr. Steve Hardy) made a guest appearance on ABC's new soap, *One Life To Live*. In the story, Dr. Hardy came to Llanview, PA at the request of his colleague, Dr. Jim Craig, to check on the medical condition of Meredith Lord, who suffered from a blood disease.

feared the worst. The foreman announced the verdict. "Guilty—in the first degree."

In the midst of these punishing days of misery, Dr. Phil Brewer returned to town, pledging to find the evidence to set his beloved Jessie free. Phil suspected that Dr. Prentice committed suicide and he tested his idea with Polly.

"My father would never do such a thing. Impossible!" she exclaimed. Hmmm....Polly's overreaction gave Phil further ideas! In exploring his theory, Phil contacted a pharmaceutical company and discovered that Dr. Prentice had been authorized to experiment with Alkaloid X34, the drug that killed him. In a heated confrontation, Phil wore down Polly's resistance, forcing her to reveal that her father had asked Polly to bring him the pills on the night he died. Polly's confession

set Jessie and Tom free. Ironically, their freedom was thanks to Phil Brewer's ace detective work.

Feeling sorry for Polly, Jessie arranged with Lee to give Polly her father's estate. Grateful for Phil's heroic efforts, Jessie stunned her friends when she announced that once again she was going to marry him.

"He's changed, Steve," Jessie informed a highly skeptical Dr. Hardy. "Phil assured me that he wants to settle down."

Was Jessie ever wrong! Within months of their remarriage, Phil was up to his old philandering ways—with none other than little Polly Prentice! Their affair was short-lived, and Phil grew disgusted with the spiteful girl. However, the damage had been done. Polly accused Phil of being the father of her child. Worse, she told the shocking secret to

The Complete Stories 1963-1970

Jessie! Desperate to abort her baby, Polly took an overdose of pills. Knowing something was wrong, Phil showed up at Polly's apartment, and seeing her condition, rushed her to General Hospital. Along the way, Phil's car crashed and Polly was killed. Jessie noticed that her wayward husband was not as sorry as he might be. The District Attorney took notice too and prepared to file charges against Dr. Phil Brewer. Near a breakdown, a distraught Phil wrote Jessie a note.

"I can't bear to destroy you, Jess. I will always love you. —Phil." With those words, Phil Brewer took flight—a fugitive from justice. Ironically, if Phil had stayed in town, he would have learned that murder charges against him had been dropped. More so, Polly's diary revealed that he was not the father of her unborn child after all!

Months later, in November of 1969, word reached Jessie that 93 people had been killed in a plane crash in South America. And a passenger listed as "P. Brewer" had been one of the victims. By now, a new doctor had joined the staff of General Hospital—and he took an immediate interest in the grief-stricken widow. He was Dr. Peter Taylor, a compassionate psychiatrist. Like Phil, Peter was strikingly handsome. Unlike Phil, he was sincere and honorable. Concerned about their image, Peter made it abundantly clear to his superiors that his involvement with Jessie Brewer was friendship, nothing more.

In the months after Phil's "death," Peter Taylor became Jessie's main source of strength. In time, their friendship turned to passion and they married. Far away, in Venezuela, a critically injured accident victim by the name of Harold Williamson lay immobile in a remote hospital. Harold Williamson was none other than Phil Brewer— alive—but not well at all!

Fresh from six months in Vietnam where she aided war orphans, Audrey returned to General Hospital not knowing what the future would hold. Audrey was certain of only one thing—she wanted to "start fresh." So, before returning to town, she detoured to Mexico to secure a divorce decree.

Arriving home to start her new job as a pediatrics nurse at General Hospital, Audrey found everyone and everything the same. Still, she experienced more than one pang of jealousy every time Steve Hardy chatted with a new girlfriend, hospital volunteer Denise Wilton. Determined to prove to herself that she was over Steve, Audrey married Dr. Tom Baldwin and soon became pregnant with his child. Their union was rife with tension because, almost immediately, Audrey realized that she had made a terrible mistake by marrying the surly and intolerant doctor. Disillusioned and carrying the child of a man she despised, Audrey sued Tom for divorce, then left town again.

Meg and Lee Baldwin's once-idyllic marriage began to come apart at the seams upon the arrival of Meg's old nursing school friend, Iris Fairchild. Having suffered through one failed romance after another, Iris began to drink heavily. Booze ruined her nursing career, and might have taken her life had it not been for Lee's intervention. A recovering alcoholic, Lee counseled Iris in her time of need, and gave her a job as his secretary. Meg grew increasingly jealous as Iris and Lee spent their days together in the office and their nights attending Alcoholics Anonymous meetings. Finally, Meg confronted Iris, accusing her of having an affair with Lee!

Stinging from Meg's attack, Iris offered to quit her secretarial post, but Lee would not allow her to bend to Meg's unfounded accusations. For a time, the Baldwins separated, but they reconciled when Lee donated his kidney to save Scotty's life. The crisis brought Lee and Meg back together.

In 1970, Meg received an unexpected telephone call from her stepdaughter, Brooke.

"Can I come home?" she sheepishly pleaded to Meg, who was stunned that Brooke would have the gall to even ask such a thing. After all, it had been four years since the then-teenage Brooke seduced and married Meg's fiancée, Noel Clinton. Now, that marriage was over. Meg dreaded Brooke's return but when the girl begged for forgiveness, Meg chose to give her another chance. With reservations, Meg agreed to let Brooke live with them.

Lee and Meg's marriage would once again be put to the test when Meg received devastating news about her own health. She was suffering from breast cancer. After undergoing a radical mastectomy, Meg could not shake a deep and unabating melancholy. And it certainly didn't help her situation to have sexy Brooke Clinton running around the house. Meg, overcome with jealousy and depression, suffered a nervous breakdown. Lee, devastated, was forced to institutionalize his wife.

The new decade brought a new corps of doctors and nurses to the forefront at *General Hospital.* Nurses Jane Harland and Sharon McGillis (who began her career at GH as a candy striper) displayed youthful exuberance as they cheerfully carried out their duties caring for the sick on General Hospital's seventh floor. Both were blonde, spirited and beautiful, but their respective men were less than stellar specimens of manhood. Jane was engaged and later married to an irresponsible louse by the name of Howie Dawson. Inherently lazy, Howie wanted a responsible desk job even less than he wanted children. He did his best to avoid both—even going as far as to undergo a vasectomy without telling Jane. Behind her back, Howie flirted with every "pretty thing" who crossed his path.

Pert and always upbeat, nurse Sharon McGillis was involved with an unlikely mate. Henry Pinkham was a tall, shy and awkward intern who rarely smiled, let alone spoke to his hospital colleagues. When he was especially nervous, Henry stuttered. And when pert and sassy Sharon kissed him in the medicine room, a thoroughly flustered Henry found himself unable to string two words together! Henry was born into a rich and snooty family, and he lived in fear of his domineering Uncle Henry. Dr. Pinkham

GREAT MOMENTS

"Oh my," exclaimed a delighted Lucille March when long-time beau Al Weeks presented her with a sparkling engagement ring. Al and Lucy's golden-years romance was a favorite of General Hospital *fans in the early 1970s.*

Henry and Sharon Pinkham were the hospital's original odd couple. She was a sassy and gregarious nurse. He was a shy and bumbling doctor. Somehow they found each other and fought their way through four stormy years of marriage.

knew that his uncle would not approve of his becoming involved with a woman until he became a full-fledged doctor. Only Steve Hardy knew that Henry and Sharon had secretly married!

The new crop of nurses lived in fear of brusque, no-nonsense senior nurse, Lucille March. Her screeching shouts of *"McGillis! What are you doing?"* sent shudders down Sharon's spine. Yes, Lucille was brusque, but anyone who really knew her understood that beneath her armor beat a heart of gold. One man who knew, but rarely saw, Lucille's softer side was widower Al Weeks, who had joined the hospital staff as custodian. Though she would never, ever admit it, Lucille adored good ol' Al! Eventually, they would decide to spend their golden years together as man and wife.

In February of 1971, Lucille was surprised when out of the blue, her sister Audrey returned to town—without her baby.

"My baby was born dead," a seemingly grief-stricken Audrey told Lucille and Steve. Still married to Tom, Audrey wasn't telling the truth. Her baby son, whom she called "Stevie," was very much alive—and living with a nanny, Peggy Nelson, in a seedy part of town. Audrey spun an elaborate web of lies to keep her loser-husband Tom Baldwin from contesting their divorce action. She was certain that Tom would never give her up if he knew about their son! According to her plan, Audrey would tell Steve that Mrs. Nelson's baby was a foster child—the son of her cousin. Eventually, Audrey and Steve would arrange to adopt the child. It was a brilliant scheme that might have succeeded had it not been for Mrs. Nelson's greed. When the elderly nanny learned of Audrey's plight, she began to use her leverage to get more and more money out of Audrey. It was blackmail! Over a period of months, Mrs. Nelson began to put the squeeze on Audrey. Finally, the avaricious old woman handed down an ultimatum.

"My dear, you must either agree to pay me $500 a month or I'll have to take a drastic measure."

Audrey knew exactly what Mrs. Nelson was implying—she would reveal Audrey's secret! In addition, she demanded that Audrey buy her a gun, claiming that she needed protection in her tough neighborhood.

On the night of September 24, 1971, Audrey returned to her apartment in an agitated state. In one arm, she carried a suitcase. In the other, she held her baby. Rushing into the bathroom, she took out a pistol and, in a moment of panic, hid it in the water tank of her toilet. Across town, Mrs. Nelson lay dead—the victim of a fatal gunshot wound! Did Audrey do it? Her secret revealed, all the evidence pointed to Audrey, who steadfastly maintained her innocence.

"I didn't do it, Steve. You must believe me!" Dr. Hardy truly believed that the woman he loved would never commit such a horrible crime. Throughout the ordeal, Steve was Audrey's rock. As always, he was solid, solemn and a voice of reason. Charged with the murder, Audrey nearly went to prison for life, until some late-breaking detective work unearthed the real culprit—Peggy Nelson's ex-husband, Arnold.

Audrey was set free, only to suffer a fate worse than prison—marriage to Tom. Given her myriad of lies and deceits, Audrey discovered that the only way to keep possession of her baby was to move back in with her hateful husband. Steve was destroyed when Audrey chose to forsake his love and return to Tom. At home with his new family, Tom Baldwin ruled the roost with an iron hand, hiring a tough babysitter, Florence Nelson, to care for his son, who was now known as Tommy. He also instructed Mrs. Nelson to keep an eye on Audrey's every move around the child. Ironically, it was Audrey who should have been watching Tom! One night, Audrey returned to her apartment, only to find the place strangely silent. Suddenly, it dawned on Audrey—Tom had kidnaped the baby! As Audrey collapsed in sobs, Tom and Mrs. Andrews drove off into the oncoming night.

Night after night, Audrey prayed for Tommy's safe return. Months after her baby disappeared, Audrey's prayers were answered when Mrs. Andrews reappeared with Tommy in her arms. She brought stunning news—Tom Baldwin had died of a heart attack in Mexico. Young Tommy's return came just in the nick of time, because the youngster was in desperate need of open-heart surgery. Steve Hardy called upon the brilliant heart surgeon, Dr. Jim Hobart, to perform Tommy's vital, lifesaving surgery. In no time at all, the boy was back on his feet—thanks to the renowned Dr. Hobart's skillfully heroic efforts in the operating room. Audrey was eternally grateful, and showed her appreciation by dating the eligible doctor. In rapid time, she married him, much to the consternation of Steve Hardy and Lucille, who were certain that Audrey had tied the knot with Jim out of gratitude, not love.

Tommy's surgery would be one of the last operations performed by Dr. Jim Hobart. His distinguished surgical career came to a screeching halt when Jim's left hand was irrevocably damaged in a terrible accident. Deeply depressed, Jim went on a self-destructive bender, which left him impotent and hopelessly drunk. Once again, Steve Hardy watched helplessly as his true love, Audrey, suffered through another tragic marriage.

On a brighter note, Lee Baldwin rejoiced at the news that Meg was to be released from the mental institution. Supposedly recovered from the mental breakdown, Meg now suffered from a severe case of hypertension. At General Hospital, a strikingly beautiful female doctor was assigned to Meg's case. Dr. Lesley Williams assumed Tom Baldwin's practice and immediately distinguished herself with her winning bedside manner. But an insanely jealous Meg began to suspect—wrongly—that Lesley was trying to work her way into her husband Lee's bed!

One day, the whole of Meg's deranged anger erupted and she lashed out at Lee. In the middle of

Assuming a new identity, a bearded Phil Brewer returned to town in 1970. Believing he was still a wanted man, he went to work as a dishwasher in a restaurant near General Hospital and moved in with waitress Diana Maynard.

the argument, Meg keeled over and died—the victim of a deadly stroke. Meg's death left Lee inconsolable, yet he remained strong enough to fight off his desire to take a drink. Fighting back tears, Lee knew he had to be strong—for Scotty.

Fully recovered from the injuries he sustained in a Venezuelan plane crash, Dr. Phil Brewer ducked back into the country. Still believing he was a wanted man, he grew a scraggly beard and used his assumed name, Harold Williamson. Taking a job as a dishwasher at a restaurant not far from General Hospital, Phil befriended a beautiful young waitress, Diana Maynard, who took a liking to the shy and quiet laborer. As the months passed, Phil pined away for Jessie, occasionally spying on her, but knowing he could never reenter her life. Meanwhile, Diana fell hopelessly in love with "Harold." They became lovers. When Diana accidentally stumbled upon Harold's real identity, she was torn by the realization that she could lose the man she loved. After all, like everyone in town, Diana knew that Dr. Phil Brewer had been cleared of the murder charges in the death of Polly Prentice.

For months, Diana agonized over keeping the news from Phil—until the day the secret blew up in her face. Searching through old newspapers in the local library, he discovered the shocking news all by himself. The joy of knowing he was a free man was tempered by the anger he felt toward Diana for keeping the news secret for so long.

"How could you do this to me?" he shouted

irately at Diana before rushing to his car, intent on seeing Jessie. Phil parked in front of the Taylor house, waiting for Jessie to come home. Then he saw her—walking arm in arm with her husband, Peter. Lurking in the shadows, Phil was pained to see how happy and amorous they were. Tortured, he floored the gas pedal and roared off. Driving blindly into the night, Phil crashed his car. Critically wounded with severe head injuries, "Harold Williamson" was rushed to the emergency room at General Hospital.

With his head wrapped in bandages, Phil was moved to the ICU. Diana panicked when Jessie made her way into his room. To Diana's relief, Jessie didn't recognize the patient! While waiting for him to regain consciousness, Diana made a stunning discovery—she was pregnant with his child. Now more than ever, she needed him! And he needed a miracle to make it through delicate brain surgery. For a few touch-and-go moments, it appeared that he would die, but amazingly, the patient lived. Slowly, his bandages were removed. One day, Jessie walked into the room, took a long look into the piercing blue eyes of the man she'd come to know as Harold Williamson, and stopped dead in her tracks.

"Oh my God, Phil!" she exclaimed, before passing out! Upon regaining her wits, Jessie absorbed the fact that her husband was alive and her marriage to Dr. Peter Taylor was invalid. In an even more stunning decision, Jessie and Phil reconciled yet again! Left out in the cold, Peter Taylor and

The Complete Stories 1970-1975

Diana Maynard grew close as they commiserated in their shared grief. When Diana confided the news of her pregnancy with Peter, he nobly asked her to become his wife in order to "give the baby a name."

This time, Phil and Jessie's reconciliation was shorter than ever! After a decade of strife, deception and lies, they simply could not bring back the old magic. Making matters worse, Phil had been rendered impotent as a result of his near-fatal auto accident. The final blow to the Brewer marriage came when Phil discovered that Diana was pregnant with his child. Leaving Jessie, Phil hoped to become a family with Diana and his soon-to-be-born baby, but he was too late.

"I love Peter now," Diana declared to Phil—and she meant every word of her short but precise statement. Soon after, Diana gave birth to Phil Brewer's son, and together with her new husband Peter, she picked out a name for the child.

"Tracy Taylor! Doesn't that have a nice sound to it?" asked Diana when she held her baby for the first time. Phil cringed when he heard his son's name.

"Tracy is a girl's name." Sorry, but Diana made it abundantly clear that Phil had no voice in the naming of "her child." Diana grew to detest Phil, and her feelings for him may have cost her baby his life. When Tracy became ill while Peter was out of town, Diana refused to take the child to the hospital, where she knew she would run into Dr. Phil Brewer. Tracy died of pneumonia, leaving Diana devastated and guilt-ridden.

As the months passed, Phil grew increasingly bitter and dejected over his botched and hopeless life. Impotent and alone, he became more obsessed than ever over Diana. One fateful night, he forced his way into her apartment, wanting to talk with her. Suddenly, he felt a stirring in his loins. Could it be?

"I'm a man!" he declared—to his own amazement. Phil's spirits suddenly rose with utter delight upon seeing that his impotence had finally abated. Overwhelmed by the enormity of this incredible moment, Phil embraced Diana. Out of control, unthinking, he kissed her. Fearful of what was happening, she pushed him away, but Phil was so much stronger. In a heinous and horrible display of "manhood," Phil forced himself upon Diana, raping her. Fearing repercussions, she kept the encounter secret from Peter, vowing never to see Phil Brewer again. Ten weeks later, Diana Taylor discovered that she was once again pregnant. Counting back the weeks, she understood the terrible truth that the baby must belong to Phil. Telling no one—especial-ly not Peter—her secret, Diana gave birth to a baby daughter, Martha. She breathed a sigh of relief when Phil, never suspecting that the child was his, left to take on new doctoral duties in Nairobi, Kenya.

Diana tried to pass off Martha as Peter's baby, but powerful secrets like this one never seem to stay secret for very long in the whisper-filled corridors of General Hospital. Phil's jealousy got the better of him, and he blurted out the stunning truth to Peter. The news that Martha was *not* his daughter stunned Dr. Taylor who, in a hail of accusations, rejected Diana. Though he loved her deeply, a cold and distant Peter simply could not forgive his wife for her betrayal. Even after Phil left town, Peter would not allow Diana back into his life or his bed. For months, they lived in the same house, sleeping in separate beds and barely speaking. Believing that their marriage was over, Diana filed for divorce.

In 1972, Jessie Brewer suddenly found herself with a house full of teenagers. When Jessie's widowed brother died in Auburn, N.Y., Jessie became guardian for his teenage children, Kent and Caroline Murray. At the same time, she began treating a hepatitis patient, Teddy Holmes, on General Hospital's seventh floor.

General Hospital received an infusion of youth when Caroline and Kent Murray relocated from Auburn, New York to Port Charles and moved in with their aunt Jessie Brewer in 1972. The following year, Caroline abruptly left town—on the arm of Jessie's beau, Teddy.

Teddy, a prize-winning journalist, charmed Jessie like … well, he charmed her just like Phil! In many ways, Teddy Holmes was a Phil Brewer clone. He was dashingly handsome, younger than Jessie, and oh-so-smooth with the ladies. Inevitably, a trusting Jessie would fall in love with him.

When her fetching patient recovered sufficiently to be released from the hospital, she invited him to recuperate in her home. Believing Teddy's story that he had always dreamed of opening his own motorcycle shop, Jessie agreed to co-sign a $25,000 loan for him. Living in Jessie's comfortable home, Teddy Holmes came into close contact with 17-year-old Caroline Murray. The news that Caroline would receive a huge inheritance on her eighteenth birthday intrigued the greedy Mr. Holmes. Short of cash, he had to find a way to get his hands on that money! While courting Jessie, Teddy began a very subtle seduction of her niece. He convinced the impressionable girl that Jessie was an ogre whose decision to take the Murray children into her home was motivated by money, not love. Then, he "confessed" his love to Caroline, and convinced her to run away with him. Teddy and Caroline's midnight exodus left Jessie devastated—and stuck with a huge debt to pay back. Once again, Jessie Brewer had been deceived and destroyed by a handsome man!

At General Hospital, nurse Jane Dawson found herself immersed in situations not at all unlike those faced by Jessie. Howie Dawson thrived on his excesses—he loved fun, he loved women—and most of all he loved fun women! Through it all, Jane loved Howie. She constantly gave the benefit of the doubt to her wayward husband even after he had frittered away her hard-earned money on a "sure-thing"—a horse named Blue Streak! She forgave him for his romantic dalliances with vamp Denise Wilton—even after Denise's estranged husband named Howie as corespondent in their divorce. Jane turned the other cheek when he canceled their planned lunches in order to spend a lazy afternoon with Beverly Cleveland, the sexy secretary he worked (and played) with at his company, Universal Plastics. Jane very nearly divorced Howie upon discovering that he had secretly undergone a vasectomy to spare himself the responsibility of fathering a child.

"I'm sorry, Janie. It will never happen again." Over and over, Jane Dawson heard those very words, always giving the benefit of the doubt to her now-contrite husband.

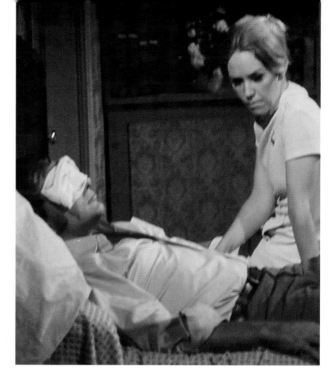
Nurse Jane Dawson put up with the endless antics of her wayward husband, Howie. When lazy Howie wasn't flirting with women or betting on horses, he was getting over a vicious hangover.

"Forgive him, Jane. Howie's a good boy," pleaded Howie's mother, who lived with the Dawsons in their tiny apartment. When a penitent Howie underwent a successful procedure to reverse his vasectomy, the Dawsons became the parents of a darling daughter, Joanne. The responsibilities of parenthood still didn't curb Howie's childish, self-destructive ways. When he played around with the alluring Brooke Clinton, Jane finally put her foot down.

"I want a whole marriage—or none at all!" Howie tried to melt away her ultimatum with his charm, but was hurt and shocked to find out that this time Janie really meant it! Determined to turn over a new leaf, he took Brooke out (on her birthday) for a final spaghetti and wine dinner at a local restaurant, Jo's Place. Afterward he took Brooke home, dropping her off outside her apartment. It would be the last time he would ever see Brooke alive. Entering her apartment, she encountered her other boyfriend (and ex-boss) Burt Douglas. Crazed with jealousy, he glared at Brooke.

"You're sleeping with him, aren't you?" Burt screamed, demanding an answer. When she refused to confirm or deny anything, he struck her in anger. Brooke fell, hitting her head! Startled, Burt realized he had killed her! In a panic, he wiped away all fingerprints and other traces of his presence and fled town. Howie, the chief suspect in the case, sweated it out while the police investigated Brooke's murder. Fortunately, he got off the hook when he recalled

The Complete Stories 1970-1975

In 1974, nurse Augusta McLeod killed Dr. Phil Brewer with a paperweight because she feared that he would tell Diana Taylor that she was pregnant with Diana's husband Peter's child. To silence Phil, Augusta hit him over the head and, after finally confessing months later, she went to jail—where she gave birth to her baby.

seeing Burt Douglas at the scene of the crime, and the guilty party was apprehended.

Breathing a sigh of relief, Howie Dawson promised to become a model husband. For a while, the beer-guzzling, pot-bellied Lothario even managed to give up his womanizing and excel at his new job in the public relations department at General Hospital. But this lazy leopard was not about to change his spots. Dr. Steve Hardy saw through Howie's put-on charm and challenged him at every turn.

"I'm sick and tired of you telling me what to do," Howie exploded at Steve. Realizing he was certain to be canned, Howie quit his job and left town, leaving his mother stricken—and Jane amazingly

relieved. Alone at last in the fall of 1974, she began to enjoy the company of Dr. Henry Pinkham. Henry found himself facing similar circumstances when his wife, Sharon, suddenly left town to nurse her mother (who had suffered a broken leg) back to health. Two months later, a stunned Henry received a "Dear John" letter in which Sharon informed him that she had fallen in love with an old childhood beau. As for Howie, he returned only once to attend the funeral of his infant daughter, Joanne, whose sudden death devastated poor Jane. Fortunately, she now had a man who could give her the security, comfort and compassion she so desperately needed in her time of grief. Seeking a fresh start away from the painful memories they felt inside the halls of General Hospital, Henry and Jane transferred to nearby Mercy Hospital.

Dr. Peter Taylor's injured pride continued to keep him from reconciling with his wife Diana, who was now a staff nurse on General Hospital's seventh floor. In faraway Kenya, Dr. Phil Brewer dreamed of someday winning back Diana's affections. Aiding Phil in his long-distance quest to keep the Taylors apart was Jane Dawson's ravishing cousin, sexy vixen Augusta McLeod, R.N. The curvaceous Augusta sashayed into General Hospital and immediately demonstrated exactly how to adeptly use sex as a weapon to lure an eligible man. While Augusta seduced Peter into a meaningless affair, Diana was pursued by another dashing arrival, Dr. Joel Stratton, whose older brother, Owen, was a cardiac patient at General Hospital. Though they loved each other deeply, Peter and Diana were headed for divorce court. At the last minute, they managed to put aside their mutual hurt and reconcile. In a moving scene, Peter pledged his love to Diana and admitted he loved her daughter, Martha, as if she was his own child.

Learning that Peter and Diana were reconciling, a desperate and hysterical Augusta wrote Phil in Kenya, urging him to return to town. She had good reason to seek Phil's assistance—for Augusta was pregnant with Peter's child! Heeding Augusta's call, Phil made a bee-line back to town. But his stay would be short. No one was happy to see surly Phil Brewer again. More than anyone, Peter Taylor dreaded the return of his longtime rival. Cockily, Phil summoned Peter to meet him late one night and delighted in revealing to him that Augusta was carrying his child. The unexpected news shocked Peter! When Phil threatened to reveal the secret to Diana, Phil knocked him down just in front of the seventh floor nurses' station.

"Stay away from Diana or I'll kill you!" Peter's shouts caught the ear of staff and patients alike. Later that night, Dr. Steve Hardy walked into Dr. Lesley Williams' office and stopped in his tracks. In front of him he witnessed Jessie, on her knees, bending over a fallen Phil. He was dead—the victim of a vicious blow to the head! On the night of December 6th, 1974, Phil Brewer's long reign of terror and deceit had finally come to an end.

"I'm sorry. I'm so sorry," repeated Jessie as she kneeled over Phil's limp body. Did she kill the man who had made her life a living hell? Or had Peter Taylor's hatred driven him to take his rival's life? Who would do such a thing? And where was the missing murder weapon? Peter and Jessie were not the only people who wanted Phil Brewer dead. Diana, Augusta and Dr. Jim Hobart also had reasons to want the dastardly doc dead!!

The news of Phil Brewer's murder became page-one news. TV reporter Kira Faulkner (who had been dating Steve) filed daily reports on the local news, filling the scandal-hungry citizens in on all the sordid details of the horrifying whodunit. After days of speculation, Assistant District Attorney Ross Jeanelle charged Jessie Brewer with the murder of her ex-husband!

Remanded to prison, Jessie saddened her attorney Lee Baldwin when she refused to cooperate in her own defense.

"You've got to fight this, Jessie," he pleaded. Lee kissed Jessie lightly, telling her how much he cared for her. Then he kissed her passionately. The long dormant chemistry between them had suddenly returned.

At the same time, Jim Hobart began having recurring nightmares in which he killed Phil for ruining his medical career at General Hospital! In desperation, Jim tried to remember the details of the fateful night of December 6th. But he had been drinking heavily, so his memories were clouded by an alcohol-induced haze.

Did Jim murder Phil? Not according to Diana Taylor, he didn't! Just days before Jessie's case was to go to trial, Diana Taylor confessed that she was the killer. To prove her guilt, she produced the murder weapon—a bloodstained geode paperweight. Jessie was immediately set free, and Diana convicted. Still, Peter Taylor refused to believe that Diana had done it.

"She's protecting me. Diana thinks I killed Phil!" Peter explained to Lee Baldwin as they set out to reexamine the clues from the night of Phil's death. Diana's fate appeared to be sealed until Jim Hobart finally remembered that he had seen Augusta McLeod in Phil's company on the night of December 6th! Peter confronted the pregnant Augusta, coercing a startling confession.

"Yes, I did it. I did it for you, Peter" she cried out. "If you want the truth, I hit him because he was going to tell Diana about my being pregnant with your child. I didn't want her to know . . . for you, Peter, for you!" Peter listened, his reactions mixed with relief and horror.

"Now I am going to pay for this. Pay for it because I was protecting our child. Knowing that I have your baby is a secret that has kept me warm and alive. It's kept me going all these months. Without that secret . . ." Peter interrupted.

"Without that secret, that baby . . . none of this would have happened."

Augusta McLeod went to prison, where she had her baby. Not wanting to keep another secret, Peter painfully revealed the details of his affair with Augusta to Diana, who forgave him.

Kindly Caroline Chandler, an adoption agent, arranged for Augusta's baby to be placed in a foster home. While handling Augusta's case, Caroline became reacquainted with her old friend, Lee Baldwin. A widower since his wife Meg's untimely death, Lee relished the moments he spent with Caroline while they made arrangements for the adoption of Augusta's baby. When the case wrapped up, they agreed to continue to see each other. Finally, Lee had found his perfect match—Caroline was as generous and levelheaded as he was.

To the delight of their friends, Lee and Caroline became man and wife. After a short honeymoon, the newlyweds returned to town to face the disastrous news that Caroline's son, Bobby, an energetic med student, was suffering from an incurable case of Melenkoff's disease. Ignoring his own condition, Bobby worried that his young wife, Samantha, who had just become pregnant, would have to raise their child alone after his death. Miraculously, Bobby's certain fate was reversed when Steve discovered that Bobby's fatal diagnosis was wrong! The blood disease he had was not entirely hopeless. Rejoicing from the welcome news, Lee and Caroline joined Bobby in New York where he received the treatment required to combat his illness. In short order, Bobby went into remission. Another life had been saved through the miracle of modern medicine.

Dr. Lesley Williams savored those miraculous moments. As a doctor trained in the most up-to-date medical techniques, Lesley fought to preserve each and every precious moment of life. Rarely did this dedicated physician allow herself a second to savor those tiny medical victories. Without missing a (heart) beat, she was on to the next case. One of Lesley's first patients at General Hospital was Mrs. Florence Grey, who suffered from stomach ulcers brought on, she supposed, by the misery of a troubled marriage. In the course of the treatment, Florence revealed her marital history to psychiatrist Peter Taylor. Years earlier, Florence explained, her husband, Professor Gordon Grey, had an affair with a student. Together they had a daughter who died soon after she was born.

When Peter filled Lesley in on this seemingly inconsequential element of their patient's history, a cold chill ran through her body. *She* was the very student engaged in the affair with Professor Grey! Now, nearly a dozen years later, Gordon Grey had reentered her life, this time proclaiming his love. Gordon revealed to a tormented Lesley that he wanted to leave his wife to be with her. Tormented by her indecision, Lesley begged Dr. Hardy to take her off the case. In an emotional confrontation, Lesley convinced Gordon to stay with his wife during her recovery. Soon, the Greys left town. But for Lesley, the memories of giving birth to, then losing, a precious daughter, lingered on.

In her infrequent free moments, Lesley Williams dated cardiologist Joel Stratton. They fell in love and planned to marry, but Joel suddenly and inexplicably backed away from their carefully laid plans. In truth, Joel had discovered that he was dying from a fatal blood disease. Not wanting Lesley to suffer through his death, he broke their engagement without telling her why.

A heartbroken Lesley turned her romantic attentions to millionaire Cameron Faulkner. Suave and smooth, "Cam" was the Donald Trump of his day. Successful in business, he devoted much of his energy and money to good causes. Lesley's new free clinic was just such a worthy cause. Cameron became her benefactor, and soon her lover. Lesley was overjoyed when Cameron surprised her with elaborate plans to marry in Cameron's hometown of Baltimore.

"When?" she asked.

"Now!" he replied, picking her up and spinning her around. Lesley, buoyant with the prospect of marrying her millionaire, headed home to gather her belongings for the wedding in Baltimore. The sound of her front-door chime interrupted Lesley's packing. Opening the door, Lesley was startled to see Felix Buchanan, a young patient she had recently treated for ulcers at General Hospital.

"The wedding is off!" he declared, waving a pistol in Lesley's face. She recoiled in horror as Felix entered her home and slammed the door behind him. Unbeknownst to Lesley, Felix had fallen obsessively in love with her, and hearing of her impending marriage, he snapped.

"You are too good, too pure to fit into Cameron Faulkner's world," he proclaimed with a wild look in his eye. Felix hoped to reason with Lesley, but his mad methods went awry when Cameron unexpectedly arrived on the scene and valiantly attempted to wrestle the gun away. Lesley watched in horror as a shot rang out. Cameron fell to the floor with a bullet wound to the chest!! The police rushed to the scene and arrested Felix. Meanwhile an ambulance hurried the wounded millionaire away to General Hospital, where Dr. Joel Stratton performed a life-saving operation. With Lesley keeping a vigil at his bedside, Cameron pulled through. Eternally grateful, Lesley promised her groggy and brave beau that she would never forget what he'd done.

"You nearly gave your life for me," she exclaimed, just before marrying Cameron in a simple ceremony in his private room at General Hospital. Aided by Lesley's bedside charm and expert medical care, Cameron made a full recovery from his near-fatal wound. But before the newlyweds could begin their happy new life together, something incredible happened that would change the course of their marital history.

An old woman, Doris Roach, was admitted to the hospital and with her dying breath asked to speak with Dr. Lesley Faulkner. Perched at Miss Roach's bedside, Lesley listened as the elderly woman revealed that Lesley's infant daughter had not died at birth twelve years earlier at the Sullivan Clinic, a private nursing home in Detroit. According to Miss Roach (a former maternity ward nurse), Lesley's father, Walter, had bribed her to switch Lesley's living baby with the body of a dead child.

Shaken almost beyond the point of reaction, Lesley listened to every word of Nurse Roach's amazing tale. Just then, Dr. Hardy entered the room on routine rounds, and attempted to take the weak woman's vital signs.

"I must continue. Please… before it's too late," she murmured to Steve, who stayed to hear the rest of her story. Nurse Roach pleaded with Lesley not to judge her father too harshly for taking such deceitful action.

"He only wanted what was best for you, my dear," she explained, informing Lesley that her father believed that the responsibility of caring for a newborn baby would have kept Lesley from fulfilling her dream of becoming a doctor.

"Surely I know the child is alive."

Lesley pressed her further.

"Do you know the name of the child?"

"No, but I remember that the mother used her maiden name, for it was that kind of clinic. Now I am going to sleep. Thank God I was finally able to tell you the truth."

As Nurse Roach closed her eyes, Lesley leaned on Dr. Hardy's broad shoulder.

"What should I do, Steve?"

"I'm not sure you should do anything, Lesley."

Stunned by the incredible turn of events, Lesley repeated nurse Roach's tale to her new husband, Cameron, who repeated Dr. Hardy's professional opinion.

"It's better to let sleeping dogs lie," he insisted. "She's probably living with people she assumes are her parents. I'm sure she's well-adjusted and happy."

Ever the busybody, nurse Lucille Weeks disagreed.

"I know you're not asking me, Dr. Faulkner. But if I were in your shoes, I would try to find my child, just to be sure she was all right."

"Lucille, for the last time, I am *not* going to search for my daughter. But I must admit, I will always wonder about her."

"Oh, I'm sure you will, Dr. Faulkner. Every minute of every day…for the rest of your life."

Lesley paused, deep in thought. Lucille's words had sunk in. If she was ever to have peace, she must find her child! At Lesley's urging, Cameron assigned his assistant Mac McLaughlin to the task of finding her twelve-year-old daughter. He didn't have to look far. Mac found the girl, Laura Vining, living with her parents, Barbara and Jason Vining, and younger sister Amy, in a modest home near the university, no more than five miles from Lesley's home.

A teacher, Jason Vining struggled to make ends meet. Like any typical twelve-year-old girl, Laura had the usual differences of opinion with her parents. Their chief source of conflict was money— Laura wanted new clothes, a ten-speed and most of all, she had her heart set on getting a new typewriter for Christmas 1975.

"We'll see," mumbled Barbara, who was already struggling to stay within the bounds of this month's budget.

Lesley was not satisfied simply with the information that her daughter was alive and well. She wanted to see her! Cameron, dismayed to learn that his wife was absolutely determined to make contact, ordered Lesley to stay away from the child. Nevertheless, Lesley defiantly set out to make contact or catch a glimpse of the child she so desperately longed for. Entering a local candy store, Lesley stopped dead in her tracks. She saw a pretty golden-haired girl sitting at the soda fountain with her friend Gary. Overcome with emotion, she followed Laura into the park and halted her progress with a question.

"Do you know where I can get a decent slice of pizza?"

"Follow us," Laura cheerfully answered, pointing to her friends up ahead. Her ears perked up when Lesley offered to pay for a pizza lunch for both of them.

"Are you rich?" she asked in awe.

"Well, sort of." That was all Laura needed to hear! Instantly captivated by her new friend, Laura couldn't wait to see her again.

"She's so glamorous!" an excited Laura told her ten-year-old sister, Amy! "She said she's going to buy me a bike, and a new typewriter." Amy was jealous of Laura's fabulous new friend, while the Vinings were cautiously guarded upon hearing of Laura's mysterious benefactor. What did Dr. Lesley Faulkner possibly want with their eldest daughter? In time, the Vinings had their answer. Upon hearing the shocking news that Laura was really Lesley's daughter, Barbara and Jason vowed not to let her go.

After breaking the news to a thrilled Laura, Lesley launched a custody suit. The judge, realizing that both mothers had been wronged twelve years earlier, postponed making a decision to allow Laura time to get to know her biological mother. In a startling decision, Lesley was granted custody of her daughter for thirty days, after which Laura herself would have a voice in deciding her future. After months of turmoil, Lesley was the happiest woman on earth!

1976

With a renewed zest for life, Dr. Lesley Faulkner looked forward to the new year. And why not? She'd located her long-lost daughter, Laura, sued for custody and been granted the chance to have Laura live with her until the girl could choose which family she preferred. Lesley was even more thrilled when her husband, Cameron, reluctantly agreed to accept the child into their new life. In fact, Cameron actually began to overextend himself to please both mother and daughter, despite his early opposition to Lesley's quest to find her daughter. As the days passed, Laura grew close to Lesley, but still wasn't sure that she wanted to make her stay with the Faulkners permanent. She missed her friends, her parents and, most of all, her younger sister, Amy. At Laura's request the judge extended the temporary situation for another thirty days, at which point a decision about Laura's future would have to be made.

"I can't lose my daughter!" worried Lesley as she began to smother the girl with love and a kind of energy that bordered on hysteria.

Laura felt trapped by Lesley's overprotective love. After all, she already had a "real mother"—Barbara Vining, who provided her with everything she needed from a mother. But Cameron—now he was exciting! Laura was much more impressed by Cameron's glamour than by Lesley's smothering attempt at mothering!

Laura's two mothers came into contact with each other sooner than expected when she was rushed to the hospital suffering from what was at first diagnosed as strep throat. Exhaustive tests failed to reveal any physical reason for her illness. In the midst of her high fever, a delirious Laura called out for her adoptive mother, then went into convulsions. Lesley was horrified to learn from Barbara Vining that the child had gone through a similar episode once before when she was in great emotional pain. Not wanting to cause Laura further stress, Lesley arrived at the difficult conclusion that Laura's condition stemmed from being torn between two parents. Lesley turned to Dr. Peter Taylor for counsel and affirmation that the agony

the child was going through could be emotionally based. He concurred that it could, but Peter couldn't tell Lesley what to do. It was a decision she had to make for herself. Should she give up Laura?

During Laura's period of hospitalization, a rift developed between Lesley and her egocentric husband, Cameron. Lesley was spending all her nights in the hospital—going home only during the day to change clothes. Cameron grew more selfish—he wanted Lesley for himself, and resented her love for Laura or anyone else. It quickly became apparent to Cam that he would have to take drastically dishonest measures to win back Lesley's attention and save their marriage.

Cameron considered bribing the judge assigned to the case, but he didn't need to take such an underhanded action because Lesley made the painful decision to cancel the custody suit and return Laura to Jason and Barbara Vining. Cam, secretly triumphant that Laura was out of his life for good, dedicated himself to healing Lesley's hurt. Despite his efforts to help her overcome her grief, Lesley Faulkner remained obsessed with her daughter.

Soon after returning to her "old life" with the Vinings, Laura suffered another psychosomatic attack that prompted Barbara Vining to place a call to Lesley.

"Please don't stay out of Laura's life," she pleaded. "Let her grow up knowing your love as well as mine."

Lesley wrestled with the difficult decision. She wanted to say yes—but feared that Laura would once again be caught between two mothers. After consulting with her psychiatrist, Peter Taylor, Lesley concluded that she should see Laura again. Of course, seeing Laura meant seeing less of Cameron—and this news did not please the irritated millionaire. Behind Lesley's back, he began spending more time at the mountain retreat he bought for Lesley—and even more time in New York with his sexy secretary, Peggy Lowell.

Lesley, believing Cameron loved her daughter as much as she did, was thrilled when Laura decided to spend the summer of 1976 with them. Cameron quickly saw that his life alone with Lesley—about whom he was fanatically possessive—was going to be ruined.

"It's time to get that kid out of our lives for good!" he thought.

With that goal in mind, Cameron concocted a scheme: He flew to Detroit to see Margaret Clifford, a former nurse at the Westlake Clinic where Laura was born. Nurse Clifford was a close friend of Doris Roach, the nurse who confessed on her deathbed that she had swapped Lesley's baby—Laura—for Barbara Vining's daughter who had died.

"Doris Roach helped my wife *find* her daughter. I want you to help *lose* her!"

Cameron wanted Margaret Clifford to lie to Lesley that Doris Roach's deathbed confession was false—Laura was not her child after all. She'd invented the changeling story. For 10,000 dollars of Cameron's money Margaret Clifford promised to tell Lesley this elaborate lie that Laura was *not* Lesley's daughter after all.

Despite Nurse Clifford's claim, Lesley refused to believe that Laura was not her child. Resolving to stop Margaret Clifford from causing any more trouble, Lesley decided to go to Barbara Vining and tell her what had happened. With Cameron by her side, she headed for the Vining family home in Buffalo. Upon arrival, she found the home deserted! The family was gone. Laura was gone! As they began to leave, Lesley spotted Laura's favorite rag doll, one of the remaining items left in the house.

"Laura would never leave her doll behind," she cried to Cameron. "You've got to help me find her!" Cameron knew exactly where Laura was. He had bribed Barbara to take the girl to Canada.

In the grueling weeks after Laura's disappearance, Cameron urged Lesley to get on with her life. But Lesley was determined to never accept the fact that Laura was not her daughter.

"Not without absolute proof!" she declared defiantly.

Cameron finally convinced her when he produced a man named Russ Waverly, who claimed to be Laura's father by Barbara Vining. Lesley had no choice but to believe his claim.

Shattered by her husband's lack of sensitivity, Lesley wrestled with the question of whether she should leave Cam for good. Her dilemma was solved when she found a check from Cameron to Barbara Vining for 25,000 dollars. Lesley could not understand the meaning of the check. Just then Cam showed up and furiously discovered that his secret had been exposed. Pushed to the brink of madness by Lesley's never-ending obsession for her daughter, Cameron's anger exploded. He grabbed Lesley and threw her onto the bed. She couldn't escape Cam's powerful grasp as he brutally raped her. When Lesley tried to escape, Cameron forced her into the car. "We're going to the lodge!" he declared as he set out for the mountain cabin they'd purchased in happier times. "And I'm going to keep you there until you learn to be the right kind of wife!"

Realizing she was being kidnaped, Lesley lunged for the wheel—and the car careened off the road!

Hours later, Lesley was found wandering in shock on a mountain road. Cameron was dead! In the days after the tragedy, Lesley learned another shocking secret about her husband: he died broke, his empire crumbled beneath him in the weeks before his death. Dr. Peter Taylor made every effort to help Lesley come to grips with the guilt and pain of the horrible events. His efforts proved futile. Peter could not get through to Lesley. But in time another doctor would. His name was Rick Webber.

In March of 1976 several new characters, whose presence would be felt for years to come, were introduced to the canvas of General Hospital. Among them was Terri Arnett, whose husband David, a doctor, had been killed in Vietnam. Terri was the daughter of Steve Hardy's closest friend, the late Dr. Lars Webber. Once an aspiring singer in New York, Terri returned home when Lars and his wife Helen were killed in an accident to play surrogate mother to her two younger brothers, Rick and Jeff. Rick, a promising resident at General Hospital, volunteered for a six-month medical stint in Africa. Two months after his arrival, he was reportedly killed when the small plane in which he was being piloted to a remote village crashed and burned. Rick's dashingly handsome younger brother, Jeff, graduated from med school in the spring of 1976 along with his wife, Monica, who had once been Rick's fiancée. Dr. Steve Hardy tapped the young married doctors for a bold new experimental program at General Hospital—Mr. and Mrs. Intern!

For Steve Hardy, the intern experiment was a noble gamble. He believed that Jeff and Monica were a perfect choice. Six months into their marriage, he assumed they were ideally happy. He was wrong! Their new marriage was a wreck! Jeff had a hang-up: He feared that everyone at General Hospital was comparing him to his "late" brother

Though she was married to Jeff, intern Monica Webber still pined away for his "late" brother Rick, who was reportedly killed when his plane crashed while on a medical mission in Africa.

Rick. Fearing he would always be second best, Jeff's every thought was plagued by memories of his dead brother. Jeff missed Rick dearly—and so did Monica. More than anyone—even Jeff—knew.

The ghost of Rick Webber was no sooner laid to rest by Steve than it came alive again when Jeff and Monica were assigned to clinic duty under Dr. Lesley Faulkner. Dr. Rex Pearson, an on-the-make former colleague of Rick, was to be their supervising resident. Rex, with an eye on Monica, made a couple of tentative passes, which Monica deftly fended off. Irritated, Rex hit back by going after Jeff to goad him about not being "man" enough to handle his "willful and capricious" wife. The spotlight was getting to Jeff. He began to make mistakes—nothing critical—but alarming nonetheless. Steve confronted the young intern, accusing him of being "hung up on the ghost of Rick." Jeff accepted the blame for his errors but insisted his errant behavior had nothing to do with Rick.

"He was a great guy, but he's gone," Jeff stalwartly insisted.

Or was he?

In the remote African village of Lomonda, Rick Webber was very much alive! He was being held there, against his will, having been captured ten months earlier by revolutionaries in Lomonda's civil war. Suspected of being a C.I.A. spy, Rick was imprisoned, tortured and scheduled for execution. Before

the execution could take place, Rick's prison was hit by a bombing raid and he was set free.

With considerable fanfare, Terri opened a new nightclub, "Terri's Place," on April 30, 1976. At the height of an evening marked with many telegrams of congratulations, one arrived from Africa. The envelope stated that it was from the American consul in Lomonda City. Inside was remarkable news.

The message: "Your brother Dr. Richard Webber is alive. Details to follow."

For Jeff, the news of his brother's imminent return brought a mixture of joy and upset. Joy, because his idolized older brother was alive! Upset, because he wondered how Rick would take the news that Jeff had married the girl Rick asked to be his wife in a letter he wrote her ten months ago from Africa, just before his reported death. Monica was torn by the same mingled joy and fear. Fear that Rick's return would reveal the lie she told Jeff when news of his death came: that the letter she received *did not* ask her to be his wife. Instead, Rick had spelled out clearly that their romance was over. Unbeknownst to Monica, Rick's feelings had changed during his long imprisonment. In captivity, he realized he truly loved Monica after all, and it was this realization that kept him going through his ordeal. Rick was coming home to reclaim her!

Before departing from Africa, Rick got through by phone to Terri and learned the shocking news that Monica and Jeff had married. Monica was relieved to know that Rick didn't give away her "letter lie." Upon learning that he'd be landing in New York en route home, she secretly flew to New York to await Rick's arrival and plead with him not to reveal the truth of the letter to Jeff. Monica explained why she lied: Rick's reported death had panicked her into feeling she would be abandoned by Jeff and Terri—and Monica had a lifelong fear of aloneness. Having been raised in a foundling home and never chosen for adoption, the Webbers gave Monica the first sense of family that she had ever known. She couldn't stand the thought of losing them!

Upon his long-awaited return to General Hospital, Rick was reunited with Steve Hardy, who sensed that Rick was haunted by something. Was it, as Steve suspected, the months of imprisonment that troubled Rick? Or was he, as Terri believed, deeply troubled by the fact that Monica had married Jeff?

As for Jeff, he was wary every time he saw Monica and Rick together. His jealousy exploded into anger when he stumbled on the secret that his wife and brother had met in New York.

"I don't trust you anymore!" he screamed at Rick. "So far as I'm concerned, the brother who went to Africa never returned!"

For weeks, the climate between Monica and Jeff remained stormy. Dr. Steve Hardy thought it best to end his noble Mr. and Mrs. Intern experiment.

"Jeff, I'm separating you and Monica as a team, and assigning you to surgical service under Rick," Steve sternly told the furious young intern.

Eventually, the Webber brothers reconciled as Jeff's animosity cooled, but the volatile Webber/Webber/Webber triangle was just heating up! In mid-July, Rick and Monica suddenly found themselves locked in a passionate kiss! The smoldering flames of passion erupted on a night when Monica lost her first patient, a little boy by the name of Joey Galvin. After the kiss, Monica confessed that she never stopped loving Rick, and he also let out his feelings.

"I love you too, Monica," confessed Rick.

He cautioned her that they must put a lid on their own feelings, "for Jeff's sake." Monica reluctantly agreed. Rick did his best to stay away from Monica, but that was hardly possible in the halls—and elevators—of General Hospital. One day, the couple found themselves trapped in a stalled elevator. In a heated moment, Rick confessed his torment.

"I can't stand being alone with you, Monica. I can't trust myself!"

During this tormenting time, Rick shared his intimate secrets with an old friend, Dr. Mark Dante, a skilled Boston-based surgeon who had recently joined the General Hospital staff. Mark warned Rick that it was time to get on with his life.

According to the wise Dr. Dante, "the only way to break this is to get yourself a new girl."

The thought that Rick would be dating other women sickened Monica, who privately vowed to do everything in her power to stay close to Rick Webber.

Like Rick, Mark Dante was involved in a romantic triangle. Soon after arriving in town, he became attracted to Rick and Jeff's widowed sister, Terri. But Dr. Dante couldn't act on his feelings, since he already had a wife back in Boston. Mary-Ellen Dante had been committed to a sanitarium two years earlier suffering from severe depression that left her unable to communicate with the outside world.

Soon after taking his new post on the surgical staff at General Hospital, Mark brought Mary-Ellen to Lakecliff, a sanitarium outside of Port Charles.

Before long her depression returned full force. After a suicide attempt, Mark turned to Terri for reassurance that bringing Mary-Ellen to town had been the right thing for him to do. In the course of a tormented speech, Mark made a startling revelation.

"I love you, Red," he told Terri, who was astonished by his confession.

Dr. Rick Webber "returned from the dead" in late 1976, only to make the shocking discovery that the woman he loved, Monica, was married to his brother, Jeff.

It was an honest confession of his feelings, which Mark had privately vowed he would never make to Terri until Mary-Ellen was well and he could divorce her. The chemistry between Mark and Terri exploded in a passionate kiss. Afterwards, stricken with pangs of guilt, Mark could only ask, "God, sweetheart—what have I gotten us into?"

And there was more pain to come because Mary-Ellen soon discovered their secret passion and privately vowed to keep Mark and Terri apart.

As for Rick Webber, he needed to keep away from Monica, and that meant moving out of the Webber family home, where he lived with Terri, Jeff—and Monica. Monica offered to help find an apartment for Rick. No need—Lesley Faulkner had found one for him—in her building. Lesley! The very thought of the widow Faulkner anywhere near Rick steamed Monica. Lesley insisted that she and Rick were just pals, but just as these feelings began to blossom, Lesley felt something else. One day, she suddenly swayed and almost fainted! Horrified, she asked herself, "Could I be pregnant? Oh dear God—no!"

Yes, Lesley was pregnant—with the late Cameron Faulkner's baby.

Meanwhile, the marriage of Jeff and Monica continued to crumble, and the trouble became even more pronounced when Monica refused to consider having Jeff's baby. Realizing the inevitable, Monica called a lawyer to discuss a no-fault divorce, which was not as easy as it sounds. Monica quickly learned that it would be impossible to get a no-fault divorce without Jeff's consent. How could she make Jeff want a divorce, too?

"Easy," thought Monica. "I'll refuse to sleep with him!"

During the summer of '76, Diana Taylor found herself in need of a new nanny to care for her daughter, Martha. After interviewing dozens of candidates, she found the perfect nanny—the scheming Heather Grant! The product of a lower-class background, Heather beat out the competition the way she knew best—by cheating. Desperately wanting the job, Heather devilishly gave Diana a forged letter of reference. After winning the job and gaining the Taylor's trust, Heather admitted to her widowed mother, Alice, that she was using the Taylors. They were Heather's entrée into a world of "more important people" where she intended to snag herself a rich husband—like the doctor she'd already met in the halls of General Hospital—Jeff Webber!

Guilt-ridden Dr. Mark Dante loved Terri Arnett, but felt an obligation to encourage his mentally ill wife, Mary-Ellen, to emerge from the deep depression that had kept her institutionalized for many years.

Diana Taylor unwittingly told her troubles to her scheming new nanny, Heather Grant, who used her position in the Taylor home as an entree into a world of "more important people."

Heather set out to do anything in her power to see the handsome, vulnerable and very *married* doctor. She volunteered her spare time at the hospital where she could dote every day on her handsome prey.

Soon after, Heather received an unexpected visit from her ex-husband, Larry Joe. A sleazy opportunist, Larry Joe had heard about Heather's hospital volunteer job, and wanted her to steal a key to the hospital drug cabinet. Heather continually refused, prompting Larry Joe to steal Monica's purse. Realizing what he'd done, Heather demanded he return it. When he did so—there was no key inside—she found Rick's letter from Africa which Monica had saved. It was proof that Monica still had a yen for Rick, Heather figured.

"I'll find a way to use this" she thought, the wheels turning.

In due time, Jeff got the true answer to what was bothering Monica when Heather anonymously arranged for Rick's letter to fall into Jeff's hands. Jeff kept silent about the letter but grew increasingly tormented by it. Monica, not knowing Jeff had the letter, was mystified and annoyed by Jeff's behavior. He began taking sleeping pills at night, wake-up pills the next day to keep going—and in between he dogged her footsteps.

Jeff's suspicions grew more fierce, his thoughts clouded by the abundance of pills he took to numb his pain. The tension built until the day Jeff confront-ed his wife with Rick's letter!

"You've never gotten over Rick, have you?", he screamed as he grabbed her. "If you need sex, I can give it to you."

Monica fought him off and ran, showing up on Rick's doorstep. Outside his door, before she rang the bell, she deliberately tore her dress and when he answered the door, Monica threw herself tearfully into his arms.

"Look what he did to me!" she screeched.

Rick wrapped his loving arms around her, and they ended up in a passionate kiss. Together, they gave in to their long-held feelings and made love.

Meanwhile, Lesley's fears that she was pregnant with her late husband's child proved true. The idea that she could carry a child conceived in rape terrified her. Lesley resolved that there was no other answer for her but to make arrangements to go to the Ridgely Clinic in New York for an abortion. Terri tried to go with her, but Lesley insisted that she must go alone. Terri was rocked to learn Rick didn't even know about Lesley's pregnancy, much less that she was planning an abortion!

"Don't tell Rick, Terri!" Lesley pleaded.

It was obvious to Terri. Though Lesley denied it vehemently, she was falling in love with Rick. When he discovered what Lesley was about to do, he raced to New York, where he found Lesley, who had decided *against* the abortion after days of soul searching. Touched by his visit, Lesley told Rick that this was the tenderest gesture he could have made.

Back home, Heather made her move on Jeff. After drinking his way through the night, Heather found him the worse for wear, in no shape to report for duty at the hospital. She took the drunken doctor home for coffee, sympathy and sex! Afterward, a guilt-ridden Jeff swore that their romp in the hay was a "one time thing." But, back home, Monica and Jeff's shattered marriage grew increasingly bitter. When Jeff attempted a reconciliation, Monica blasted him.

"You don't turn me on. Find a girl who does," she taunted Jeff.

Heather, who had already announced to her mother her plans to get herself pregnant as a way to give Jeff what he wanted and land him as a husband, made capital use of Monica's rejection. She wangled her way back into his bed—with a pious assurance to Jeff that they would have a "no-strings" arrangement.

Monica, crazed with jealousy over Rick's visit to see Lesley in New York, was shocked to hear that

With Audrey's love and support, Dr. Steve Hardy began the long road back from paralysis suffered in a fall down a hospital stairwell.

Lesley was pregnant. With Rick's baby, she assumed at first, but was quickly set straight by Terri. Steamed with Lesley for trying to move in on Rick, Monica confronted her rival in Lesley's penthouse.

"Keep your hands off him. We're having an affair," she declared.

Monica's stunning declaration left Lesley reeling, not sure whether to believe her or not. But Lesley was certain of one thing—she deeply loved Rick Webber. But Rick was still seeing Monica, though their secret affair was growing increasingly less passionate and more volatile.

Late in the year, Heather arranged for Jeff to discover that Monica had stayed overnight at Rick's place. Instead of turning to Heather, Jeff disappeared. Where could he be? Rick was worried, Monica frightened and Heather, most of all, needed Jeff because she was pregnant with his baby. Meantime, Jeff showed up at a bar downtown—Barney's Place—drunk, despondent and high on amphetamines. Barney, fearful that Jeff would wander out and get himself into trouble, put Jeff up in the back room overnight. Unknown to Barney, Jeff stole a gun from behind the bar. Dr. Mark Dante showed up the next day to bring Jeff home, but upon his arrival, the sound of a gunshot shattered the early morning calm. Mark raced into the back room, where he found Jeff unconscious—with a bullet in his brain.

Rick blamed himself for everything. When he broke the news to a shocked Monica, he also said emphatically that their affair was over. And Terri, fearful that Jeff would die, went to Dr. Steve Hardy to say that her mother, Helene, on her deathbed, had told Terri of the existence of a letter. Hidden away in a safety deposit box, the letter was to be opened only in case of a life-and-death crisis for Jeff. Steve assured her that Jeff would survive. High-risk surgery saved Jeff's life, and the secret letter remained unopened—for now.

At home with her husband, Dr. Jim Hobart, Audrey faced a crisis of her own. Jim's impotence wasn't getting any better and he kept his distance from his wife, fearing that another sexual encounter would prove embarrassing. Feeling alone, Audrey turned to Steve for moral support while Jim began a secret affair with a medical student, Sally Grimes.

Audrey and Jim Hobart's failing marriage came to a climax when Jim bitterly threw his affair in Audrey's face, declaring that his impotence was really caused by Audrey's frigidity.

"You're a burned out woman! A three-time loser! Why don't you just get out of the game?" Jim taunted before walking out of her life for good.

In despair, Audrey took an overdose of sleeping pills. As she sank into unconsciousness, she was stabbed back into momentary focus by the thought of her young son.

"I can't leave Tommy!" she cried out through the haze.

Audrey tried to reach the phone to call for help, but lost consciousness with the phone dangling off the receiver. Steve, knowing Jim was drunk and on the warpath, arrived at the apartment, found Audrey and rushed her to General Hospital, where she finally pulled through. But Jim's cruel and vicious accusations had decimated poor Audrey. Steve vowed to become her motivating force and her strength. It was apparent to everyone, especially Jessie, that Steve had never fallen out of love with Audrey. But in his usually stoic style, he refused to reveal his feelings to the woman he adored so deeply. Audrey returned to General Hospital in a new position—Supervisor of Student Nurses, and finally did what everyone had hoped for. Marching into Steve's office, she declared her love for him.

"Is the rumor true?" Audrey demanded to know. "Do you share my feelings?"

"Yes, Audrey . . . Yes! Yes!" gushed Steve.

Steve and Audrey were back together at last!

The joy instantly turned to horror. Delighted by their reconciliation, Steve rushed out of his seventh floor office, rushing to keep an appointment. Taking the stairs, he tripped and fell down an entire flight, ending at the bottom, unconscious! Audrey found him lying at the bottom of a stairwell, unable to move his legs. Steve was *paralyzed!*

After touch-and-go surgery, Steve emerged with hope that someday he would walk again. Then, and only then, would he marry Audrey! With her as his personal physiotherapist, Steve began the long road back.

Audrey's young son, Tommy, was not so quick to accept his mother's plans to marry Dr. Hardy. Tommy refused to believe what he had been told—that his real father, Dr. Tom Baldwin, had died several years earlier. Young Tommy's instincts were correct! In Mexico, the *General Hospital* audience discovered that Tom Baldwin was alive and imprisoned in Mexico where, years earlier, he had been framed for a murder he didn't commit. Because he didn't want his son to grow up knowing his father was a prisoner for life, Tom bought a phony death certificate and gave it to Tommy's nurse, Florence Andrews, to bring back to the states along with the child he had kidnaped several months earlier.

Steve and Audrey walked down the aisle, oblivious to the fact that Tom Baldwin was about to reclaim his son. While the newlyweds honeymooned in Hawaii, Tom showed up in Port Charles. Cutting short their honeymoon, Steve and Audrey returned to town where they expected to find Tom as he'd been when last they met—vicious and cruel. Instead, Tom insisted that he'd changed.

"I don't want any trouble. I just want my son."

After serving time for a murder he didn't commit, Dr. Tom Baldwin received wonderful news from his lawyer that he was a free man. But upon his release, Tom returned to find his wife, Audrey, had married Steve Hardy.

or weeks, Jeff Webber lingered in a coma brought on by his self-inflicted bullet wound to the brain. Steve grew alarmed when the patient took an unexpected turn for the worse.

Jeff's sinking condition sent Terri and Steve to the bank vault to retrieve Helene Webber's letter, left there for opening only in case of a life-and-death crisis for her son, Jeff. Inside the box, Steve and Terri found *two* letters in an envelope. The one to Terri revealed that Helene and Steve had been high school sweethearts. Helene had divorced Lars with an interlocutory decree and returned to Port Charles, where she and Steve had become reacquainted and realized they were still in love. In the letter, Helene told her daughter how she and Steve had decided to marry on Steve's return from Korea in a year. Steve's letter said that the one night they spent together on the eve of his departure for the war had left her pregnant with Jeff. But when Steve was reported missing in action two weeks later, Helene returned to Lars and never told anyone that Steve Hardy was Jeff's real father. Steve absorbed the shocking news, sharing the secret with Audrey.

"Jeff is my son!" he announced with pride and trepidation.

Back at the hospital, Rick admitted to Monica what she already feared:

"It's over, Monica. Once and for all!"

Still, Monica refused to accept that they would never be together.

All of the concerned parties breathed a collective sigh of relief when Jeff regained consciousness and made a miraculous recovery. Refusing to speak with his brother Rick, Jeff accepted Monica's offer to resume their marriage. Not that she loved Jeff. Ever opportunistic, Monica saw a reconciliation as the only way she could stay on staff at General Hospital—and stay close to Rick. Back with Monica, a more cynical Jeff Webber vowed to "be a man!" Jeff laid out his plans to Dr. Gail Adamson, General Hospital's new psychiatrist who had known Monica Bard Webber ever since she was a young waif growing up in a St. Louis foundling home. Jeff insisted he was not taking Monica back to "punish" her. "No more worshiping Monica. She needs a man, and that's what she's going to get!" insisted Jeff.

Jeff wanted a baby, and Monica agreed to his request—without telling Jeff that she was secretly taking birth control pills. Jeff was in for a shock upon discovering that he already had a child on the way—*Heather's* child!

"I can't understand it, Heather. You told me you were on the pill!" bellowed Jeff after learning the news.

Jeff offered a solution to Heather's dilemma when he asked her to give the baby to him and Monica to raise. No dice! Heather was not about to give Jeff her baby. The child was worth too much to her! The news of Jeff and Monica's reconciliation crushed Heather, who faked a suicide attempt to try and win Jeff's affections. Heather's efforts were all for naught. Once she detected that Jeff still wouldn't leave Monica, she ordered him to leave her alone. Heather had plans for her baby—plans that would net her a fortune. Heather revealed her scheme to her mother: she wouldn't abort her unborn child, as Jeff wanted, but

With his marriage to Monica unraveling, Dr. Jeff Webber fell prey to the machinations of the dangerously neurotic Heather Grant, who lured Jeff into her bed and eventually into marriage.

she would have the baby, sell it to Diana and Peter, and take the money to make a new life for herself. The Taylors wanted another child. They tried to adopt—but their plan to bring foster son Mike into their family was thwarted when Diana's past involvement with the late Phil Brewer came to light. Diana desperately wanted a brother or sister for her daughter, Martha, and found herself tempted when Heather offered her baby in exchange for $10,000 in cash.

Meanwhile, Rick became even closer to Lesley as he lent a helping hand in the search for Laura. In Detroit, they learned the stunning news from Cameron Faulkner's old business partner that despite all Cam's elaborate machinations, Laura really was Lesley's child after all. But where could she be? Canada!

Lesley and Rick headed north to Haverland, Canada, where viewers saw Laura with Barbara Vining (whose marriage to Jason had broken up), who had dragged her daughter away from a commune. Laura (now played by teenager Genie Francis) was not the naive girl she'd been before entering the commune. The "new" Laura was rebellious, feisty and not about to go home.

"I'll run away if you make me go back!" she insisted. Lesley, hoping for a joyous reunion with her daughter, was crushed by Laura's attitude. "I don't want either one of you. I'm happy right where I am," she declared.

Lesley insisted that Buck, the lecherous guru of the commune, had brainwashed Laura. Not convinced, Rick hammered at the girl to change her tune. Privately, Rick vowed to win her over. In time, he succeeded in getting through to Laura, removing her from Buck's web in the nick of time before Laura became part of the cult leader's "private harem." Rick had an equally arduous time gaining Lesley's love. In the course of their search, Rick and the pregnant Lesley had grown closer. On one occasion, a heated argument even sparked a hot kiss! But Lesley continued to drag her heels, even after Rick returned to Port Charles with Laura in tow.

At home with her real mother, Laura tried to come to grips with the confused emotions that had led her to distrust all "adults." At the bottom, she came to realize that her communal experience was spawned by a feeling that Lesley no longer cared about her. Rick got through to Laura, making her see that she was truly loved, both by Lesley and her adoptive mother, Barbara Vining. Lesley was deeply touched by Rick's effort, but staggered when he declared his love with a proposal of marriage! Caught off guard, Lesley admitted she loved him too—but wondered if perhaps he might be confusing love for her with his desire to do "something constructive" with his life after Jeff's near-tragedy.

"If you think I'm asking you to be my wife just to regain my self-respect—I'm not."

Lesley's attitude infuriated Rick, who stormed out. In a short time, they mended fences, and Lesley joyously agreed to become Mrs. Rick Webber.

Monica, shaken by the news that Rick had asked Lesley to marry him, finally did what she had long feared to do. She asked Jeff for a divorce. On the rebound, Jeff asked Heather to marry him, and she accepted. But before the marriage could take place, Heather's ex, Larry Joe, set Jeff straight by exposing a flurry of Heather's insidious plots. This put Jeff in a dilemma: How could he marry such a devious girl? But how could he give up his son? In desperation, Jeff told Heather he couldn't marry her. Instead, he would keep their baby and give her money to settle down in New York. Heather refused his offer and fled to Glenville, leaving Diana Taylor destroyed by the fact that she wouldn't get the baby she so desperately wanted. Now, more than ever, Monica wanted Rick! On a rampage, Monica confronted Lesley at home and bitterly threatened her rival with an ultimatum: Unless Lesley broke her engagement to Rick, Monica would publicly air their affair and ruin Rick's career. Rushing out of the apartment, Monica didn't hear Lesley's scream as she fell down the stairs! Rick found her unconscious and rushed her to General Hospital, where surgery was performed by Dr. Adam Streeter and Gina Dante, Mark's younger sister, who had recently moved to Port Charles after the breakup with her fiancé, fellow doctor Gary Lansing. But their heroic efforts failed—the baby was dead, its blood supply compromised by extensive bleeding even before Lesley was found by Rick. Devastated by the loss, Lesley wrote Rick a "Dear John" letter and fled to Venice. Upon her return, Rick was able to convince Lesley that they belonged together, and in a quietly glorious ceremony held in a ski lodge, Lesley and Rick became man and wife!

The path to happiness was more difficult to cross for star-crossed lovers Terri Arnett and Dr. Mark Dante. Mary-Ellen Dante, newly released from Lakecliff Sanitarium, resolved to destroy their union—and that meant destroying Terri! She had a plan: Mary-Ellen arranged with her chauffeur, Lenny, to fix the brakes on Terri's car so she would crash. Once that plan was in place, she cornered Terri and attacked—accusing her of having an affair with Mark. Terri vehemently denied the accusations, but finally admitted that she and Mark loved each other—and their ultimate plans were to marry. Mary-Ellen, an evil gleam in her eye, vowed that she wouldn't give up "what's mine. I'll never divorce Mark and I'll kill you before I'll let you have him!" Terri, horrified, fled from the scene, and the victorious Mary-Ellen smiled in triumph—because Terri's car was rigged to crash!

At General Hospital, Mark Dante was forced to perform heroic surgery to save Terri's life. Awaking from her coma, at first Terri remembered nothing about her confrontation with Mary-Ellen. Eventually, the memories came flooding back.

"I'm going to tell Mark everything!" she taunted Mary-Ellen.

Desperate, Mary-Ellen slashed her wrists. When Terri heard of the suicide attempt, she backed down, vowing never to tell Mark the truth about what Mary-Ellen had done. Fearful that Mary-Ellen would kill Mark, Terri broke off with Mark, telling him that she didn't love him. She confided the truth to Rick and Steve, swearing both doctors to secrecy. Thus spurned by Terri, Mark resolved to make his future with Mary-Ellen, telling her that his relationship with Terri was over for good. Eventually, Mary-Ellen's mental illness resurfaced and she sank back into catatonia. But it was too late for Mark and Terri to have a future together. Seeking a new start, Terri moved to Los Angeles to resume her singing career.

After the birth of her baby, Steven Lars, Heather took $500 of Jeff's money and fled to New York City, where she hoped to fulfill her grand dreams of a fabulous modeling career! She found refuge in a boarding house run by Edna Hadley, a slovenly old landlady who promised to help her, but quickly revealed a shady side with involvements with a porno photographer and a lawyer with questionable ethics. Heather's fortunes were at a low ebb in New York. Mrs. Hadley pressured her into working for pornographer Cal Whedon. Jerry Sherman, an assistant director, spotted her and offered Heather a movie job in Hollywood. This was Heather's dream! She didn't know where she could get the money for the trip, but Mrs. Hadley did! Heather spilled the beans to her landlady about her original plan to sell Steven Lars to the Taylors for $10,000. "A dandy plan!" spewed Mrs. Hadley, with dollar signs in her eyes.

Mrs. Hadley arranged for Heather to see a shady lawyer who told her that a legal adoption would take 18 months in New York and suggested that a "legal" adoption could be staged for the Taylors' benefit. He assured Heather that the baby's identity would be kept a secret. The lawyer then sent a cable to the Taylors telling them that a child was available for adoption. Along with their lawyer, Lee Baldwin, who had recently returned to Port Charles, the Taylors flew to Miami, where Mrs. Hadley, posing as the baby's grandmother, handed the baby over to them. After Mrs. Hadley and the lawyer took their cut, Heather was left with only $1800 of the $10,000—not even enough for her to establish herself in Hollywood.

"Is there any way for me to get my baby back?" she asked innocently.

"Sorry, kid." answered the lawyer. "Get a job!" countered Mrs. Hadley.

Discovering that Heather was in New York, Jeff intended to bring her and the baby back to Port Charles. Learning Jeff was on his way, she decided to flee to California immediately. Mrs. Hadley recommended that she tell Jeff that Steven Lars had died, but Heather found that idea abhorrent—because it "would devastate Jeff." Before Heather could leave, Jeff showed up at her door. Heather, so shaken by his presence, couldn't bring herself to reveal the real story of Steven Lars. Instead, she told the inexcusable lie.

"Steven Lars is dead," she cried out.

Jeff, devastated, was very sympathetic to Heather's plight and asked her to come back to Port Charles with him. Touched by her apparent sadness, Jeff made the mother of his child a tempting offer.

"Marry me, Heather," he proposed. She eagerly accepted.

Back home, the newly engaged Heather began to spend considerable time with the Taylors and "Peter Jr."

In 1977, Audrey Hardy's problems were becoming ever more complicated. All she wanted was a happy married life with Steve and her son, Tommy. All she had in 1977 was the threat of a custody fight from the back-from-the-dead Tom Baldwin. Young Tommy took the news joyously, spending all his free time with his indulgent daddy. Tommy didn't want his mom to marry Steve Hardy—instead, he wanted to reunite his parents. To his friend, Mike, Tommy confided his plans to fake an illness to bring Audrey and Tom together. The boy's mysterious pains nearly worked when Steve and Audrey's relationship became strained over Tommy's "pretended" illness. At the same time, Tom begged Audrey not to divorce him.

"I'm still in love with you," he pleaded with a conflicted Audrey, who ultimately refused Tom's demands to resume their marriage.

Bitterly rejected, Tom announced to Steve and Audrey that he was leaving for a new job in Salt Lake City—and taking Tommy with him! Tom adamantly declared that unless Audrey granted him full custody of Tommy, he wouldn't allow the divorce to go through. Tommy, feeling caught between the Tom-Audrey battles, ran away! In the days after Tommy's disappearance, Tom and Audrey came to realize the damage they had done to their son. Reluctantly, Tom agreed to give Audrey her divorce. And that happy news was capped by the news that Tommy had been found.

The joy over Tommy's return was decidedly short-lived. Within days of his return, the boy fell gravely ill, this time for real! Dr. Gary Lansing discovered he had been bitten by a wood tick. After removal of the dreaded insect, Tommy quickly recovered. Tom, knowing that his stubbornness almost cost his son's life, agreed to let Tommy live with Audrey, participate in Steve and Audrey's upcoming wedding and visit Tom periodically in Salt Lake City. The autumn of 1977 brought a new marriage and new joy to Steve and Audrey—their family crisis was finally over. Still, there were more surprises to come!

For attorney Lee Baldwin, an extended visit to Port Charles meant renewing old acquaintances with his dear friends. Despite the comfort he felt with the old gang, Lee yearned to return to Florida where his loving wife Caroline lived with her son, Bobby. After counseling his brother, Tom, in the Tommy Hardy custody battle, Lee had hoped to head home to his wife but his plans changed drastically—tragically—when word came that Caroline and Bobby had been lost at sea. Lee returned to Florida to make final arrangements, but with his beloved family gone, Lee couldn't stay. Returning to Port Charles, he set up a new law practice and found comfort in long, warm and strictly platonic evenings with Gail. As they struggled with their memories—Gail had recently lost her husband, the brilliant Dr. Greg Adamson—Lee and Gail were good company for each other. Sensing Lee's devastation, Gail secretly contacted Scotty Baldwin, his stepson, urging the young law student to get in touch with the man who had raised him—the only father he'd ever known. Scotty had left Port Charles several years earlier and was now living in New York's Greenwich Village. Gail's mission worked when Scotty showed up in town. She smiled with satisfaction as father and son reunited. Scotty, agreeing to join the "establishment," accepted a clerking job at General Hospital, where he met and became instantly captivated by young Laura Webber.

Another crisis was about to devastate the city of Port Charles. During the first week of September 1977, the town was hit by a catastrophic hurricane, wreaking havoc and causing a series of dramatic events to unfold. Laura and Scotty, en route to a rock concert, were caught in the storm and forced to seek refuge in a storage shed. At General Hospital, the power failed, forcing surgery to continue in the garage, illuminated only by car headlights. Dorrie Fleming, a dynamite nurse who proved invaluable with the many hurricane casualties, was introduced, as well as two injured patients: the paralyzed David Hamilton (a former college roommate of Rick's, now a down-on-his-luck artist) and Lisa, a mysterious young girl. Diana's mother, Mrs. Maynard, and Diana's daughter, Martha, en route to an emergency shelter in Barton Falls, were

Troubled teen Laura Webber found a friend in young law student Scotty Baldwin. Love blossomed when, en route to a rock concert, the kids were caught in a hurricane and found refuge in an abandoned storage shed.

Happy moments were rare for young Laura Webber in 1977. Suffering from a bad case of growing pains, she felt that her parents and new boyfriend Scotty Baldwin treated her like a child.

involved in a serious auto accident. After many tension-filled hours, Mrs. Maynard pulled through, but little Martha died from her severe injuries. The loss shattered Diana, whose emotions had been strained so often over the years in trying to build a family.

David Hamilton wallowed in pity when he was informed that the bodies of his wife and children had been discovered in the wreckage of their house. David's paralysis puzzled the General Hospital doctors, who could find no physiological basis for his inability to walk. After several weeks, he was released from the hospital and gratefully accepted his pal Rick's offer to move into the Webber house to recuperate. In time, Lesley couldn't help but notice that there was something strange about David Hamilton.

Laura didn't feel the same way—she adored David! The maturing girl and the older man struck up an instant friendship, one that troubled Lesley Webber. Laura was experiencing severe "growing pains" which had caused her relationship with Lesley to become cold and distant—not at all like the cozy rapport she'd established with Monica and David. From the moment Laura returned to Port Charles, she rebelled against her mother's rules and edicts.

"You treat me like a child. Monica and David treat me like an adult!" Laura defiantly told her anguished mother.

Lesley became especially upset when she correctly suspected that Laura and Scotty's relationship had become a romantic one. Laura asked Dr.

Monica Webber to supply her with birth control pills, but she refused at first, urging Laura to speak candidly with her mother. Laura, insisting that Lesley "wouldn't understand," persuaded Monica to prescribe the pills. Scotty was a bit more understanding of Lesley's demands. He was willing to cool it with Laura. Laura was not, and she planned a series of deceits and intrigues designed to keep her mother off her back.

One day, Lesley became enraged when she found Laura in David's bedroom. Then, checking inside Laura's purse to see if she needed a new wallet for Christmas, Lesley found birth control pills! She kept the information to herself, but became highly distraught. When she finally confronted Laura, the girl was furious, shouting, "What right do you have to be going through my purse in the first place?"

Like Lesley, Scotty Baldwin took notice of Laura's fascination with David Hamilton. In fact, Scotty caught Laura in several lies—all having to do with her handsome houseguest. One night, a lying Laura turned down an invitation from Scotty because she claimed to be having dinner with Lesley.

Later that evening, Scotty ran into her with David. It seemed that both Lesley and Scotty had good reason to be distrustful of David Hamilton.

With his personal life back on track, Rick turned his attentions to a lifelong dream—the building of a new cardiac wing at General Hospital. But the project needed someone to foot the bill, and to that end, Steve Hardy contacted Dr. Alan Quartermaine of the Hardwick Foundation. Monica's head turned when she set her eyes on the tall and handsome financier/doctor. The son of wealthy and influential Lila and Edward Quartermaine, Alan was born with a silver spoon in his mouth. Formerly a surgeon, Alan was forced to become a general practitioner when his left hand was injured. Working for the Hardwick Foundation, Alan was in Port Charles to determine whether Rick's new project was worthy enough to receive funding. In typical fashion, Monica landed a plum assignment assisting Dr. Quartermaine with evaluation. Right from the start, the two doctors butted heads. Alan found Monica appealing and she was certainly attracted to him, but she found his evaluations on the project not at all to her liking.

"You're pigheaded!" she told him after just a few weeks of close contact.

The war between Alan and Monica had begun!

1978

In early 1978, the corridors of General Hospital were abuzz with the news that celebrated industrialist Lamont Corbin had been admitted to the hospital for a risky operation. Dr. Hardy assigned his best surgeon, the no-nonsense Mark Dante, to the case. Mark bristled upon hearing that the wealthy and influential Corbin would be receiving preferential treatment. Dante had more than a passing interest in the case—he knew Lamont's wife, Kathryn.

"Katie and I were street brats in Boston," he told Steve Hardy.

That was a slight bend in the truth. Mark and Katie had been childhood sweethearts on Boston's north side—and when their paths crossed again at General Hospital, it was clear to both that the old spark was still there.

Lamont, facing the eventuality of his death, made elaborate plans. His plans included pairing off Katie with Mark Dante. Mark and Katie acknowledged their deep feelings for each other, but agreed that their immediate concern was to pull Lamont through the difficult surgery. They allowed themselves one passionate kiss, but Mark admonished that it must be their last. Remarkably, Lamont pulled through the operation and began a slow but steady recovery. Because Lamont's health could influence the price of Corbin Ltd. stock, his medical condition was kept a closely guarded secret from the media. Sensing an opportunity to make a fast buck, David Hamilton made a deal with Cates, a shady investor, that through his ties with Rick Webber, he would be kept up to date on Lamont's condition. With the clear sound of a threat in his voice, Cates advised Hamilton that "your information had better be correct—you're playing in the big leagues now!"

In time, Mark and Katie admitted their love for each other and resolved to tell Lamont as soon as he was strong enough. Now that he was no longer a dying man, Lamont's feelings about Mark and Katie changed. He became tremendously possessive of his wife as he instructed his business associate, Dan Rooney, to tail Katie and Mark at all times. In the meantime, Lamont continued to do "good works" for General Hospital while engineering a behind-the-scenes smear campaign against Mark Dante. Finally, the scheming Lamont threatened Katie by declaring that unless she came back to him, he would destroy Dante's career.

Fleeing to Boston, Katie felt she had no choice but to give in to her husband's emotional blackmail. But Mark wouldn't give up on Katie! Eventually, with Dan Rooney's assistance, he was able to convince his "fair Kate" to leave her husband. Together, they broke the news to Lamont, who felt he had no choice but to allow his wife to be with the man she loved. Lamont's subsequent death cleared the way for the long-ago lovers to be together—in marriage—at last!

Dr. Monica Webber's combative relationship with Dr. Alan Quartermaine began to mellow and blossom into romance early in 1978. But Alan's stay at General Hospital was scheduled to be a short one. When his evaluation of the cardiac wing concluded, Alan made

Dr. Alan Quartermaine agreed to make Port Charles his home base after falling in love with his colleague, Dr. Monica Webber. They began a serious relationship, but Alan remained deeply concerned that Monica was still in love with Rick Webber.

preparations to wind up his affairs in Port Charles and return to his family home in Southampton. While packing to leave, Dr. Quartermaine discovered, to his amazement, that he couldn't exactly "wind up" his relationship with Monica.

Just before departing Port Charles, Alan confessed his strong feelings for Monica, who admitted that she, too, cared for him. Monica's confession persuaded Alan to make Port Charles his home base. And soon his eccentric family followed him to town. The upper-crust Quartermaines were one of the wealthiest and most prominent families in the state of New York. The crusty family patriarch, Edward, had amassed a great fortune through his world-renowned conglomerate, ELQ.

"Making money keeps my arteries open," he often announced to no one in particular.

Edward's kindhearted wife, Lila, was as shrewd as she was wise. Their haughty daughter Tracy was a spoiled "bitch" who felt, by birthright alone, that she deserved her rightful share of the family fortune. Unlike her brother Alan, Tracy had a natural affinity for big business—but "daddy" Edward refused to recognize her prowess. As a result, spiteful Tracy was always at odds with the rest of the family. The Quartermaines were a rich—and quirky—bunch.

Almost immediately Alan's insecurities began to play a major role in his rocky relationship with Monica—and Rick was the cause of his anxiety. While Alan genuinely seemed to like Rick and respect his abilities as a doctor, he neurotically distrusted Monica, incessantly questioning her "close" working relationship with Dr. Webber.

"I'm over Rick Webber," she assured Alan.

Privately, Monica had her doubts, even as she planned a June wedding to Alan! And Alan struggled to keep his jealousy a closely guarded secret, which proved difficult—especially from his sister, Tracy. Tracy Quartermaine knew her brother like a book!

Feeling pressured by her confrontation with Laura over the birth control pills, Lesley decided to make peace with her daughter. With a firm resolve she chose to be Laura's friend as well as her mother. Laura, too, made every effort to achieve a better relationship with Lesley. David Hamilton's presence in the house continued to unsettle the Webber clan. David's self-serving, darker side began to surface as did his obsession with Lesley. An artist, he began to spend hours sketching her portrait. That was

understandable. But why was he carrying Lesley Webber's photograph in his wallet?

After several weeks, David moved into his own apartment, but his obsession grew more pronounced. Alone with Lesley, he smoothly attempted an all-out pass! Lesley would have none of it. When Lesley rebuffed his advances, David exploded, confessing how much he hated his "best friend" Rick. She fled out the door, and although she wanted to tell Rick immediately, she decided to wait until he returned from New York where he was working with Monica on the new cardiac wing. Upon his return, Lesley couldn't bring herself to tell Rick about David's attack because his plans were going so well for the cardiac wing that she was loathe to destroy his happiness. Instead, Lesley told Jeff about the episode, swearing him to secrecy.

Rejected by Lesley, David moved in on her teenage daughter, Laura. Luring her to his apartment, he shocked the impressionable youngster by telling her that Lesley had made a play for him. Laura didn't fight her attraction when the handsome artist took her in his arms and kissed her on the lips. Over a period of weeks, David and Laura continued to meet secretly, and their relationship became romantic—at least in Laura's eyes. David had an ulterior motive in charming Laura. He kept her notes and poems, feeling he could use them against Rick and Lesley at the proper time.

More and more Laura fell under David's spell, neglecting her family, schoolwork and friends. Rick became increasingly concerned over his adopted daughter's violent mood changes and inconsistencies in explanations of her daily whereabouts. Feeling the pressure mounting at home, Laura pledged her love and pleaded with him to whisk her away from Port Charles. What Laura didn't know was that David was up to his ears in an illegal land scam and planning to beat a hasty retreat out of town. Discovering the depth of his friend's deception, Rick confronted David, and a violent argument ensued between the men.

"I've always hated you, Rick!" screamed David, as he taunted his "old friend" with insinuating remarks about Lesley and Laura.

Losing his temper, Rick punched David and stormed out! Laura called David at his apartment and begged him to take her away with him—now! With that, she scribbled a note for Lesley, telling her she "loves David and is leaving with him." When Laura arrived early at his apartment, David let her have it!

"I never really loved you! It was your mother who turned me on!"

In her fury, a horrified Laura lashed out at David, pushing him with every ounce of her strength, before fleeing the apartment in tears.

Laura's potent push had caught David off guard. Falling back against the fireplace hearth, he hit his head, sustaining a critical injury. Dazed and bloody, he struggled to reach the phone, but passed out before he could call for help. Finding Laura's note, Lesley dashed to David's apartment and found a hysterical Laura bolting from the scene. Telling Laura to remain in the hall, Lesley went inside and found David—dead! Returning to the hallway, an astonished Lesley discovered that Laura was gone! Coolly demonstrating the extent to which a mother will go to protect her child, Lesley cleaned the apartment, removing all fingerprints and carefully placing her own on the marble statuette she found beside David, which she believed to be the murder weapon. With steely determination, Lesley picked up the phone.

"This is Dr. Lesley Webber," she told the police dispatcher on the other end of the phone. "I'm calling to report that I accidentally killed a man."

With her lawyer, Howard Lansing, by her side, Lesley informed Detective Burt Ramsey that David had lured her to the apartment by saying that Rick was there unconscious. Once there, David, drunk, tried to rape her. But certain aspects of her story didn't coincide with the coroner's report. For one, the police determined that David wasn't killed by a blow from the statuette and wasn't drunk at the time of his death. But what about Laura? That horrifying encounter proved too much for the troubled girl, causing her to block from her mind the entire night of the murder. Lesley's well-crafted tale did not fool the Port Charles police chief Burt Ramsey who suspected that either Lesley was trying to protect someone else or she and David had been having an affair. A Grand Jury assembled and indicted Lesley Webber for murder.

From her prison cell, a valiant Lesley kept mum even as the prosecution painted a vivid picture of her as a vengeful woman who had been rejected by her forbidden lover. She kept mum, stressing to Laura that she must never reveal to anyone—including Rick—that she was at David's on the night of the murder. With memories buried deep in her psyche, Laura began suffering terrible nightmares. Through intensive therapy sessions with Dr. Peter Taylor, she gradually began to recall glimpses of the tragic encounter with David. But when Laura's horrifying memories came flooding back, panic set in!

"Oh my God, I killed David!" she realized.

Skipping town, she took a bus to New York City.

"Oh Laura, where are you?" worried Lesley in her prison cell.

Scotty Baldwin was wondering the same thing about his former girlfriend. Though he and Laura had gone their separate ways, Scotty still carried a torch for his forlorn friend. To locate Laura, Scotty enlisted the aid of his best friend, Bryan Phillips, and together they set out for New York. In the East Village, Bryan and Scotty found Laura, who was about to join a seamy drug and prostitution ring. Much to Laura's horror, Rick informed his daughter that he knew of her affair with David. Laura then visited Lesley and told her that *during* her last session with Peter, she remembered killing David! All charges against Lesley were dropped, but her worst fears were realized when Assistant District Attorney Mitch Williams released the real story to the press in order to further his political ambitions. Soon after Lesley was set free, Laura was taken to juvenile court, then released on six months' probation in the custody of her parents—making for a very uncomfortable Webber household! The one good thing in Laura's young life was Scotty, who helped her endure her probation by courting her all over again! Still, Laura felt that Rick and Lesley were her jailers, and she trusted no one. Lesley, her nerves shattered by the experience, had difficulty responding to Rick's gallant attempts at patching up the relationship.

Heather left her dreams of becoming a model behind in New York and returned to Port Charles,

Dr. Monica Webber paid a prison visit to Lesley Webber, who was awaiting trial for the murder of David Hamilton—a crime that she did not commit. To protect her daughter Laura, Lesley had confessed to the murder.

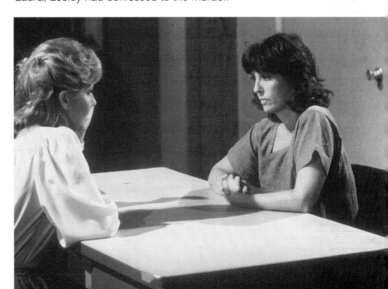

where she spent precious time with her son, Steven Lars, or "P.J." as he was known by his new family, the Taylors. Living in an apartment that her fiancé, Jeff, had rented for her, Heather began receiving threatening, anonymous calls warning her to leave Port Charles. Gripped by fear, she concluded that someone had learned the truth about Steven Lars. She considered heeding the sinister warnings, never realizing that the calls were the handiwork of Jeff's patient, the mentally disturbed Lana Holbrook. Lana nearly made good on her threat by attempting to kill Heather, but Jeff raced to her rescue, and saw to it that Lana was given proper treatment at a private hospital on Long Island.

With that crisis out of the way, Heather began to devote more and more of her time to "P.J." As the boy's nanny, she was able to see her son every day, but Heather's all-consuming interest in the child's welfare alarmed Peter and Diana. Fearing her interest was unhealthy, Peter and Diana dismissed Heather. Still, she discovered ways to see her beloved son. During an "adoption celebration for P.J." at Peter and Diana's, Heather's mother, Alice Grant, made a stunning realization—that P.J. is really Steven Lars! Confronted with her incredible lie, Heather fled the party and decided to leave Port Charles. Jeff, not knowing the true reason for her quick exit, enticed her to stay in town by offering Heather a job in General Hospital's new library— another gift from the late Lamont Corbin.

Head writer Douglas Marland gave *General Hospital* a dose of vitality when sexy student nurse Bobbie Spencer arrived on General Hospital's seventh floor in 1977. Bobbie desperately tried to keep her sordid street-walking past a secret from her new friends and colleagues at the hospital.

A new job, a new lease on life, and a new husband for Heather! Her wish came true when she married Jeff Webber, but early in their marriage the newlyweds saw little of each other because of Jeff's hospital duty and long hours of study for his license. Happy in marriage, Heather Webber had no inkling that her troubles were just beginning! A lowlife mobster by the name of Cal Jamison came to town armed with a deadly threat aimed at Heather. Meeting with Jeff, Jamison made the incredible claim that Steven Lars didn't die in New York. Panic-stricken, Heather couldn't find a way to stop him. With Steve, Jeff journeyed to New York City where, oddly, he located Steven Lars', death certificate. Unable to contact Jamison, Jeff gave up the search, firmly believing what he'd thought all along—that his son was dead.

Upon Jeff's return, Heather felt a sense of comfort—but it proved temporary because she began experiencing dizzy spells and nausea. Could it be? Yes! Heather was pregnant—but not 100% happy! Conversely, Jeff was overjoyed.

"If it's a boy I want to name him Steven Lars!" he gushed to his stricken new wife.

Several newcomers staked their claim to a piece of Port Charles in 1978. Heather's flirtatious cousin, Susan Moore, arrived in town and took an immediate interest in the handsome and very-married Dr. Peter Taylor. Heather noticed how her sexy cousin grabbed every opportunity to spend time with Peter, who didn't respond to her heated overtures. In rapid time, Susan's preoccupation with Peter was diverted to Assistant District Attorney Mitch Williams, who found the brunette beauty equally attractive. But Susan had stiff competition in her quest to bed the studly D.A. Her competition was feisty and rich Tracy Quartermaine—who stopped at nothing to get what she wanted—and Tracy wanted Mitch very badly. Perhaps she would not have been so eager had she known that sleazy Mitch secretly maintained close ties to the Port Charles mob!

And then there was Barbara Jean Spencer, or simply "Bobbie" as she was known to her friends. The flame-haired student nurse with the bright smile and bubbly personality found herself smitten with law student Scotty Baldwin, who was in the midst of a stormy courtship with Laura. Between his law studies and his support for his stepfather Lee (who had fallen off the wagon and once again battled alcoholism), Scotty had little time to spend with Laura. And Laura's infatuation with David Hamilton irritated Scotty. After one of Laura and Scotty's squabbles, Bobbie was there to pick up Scotty's spirits by taking him home to her rooming house—which was strictly against house policy. Bobbie paid a heavy price for taking in her overnight guest: eviction. With no place to turn, she accepted Jessie Brewer's generous offer to move into her spare room.

One day at the hospital, a startled Bobbie ran into Cal Jamison, the very same scoundrel who was attempting to extort money from Jeff Webber. He vaguely recognized Bobbie, and she nervously tried to hide the fact that she recognized him. Jamison's presence unnerved Bobbi—she knew that it was just a matter of time before he would recall where they'd met. Weeks later, Bobbie's fears were realized when she received a special-delivery letter from Cal Jamison threatening to expose her former lifestyle—as a hooker! And he had the pictures to prove it. To keep Jamison at bay, a jittery Bobbie began to send him hush money.

With the publicity of the David Hamilton murder taking a toll on the Webber household, Laura experienced bad times and bad grades at school, while Lesley, troubled by frigidity in bed with Rick, wondered if their marriage would ever work again. Late in the year, Lesley began to suspect—helped along by Laura's constant name-dropping—that the Rick/Monica relationship was more than just a working one. At the hospital, Alan caught Monica and Rick in an innocent, yet joyful embrace. Poker-faced, Alan told Monica, "Of course I have no reason to be jealous. I understand your relationship now."

But did he—*really?*

The Bobbie/Scotty relationship began to fail when Scotty chose to devote more time to Laura. He tried to be honest with Bobbie, sharing his feelings about Laura with her. But Bobbie simply refused to listen. She had feelings for Scotty—in fact, Scott Baldwin was the first man Bobbie Spencer had ever slept with whom she truly loved. Believing that Scotty's change of heart was all Laura's fault, a scheming Bobbie set out to destroy her rival! Bobbie placed a call to her older brother, Luke, asking for his help in sending Laura to reform school!

"This chick has been trouble for me for a long time. I want her sent to reform school!" she told Luke.

Bobbie engineered a plan designed to make Laura break her curfew. And she convinced Luke to

Luke Spencer's debut: In the fall of 1978, Bobbie Spencer deviously called upon her hoodlum brother Luke to assist in her sneaky scheme to break up Scotty and Laura.

do the dirty work! Knowing that Scotty planned to take Laura for a "special dinner" at the Lakeview Lodge, a hotel and restaurant 40 miles from Port Charles, Bobbie coerced her brother to sneak into the restaurant parking lot, lift the hood on Scotty's car and tamper with the engine so it would break down on the road back to Port Charles. No problem for Luke! He'd made a career out of performing low-level crimes much more difficult than this!

"There ain't no mechanic up here in the boondocks who is ever gonna figure out what I did with that carburetor," he boasted in a phone call to Bobbie.

Bobbie added to the scheme by calling the Lakeview Lodge to make a reservation in Scotty Baldwin's name.

"This way it will look like they had more than dinner in mind!"

Bobbie's plan worked like a charm! Of course, Bobbie put the finishing touches on her scheme by secretly placing a call to John Higgins, the court-appointed investigator, alerting him to Laura's probation violation. Thanks to Luke, who assisted Bobbie in scheme after scheme, the threat of reform school became a stark reality. And if these maneuvers didn't work to get Laura out of Scotty's mind, then Bobbie had one more trick up her sleeve—pregnancy!

For a time in early 1979, it appeared as if Bobbie had won her war against Laura Webber by claiming to be pregnant with Scotty's child. And to ensure that her scheme would work, Bobbie saw to it that all the bases were covered—even producing a positive pregnancy test (a simple test-tube switch) that convinced Scotty she was telling the truth. By tricking Scotty into a marriage proposal to give their baby a name, Bobbie opened up the old wounds of Laura's mistrust of people. Scotty reluctantly agreed to marry Bobbie, but not to sleep with her ever again! Fortunately, their wedding would never happen. Just days before the nuptials were to take place, Lesley's secret

Laura got a job at the Campus Disco, which put her in close proximity to Luke Spencer, who managed the disco as a front for the mob.

sleuthing proved that Bobbie was never really pregnant. A relieved Scotty blasted Bobbie for her trickery, then raced back into Laura's open arms.

Bobbie, not one to take defeat lightly, continued to make plans for revenge on all those people who had caused her hurt and humiliation. She was more desperate than ever to break up Scotty and Laura and continued to put out SOS calls to the master, Luke, to help her with the dirty work. But Luke was becoming bored with her vengeance plots. Was his once-cold heart beginning to warm toward his former enemy, Laura Webber? As manager of the Campus Disco, Luke's offbeat and engaging personality was given a chance to shine. To the people of Port Charles, Luke Spencer and his partner, Roy DiLucca, appeared to be honest and respectable businessmen. Luke was a child of the streets, always reaching to get himself out of the gutter. Never allowing poverty to crush his spirit, Luke reacted to his humble environment by cultivating ambition. The Port Charles mob, run with an iron hand by the ruthless Frank Smith, offered Luke a way out. Running the mob-owned disco—used as a cover to launder organization money—gave Luke the kind of prestige, money and power that he'd never experienced before. Smith saw in the eager Luke Spencer an opportunity to take a young street punk and groom him for bigger things. He had Luke right where he wanted him—under his thumb. Luke and Frank were a match made in hell. In March, Luke finally met the young woman who had been the object of his "dirty tricks." For Luke, it was love at first sight. But, not for Laura! Troubled and nervous as she prepared for a court hearing on her probation, Laura hardly noticed Luke when they met in the campus coffee shop.

Scotty and Laura made plans for a June glorious wedding, never expecting that her father, Rick, feeling that Laura was still too young, would vehemently oppose the union. Laura was angered and upset by Rick's refusal to permit a June marriage to Scotty, often taking out her frustration on her fiancé. Rick and Lesley's troubled marriage went from bad to worse early in the new year. The David Hamilton escapade had seemingly done irreparable damage to their union. Lesley's frigidity intensified. Through group therapy, led by Dr. Irene Kassorla, Lesley made great strides in reaching a new understanding and she began to see real hope for her marriage to Rick—as soon as he came out of quarantine!

In the winter of 1979, Dr. Steve Hardy was forced to place General Hospital under quarantine due to an outbreak of a rare and mysterious disease known as Lassa Fever. Steve, Rick, Alan, Audrey, Jeff and Monica were among the hospital staff, employees and even visitors who were quarantined within the walls of the hospital for weeks while the Bureau of Disease Control in Atlanta worked to isolate the deadly disease. A patient, Beatrice Hewitt, was the first to die from Lassa Fever. Then Lee Baldwin was stricken with the mysterious illness. Within days, the disease reached epidemic proportions.

After weeks of exhaustive work, Dr. Steve Hardy fell ill with the potentially fatal disease. Flushed and weak, Steve continued to treat the infirmed before passing out. With Audrey by his side, a feverish Steve murmured, "Jeff, my son... my son...."

Audrey understood the long-buried secret Steve was sharing in his semi-conscious state. Believing that Steve was on his deathbed, Audrey stunned Jeff with the fact that Steve was his real father! Audrey begged Jeff not to tell Steve that the dark secret of his true parentage was out in the open. Near tears, an embittered Jeff ran off to absorb the incredible news. Upon Steve's recovery, Audrey gently informed him of the information he had blurted out in his delirium.

"Audrey, how could you tell Jeff?" said an angry Steve to his anguished wife.

After days of silence and separation, the Hardys reconciled. But the news of Jeff's true parentage would carry everlasting wounds. When the newly-acquainted father and son tried to patch things up, Jeff made it abundantly clear that their relationship would be a professional one—for now.

Confined to close quarters during the epidemic, Monica and Rick struggled to maintain a professional relationship themselves. But as the days passed and death filled the air, Monica turned to Rick, not Alan, for comfort, often sobbing in his arms. After several electric moments, she transferred out of Rick's service, telling her best friend, Gail, that she desperately needed to get him out of her heart.

"I'm married to Alan. I do love Alan," she constantly reminded herself.

Like Jeff, Rick Webber had idolized his late par-

ISSUES

Over the years, General Hospital *has often dealt frankly and realistically with the psychological problems of the residents of Port Charles. On several occasions, Dr. Irene Kassorla, a real-life psychologist, has led on-air group therapy sessions. Unique to daytime drama, the scenes were freewheeling and virtually unscripted.*

Here, Dr. Kassorla spearheads a 1978 encounter group involving Lesley Webber's troubles with her teenage daughter, Laura.

ents, Lars and Helene. So the bombshell news of his mother's long-ago affair with Steve Hardy had a profound impact on him. He began neglecting his hospital duties. Monica was concerned about Rick's bad attitude, while worrying about Alan, whose feelings of jealousy were renewed. With the quarantine lifted, Rick quickly exited the hospital and retreated to a remote fishing shack far from Port Charles—followed by a frightened but concerned Monica. Would their self-control hold out this time—or would passion overcome them?

Alone together, Rick grabbed Monica and kissed her. But cooler heads quickly prevailed and he insisted that they must fight what they feel for each other. Without making love, they left the shack and returned to Port Charles where Rick confessed to his wife that he had been away with Monica, then moved into the guest room.

"I love you," Rick whispered to Lesley, but when he kissed her, he could only think of Monica.

Instead of telling the truth to her husband,

Monica lyingly informed Alan that she had spent the night at the hospital—which served to fuel the flames of his jealousy even more!

As the weeks passed, Rick continued a downward spiral. Under tremendous personal and professional strain, he could not complete an emergency operation, handing the job over to Monica before fleeing to a local hotel to drown his despair in alcohol. Again she followed, and, in the charged atmosphere of anguish, attraction and mutual need, they finally made love. After a night of passion, Monica declared her total commitment to Rick, but he persuaded her that they both needed time to put their lives in order and to make absolutely sure of their feelings.

In the spring of 1979, Scotty kept assuring Laura that he was doing everything in his power to bring about a June wedding, but she lost confidence that they would ever be together. Disillusioned, Laura returned her engagement ring and set out to make new friends. Laura's disregard for his feelings sent Scotty into a tailspin.

"I've lost her," he moaned to his best friend Bryan.

In despair, Scotty turned to drink. Thankfully, Bryan and Lee, both recovering alcoholics, pulled him out of the trap—but not before Bobbie hatched another elaborate scheme designed to snare Scotty once and for all. Bobbie convinced her sometime boyfriend, Roy DiLucca, as a practical joke, to lift the ring from Scotty's pocket, and one night at the disco persuaded the bartender to slip a mickey to Scotty. Bobbie then took a semi-conscious Scotty back to his apartment and awaited Laura's appearance.

When the doorbell rang at his apartment, Bobbie dimmed the lights, messed up her hair, then made certain that Scotty's ring was on her finger before opening the door to a stunned Laura.

"Why do you look so surprised?" taunted Bobbie. "How long did you think you could treat Scotty like dirt without him turning to someone else?"

With tears in her eyes, Laura ran blindly into the night—but she would never make it home! In her fraught emotional state, Laura crashed the car and was rushed to General Hospital. When the scheduled surgeon was incapacitated at the last moment, Rick was forced to perform life-saving emergency surgery on his daughter. Upon her recovery, Laura's prayers were answered when she received permission to marry. As a special bonus, all charges relating to the Hamilton murder were dropped, freeing

Young lovers Scotty Baldwin and Laura Webber overcame many obstacles to marry in a casual June wedding held in Port Charles Park. Moments before the long-awaited wedding, Laura nearly panicked when Scotty was nowhere to be found! Due to a mixup, he arrived just in time to take Laura as his teenage bride.

her to begin frenzied wedding plans. Scotty feared he wouldn't pass his exams, making marriage impossible, but he did, graduating at the top of his class. In a casual, country-style wedding, Scott and Laura were married in the park.

Very much in love, the newlyweds traveled to Hollywood for their honeymoon.

Laura's accident shook Rick back to his senses. The fight to save his daughter's life, and his subsequent realization that he and Lesley shared a mutual need, put Rick's own life back in perspective. He informed Monica (who had separated from Alan) that despite their deep feelings they must acknowledge that the life they had planned together was a wild and impetuous dream. Knowing she would never love anyone in the same way she loved Rick, at first she declined Alan's attempts at reconciliation. What to do? For advice, Monica turned to her mother-in-law, Lila Quartermaine, who told her that despite Edward's infidelity, one that produced an illegitimate son, she had made a very happy life with him. Resigned to her fate, Monica went back to Alan, only to discover she was pregnant!

Tracy Quartermaine seethed upon learning that her brother had reconciled with Monica. There was no love lost between these two women! As the weeks passed and Monica announced her pregnancy to the Quartermaine clan, Tracy stepped up her vendetta against Monica by trying to fan the flames of Alan's jealousy of Rick. Tracy felt threatened, figuring correctly that Alan's first-born male heir would inherit the Quartermaine fortune instead of her son, Ned, who was tucked away in boarding school. The only way to keep Ned's legacy alive was to prove to one and all that Monica's baby was fathered by Rick, not Alan. At the same time, knowing that Edward wouldn't give her more money until she found herself a husband, Tracy nudged her fiancé, the corrupt, mob-tied assistant District Attorney, Mitch Williams, into marrying her. Enticed by the Quartermaine fortune, Mitch married Tracy, but continued to two-time her with Susan. By now, the upwardly mobile Mr. Williams (who remained in the mob's pocket) was running for the State Senate using Tracy's megabucks to finance his campaign. With her controlling the purse strings, Mitch had no choice but to give in to her demands to crack down on organized crime—starting with the mob's rumored control of the Campus Disco!

The Disco was quickly becoming a hub of the Port Charles community. By day, exercise guru Richard Simmons conducted classes attended by Tracy Quartermaine, Susan Moore, Laura and her best friends Claudia Jennings and Beverly DeFreest. At night, the atmosphere changed, as the club rocked to a disco beat. Luke and Roy tried to keep the Disco clean, but their hopes were dashed when money-hungry mob boss Frank Smith began to take a personal interest in the establishment.

Ruby Anderson, an ex-hooker grown too old for the profession, got a job at the hospital with Jessie's help. Salty, savvy and good-hearted, Ruby was Luke and Bobbie's aunt, the kind of person who had seen and done everything—twice! Thanks to her warmth and kindness, Bobbie and Luke enjoyed a sense of family for the first time since their youth in Jacksonville. Bobbie had undergone a major metamorphosis in the days following Laura's accident. When she realized how close to death Laura came, Bobbie was shaken to the core and truly repented her past scheming. Free of her obsession for Scotty, Bobbie found herself falling in love with Roy DiLucca. Within weeks, they were engaged. To add to the rosy scenario, Bobbie soon became a full-fledged nurse, to the delight of her mentor, Jessie Brewer.

Bobbie's private life was in turmoil. Her scandalous past life as a hooker came back to haunt her. Now, blackmailer Cal Jamison demanded $1,000—or he swore to provide Audrey with explicit details of her past, including pictures.

Upon their return from California, the honeymoon appeared to be over for Laura and Scotty as tension began creeping into their union. Scotty, pressed by his lack of money and the demands of his new job working with Lee, had precious little time to spend with his lonely new wife. Laura and Scotty's life became more turbulent upon the arrival of Laura's stepsister, Amy Vining. It cost Scotty a bundle to entertain the engaging 16-year-old, and Laura didn't exactly enjoy losing the center of attraction, especially in her parent's home, where Rick and Lesley were delighted to have Amy as a guest. Bored and seeking a challenge, Laura convinced Luke Spencer to give her a job as a waitress at the Campus Disco. She could certainly use the money to repay her huge credit card bill, as well as to fulfill her wish to buy Scotty a new set of law books. A friendship quickly followed between Luke and Laura—and one of the most amazingly complex romances in soap opera history was about to begin!

Working together in the disco, Luke and Laura developed a comfortable rapport. He found her easy to talk to.

"My life and Bobbie's, it's like we've always had to settle for second best—and I'm sick of that," he confessed.

Laura came to see the good in Luke.

"You're a pretty special person, Luke Spencer," said Laura. "You never let anyone down, ever."

Luke's intense feelings for Laura were unmistakably love. He began to fantasize about her, and in rapid time, those feelings grew into an obsession. At the same time, Laura developed an uneasy fascination with this adventure-seeking rebel. After hours at the disco, he began to air his intimate feelings to a shocked Laura. Pulling back, he apologized for overstepping his bounds, and promised Laura that they would always be "just friends."

Pressure began to mount when Luke learned that Frank Smith planned to test his loyalty by asking him to murder Mitch Williams on election night. Instantly, Luke understood the cold facts: This was a suicide mission, and there was no way he would leave the scene of the hit alive. And if he refused the assignment, he would be rubbed out by the mob. Either way, Luke was marked for death!

As counterpoint to this action, Bobbie found herself confronted in the hospital by a former "john," and the shocking truth that Bobbie was once a hooker finally came out for all to hear. When Roy found out, he beat the man up and furiously confronted Bobbie. Hopelessly embarrassed, Bobbie gave Roy back her engagement ring.

On that same evening, Scotty Baldwin opened a bill from the credit card company and saw that Laura had once again exceeded their budget—by $500! A terrible quarrel resulted, and Laura rushed out to work, feeling that her marriage was over. At the disco, a hopeless Laura found herself flirting with Roy. Later, as Laura waited for Scotty—who had promised to pick her up after work—she began feeling even more hopeless.

"Maybe he really does want our marriage to end," she thought, waiting for his arrival. As the last of the employees left the disco, a drunken Luke entered the bar area and silently began to cry. "I found out something tonight. Within a month, I'll be dead," he confided to Laura. His life and his dreams were over. In a bitter outpouring of love, jealousy, sexual tension and unbridled rage, Luke confessed the depth of his feelings for her.

"I dream about you. I dream about holding you in my arms and making love to you. Laura, you are my life!"

Fear and fascination in her eyes, Laura again stressed that they could be nothing but friends.

"I don't want to be your friend, Laura—and I can't have you," he countered. "You don't belong in my world and I don't belong in yours. Look what you've done to me! I'm not going to die without holding you in my arms just one time. Dance with me, Laura."

Luke reached out and took Laura's hand and together they swayed to the pulsating beat of Herb Alpert's sultry song, "Rise." Luke drew her close, and his grasp became urgent and fierce.

"No, Luke, no!" exclaimed Laura, as they sank to the floor.

Moments later, it was over.

Oh my God, what have I done? thought Luke as he looked at Laura on the floor. Her clothes ripped and her body bruised, she ran sobbing into the night. A policeman found her, crying and disheveled, in the park and asked if she had been raped. Laura replied that she had, but didn't reveal the identity of her attacker. When she was admitted to the hospital, Laura lied, telling everyone she couldn't remember anything except that a man grabbed her in the park. This was a tense time for Luke, who deeply regretted what he'd done. Luke was placed under additional mental strain

when Roy was picked up by the police as a suspect in the case. Scotty, enraged, confronted Roy in the disco, looking as though he had every intention of killing him. But Luke broke up the fight. Terrified of being sent to jail, Roy asked Bobbie to provide him with an alibi, and still in love with Roy, she agreed. Laura soon realized that she must clear Roy and so she lied again, giving the police and her friends a phony description of the rapist. After Roy was cleared by Laura, he forgave Bobbie for her past, and they made plans to marry.

In the aftermath of the rape, Scotty and Laura's marriage was more strained than ever. Laura, trapped by her own lies and feeling dirty and guilt-ridden, didn't want Scotty or any man to touch her again. Encouraged by Scotty, Gail and her parents, Laura entered group therapy at the rape center. Still, she insisted on keeping her job at the disco, for she still owed Luke money she had borrowed to purchase Scotty's law books. Laura's presence in the disco proved to be awkward and uneasy for both of them. Luke's tensions increased further as election night approached. Mitch Williams, surmising from rumors in the underworld that Roy DiLucca was to be his assassin, called on a surprised Luke at the disco.

"If DiLucca tries anything, he's a dead man," warned Mitch.

Laura overheard the threatening words and realized that Luke and Roy were in some sort of trouble. Facing Luke, Laura took a strong position.

"I will not stand by and see you hurt or destroyed again! I'd like . . . to be your friend." Luke's heartbreak was apparent.

Amazingly, she was still there for him in his time of need.

As election night approached, Luke grew more hopeless and used his payoff money to buy an insurance policy on his life, so that Bobbie and Ruby would be taken care of. In turmoil, Laura found herself deeply torn, for although she loved Scotty, she was stricken by one fear: Did she encourage Luke that fateful night in the disco, or had he brutally raped her? In an ironic twist, Luke was asked by Scotty to drive Laura home on election night. Laura, having picked up on enough information to know that Luke was involved in something very dangerous, threw his car keys out the window to prevent Luke from doing whatever "job" it was that threatened his very life. Luke was aghast, crying out, "You've just put a bullet in my head!"

In a race against time, Luke phoned Roy to pick

him up so that he could complete his assignment to kill Mitch Williams. But Roy decided to do the job himself! Finding the gun in Luke's office, Roy left for the victory celebration with Bobbie in tears begging him not to go. Roy raced to the hotel, and, as Mitch descended in a glass elevator, Roy fired a shot, barely wounding the new state senator. Roy, shot by the security guards, stumbled his way to the front of the hotel, where he died in Bobbie's arms.

Luke and Bobbie were able to get away unseen. Together they fabricated a story for the underworld bosses, who accepted it. Luke's life was spared. He asked Smith to let him out, but he refused. Concluding that if he had to stay in the organization, Luke proclaimed that he would make it pay for Bobbie and himself—and he vowed to have Laura too!

Luke Spencer wasn't the only resident of Port Charles immersed in deceit and secrecy. A pregnant Monica struggled to hide the fact that she had slept with Rick from her sister-in-law, Tracy. This became especially difficult after Rick and Monica were forced, under oath, to admit their union while giving a deposition in a malpractice suit. The court papers were sealed, and Tracy—whose own marriage was in shambles after she discovered Mitch in bed with Susan Moore—struggled to get her greedy hands on the elusive document.

Across town, Heather Webber tried desperately to win her son, Steven Lars, away from Diana Taylor—by driving Diana insane! Over a period of months, Heather craftily conducted a behind-the-scenes gaslighting that nearly succeeded in making Diana feel incompetent as both a nurse and a mother. Increasingly, Diana grew more dependent on—who else—Heather!

In one final diabolical move designed to destroy Diana, Heather purchased LSD and planned to give it to her moments before Diana kept an appointment with a psychiatrist. She hoped that, during her session, Diana would begin to hallucinate and be committed to a mental institution, thus giving P.J.—who was really Jeff and Heather's natural child Steven Lars—back to them. Heather placed the LSD into a glass of iced tea, putting it alongside another glass on a lazy susan. P.J. toddled in and, unseen by anyone, turned the lazy susan and mixed up the two glasses. By mistake, Heather drank the LSD and began to wildly hallucinate. Jeff had no choice but to ship his wife to Forest Hills sanitarium. Heather's reign of terror was over—for now!

In November 1979, Laura's after-hours liaison with her boss and "friend," Luke Spencer, ended in rape.

LUKE
Look what you've done to me. I'm not going to die without holding you in my arms just one time. Dance with me Laura.

LAURA
No.

LUKE
I said dance with me.

Reeling from the shock of Heather's mental collapse, Jeff found solace in his newly warm relationship with his father, Seve Hardy. Steve shed a tear when Jeff called him "Dad" for the first time. Jeff grew close to his new roommate, Joe Kelly, who had fallen in love with a virginal nurse, Annie Logan. Annie, who was Audrey's niece and a registered nurse, had recently adopted an orphaned child prodigy, Jeremy Hewitt, whose grandmother was first to die in the Lassa Fever epidemic. Annie enjoyed dating Joe, who wanted more. He wanted to sleep with her! Annie said she preferred to wait for marriage. But it became increasingly apparent to Audrey that what Annie was really waiting for was a romantic overture from Jeff.

In a shocking revelation, Dr. Peter Taylor learned from Heather's mother, Alice, that P.J. was actually Steven Lars. Peter, not feeling well and in a state of shock, journeyed to Pine Circle to see Heather, returned to GH, then suffered a heart attack and, later,

GREAT MOMENTS

"I love you," were the last words spoken by Bobbie Spencer's fiancé, Roy DiLucca, who was gunned down by security guards after his failed attempt to complete a mob-ordered hit on newly-elected State Senator Mitch Williams. Mortally wounded, Roy stumbled to the street and died in Bobbie's arms.

several strokes. Peter died, trying vainly to tell Jeff that he knew something about Steven Lars. So the secret of P.J.'s identity remained only with Mrs. Grant and Heather. Jeff, realizing that Heather told Peter something about Steven Lars, traveled to the sanitarium, but Heather was so ill that Jeff wasn't allowed to see her. He called upon his private detective friend, Joe Kelly, who found Mrs. Hadley in Chicago. Finally there was a breakthrough in the search for Steven Lars. Diana, going through Peter's old clothes, found the fateful note he wrote only moments before he died—"P.J. is Steven Lars." In shock, she realized she could lose the child she loved so dearly. That is, unless she married Jeff Webber. Then they would both have what they want—P.J. and Steven Lars!

At the Webbers, Rick and Lesley began discussing Lesley's becoming pregnant. Their hopes were dashed when Lesley was told that conception might be impossible: Carrying a baby would be extremely risky to her life. At the Quartermaines, a baby was about to be born. One night in late December, Lesley and Gail visited Monica, who had been ordered to stay in bed until the birth of her baby. They arrived in a horrendous snowstorm just as Monica's labor was beginning! Phone lines were down, electric power had failed, and slowly but

surely, Monica's baby was being born. By candlelight, Lesley, with Gail assisting, delivered the premature boy—a breech birth and a painful delivery. During the emergency delivery, a near-delirious Monica, believing that she was dying, muttered aloud that Rick was the father of her child!

The snowplows made a path to the Quartermaine's Georgian mansion, and Alan and Rick arrived in time to get Monica and the baby into the ambulance. Lesley, in a state of silent shock, rode along to the hospital, still loyal to her medical responsibilities—even when they involved the woman who was bearing Rick's son—the son Lesley herself could not give him.

At the hospital, Rick made a fateful decision to tell Lesley the truth of his night with Monica. But Rick was soon thunderstruck when a fiery Lesley reported to him that she already knew the horrible truth. Rick agreed to a separation from Lesley and left the house, while saying a definite "no" to divorce. Despite his leaving, Rick loved Lesley completely and the year ended with both of them angry, yet heartbroken. Unknown to both, gossipy nurse Amy Vining had eavesdropped on their vital conversation!

Immediately after the birth of her son, Alan Jr., Monica felt utterly hopeless! Facing a life of secrecy and blackmail, and knowing that Alan could be jealous and cruel, she had no desire to live. Lesley and Rick faced a medical and personal decision and agreed that Rick must give Monica some hope by telling her he loved her. Monica, overjoyed with Rick's expression of love, made a successful recovery. Lesley asked Rick if he did in fact love Monica.

"Monica and I have a long history together," he answered cryptically.

Behaving nobly, Monica informed Rick that she would continue her marriage to Alan.

"Alan now has what he's always wanted—an heir," she informed him coldly.

But Rick sensed that Monica was lying. He knew in his heart that she still loved him. Rick waited for Monica to admit that the child was his. The twist to this tale was that Monica herself didn't remember her confession to Lesley during labor. Only Lesley and Rick knew what Monica had blurted out during childbirth. More than anyone, Tracy Quartermaine wanted to prove that Monica's baby was fathered by Rick. If the baby was Rick's, then greedy Tracy's son Ned would be first in line to inherit Edward Quartermaine's vast fortune!

1980

Unable to resolve their mounting marital difficulties, Rick and Lesley began the new year apart. Rick, unsure of what he wanted to do with his life, left Port Charles with no plans to return. While away, he hoped to find the answer to the question that plagued him early in 1980: "Could I possibly be in love with two women—Lesley *and* Monica?"

Monica, seeing that her future with Rick was an impossible dream, returned to Alan, and, after he reassured her of his love, she began to feel more secure. But that feeling of well being came to an abrupt end when Alan managed to get his hands on the elusive deposition from Rick's malpractice hearing in which, under oath, Dr. Webber was forced to reveal the sordid details of his affair with Monica. Seething, Alan covered his rage and began a quiet terrorization of Monica, throwing her into a state of panic and confusion.

Does he know or doesn't he? she thought to herself in every waking moment.

With an air of mystery and foreboding, Alan began to make elaborate plans to build a nursery at the top of the Georgian mansion.

The plot took a further upsurge when it was discovered that Alan Jr. had developed a heart problem which had to be surgically corrected or the child would die. In a race against time, a call went out to Rick, who returned to skillfully perform a lifesaving operation. Later, panic broke out in Intensive Care when the baby needed a blood transfusion. Monica was terrified for, once again, she feared that Alan would find out that her son belonged to Rick. But Alan, still in the lab, ignored frantic pages to come to ICU. At that very instant, a shocked Alan was reading lab records offering proof that the baby was Rick's, since they shared the same blood type. Rocked by the information, Alan left the hospital in shock while Rick gave blood to the baby, but in a routine way so that no one suspected that he was Alan Jr.'s father. At home, Alan continued to pretend that he didn't know of Monica's affair and the paternity of his child, while waging a war of nerves against Monica, keeping her in fear and doubt. The work progressed on the attic nursery, and he formulated his vengeful plan to collapse the roof on Rick and Monica on the day of the baby's christening!

Despite all they had been through in the last few months, Luke and Laura continued to be drawn to each other. When Laura needed a confidante, she reached out to Luke. There was a bond between them. Still, her confused feelings led to some tense times for the troubled twosome. The sexual tension of working side by side at the disco eventually proved too much for her fragile psyche.

"I'm going home to my husband, and I never want to see you again," Laura declared to Luke. She gave him two weeks' notice.

At the same time, Scotty was growing closer to the truth about the night of Laura's rape. He now believed that Laura knew her attacker, and that it was probably a friend who committed the crime. Luke still loved Laura, but dated Jennifer Smith, Frank's naive daughter, in an effort to forget his feelings for another man's wife. Laura, for her part, suffered terrible twinges of jealousy whenever she saw Luke and Jennifer together.

At Forest Hills Sanitarium, Alice Grant was overjoyed to witness her daughter Heather's emergence from catatonia. But it was all an act.

On her last night of work at the disco, Laura accidentally locked herself in Luke's closet where she overheard an incriminating conversation between Luke, Smith and his right-hand man, Bill Watson. When the mobsters discovered that Laura had overheard too much, Smith took action. This was not going to be Laura Baldwin's last night of work at the disco.

"Get her back!" Smith ordered Luke.

In time, Luke learned the horrible truth—that Smith had marked Laura for death! To save her life, Luke agreed to pay a heavy price: marrying a woman he didn't love—Smith's daughter, Jennifer!

Diana Taylor, now aware that P.J. was Steven Lars, tried to keep Jeff from discovering the truth. In Chicago, Jeff reached another dead end when he questioned Mrs. Hadley, who provided no information to help him. He might have learned the truth if it hadn't been for an anonymous phone call from Diana to Mrs. Hadley warning her of Jeff's visit. Back in Port Charles, Diana tried to woo Jeff, but the handsome young doctor was already seriously smitten—with nurse Annie Logan. The young lovers hoped to marry, but of course, Jeff was already married to Heather, who had been committed to an institution. Their romance suffered an unbearable blow upon Jeff and Annie's discovery that they would have to wait five years to marry—the time required for the annulment of Jeff's marriage to Heather. Jeff, feeling the pressure of the five-year wait, began making regular visits to Heather in hopes of bringing her back to reality. At the same time, the sexual pressure was getting to Annie Logan, who was caught in a struggle between her religious beliefs and her sexual desires. And as a counterpoint to this scenario, Heather emerged from her delusional state, only to overhear a nurse say that she might have to face charges when she recovered for what she did to Diana Taylor. Thus, in a private panic, Heather faked catatonia and began to formulate a plan to escape from Forest Hills Sanitarium.

Aided by her fellow patient and confidante, Sarah, Heather impersonated Shelly Vernon, a nurse she resembled, and escaped Forest Hills. With fierce determination, she headed for the Hardys, where, looking through the window, she saw Anne in Jeff's arms! Listening horrified to their conversation, she overheard Jeff tell Audrey and Steve that he planned to ask Heather for a divorce when she was emotionally ready. Throughout the summer, Heather contin-

In 1980, Jessie Brewer's world was brightened by Dan Rooney, the new hospital administrator. To the amusement of their hospital colleagues, Dan and Jessie entered into a "trial marriage" to test their compatibility.

ued her "Shelly Vernon" ruse, paying regular and highly secretive visits to Port Charles, where she spied longingly on Jeff and Steven Lars. At Forest Hills, her condition began to slowly progress, and her act proved so convincing that Dr. Nelson, Heather's psychiatrist, felt she was ready to be released. Heather Webber was going home!

At the hospital, nurse Jessie Brewer found her workday routine interrupted by increasingly regular visits from Dan Rooney, the new hospital administrator. Dan, smitten with Jessie, offered to take her for a weekend of romance.

"Oh, Dan. I couldn't," blushed Jessie, who hadn't allowed herself to be courted by a man in nearly a decade.

Through persistence and always charming requests, Dan managed to wear down Jessie's resistance. Alone together, a nervous Jessie tried to sleep with her gallant suitor, but simply couldn't go through with it. Back home in Port Charles, Dan and Jessie devised an innovative "trial marriage" to see if they were indeed compatible. To the amused glances of their colleagues, he would spend his days with Jessie in her apartment and at the hospital—but would sleep at home.

With steely determination, Alan awaited the dark day of Alan Jr.'s christening. With the attic nursery completed—and the roof rigged to collapse—he put his plan into motion. On the big day, Alan sent Rick and Monica up to the nursery, telling them he had a "lovely surprise" for them. But, in the study, Alan realized that Lee Baldwin had begun to suspect him of foul play—and there were only three minutes left until the attic roof would collapse. Alan panicked, made his way through the crowd of guests, arriving in the attic in time to push Monica and Rick aside as the slate roof came crashing down. In the wake of this near-tragedy, Alan was viewed by all as a hero, and this newfound glory only served to reinforce his unquenching desire to set up Rick and Monica for the kill.

Only one person—Tracy Quartermaine—was convinced that there was "foul play" involved in the roof collapse. Tracy knew in her cold heart that Alan had tried to murder Monica and Rick in the attic, but she simply couldn't prove it. Still hoping to ensure her own inheritance by proving that Monica's baby belonged to Rick, Tracy brought a paternity suit against Monica. Her father, Edward, infuriated with his renegade daughter, drew up a new will—disinheriting Tracy!

Rick, desperate to claim Alan Jr. as his own, resolved to tell Alan the truth about the baby's parentage. Of course, Alan already knew this piece of highly volatile news! Lesley supported Rick in his actions, and Monica, terrified of losing her child, begged her to stop Rick from going to Alan. Lesley steadfastly refused. With her heart breaking, Lesley went to the courthouse to file for a divorce so that Rick could eventually be free to marry Monica.

Believing that the truth about his son's paternity was about to come out anyway, Rick went straight to Alan and told him that he and Monica were lovers and that Alan Jr. was his own son. Alan pretended shock and begged for time to make up his mind regarding what he would do. But Alan knew *exactly* what he wanted to do! Privately, he vowed that "Rick and Monica will die."

Playing out his game, Alan secretly purchased a gun, set up target practice in the basement of the mansion and began to fantasize what his legal defense would be.

"You see, your honor, it was unpremeditated. I found my wife and Rick making love. And so I killed them."

Against this lethal pattern of Alan's, Monica and Rick began to share some hope for their future.

The day of destiny arrived. Believing that Rick and Monica planned to make love, Alan followed them, in a jealous rage, fantasizing about killing the lovers every step of the way. Knowing that he must

After cracking the code to Frank Smith's black book, Luke's life nearly came to an end when he was gunned down in front of the statue of the Left-Handed Boy. Laura raced to Luke's side only to gratefully discover that a bulletproof vest had saved his life.

make it look like a crime of passion, he controlled his anger, stalking them from the beach to the harbor to Paddy Kelly's fishing boat and, finally, to their rented cottage. Alan gave them enough time to start making love, then started up the stairs, gun in hand. At that instant, fate intervened in the form of a terrific explosion! The force of the explosion—caused by an unforeseen gas line break—knocked Alan off the stairs. Monica, stunned by these events, found the gun near Alan's body and knew he had tried to kill them. But faced with the facts, he presented a series of foolproof answers that cast doubt on his guilt. Desperate to prove Alan's crime, Rick and Monica set out to prove that he was a liar.

"It's the only way to free us from him!" he told a willing Monica.

Rick then came up with one more way.

"The hell with the scandal," Rick threatened Alan. "I'm going to force the issue by telling Tracy the truth that Alan Jr. is my child!"

Without flinching, Alan let Rick know that if he

did that, Alan would keep the child forever, for the baby was legally his. The battle lines were drawn.

Laura found herself in the midst of another kind of battle—an internal battle of her own feelings on the day that Luke and Jennifer Smith's engagement was announced. Deep in her soul Laura loved Luke, but she could never admit that fact to anyone—especially herself. She was further unsettled by an invitation from Jennifer Smith to go sailing. Luke nobly prepared to marry Jennifer, but hoped to use this sailing trip as a chance to be alone with Laura to prove, once and for all, that she loved him.

On the day of the sailing trip, Luke called upon Bobbie to delay Scotty and Jennifer's arrival, giving him time to be alone with Laura on the boat. After luring her into the sailboat and lying that the door had jammed, Luke artfully and smoothly started seducing Laura.

"Listen, I know you love your husband. I know you love Scott, but you can't tell me that there aren't nights when you lay in that bed and turn over and touch him and wish that he were me. And wish that I was holding you. You wish that I was making love to you, Laura. Laura, doesn't that precious truth that you claim you want so much, doesn't that tell you anything? Doesn't it tell you that you're in love with me? You need me. Doesn't it tell you? I won't touch you unless you want me to. But Laura, you have to say the words. I love you. I love you. I want to hold you in my arms."

Swept away with passion, Laura responded breathlessly, "Yes. Yes. I want you to make love to me."

Suddenly and without warning, Luke turned ice cold!

"Here. Take this, the key to the door. You're free to go. Go on. Go tell Scott that that night in the disco was rape!"

Laura, now fully aware of her feelings for Luke, and horribly ashamed by them, ran off.

In her desire to free herself from him, she wrote a letter of release to Luke—but it sounded very much like a love letter. On the day of Jennifer and Luke's wedding, Scotty found it, and learned at last the identity of Laura's rapist. Calling Laura a "tramp," Scotty rushed out in search of Luke, only hours before his wedding was to take place on Frank Smith's yacht.

Luke demanded of Smith that the price for marrying Jennifer would be a contract giving him title to his businesses that weren't involved in organized crime. The key to getting what he wanted was Smith's little black book, which contained the names of the key players in the Port Charles mob. At the 4th of July picnic, Bobbie covered for Luke's absence while Luke searched Frank's office and found the little black book. He successfully photographed its contents, but realized that his mission was not yet complete because the book was in code. Just before the wedding, Luke confronted Smith with his evidence.

"You draw me up a new contract, you keep your word to me, and nobody will ever see these pictures," he threatened.

Looking into Luke's steely eyes, Smith countered with a threat of his own.

"You can walk out of this wedding. Cause me any more trouble, and you're a dead man."

Luke did not need to walk out of the wedding. Scotty did the work for him when he leapt aboard the yacht and lunged at Luke. The guests backed away in horror as the two men pitched themselves in a brutal fistfight. Punch after punch was thrown until finally Scotty hit Luke in the head with a mighty blow—sending him overboard, dazed and disoriented, into the water below.

A frantic Laura followed Scotty to the yacht, and as she wandered toward the scene of the fracas, a hand reached up from the dock and grabbed her leg. It was Luke—alive—begging for help.

"Get me out of here, Laura," he pleaded. "This is our chance! Our chance!"

Feeling her marriage was over, Laura accepted Luke's offer to run. Scotty had gotten even with Luke, but by stopping that wedding, he threw Laura into Luke's arms for a summer they'd never forget.

They set off on an incredible odyssey, hiding from the handsome hitman, Hutch, who had been hired by Smith to kill them. Their mission: to decode Smith's black book and solve the mystery of the left-handed boy, whose existence Luke had learned about by overhearing one of Frank's private conversations. Who was the left-handed boy? What was he? Luke knew only that the left-handed boy could break the power of the Port Charles mob. Smith, in an effort to smoke Luke out of hiding, had Aunt Ruby beaten up and Bobbie harassed when a gift-wrapped dead rat was delivered to her.

"COUPLE WANTED FOR QUESTIONING" screamed the headlines of the *Port Charles Herald.* Luke and Laura were front-page news! Before

After discovering that Luke was the man who raped Laura, Scotty boarded Frank Smith's yacht and attacked Luke, sending him plummeting into the water below. Luke was presumed dead, and Scotty faced murder charges.

departing on their journey to find the left-handed boy, the pair ducked for the night into Wyndham's Department Store to hide. And it proved to be one of the most fantastic nights of their lives. Dressed in formal attire, Luke and Laura shared champagne and a candlelight dinner as they cast their fears aside for one night of pure fantasy. But Laura wouldn't sleep with Luke, who adored her. She was determined to prove that she was not the tramp that Scotty thought she was. The next morning, Luke and Laura found the night watchman dead and they realized the hitman was in the store with them. Racing to the bus station, they headed for the town of Fair Oaks, stopping along the way in the farm community of Beechers Corners. Hot on their trail was the hitman, who by now had learned that a secret supply of gold bullion was hidden in the hand of the left-handed boy—which was actually a statue. And Luke and Laura were going to lead him to it!

Luke and Laura, broke, pretending to be a married couple—Lloyd and Lucy Johnson—spent their first romantic night in a barn belonging to a friendly farm couple, Agnes and "Whit" Whitaker.

Wrapping Laura in his arms, Luke dreamed of a life together.

"We're going to be together one night. I swear we will, but it's going to be right. It's going to be absolutely right. It's going to be just the way you want it. And I can wait, you crazy lady! But I'll tell you something. I hope you sleep as miserably as I'm going to!"

The sexual tension was thick.

"Luke, I hope you understand," said Laura.

"I understand one thing very, very clearly. You may be only 18 years old, but when you kiss me you are a full grown woman and . . . it's . . . driving . . . me . . . out . . . of . . . my . . . mind!"

The next morning, the Whitakers rented "the Johnsons" a room, but Laura insisted that she could sleep with Luke. Building the "Walls of Jericho"—a blanket hanging over a rope—Laura divided the room in two to ensure that Luke kept his distance.

"With that blanket up there, what do I sleep under?" feigned an anguished Luke.

"It's the middle of August—you don't need a blanket!" laughed Laura.

For the first time, Laura told Luke that she loved him. And Luke, holding to his dream that they could be together forever, made up his mind that he could wait awhile for "the Walls of Jericho" to come down.

Smith's double-crossing hitman, Hutch, arrived in Beechers Corners and, turning on the homespun charm, fooled Luke and Laura into believing he was their friend.

Hutch, Luke and Laura got jobs in Calhoun's Diner—before the arrival of another hitman sent them scurrying off to Fair Oaks, where they believed the left-handed boy to be. Back in Port Charles, Frank Smith was getting increasingly agitated as the summer wore on and the elusive Luke and Laura remained at large. When detective Joe Kelly got too close to Smith's secrets, Frank ordered another hit man, Vic Gower to snuff him out. But Gower hit the wrong man—knifing and killing Joe's father, Paddy. Gower moved on to Beechers Corners, where he had been ordered to kill Luke, Laura—and Hutch. But it was Gower who was to die! Before leaving for Fair Oaks, Hutch committed a crime (that would later come back to haunt him) when he killed Vic Gower and buried him in the Whitakers' cornfield.

Lesley, now divorced from Rick, plugged away at the single life while supporting him in his efforts to gain custody of his son. Edward Quartermaine was equally determined to lose a daughter. When the senior Quartermaine discovered that Tracy disobeyed him and went back to court to try and get the judge to administer blood tests to prove Alan Jr.'s paternity, he'd had enough. "It's time to pay Tracy back!" he harumphed to himself.

Edward devised a plan to test her true colors. Edward approached Tracy with his new will, which disinherited her. As he began to sign the document, Edward suddenly slumped over with a heart attack. Clutching his chest, he begged Tracy for his medicine.

GREAT MOMENTS

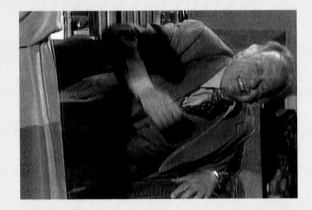

EDWARD
"For God's sake. Help me, Tracy! Give me my pills!"

TRACY
"Only if you promise not to sign that will, daddy."

In perhaps the most cold-hearted moment in General Hospital*'s long history, Tracy Quartermaine refused to give her dying father Edward his heart medication until he agreed not to sign a new will which disinherited her. Little did Tracy know that Edward's heart attack was merely a trick to test her true colors. Failing the test, Tracy was banished from the Quartermaine mansion for the next decade.*

"For God's sake, help me, Tracy!" he cried out.

She stood immobile, refusing to move as he slumped to the floor, apparently dead. Then, roaring with laughter, Edward jauntily sprang back to life and signed the will. Tracy had failed the test miserably. Later, he relented, giving Tracy two million dollars, insisting it could be spent only on Mitch's race for the governorship. Tracy went to Mitch and told him he could have the money only if he dumped his lover, Susan, and took her back. Forced to choose between his love for Susan and Tracy's money, Mitch opted for the bucks. Defeated and humiliated, Tracy joined her husband, Mitch, in Albany.

Monica made a startling discovery when she observed that Alan Jr. bore the same birthmark that Alan had. Alan's mother, Lila, confirmed that the oddly shaped mark was a Quartermaine family trait. Horror stricken to think that the baby might belong to Alan, Monica made an appointment with a hematologist and discovered, after tests, that through a rare medical phenomenon, the Bombay Phenotype Syndrome, that the baby was indeed Alan's. Armed with this news, Monica was now even more desperate to free herself from Alan and marry Rick. After taunting Alan into confessing that he tried to kill Rick and her, Monica presented him with his confession—on tape.

"I'll give the whole world a copy unless you give me a divorce—now!"

His back against the wall, Alan saw no alternative but to bow to Monica's wishes. Monica took her baby and strutted out of the Quartermaine mansion—triumphant at last.

Monica's victory over Alan proved to be short and hardly sweet. Seeking to keep her latest secret, she arranged for the hematologist, Dr. Henry, to take a new job far away from Port Charles. But before leaving, Dr. Henry informed Alan that the blood tests proved he was the father of Alan Jr. Stunned but gratified, Alan kept his knowledge secret, waiting for an opportune moment to publicly humiliate Rick and Monica. He knew just the occasion—a fund-raising party to be given on the day before Monica's divorce was to come through. Arranging for almost all of General Hospital to be present, Alan made his announcement.

"Through the wonderful research of people like Dr. Henry, I now know that Alan Jr. is my son," he told his well-heeled audience.

The embarrassing truth was out—Alan Jr. was truly a Quartermaine! Reeling from the humiliating revelation, Rick rejected Monica and left town to buy medical equipment for his waterfront clinic. Monica, desperate to regain Rick's love, still wanted her divorce. But Alan wasn't going to be so obliging. At the last minute, he contested the decree, demanding that Monica return the child. Having lost her last witness to the fact that Alan tried to kill her, Monica bowed to the inevitable and moved back into the Quartermaine mansion.

In search of the left-handed boy, Luke, Laura and Hutch moved on to Fair Oaks, where they got jobs in a bar run by Sally Armitage, who was actually a member of Frank Smith's hit squad. With her prey close at hand, Sally called Smith to inform him that as soon as she could get the black book away from Luke, she would kill Luke, Laura and Hutch. Suspicious of Sally, Luke searched her room and made two startling discoveries: Number 1: Sally was a member of Frank Smith's hit squad; Number 2: Sally was a man in disguise!

Frantic, Luke ran to the nearby plaza and spotted Laura just as she was boarding a bus with Sally. Just as he was about to tell Hutch who Sally really was, Hutch made a slip and Luke realized that he had located *both* hit men assigned to kill Laura and him. Hurrying back to Sally's bar, he looked into a fountain and couldn't believe his eyes when he saw—a statue! Luke stood in wonder, gazing at the statue which appeared to be a boy—a left-handed boy! He further realized that through the inscription on the statue, he could finally decode Frank Smith's black book. Electrified, he hastily told Laura that he had found the left-handed boy and put a very reluctant Laura on the bus to Port Charles.

Unknown to Luke, Laura got off the bus as soon as it turned the corner and ran into Hutch, who exposed his true colors by holding her hostage in an abandoned magic shop. "You're never going to see your lover again unless he gives me the gold," Hutch threatened Laura as he tied her up. Then, calling Luke, Hutch offered a deal—Laura for the gold.

With a knife, Luke loosened the square under the word "gold" in the inscription of the statue, and found Smith's private stash of gold. Then Luke used his powerful charm to convince Sally, by lying about his mailing the black book, to help him save Laura in exchange for the gold—a more lucrative deal than the contract on their lives. In a shootout at the statue of the Left-Handed Boy, Hutch and Sally ended up shooting one another. Laura watched in horror as Luke fell to the ground—with a bullet to the chest!

"Luke, Luke, Luke! Somebody please get me an ambulance. Help me!" cried Laura as she raced to her stricken lover. To her surprise, Luke opened his eyes and said, "Chill out! I'm OK! What do you think you're dealing with here? You buy blue jeans, right? I buy bulletproof vests! Now, let's get out of this town. It bores me."

Looking back, they saw that Sally had been killed, and Hutch critically injured. Looking forward they saw their own bright future—a future they could finally share. As the sun rose over Fair Oaks, Luke and Laura triumphantly hopped onto a nearby motorcycle and roared back to Beechers Corners

"where the Walls of Jericho" came tumbling down in a loving night of pure passion.

With the black book decoded, Luke had the goods to put Frank Smith behind bars for years to come. Returning to Port Charles by police escort, Luke and Laura stopped at a drugstore outside of town where he seized the opportunity to buy a cigar, slip off the band and slip it on Laura's finger. In a simple yet poignant ceremony, they spoke their vows, reaffirming the commitment they had made the night before. Together at last—well, at least for a few more hours.

At police headquarters, Laura wasn't prepared for the onslaught of media who greeted the runaways. Facing her in-laws, Lee and Gail, and a press hungry for scandal, Laura panicked. In a weak moment, she silently slipped the cigar band off her finger.

"I'm still Mrs. Scott Baldwin," she told the crowd of reporters.

Luke was rocked by Laura's stunning statement. Feeling betrayed and rejected, he refused to speak with the woman he loved. And Laura returned to her apartment to ask Scotty for a divorce—only to discover he had left her. In desperation, she tried to contact Luke, but he tore up the letter, vowing to not let Laura Webber Baldwin back into his life.

Finding himself too "notorious" for respectable employment, Luke found that the only place he could get a job was Kelly's Diner, run by Rose Kelly, whose late husband, Paddy, had been killed by the mob. As for Laura, losing two men in one year forced her to make some major changes in her life. For one, she made a pledge to herself to stop living her life by other people's rules. Second, she was determined to make it on her own. Refusing help, she was determined to prove to Luke that she was a mature woman. In need of her own place, she found a shabby apartment that she agreed to paint in exchange for three months' free rent—unaware that Luke was living in the same building. When Laura learned that Scotty had agreed to a divorce, she was finally encouraged that everything would work out. But before the papers could be drawn up, Scotty disappeared without a trace.

Torn apart by love and pride, Luke and Laura ran into each other occasionally, but displayed a facade of happiness which kept them from getting together. Just as they were finally settling down, a new arrival—Alexandria Quartermaine—was about to bring new conflict and adventure into their lives.

1981

In the opinion of her psychiatrist, Dr. Nelson, Heather Webber's mental health had improved enough to let her come home to Port Charles. Pretending that she had no memory of her wild past, this "new" Heather impressed people with her sweet and engaging personality. Only Diana Taylor, Anne Logan and Heather's mother, Alice Grant, suspected that Heather was as "possessed" as ever. Diana's worries escalated when a prowler entered her apartment and threatened her with a gun. Jeff, who was in the corridor, heard her screams and rushed to her aid. Jeff grappled with the prowler, but the mystery man made his escape. Fearing that something might happen to her, Diana changed her will, naming Lesley Webber as P.J.'s guardian instead of Jeff and Heather. In the wake of Diana's mounting anxiety, she confronted Heather in the Floating Rib and accused her of killing Peter.

"If it wasn't for you, my husband would be alive today!" screamed Diana before collapsing from the effects of the stressful encounter.

Alice Grant had been observing her daughter rather closely during her stay in Port Charles, and, as time passed, she became highly suspicious of Heather's motives. Unlike most, Alice Grant was not convinced that Heather was a new person with no memory of the past. Sensing what Heather was "up to," Mrs. Grant presented her with an ultimatum.

"If you pull another trick, Heather, I'll go to Diana and Jeff with the entire truth about P.J.'s identity!" she threatened.

As usual, Heather wasn't about to give up. She had yet another "deadly" scheme up her sleeve.

After stealing a gun from the Webber house and faking hysteria, Heather convinced Lesley, Rick and Dr. Nelson that she must return to Forest Hills. Only there could she safely carry out her plan to murder Diana Taylor! Once back at the sanitarium, Heather hid the gun in the body of her deeply disturbed friend Sarah's baby doll. Then, when the moment was right, she slipped out of Forest Hills and headed straight for Port Charles with murder on her mind. Entering Diana's apartment with a set of stolen keys and a drawn gun, she stood frozen at the sight of Diana and Jeff, who had been rejected by Anne, making love!

Returning to Forest Hills without carrying out her murder plan, Heather became more determined than ever to kill Diana and claim her son. Knowing that Diana planned to sign a new will changing guardianship of P.J. from Jeff and Heather to Lesley, Heather returned to Diana's apartment and snatched both copies of the will, ripped them into tiny pieces, and, back at Forest Hills, used the scraps in an arts and crafts project. It was time to carry out her devious plan.

Diana, meanwhile, hoping for a future with Jeff, finally revealed to him the secret she had known for months.

"P.J. is Steven Lars, your son," she declared.

And to prove her claim, she handed Jeff copies of P.J.'s birth footprints and suggested that he compare them with those of Steven Lars, whose prints were on file at General Hospital. Jeff, bewildered and angry that Diana had kept the truth from him for so long, stormed out of the apartment. At wit's end, Diana pleaded with him from the open door to stay.

"Make love to me!" she cried out in panic.

Anne, unseen by them, arrived in time to overhear the bitter exchange. Seeing Jeff, then Anne, leave the building, Heather entered for the kill.

Within moments, Diana's body lay lifelessly on the kitchen floor. In the final step of her elaborate frame-up, Heather wrote Anne's name, in blood, next to Diana's body.

"Now there are two victims!" she chuckled to herself as she scrawled the incriminating letters on the floor, then slipped out the door.

Police Chief Burt Ramsey mounted a clear-cut case against a frightened Anne Logan. The clues pointed directly to her: "Anne" spelled in blood on Diana's kitchen floor, her wallet found outside Diana's door, and witnesses who saw her at Diana's. But Heather hadn't counted on one crucial fact—Diana had died instantly! Anne and Jeff breathed a collective sigh of relief when forensic experts determined that Diana could not possibly have had time to write Anne's name in blood. Anne was set free—but a terrifying question remained unanswered. Who had tried to frame her?

Chief Ramsey agreed to assign Joe Kelly as a special investigator on the case. Jeff and Joe, suspecting Heather of murdering Diana, set out to uncover the missing pieces. Heather remained confident since she had an alibi: Her roommate, Sarah, insisted that Heather was safely tucked away in bed at Forest Hills when the murder was committed. Meanwhile, she fooled Dr. Nelson into believing that she was getting well and wanted to become an outpatient so that she could spend time with her son. With Heather about to be released, Jeff and Anne feared for P.J.'s safety. Heather's actions forced them to make a painful decision: Jeff must take P.J. and leave town. Steve Hardy arranged for his son to join the staff of a hospital in Nevada, where he could quickly be divorced once Heather was well. With a tearful goodbye, Dr. Jeff Webber, his young son in his arms, departed from Port Charles.

Suspecting her of the murder, Joe Kelly befriended Heather Webber in an attempt to maneuver her into some sort of confession. But it was busybody Amy Vining's admission that she told Heather about the friction between Anne and Diana that provided the necessary motive for the crime. Heather steadfastly denied any knowledge of the crime, but Kelly picked up another crucial clue when Heather's sanitarium friend, Sarah, informed him that a hairpin found in Diana's apartment belonged to nurse Shelly Vernon—the very same nurse Heather impersonated in her many escapes from Forest Hills. His heart racing, Joe concluded that Heather sneaked out of Forest Hills dressed as Shelly! Still, there was a missing link. How was Heather able to get back into the sanitarium? And there was another complication: In the course of his contact with Heather, something incredible was happening to Joe—he was falling in love with her!

Throughout the investigation, his stomach was in knots. How can I care for a woman who may be a cold-blooded killer? he wondered while trying to link Heather to Diana's murder. Anguished and tired, Joe considered removing himself from the case, but Ramsey insisted he stay on. In a pep talk, Ramsey told him "You're the only one who can see this case through!" After Sarah handed over Heather's gun, Joe had no choice but to recommend that Heather be arrested for murder. But in a stunning twist, the police

were forced to release her when they discovered that this was not the gun that killed Diana. Free from prison, Heather's elation was tempered by a letter from Jeff asking for a divorce. But not because he wanted Anne!

"I've found someone else to share my life with," the note said.

Heather snickered between her tears when she realized that she'd lost the man she loved, but so had Anne Logan.

Joe, in love with Heather, refused to believe Ramsey's theory that there was a second gun involved in Diana's murder.

"Burt, you can't believe that Heather did it!" Joe pleaded.

Did she? Yes, there was a second gun involved and Heather was about to find it—in her mother's apartment! Hiding the incriminating weapon in her purse, Heather sped home, only to be stopped by a cop. Noticing the gun, the cop took Heather to the station, where ballistic tests confirmed that this was the pistol that killed Diana Taylor. Ramsey, satisfied, booked Heather for suspicion of murder. To the Port Charles police, the case was over except for the trial. To Joe Kelly, who believed strongly in Heather's innocence, there were still significant questions to be answered.

Hitting the streets, Joe questioned a bus driver on duty the night of Diana Taylor's murder, and he learned that a middle-aged woman had flagged his bus down from the middle of the street. Witnesses identified a picture of the woman—it was Heather's mother, Alice Grant! Joe confronted her and, in a bizarre turn of events, she admitted going to Diana's apartment to put a stop to Heather's reign of terror, only to witness a bitter exchange between Heather and Diana. When Heather aimed her weapon, Diana pulled out a pistol of her own. Afraid for her daughter's life, Alice killed Diana while trying to wrestle the gun away from her.

"She was going to shoot my Heather!" cried a distraught Alice.

Citing extenuating circumstances, the D.A. dropped the charges against Alice Grant, but Heather wasn't so lucky. Or maybe she was. Placed on probation for her crimes, she learned that in six months she would go to jail, a mental institution or go free.

Alan and Monica's marriage continued to be as volatile as ever in 1981. But Monica became hopeful that she could get Alan off her back when he

Edward Quartermaine's enchanting niece, Alexandria, relocated to Port Charles ostensibly to work on a business deal with her uncle. But Alex was actually interested in locating an ugly little black statuette known as the Ice Princess, and she hired Luke Spencer to find it.

reached a financial agreement with Susan Moore to finance her purchase of the Campus Disco from Frank Smith, who had been shipped off to jail. Monica saw this "partnership" as her gateway to freedom—freedom to be with Dr. Rick Webber, who was now working (alongside his ex-wife Lesley) at the new Waterfront Clinic. Rejected by Monica, Alan turned to Susan and they began a tumultuous affair in a waterside cottage paid for by Alan. In rapid time, Susan was pregnant with Alan's child.

"We must be discreet," answered Alan to Susan's confession of her "delicate" condition.

Divorce was, in Alan's words, "out of the question."

The arrival of the shrewd and glamorous Alexandria Quartermaine was met by enthusiasm from her uncle, Edward, and wariness from Monica. Edward, exhilarated by his niece's presence, decided to come out of retirement and go into business with her on a secret project. Within days of her arrival, Alexandria hired Luke to do some investigative work. His mission: to locate Alex's competitors, the Cassadines, who were thought to be living in Port Charles under assumed names. Alexandria assured Luke that the job was strictly legitimate, but he remained wary of both on a professional level. While he was prepared to accept her money, Luke was not willing to give in to Alex's sexual overtures. He could smell, see and feel that the sex-crazed Alex had more on her mind than just international commerce. And Laura, aware of every one of Alexandria's blatant moves, grew more jealous by the day.

Luke's suspicions about the nature of his supposedly "safe" job with the Quartermaine's were confirmed when he entered his ransacked apartment and came face to face with a man who held him at gunpoint.

"I've been waiting for you. Close the door. No sudden moves or I'll blow your head off," the man threatened.

Luke could see that his uninvited houseguest was no ordinary waterfront thug. He was suave, cool and spoke his quietly menacing words in a smooth Australian accent.

"Now, I want information about the Ice Princess," he demanded.

Luke, baffled by his questions, tried to disarm the Australian with a karate kick but wound up unconscious himself when an accomplice emerged from the bathroom and knocked him out.

Luke awakened and, in a fury, headed straight for Alex's office at ELQ International to resign—only to find Laura working there as receptionist. He quit, but not before he described his attacker to Edward and Alex, who were now aware that the Cassadines were not their only competitors. In time, Luke discovered that his Australian attacker was none other than Robert Scorpio, an international financier and well-known bon vivant.

What did Scorpio want? Whose side was he on? In search of answers, Luke decided to pay an unannounced visit to the dashing Australian. Scorpio entered his penthouse and found himself face to face with Luke, who held him at gunpoint. Scorpio evaded Luke's questions about the Ice Princess and made the mistake of going for the gun, giving Luke the opening he had been waiting for. This time, Luke

Laura made Luke insanely jealous when she dated mysterious new arrival, Robert Scorpio. In March 1981, Robert and Laura attended the Port Charles Bicentennial Parade together.

conked him on the head and left Scorpio unconscious. A strange friendship had been born!

Luke wasn't the only Port Charles resident to become acquainted with Robert Scorpio. Laura used her own friendship with the charming Aussie to pique Luke's jealousy. Luke was astonished to see the woman *he* loved dining with Scorpio at Port Charles' elegant Versailles Room. Interrupting their evening, Luke made a nuisance of himself with his crass and crude comments. This was exactly the reaction Laura wanted, and she continued to allow Scorpio to squire her around town.

Laura surprised Luke with a show of independence when he tried to persuade her to quit her job as receptionist for E.L.Q.

"I won't allow you to scare me off. Besides, I need this job," countered Laura.

Luke and Laura desperately needed to clear the air and decided to make their peace by braving the stares of friends and family at the Floating Rib. Laura confessed to Luke that she lied about the rape and admitted that she had loved him on that fateful night in the disco.

"I was too immature to admit it, even to myself," she confessed.

The depth of Laura's confession proved too painful for Luke to respond. He needed time to decide whether to start their stormy romance all over again.

Learning from Scorpio that the Ice Princess was a statuette, Luke forced Alex and Edward to level with him. He agreed to help them find the missing statuette—for a price! But Scorpio wanted it too, and

he offered Luke $50,000 to find the statuette, actually a huge uncut diamond which Alex had painted black, mounted on a pedestal and shipped from Rio de Janeiro to Port Charles. But when she went to the docks to claim the crate, Alex was horrified to discover that it had been stolen! Now everyone was after the prize—Luke, Scorpio, Alex and Tony Castle, who lived on a huge yacht and dated Lesley Webber. Unbeknownst to the people of Port Charles, the urbane and sophisticated Tony Castle was in reality Tony Cassadine, one of the notorious brothers who wanted to get their greedy hands on the Ice Princess. Tony Castle and Robert Scorpio were partners, but Scorpio's phone conversations indicated another secret alliance. Who was he talking to?

With the help of his cabby friends, Luke encountered a blonde bimbo by the name of Emma Lutz who could be the missing link in the dock thefts. Emma's husband, Charlie, was a cab driver with too much money—earned, Luke thought, by pilfering shipments from the Port Charles docks. Emma did indeed have the Ice Princess in her possession at one time, but hoping to join "high society," she gave the ugly black statuette to Lila Quartermaine, who was sponsoring an art auction to benefit General Hospital. Luke, Robert, Alex, Edward and Tony all planned to steal the statuette on the night of the auction.

The Ice Princess was more than just an ugly statuette. It was the world's largest uncut diamond—with a secret formula in its base.

Luke and Laura were brought together by the news that Hutch had been given a lengthy prison sentence. Although Hutch maintained a cheerful facade, he feared for his life in prison. Laura and Luke were an inspiration for him, and both realized how fortunate they had been since their infamous summer on the run. Luke, desperate to get his stake, felt that the Ice Princess caper would finally enable him to have a normal life with Laura. Convinced that his plan to snatch the statuette couldn't fail, a buoyant Luke took Laura out for a night on the town. Their romantic evening began at the Versailles Room, topped off by a celebration on the docks—complete with a bottle of the bubbly, and glowing candles placed atop a crate. Back at Laura's apartment, Luke astounded himself by asking Laura to marry him. "Yes, oh yes!" she answered ecstatically.

Laura placed ads in Mexican papers so she could find Scotty and get a divorce. Luke wanted to find the Ice Princess, especially after Scorpio's warning that if the statue fell into the wrong hands it could cause cataclysmic global problems. On the night of the auction, the stakes were high and the bidding brisk when suddenly the lights went out! When they came back on, the Ice Princess was gone—and so was Luke! A frustrated Scorpio phoned his secret accomplice and agreed with the voice on the other end who said, "Luke Spencer must be silenced if he is found by the Cassadines."

Weeks later, Luke surfaced again, telling his friends that he didn't have the Ice Princess in his possession. So who did? Scorpio desperately wanted to know, and, once again, he teamed up with Luke and together they pledged their allegiance to finding the Ice Princess. Unknown to anyone else, Alexandria Quartermaine held a clandestine meeting of her own—with Tony Cassadine! Together they forged a partnership, rekindled their once-hot affair and confirmed that the Ice Princess had inestimable value because it contained a secret formula hidden in its base. But a formula for what? Again, Alex had the answer. She had secretly worked with a noted scientist, James Duvall, on a secret formula for the manufacture of synthetic diamonds. But this was also a formula for a powerful weapon that could give the Cassadine brothers the power to hold the world hostage! When James Duvall discovered that his priceless formula was missing from the base of the statue, he lost his temper and bitterly attacked Alex.

In retaliation, she hit him over the head with the Ice Princess—killing him! After finding the formula, Alex rushed to the yacht where she was greeted by Tony and his younger brother, Victor Cassadine.

At Scorpio's penthouse, Robert finally revealed to Luke and Laura his real purpose in pursuing the elusive statue: He was an agent for the World Security Bureau, and it was imperative to locate the Ice Princess and keep it from falling into the wrong hands. Robert's fellow WSB agent, O'Reilly, hid on the waterfront waiting for some indication that the Cassadine yacht would set sail. For agent O'Reilly, an elfish elderly woman with a quick tongue and a zest for life, this was just another dangerous mission. She had been on many such assignments with Robert, whom she had affectionately dubbed "Sonny." This mission was different; it would be O'Reilly's last. In a shootout on the docks, Victor Cassadine recognized O'Reilly and gunned her down. In a tearful farewell, Scorpio held his dying friend, vowing revenge on the evil Cassadines.

After a poignant goodbye to Laura, Luke joined Scorpio in his plot to sneak aboard the Cassadine yacht. From a hiding place on the dock, he and Luke watched the Cassadine entourage board the massive vessel. Victor Cassadine arrived with his latest passion, Tiffany Hill, a B-movie actress. The rest of the

Actress Tiffany Hill, a member of the Cassadine entourage, accidentally bumped into Robert Scorpio on her first foray above ground on the tropical island. Their sizzling encounter triggered Tiffany's ultimate decision to defect from the Cassadine fold.

evil ensemble included English engineer Nigel Penny-Smith, General Konrad Kaluga and his beautiful blonde girlfriend, Corinne. World leader Maximillian Von Stade and his wife, Noel, were also on board to handle the distribution of the diamonds. Waiting in an underground command center located under a tropical island was the mastermind of this scheme—the brilliant but diabolical Mikkos Cassadine.

Luke and Robert managed to stow away on the boat and quickly discovered they were not alone—Laura had found a way to sneak aboard to join them on this adventure of a lifetime. One week later, the Cassadine party arrived on the tropical island and moved into their beautiful underground accommodations. When the coast was clear, Luke, Laura and Scorpio swam ashore and spent a miserable first night on the island. The next morning, the trio discovered that Cassadine's factory was underground, protected by an alarm system. There, Mikkos Cassadine gathered his guests in his spectacular Crystal Room and revealed his fiendish plans to build a massive weather machine capable of producing a substance called carbonic snow, with which he could freeze the world! With a psychopathic gleam in his eye, Mikkos told how he would force global leaders to yield to his will by freezing a sample city—the northern New York mecca of commerce, Port Charles.

"The entire world will live by my rule. I will be in supreme command!" he boasted to his guests.

Some were thrilled by the plan. Others, like Tiffany Hill, were repulsed. Below the island, the Cassadines plotted their deep freeze. Above ground, Luke and Laura found time to enjoy their island paradise by making passionate love in a breathtakingly beautiful oasis, complete with a flowing waterfall. Scorpio ventured out, ran into Tiffany Hill—and found instant and mutual attraction. With Tiffany's help, the trio plotted to break into the underground command center and destroy the weather-making machine before the maniacal Mikkos wreaked havoc upon the world.

On the Island, Luke and Laura finalized plans while Scorpio, ever the thrill-seeker, secretly decided to break into the compound—alone! Back in Port Charles, the temperature began to drop drastically as Mikkos informed the WSB that he would not negotiate. As Mikkos grew impatient, he moved up the deadline, lowering the temperature even more. Gripped by a blizzard, Port Charles was declared a disaster area! Furious that Scorpio had gone off to stop Cassadine alone, Luke and Laura entered the underground command center through an air vent leading into the factory. Stealing worker's uniforms, they made their way through the plant into the control room. Suddenly, the piercing sound of an alarm filled the air. The guards had detected the intruders.

Racing through tunnels, Luke and Laura suddenly stumbled upon an ice chamber containing the frozen bodies of Max, Noel, Alex and Tony. At this moment of horror, they were captured and taken into custody. Once inside the control room, Luke and Laura were brought before Mikkos and reunited with Scorpio, whom the guards had captured earlier. Thinking quickly, Luke pretended to side with Mikkos, promising him that he would convince the WSB to capitulate. But during a radio transmission, Luke began to reveal their whereabouts, prompting Mikkos to turn off the radio, but not before Luke uttered a clue.

"We're somewhere off the coast of Ven-."

Mikkos exploded in anger and lunged at Luke. A vicious scuffle followed as Mikkos attempted to hurl Luke into the ice chamber. But in a bizarre twist, Mikkos fell into the deadly chamber and was instantaneously frozen to death!

Luke tried desperately to release the lever controlling the weather that Mikkos had programmed into the "lock" position. After several unsuccessful attempts to decode the computer, he entered the words "Ice Princess" and the weather machine shut down! The freeze was off! The courageous efforts of Luke, Laura and Scorpio saved Port Charles—and the entire world—from disaster! It was time to go home—to plan a wedding!

So much had changed in the months Luke and company were off saving the world. Working closely in their waterfront clinic, Rick and Lesley had found their way back to each other and in the fall of 1981, they busily planned both a wedding and a new waterfront sports center. On the homefront, they began proceedings to adopt a young waterfront orphan, Mike, who had recently entered their lives.

Bobbie was now romantically involved with a dashingly hip new surgeon, Noah Drake. Their romance swiftly progressed to the serious stage, but Bobbie's past was about to catch up with her. After they made love for the first time, she moved some of her belongings into Noah's apartment. Still, the roving Romeo could not bring himself to make a

Working side by side in the waterfront clinic, the divorced Webbers found their way back to each other in 1981. Together, Rick and Lesley planned both a wedding and the opening of the new waterfront sports center.

commitment. Frustrated by the fact that Noah couldn't say "I love you," Bobbie faked blindness to gain his affection. Although Noah admitted his love in a moment of panic, he later recanted his confession.

"No one can force another person to love them," he coldly told Bobbie. Heartbroken, she split up with Noah and prepared to leave Port Charles.

A medical crisis at the Quartermaines nearly took the life of young Alan Jr. When the child fell ill with a recurrence of his ailment, Rick stepped in and successfully performed delicate open-heart surgery. The emergency brought Alan and Monica closer together, but their truce came to an abrupt end when Alan discovered that Monica had hired a private detective to investigate him. Susan, pregnant with Alan's child, relocated temporarily to New York, where she gave birth to her baby, Jason, in secret. Alan chased Susan down and persuaded her to come back to Port Charles with him. Still, Alan was reluctant to ask Monica for a divorce, fearing she would gain sole custody of their son. It wasn't long before Monica's private investigators filled her in on Susan's secret love child and Monica confronted Alan, telling him, "I know all about your girlfriend—and your baby!"

In retaliation, Monica demanded exactly what Alan feared—total custody of Alan Jr.!

"And *I* don't care if I have to create a public scandal," she threatened.

The stage was set for another war between the Quartermaines!

On a brighter note, Luke and Laura hurriedly planned their November wedding. The lovers hoped to have a private ceremony, but their friends and family simply wouldn't have it. They insisted upon a lavish celebration, so Luke and Laura reluctantly agreed to hold "the wedding to end all weddings."

The last obstacle the pair faced before tying the knot was Laura's divorce from Scotty Baldwin. Living in Mexico, Scotty agreed to give Laura a divorce. But the papers still hadn't arrived two days before the wedding. Luke discovered that the culprit wasn't Scotty but his alcoholic stepfather, Lee Baldwin. Bitter over Laura's betrayal, Lee burned the divorce papers—leaving Laura no choice but to obtain a last-minute "ex-parte" divorce decree which involved a key risk: If Scotty contested the divorce, Laura could be charged with bigamy. Faced with this dilemma, Laura decided to follow her heart and go through with the wedding.

Meanwhile, Luke and Laura were the toast of the town! The people of Port Charles expressed their thanks to the heroic couple by showering them with gift after gift—topped off with the grand prize—the Cassadine yacht!

The mayor's wife had graciously offered the sprawling lawn of the mayoral mansion for the ceremony and Agnes Whitaker and her Beechers Corners friends decorated the site with a country flair. Too exhilarated to be nervous, Laura awoke on

Bobbie Spencer shared a relaxing evening with handsome surgeon Dr. Noah Drake. Bobbie hoped to marry Noah, but the blue-blooded Romeo couldn't bear the thought of settling down.

At their wedding reception, Laura and Luke shared a bit of the bubbly with Slick, Robert and Bobbie—all members of their wedding party.

her wedding day prepared to become "Mrs. Luke Spencer." Luke was equally excited to marry the woman he loved. Waking on November 16, 1981, he stepped out on his balcony to breathe in the crisp morning air and shouted for all of Port Charles to hear: "Lucas Lorenzo Spencer, King of the Single Life, is giving it up today!"

On a beautiful Indian summer day, Luke and Laura joined each other under a gazebo and were triumphantly pronounced man and wife. Unbeknownst to anyone, a bejeweled woman stood in the shadows, staring coldly at the couple as they spoke their vows. The uninvited guest was none other than Mikkos Cassadine's widow, Helena, who vowed revenge on the newlyweds for killing her husband.

"A curse on you, Laura and Luke," she uttered under her breath before vanishing from the scene of their glory.

As Luke and Laura were about to find out, Helena Cassadine was not the only uninvited guest to crash the wedding. At the reception, Luke met Laura on the balcony overlooking the garden where she prepared to toss the bride's bouquet.

"Amy! Claudia! Ready?" shouted Laura to the women gathered below.

Laura spun around and tossed the bouquet—into Scotty's waiting hands!

"There is no marriage!" shouted the now-bearded Baldwin.

Before Laura could stop him, Luke jumped down from the balcony and in a vicious exchange of blows, knocked Scotty out. With that, the bride and groom took off—prepared to start their life anew! Luke and Laura left for their honeymoon at the Whittaker Farm. The Whittakers were out of town, so Luke and Laura tended to the farm duties.

Their homespun honeymoon in Beechers Corners was interrupted by a phone call from Rick Webber, who informed them that Helena Cassadine insisted on a meeting with Luke. Unaware that Helena had cursed them at their wedding, Luke agreed to a meeting. When Luke returned to Beechers Corners, he described the "strange burning sensation" he experienced when Helena compared him to Mikkos and put her hands on his shoulders. Luke's best man, Robert Scorpio, was equally perplexed by this—and by Helena's gift of $10,000,000 to General Hospital. Just what was she up to?

Tiffany insisted Laura accompany her to New York to visit her agent, Mickey Miller. Mickey, who had a keen eye for beauty, took one look at Laura and offered to make her a star. "Miss Star Eyes," in fact—the international spokesperson for an exclusive cosmetics line. Although Luke was at first opposed to Laura's new career, he finally relented and wished his new wife the best of success. In New York for her screen test, Laura grew apprehensive, feeling she was being watched. Her suspicions were indeed correct. A stranger, David Grey, was tracing her every move!

Mikkos Cassadine's widow, Helena, arrived in Port Charles to make a sizable donation to General Hospital. The bewitching Madame Cassadine requested a private meeting with Luke Spencer, the man who killed her husband.

1982

*L*uke and Laura's idyllic life aboard the new yacht (now dubbed The Haunted Star, a floating cabaret) came to an early end when the golden couple began to have marital difficulties fueled by Laura's constant trips to New York to fulfill her "Miss Star Eyes" obligations. In early January, she completed a modeling shoot with photographer Mel Wilson and then planned to head home on an early plane to Port Charles. As Laura left the photography studio, she walked by another blonde model, and both young women smiled as they noticed their resemblance.

"Hi, Laura" said Mel, greeting the pretty girl. Laura? Another Laura?

Walking into a New York restaurant where "her husband" had sent a message telling her he would be, Laura Spencer was surprised to be met by Scotty, not Luke! He quickly apologized for the deception. "I need time to see you alone."

Persuading her to stay, Scotty apologized for his behavior and asked her forgiveness. Touched, Laura accepted his gesture, then headed home on the same plane with him. The model whom Laura had seen in the studio was also on the flight, as was the mysterious David Grey, whom Laura had noticed earlier in the restaurant. Lurking in the shadows, this tall, dark and handsome man stared intently at the two Lauras as they walked off the aircraft.

Scotty and Laura parted company at the airport, and she hurriedly headed home to see Luke. Arriving early, Laura discovered that he was nowhere to be found and the phones were dead. This was nothing new. For weeks, strange things had been happening aboard their "haunted" ship. Fog covered the docks as Laura headed out to a nearby phone booth. Shrouded by the mist, David Grey approached in silence. Laura tried to call Tiffany, but there was no answer. She attempted to phone her parents. Again, no luck—Amy was busily talking to a reporter about what it was like to be the sister of "Miss Star Eyes." Giving up, Laura left the booth and ventured out into the eerie night. Walking along the misty docks, she grew anxious, feeling another presence. Was she being followed? Turning quickly, she saw the hand-some man with the haunting eyes staring at her through the mist. Upon his hand he wore a sapphire ring, which he raised slowly into the mist. Laura shrieked in dread as she sank to the ground.

At the airport where he waited for Laura's flight—the flight she was supposed to take—Luke had a foreboding sense that something was wrong! Heading back to the yacht, he discovered Laura's suitcases—but where was Laura? He went to Kelly's Diner but she wasn't there. As Luke walked on the foggy docks, he grew frantic with worry. Just then, he heard a girl cry out: "Help me! Somebody help me!"

"Laura?" he screamed. The young woman—the other Laura from New York—froze at the sound of her name—then ran off! Luke, perplexed, fell to the ground, letting out his frustrations in a blood-curdling scream, "Laura!"

But she was gone—perhaps forever!

The disappearance of this second Laura, identified as Laura Templeton, shook the residents of Port Charles. When a third Laura, also blonde, was rushed to General Hospital with severe facial lacerations, folks couldn't help but wonder—is some nut out to attack women named Laura? The search was on. Luke, Robert Scorpio (who had traded in his trenchcoat for a police commissioners's badge) and Tiffany Hill were joined in their quest by Laura Templeton's older sister, Jackie, a sassy, auburn-haired investigative reporter for the *Advertising Times* in New York City. Jackie was a tough, determined young woman who demonstrated considerable savvy in tracking down a story. Now she was forced to call upon her expertise to track down the missing Lauras. Soon after arriving, Jackie ascertained that a "Mr. D. Grey" was somehow connected to the mysterious disappearances, and she made it her mission to find out who he was.

The sinister David Grey was on a curious mission of his own. A priceless exhibition was on its way to the Port Charles Museum and, using a secret ingenious invention of Mel's, David planned to pilfer the valuable objects and replace them with three-dimensional holograms. Protective of his grand scheme, David hypnotized Mel's girlfriend, Laura

Templeton, so that she would remember details of the plan on cue: by responding to the words "star sapphire." Through the power of suggestion, David was able to secretly regulate Laura T's actions, control her behavior and force her to do his bidding.

Jackie confessed to her comrades that her sister was a kleptomaniac who had a passion for stealing from local department stores. Armed with this shred of a clue, they visited several department stores—and hit paydirt. Although Laura T. had a cap on to cover her long platinum locks, Jackie recognized her at Gorhams' Department Store and took off in hot pursuit. David stepped out of the shadows, grabbing Jackie, but she pulled free and ran after Laura. Spotting her sister on a nearby bridge, Jackie ran after her. Arriving at the spot, she collided with two rollerskaters who sent her toppling over the side of the bridge! Clinging to the railing, Luke arrived just in time to pull her to safety. Their eyes met in relief. Then they shared an electric moment when he threw his arms around her. Jackie

was safe, but both Lauras were still missing. Their hopes momentarily dashed, Luke, Jackie, Robert and Tiffany drew closer as they renewed their solemn vow to locate their loved ones and bring them home safe and sound.

At the Quartermaines, the battle lines in the war between Alan and Monica were drawn even closer when a humiliated Alan, suitcase in hand, returned home to the mansion—after having been thrown out of his love nest by Susan Moore, the mother of his love child! Monica, taking every opportunity to needle Alan, guessed correctly that Susan, fed up with Alan's broken promises, had tossed him out on his ear. One look at Monica's smug face convinced Alan that he had to do what he dreaded—file for divorce. In retaliation, Monica vowed to put the mansion up for sale.

"What?" bellowed Edward.

"How could she?" wondered Lila.

Easy—the mansion belonged to Monica. Alan, in a gesture of good will, had gifted his wife with the spacious estate years earlier—and she was ready to

Luke Spencer and Jackie Templeton grew closer in their quest to locate two missing Lauras—Luke's wife and Jackie's sister—whose disappearances had been orchestrated by the mysterious David Grey. In the course of the search, Jackie fell in love with Luke's pal, Robert Scorpio.

cash in the prize. Alan, as anyone might guess, was furious at his ungrateful soon-to-be-ex-wife.

Back with his greedy girlfriend Susan, Alan developed a problem—impotence! Extensive tests and psychiatric evaluations from General Hospital's new resident shrink, Dr. Katz, revealed that Alan's plumbing was in fine working order. It seemed that his impotence was caused by the simple fact that Susan no longer turned him on! To his astonishment, Alan came to realize that there was only one woman who got his fires burning—Monica! As he continued to disappoint Susan in the bedroom, Alan admitted to Dr. Katz that he was "excited by the thought of a woman I hate!"

Alan's passionate contempt for Monica intensified when she returned from a jaunt to Paris looking stunningly beautiful. Alan could hardly keep his eyes off Monica, but continued in the role of the bitter estranged husband. To make matters worse, Alan grew incredibly jealous of Monica's handsome new French friend, Phillipe, and Monica fanned the flames of desire by flaunting the studly Frenchman in Alan's face. Still, Alan stoically insisted to Edward that he loved Susan, not Monica, and was moving out of Susan's home to aid his custody battle for Alan Jr.

Monica continued to threaten to sell the mansion, but her actions proved unnecessary because attorney Lee Baldwin came up with proof indicating that the mansion was not Monica's to sell until Alan was dead. With that small victory in hand, Alan moved back into the mansion. Although Monica was adamantly against the idea, she finally relented, hired shady lawyer Scotty Baldwin to represent her and proceeded to section off the house—Alan on one side, Monica on the other. And Monica smugly made sure that Susan was aware that she wasn't moving out of the mansion. Susan was furious with Alan but reluctantly accepted his story that he was moving home to help with his custody battle. To add fuel to this comical matrimonial mess, Monica invited Phillipe to stay with her, shocking Alan. Crazed with jealousy, Alan assumed Monica had slept with him but came to realize that she was just playing some kind of vicious game. As for that handsome Frenchman, his stay with the Quartermaines was short-lived because Edward convinced Phillipe that Alan's jealousy could prove fatal! Alan sent Susan on a cruise and promised to meet her on St. Thomas, while maintaining to Monica that he must attend a medical seminar in New York. But Monica immediately doubted the validity of Alan's traveling tale and did a little "research." Upon his return, Monica greeted him with warmth and kindness, then shocked Alan with pictures of Susan and him

Seemingly on her death bed after a terrible car accident, Susan Moore called upon Scotty Baldwin to marry her. With Dr. Mark Dante looking on, they became man and wife in the hospital ICU. Miraculously, Susan recovered from her injuries, only to be gunned down later in the year.

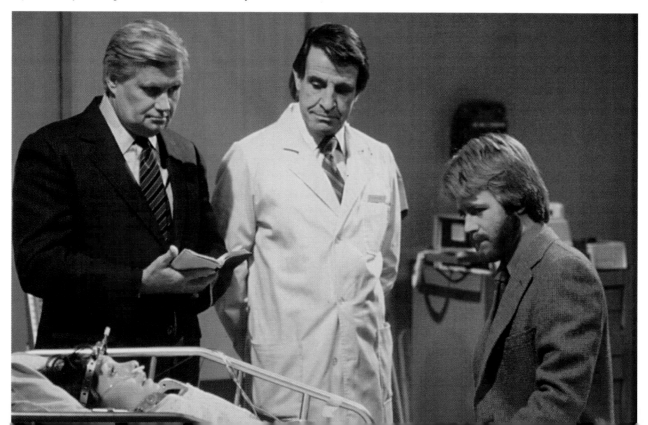

on board the ship! All-out war ensued between the quarreling Quartermaines.

Edward convinced Alan that Monica's pictures would ruin his chances for custody of Alan Jr. Alan's wise old father offered up one other piece of advice to his son: "Sleep with Monica!" Although Alan was against this at first, he spent the night in Monica's boudoir—with upstanding results! The old chemistry was there between them. Alan confessed to Monica that he was still excited by her and wanted to work things out.

"Not while Susan Moore is still around!" Monica countered.

It was time for Alan to have a little talk with Susan. With Monica's support, he coolly informed Susan that their relationship was over. Furious, Susan sued him for millions on behalf of her infant son, Jason—and won a million dollars of Quartermaine cash for Jason, but only $100,000 for herself. Bitter and disillusioned, Susan drowned her sorrows in drink. Relieved that the lawsuit was over, Alan and Monica went straight to bed.

For Scotty Baldwin, Susan Moore offered a chance for him to make his mark as an attorney in Port Charles. Motivated by the almighty dollar, Scotty lied, cheated and pulled from his bag of dirty tricks to win the case. In the process, he made a mint of money for himself—but Scotty wanted more. He wanted a piece of Susan's newfound fortune. Teaming up with Susan's cousin, Heather, Scotty encouraged the rich-but-bitter Susan to start drinking. At the same time, Scotty began to sleep with Heather—behind her boyfriend, Joe Kelly's, back. Heather's dream of spending her life with the handsome and moral Joe Kelly shattered when Amy blabbed to Joe that Heather and Scotty were having an affair. Joe, his Irish temper on the rise, barged into Scotty's room and found Heather and Scotty in bed together.

"You make me want to puke!" he screamed at Heather.

In a rage, Joe punched Scotty, then stormed out! Heather and Scotty were through forever. Scotty informed Heather that if Susan didn't clean up her act, the court could appoint a new guardian to administer Jason's million-dollar cash settlement. Together they schemed to make this come about by encouraging Susan to drink her way into oblivion. Seeing Susan going downhill fast, Alan attempted to take custody of Jason. But Monica adamantly forbade Alan to bring his love child into the house.

"I will not raise your illegitimate son!" she

Former gang member Blackie Parrish provided Luke Spencer with many a laugh with his penchant for tall stories. Upon his arrival in 1982, the handsome teenager added a youthful zest to the *General Hospital* canvas.

bellowed.

When Susan kicked Heather out of her home, Alan feared that Jason wouldn't get any care at all. When the judge ordered a soused Susan to pick a guardian for the baby, Heather and Scotty fought each other for the honors. Scotty won the battle by marrying Susan. Seriously injured in an automobile accident, she called Scotty to the ICU at General Hospital and asked him to become her husband. While Susan recovered, Scotty gloated to Alan and Heather that he had managed to gain custody of Jason. "You may have my son, Baldwin, but you won't have his money!" warned an angry Alan.

For Rick and Lesley Webber, 1982 was a year of uplifting highs and low lows. After Laura's disappearance, the grief-stricken Webbers poured their energies into the opening of the Waterfront Sports Center and their newly adopted six-year-old son, Mike. Amy's New Year's resolution to "stop gossiping and get a boyfriend" came partially true when she fell in love with a handsome boxer, Johnny Morrissey. Sadly, Amy's stormy romance came to an end when, after the death of his manager, Packy, Johnny left Port Charles.

In late winter, new turmoil arrived in Rick and Lesley's lives in the form of a sixteen-year-old street urchin by the name of Blackie Parrish. The tough-talking gang leader boldly claimed that Rick Webber's new Sports Center was on "his turf." With a can of spray paint in hand, he proceeded to vandalize the newly renovated establishment. Rick, not taking Blackie's guff for a moment, promptly kicked him out by the seat of his pants. In time, a strong bond formed between Rick, Lesley and the not-so-tough Blackie

With a wild look in his eye and the precious Sword of Malkuth in his hand, Luke avenged the supposed death of his beloved Laura by engaging in a life-and-death encounter with her kidnaper, David Grey.

Parrish. When Blackie's mother died from the effects of alcohol, they graciously took him into their home—and the Webbers were ill-prepared for the added spice this teenage terror would bring to their lives.

At the hospital, Anne Logan chose to make a new start away from Port Charles. Months of harassment from her surly superior, Dr. Arthur Bradshaw, had frayed Anne's nerves, as did the failure of romances with Joe Kelly and Noah Drake. After "one-upping" Dr. Bradshaw by successfully charging him with negligence in the death of a patient, Anne happily watched the dastardly doctor resign his post at General Hospital. Feeling vindicated, Anne then decided to take a leave herself. Along with her adopted son, Jeremy, she left General Hospital to live in peace on her Aunt Lucille's farm.

On the rebound from Bobbie and a short dalliance with Anne Logan, Dr. Noah Drake ignited sparks with sexy Tiffany Hill early in 1982. Seeking a steady commitment from the playboy doc, Tiffany successfully made Noah jealous when her old boyfriend, Tom Clark, came to town for a short visit. But the tables soon turned on Tiff when Nurse Bobbie Spencer returned to the hospital. Everyone, except Tiffany, was happy to have Bobbie back. The hospital staff also welcomed back Dr. Mark Dante, who was mourning his wife, Katie, who died in an automobile accident in Europe. Mark's spirits brightened considerably when he walked into Kelly's Diner and encountered the radiant smile of its proprietor, Rose Kelly.

Throughout early 1982, the search for the missing Lauras yielded few clues. To keep his pursuers at bay, the sinister David Grey sent Luke and company on several wild goose chases. Luke followed one set of clues to an airborne plane but when, much to his dismay, he discovered that the blonde he was chasing was not his Laura, Luke parachuted out of the plane and took off after the notorious David Grey!

Laura Templeton dated Scott Baldwin. But greedy Scotty chose money over romance when he married the wealthy Susan Moore.

Luke went on a camping trip where he stumbled upon the exquisite form of a young Englishwoman, Holly Sutton, enjoying a morning swim.

Back in Port Charles, Luke joined Robert and Tiffany in planning a gala benefit on behalf of Rick Webber's new Waterfront Sports Center. On this very night, David, having no more use for Laura Templeton, erased all memories of heists and holograms and set her free. Back at the Haunted Star, Luke and the gathered guests were being entertained by an evening of magic and comedy when suddenly the lights went out! When they came back on, Laura Templeton appeared in the center of the room, remembering nothing of her whereabouts for the last several months. Jackie was jubilant, but Luke dismayed. As the clues mounted, Luke began to fear that Laura was dead. First, a pendant that Luke had given his wife turned up as part of the wreckage from a boat lost at sea. Then a raincoat turned up and Lesley Webber recognized it as her daughter's. Heartbroken and vengeful, Luke knew in his heart that David Grey, who Luke discovered was a member of an ancient cult, was somehow involved in Laura's disappearance—and Luke was determined to destroy him!

David Grey was not alone in his grand plans to steal the crown jewels of the faraway kingdom of Malkuth. Robert Scorpio suspected correctly that Grey was part of a large, sophisticated organization that was attempting to overthrow the kingdom. The overthrow efforts, spearheaded by the notorious Magus, a cold-hearted international criminal, could only be successfully accomplished by gaining possession of several Malkuthian treasures, including a priceless sword and helmet.

Eventually, Luke gained the upper hand by acquiring the precious Sword of Malkuth. In hot pursuit of his prize, David and his goons held the Haunted Star captive, demanding the Sword of Malkuth be returned. Luke, Scorpio, Laura, Jackie and their cabbie pal, Slick, were bound and gagged, their lives in dire jeopardy. Giving in to their demands, Luke consented to retrieve the sword from its underwater storage and managed to get away—chasing after David Grey. Finally, they met face to face. Holding the sword in his hand, a steely-eyed Luke began a deadly battle with David, who crashed through the window and plummeted to his death.

A crisis was over—and Luke sadly came to accept the fact that his beloved Laura was never coming back. In the course of this dangerous escapade, a new relationship formed. Scorpio admitted to Luke that he was in love with Jackie Templeton, and he insisted that she stay in Port Charles. Jackie went to work at the *Port Charles Herald*. Her sister took a job there too, getting romantically involved with both Blackie Parrish and Scotty Baldwin. Luke, exhausted and disheartened, just needed to be alone. Packing his knapsack, he headed into the mountains to go camping. Of course, he had no inkling that a new adventure was about to begin.

After a restful, mind-clearing night of sleep, Luke awoke to the peaceful sounds of chirping birds, creaking crickets—and a curious splashing sound coming from a nearby pond. Getting up to investigate, Luke was delightfully stunned to discover a beautiful girl enjoying an early morning swim—naked! Luke was instantly smitten with this skinny-dipping nymph, who avoided his glance and ran off at the first opportunity. Later, he came across her sunbathing, but once again, she retreated hastily into her shell of solitude. Luke, bewildered but fascinated, finally coaxed her to reveal her name, which she announced with a "veddy British" flair: "Holly Sutton."

Luke and Holly went their separate ways. But fate would intervene once more. While hiking, Luke came across her once again. She had injured her knee and, while he tended to her injury, the chill slowly began to thaw. As night fell, the sexual tension grew ever more palpable. The star-crossed pair drew closer, fell into each other's arms and made passionate love beneath the stars.

The next morning Luke awakened to find his sexy siren had slipped away from the campsite. Angry and confused, Luke was left with unanswered questions. Who was this Holly? Was she a fantasy? Would they ever meet again? When next seen, Holly was luxuriating in an elegant penthouse, reporting to someone on the phone that her initial contact with Spencer was successful.

"I'm heading for Port Charles to begin the second round of our plans. Soon we will have Luke Spencer right where we want him," she told the man she affectionately called "Daddy."

Of course, she carefully neglected to tell her father that she had slept with Luke. Obviously, there was much more to the beautiful Holly Sutton than met Luke's discerning eye!

Invigorated by his vacation, Luke arrived home. Robert noticed that his dear friend had obviously recaptured some of his old spirit, and that spirit was evident when Luke was called to the police station to bail out someone who had been charged with vagrancy. It was Holly! At first, Luke denied knowing the girl who had deserted him days earlier.

"But what about our night together?" she asked.

"Must have been a dream!" answered a hurting Luke.

After allowing her to "rot" for a night in jail, Luke paid the fine and Holly was freed. Upon her release, the beguiling Holly wove her tale, explaining to Luke, Robert and Jackie that she had come to Port Charles to claim some property that her father left to her in his will. Upon investigating the site—a local swamp—Luke stepped in a sticky black substance. Reaching down to touch the mess, Luke realized instantly that he had struck it rich. Oil! Soon, Luke and many others—including Edward Quartermaine—were swallowing the bait and investing their hard-earned dollars to develop Port Charles' very own oil field.

Unbeknownst to anyone, Holly was a con artist. A swindler. As a key player in a well-planned oil scam, she joined with her father, Charles Sutton (using the alias Charles Corso) and his cousin Basil to bamboozle the residents of Port Charles. Early on, all went exactly as planned except for one thing—Holly had fallen deeply in love with Luke. Steeped in an ugly deception, Holly longed for the honesty she had experienced on her trek into the wilderness. These feelings led her to experience conflicting loyalties. Charles took notice of Holly's troubled demeanor and asked her if Luke was the cause. She denied even liking Luke, feigning instead an interest in Robert Scorpio.

As the prospect of instant wealth loomed, the residents of Port Charles poured more and more money into the pockets of the scam artists. Luke and Robert even mortgaged their business to join in the bonanza. Others, like General Hospital's Chief Administrator Dan Rooney, were a bit more skeptical. Eventually, Dan confronted Luke with his suspicions that Holly was part of an oil swindle. Luke refused to believe him, forcing Dan to dig for more evidence. Later, when Rooney unearthed evidence confirming the scam, Basil silenced him with a knife in the back and framed Luke for the crime. Luke panicked, grabbed Holly's hand and headed off for a roller coaster of an adventure at the Mystery Mountain Theme Park—with Holly's uncle Basil and his henchmen hot on their trail.

On the run, Holly finally admitted the painful truth to Luke: His dream of riches was nothing more than a scam spearheaded by her father, Charles. Luke listened in silent shock as Holly qualified that she was involved only to protect her ailing father. "But I hate what I've done, Luke. I hate it," she cried.

Luke came to believe Holly's story, and they made passionate love with a new fury not experienced before.

His life once again in danger, Luke placed an urgent call to Robert Scorpio, who arrived in time to join in the chaos and battle the bad guys. But our heroes lost the battle this time when both were knocked out. When they awoke, Holly was gone. A bump on the head didn't deter Luke Spencer! With renewed vengeance, he vowed to rescue Holly and return the stolen money to his friends in Port Charles. With Scorpio at his side, Luke journeyed across the Canadian border to Vancouver, where the daring duo saved Holly and succeeded in completing their mission. Luke, Robert and Holly returned to Port Charles, where they were met by angry crowds demanding their money back. Holly, who had been promised immunity, was suddenly charged as an accessory to attempted murder, and she seemed destined to serve a long jail sentence. It was only when Holly's father, Charles, made a deathbed declaration of his daughter's innocence that Holly was set free.

Settling into a "normal" life proved difficult for Luke and Holly. After just a few days back in Port Charles, they were at each other's throats. The issue was trust. After one terrible fight, Luke stuffed his belongings into a knapsack and announced he was heading into the mountains.

"Don't follow me!" he warned.

Luke Spencer would live to regret those words!

1983

A hiking trip was just what Luke Spencer needed to clear his head. Refreshed by the cold mountain air, he awoke whistling on his first day. As he prepared an open-air breakfast, Luke was oblivious to the fact that he was being watched. A mountain bum sat poised and ready to pounce on the unsuspecting Spencer. Luke was caught off guard when the man attacked him with a fierce karate chop, knocked him out and stole all his belongings. Awakening with a headache, Luke groggily began to follow the footprints in the snow—but stopped suddenly when he heard an ominous rumble above him. Looking up in horror, he saw a mountain of snow plummeting toward him. Within seconds, a menacing blur of white poured over Luke.

Back in Port Charles, Holly received word that some civilian hikers had been killed in an avalanche. "No, it can't be," she thought to herself, sharing her fears only with Robert. Soon the word came—Luke's badly mutilated body had been found buried in the snow. With Robert by her side, Holly rushed to the ranger station morgue room and identified the remains as Luke based on the fact that the dead man was carrying Luke's wallet. Back in Port Charles, word spread quickly. Blackie took the news very hard, burying his sorrows by getting drunk at the Bucket of Blood. Bobbie and Ruby were equally devastated, and together they made plans to hold a commemorative gathering for their loved one.

Luke's friends gathered to share their respects, unaware that the man they revered was alive, but not so well, in a remote mountain hospital suffering from a broken back. After hearing that his hometown believed him dead, and imagining what life would be like as a cripple, a despondent Luke decided not to reveal his identity. As Holly grieved for the man she loved she couldn't shake the sick feeling in the pit of her stomach, but it had nothing to do with Luke's "death." Holly was pregnant!

Robert spent hours consoling Holly, a fact that infuriated his girlfriend, Jackie Templeton. As the days passed, Robert became more and more preoccupied with Holly, which got Jackie so enraged that she broke up with him. To complicate matters, Holly received word from Dan Rooney that she was about to be deported. Without a green card, she would have to leave the country within days. With nowhere to turn, a forlorn Holly decided that the only solution to her predicament was to pack her bags. Robert, on the other hand, had a better idea. Hoping to calm her hysteria, he shouted, "Marry me!"

"Preposterous!" she countered, rejecting his wild scheme.

After writing thank you notes to her Port Charles friends, Holly boarded a plane bound for England. When Robert found out, he raced to the airport, intercepted the plane and persuaded Holly to be his wife, assuring her that the marriage would only be temporary. Over her protests, Robert insist-

GREAT MOMENTS

Avalanche! While on a hiking trip in the mountains in 1983, Luke Spencer suddenly heard a strange rumbling noise. Looking up, he was horrified to see a wall of snow descending toward him! Hit by the full force of the avalanche, Luke was paralyzed.

ed that, "After you're a U.S. citizen and have Luke's baby, you can have a divorce."

Holly reluctantly agreed to Robert's gallant act of kindness. In a quick and somber ceremony held in the mayor's office, Holly Sutton became Mrs. Robert Scorpio. Unknown to the newlyweds, Luke continued to suffer from paralysis, refused to give anyone his correct name and was moved to a state hospital.

A new husband, a baby on the way and a brand new townhouse weren't enough to shake Holly's malaise. She missed Luke dearly. Awkward and unsure of herself, she was plagued with the notion that her marriage of convenience was a terrible betrayal of her love for Luke. One day she went on a wild shopping spree, overexerted herself and, experiencing pain in her abdomen, was rushed to General Hospital. It was too late. Holly had lost the baby—a fact that sent her sinking into the lower depths of depression. Robert convinced Holly that even without the baby she must stay married to him for a year to convince immigration that their marriage was not one of convenience. Holly, realizing that she had a dear friend in Robert Scorpio, promised to make the best of things. Her attitude and appearance improved greatly over the next few weeks as she began to help Robert in his private investigation business. Mr. and Mrs. Scorpio made a great team as they examined the clues in the biggest mystery to hit Port Charles in years. The question on everyone's tongue was "Who killed Susan Moore?"

Over the course of the past year, Susan had invoked the ire of many Port Charles residents. Among them was her former lover, Alan Quartermaine, the father of her infant son, Jason. Once she realized that she would never win Alan away from Monica, Susan used innocent young Jason in a vicious game of blackmail aimed at the entire Quartermaine family. After suffering a near-fatal auto accident, Susan married her greedy attorney, Scotty Baldwin, whose only interest was gaining control over the $1,000,000 trust fund that his new wife had won, in Jason's name, from Alan. When Susan revoked Scotty's power of attorney, he grew angry, deceitful—and of course, vengeful. Susan's cousin, Heather Webber, also had designs on Jason's trust fund, and she already had her claws into Susan's man. Heather, ever the manipulator, had been having a torrid affair with Scotty Baldwin.

To exact her revenge stratagem against the Quartermaines, Susan hooked up with an elderly new arrival in town—Crane Tolliver. Crane came to Port Charles harboring a long-buried secret—he was Lila Quartermaine's first husband, and they were still married! When Tolliver whispered that he and Lila had never been divorced, that meant Alan and Tracy were illegitimate—and the entire Quartermaine trust was in question! Satisfied that she could use this information to do her bidding, Susan formed a partnership with her crotchety new friend. Gleefully summoning the Quartermaine clan to her cottage, Susan delivered the news.

"You're all illegitimate!" she declared to the devastated family.

"Illegitimate" was certainly the most popular word in the Quartermaine household in early 1983. Just after the new year, a handsome young man with piercing blue eyes roared into town on his motorcycle. His name was Jimmy Lee Holt and he'd come straight from Indiana to deliver the shocking news that he was Edward Quartermaine's illegitimate son. When the facts backed up his claim, Edward was forced to accept the truth that he had fathered a son by a long-ago lover, Beatrice LeSeur. Alan also feared that Jimmy Lee was after the Quartermaine money. But the jean-clad muscleman insisted that he was only in Port Charles to make friends with his father. To drive him away, Edward attempted to buy Jimmy Lee, but he quickly countered that wasn't interested in money. It seemed that Jimmy Lee Holt enjoyed watching the Quartermaines squirm! Of course, so did Susan Moore.

Over the month of January, Susan and Tolliver turned the screws tighter on the Quartermaines with their blackmailing scheme as Heather and Scotty plotted against Susan by illegally spending Jason's money on a mob-fronted waterfront mall, which was replacing the closed-down Sports Center. Both Lila and Alan tried to reason with Susan, but she wouldn't listen to their pleas. Monica tried to talk some sense into Susan, but ended up so angry that she threatened to kill Susan. Alan became increasingly aware of a loaded gun he kept in his desk drawer, as did Edward and Monica, and this gun was later stolen by a shadowy figure. Tolliver forced Susan to demand two million dollars from the Quartermaines in exchange for Lila's unsigned divorce papers and marriage certificate to Tolliver. Susan scheduled the exchange for Friday night, and invited reporter Jackie Templeton to attend the meeting. In the meantime, Susan learned that Scotty had forged power of attorney papers and had invested Jason's money in the mall. This revelation led to a huge fight between Susan and her new husband just before the Quartermaines and Jackie were expected to arrive. Alice Grant (who had overheard Monica's threat to kill Susan) witnessed the fight, and heard Scotty tell Susan, "I wish you were dead." On this fateful night, Alan, Monica and Edward all sneaked out of the Quartermaine mansion, each going their own separate and secret way. Heather went to see Susan, intending to talk her out of prosecuting Scotty for forgery. While Susan was upstairs taking her bath, Heather entered the cottage and found a note that Susan had written to herself as a reminder to call the bank regarding the forgery. Heather tucked the note away, but dropped her lipstick in the process. Sensing the presence of an intruder in her cottage, Susan went to investigate. Moments later, she let out a blood-curdling scream. A shot rang out, and Susan Moore was dead.

With her freshly dead body sprawled on the floor, Jackie arrived, followed quickly by Alan, Monica and Edward. Assisted by his wife, Holly (who was quickly proving her abilities as a super-sleuth), commissioner Robert Scorpio began his investigation of the murder, unearthing clues that proved that several key players had a motive to murder Susan. Robert discovered that Scotty had forged Susan's power of attorney papers, and that Heather had been hiding in the closet at the time of Susan's murder, and he uncovered information that the gun used to kill Susan was registered in Alan Quartermaine's name. To complicate matters, Alice Grant's fingerprints were found on a watch pin found at the scene. Scotty was arrested, then released. Next Heather (who hired attorney Jake Meyer to represent her) was charged with the crime. Eventually, Scorpio came to realize that Alan, Monica, Edward, Scotty and Heather had all been to see Susan on the night of the murder! And so had Crane Tolliver—but Robert couldn't prove he killed her. Shrewdly, Robert developed a plan to trap Tolliver by having the old man overhear that Heather had been an eyewitness to the murder. As Robert had hoped, Tolliver made a bee line straight for Heather and confessed to the murder as he lunged at her with a knife! In the nick of time, Scorpio arrived to save Heather and arrest Tolliver. Upon Scotty's arrival, a brief commotion enabled Tolliver to escape, but not before Scorpio fired his gun and wounded him. With his last ounce of strength, Crane hobbled to the

Who pointed a deadly weapon at sassy Susan Moore, then fired the shot that killed her? Susan's husband Scotty, cousin Heather and ex-lover Alan were among the suspects. The killer turned out to be elderly Crane Tolliver—Lila Quartermaine's first husband and Susan's partner in crime.

Quartermaines, where a party was being held for Jimmy Lee. Just before collapsing, Tolliver secretly handed Jimmy Lee the unsigned divorce papers.

With the murder mystery solved, the only mystery remaining was the whereabouts of Lila's missing divorce papers and marriage certificate. Jimmy Lee opened the papers that he received from Tolliver and realized their importance. After Tolliver's death, Robert revealed that the old man had come to Port Charles with a plan to extort money from the Quartermaines and killed Susan when she tried to double-cross him. With the mess behind them, *Edward and Lila were legally married.* Meanwhile, another Quartermaine arrived in town.

After recovering from a paralyzing injury, Luke shocked Holly with his return from the dead. Luke was equally stunned to discover that, in his absence, Holly had married his best friend, Robert Scorpio.

Distant cousin Celia, a beautiful young woman and a gifted artist, set up residence in the Quartermaine mansion. Celia was enchanted by the gruff Jimmy Lee Holt, who returned the attraction. But she played it cool, reminding him that she was engaged to another man—all-American surgeon Grant Putnam. But Jimmy Lee was not discouraged. As spring arrived in Port Charles, he kept close tabs on the "new girl in town."

With her husband-to-be, Grant, working long hours at General Hospital, Celia found any excuse to spend time with Jimmy Lee. The waterfront became Celia's new hangout when she learned that Jimmy Lee lived above Kelly's and she rented an art studio there. In time, Grant became jealous and sensed that something was up between the two. Grant Putnam began to make moves that belied his normally upbeat nature. One day, he made a mysterious phone call stating to the person on the other end of the line that his wedding to Celia was "all set." Who was he talking to? Meanwhile, the sexual tension between Jimmy Lee and Celia grew even stronger when Jimmy Lee, his chiseled torso hardened by a new job as a construction worker, agreed to let Celia sculpt him. Alone in the studio for their first sculpting session, they finally kissed. Reeling from the spontaneous moment, Celia insisted the kiss was "nothing more than a fantasy." Jimmy Lee knew it was more!

Robert and Holly's "marriage of convenience" began to take on new dimensions in the spring of 1983. Drawing a close to the Susan Moore investigation, Mr. and Mrs. Scorpio began acting more and more like man and wife—everywhere but in the bedroom. When Robert's old flame, WSB agent Constance Townley, arrived in town, Holly urged Robert to ask her out on a date. Privately, Holly hoped he wouldn't, for she had fallen in love with her own husband! Scorpio shared the same feelings and, as their mutual desire remained unspoken, the air grew thick with sexual tension.

Far away in his mountain hideaway, Luke began to make a miraculous recovery. With the aid of his physical therapist, Natalie Dearborn, Luke struggled through grueling daily sessions aimed to get him back on his feet. Once he was "whole" again, Luke planned to walk back into Holly's arms. Meanwhile, Holly became jealous of Robert's relationship with Connie—and told him so.

"It's not Connie I care about. It's you, Holly. I love you," he confessed with his Australian lilt.

Scooping her up in his arms, Robert carried Holly off to bed and they made love for the first time. The next morning, Luke, walking with a slight limp, arrived at his best friend's apartment and was greeted by a maid who informed him that Robert was not at home, but "Mrs. Scorpio is." Mrs. Scorpio? Luke barely had time to say the words when he spied a stunned Holly at the top of the stairs.

Realizing that the woman he loved had married his best friend, a humiliated Luke rushed out the door before Holly could explain.

Bobbie Spencer greeted her brother Luke's return with a mixture of shock and joy. Bobbie's own love life had taken a dramatic turn after saying goodbye, once and for all, to Dr. Noah Drake.

Alone and dismayed, Noah left General Hospital for a new surgical position in Atlanta. Soon after, Bobbie met tough-as-nails investor D.L. Brock and the pair struck up an immediate rapport. In their first meeting, Bobbie poured out her heart to Brock, confessing that she felt "put down" by people like snooty Tiffany and blue-blooded Noah. "Stick with me, kid. I'm from the same side of the tracks that you are," assured Brock. By the end of their pleasant evening, Bobbie and Brock were clearly looking forward to spending more time together.

Blackie Parrish enjoyed the company of a young runaway girl, Louise "Lou" Swenson. Blackie did his best to straighten out the gutter-mouthed, ill-dressed girl who had captured his fancy. She joined Blackie, a talented drummer, in the formation of his new band, "Blackie and the Riff Raff."

Rose Kelly became Lou's guardian, while her lawyer, Jake Meyer, flirted with Rose, who enjoyed the attention. What she didn't fancy were the whispers their budding relationship was garnering among their families because Rose was Catholic and Jake Jewish. Rose's dear family friend frowned upon her new man, while Jake's beloved "Uncle Isaac" thought that Rose was wonderful—but not for Jake!

Longtime lovers Bryan Phillips and Claudia Johnston fared better in the romance department. Still, their April wedding nearly failed to happen when the groom suffered a case of last-minute jitters. Rick Webber soothed his nerves and Bryan showed up—only to forget the ring! Claudia wrongly believed that Bryan had given up on her. Worse, her wealthy father was just about to call off the wedding when Bryan appeared out of the blue—and the wedding was on!

Reeling from the shocking news of Robert and Holly's wedding, Luke Spencer poured his energies into several new causes. To get his mind off Holly, Luke began dating the blonde and beautiful WSB agent, Constance Townley. In addition, he opened a gambling casino and (urged on by D.L. Brock) announced his candidacy for mayor of Port Charles. Luke's opponent was Lee Baldwin, whose campaign was spearheaded by Scotty Baldwin. In his usual underhanded and lowdown way, Scotty artfully began using smear tactics to discredit Luke. He even threatened to expose Bobbie's past life as a hooker in an attempt to persuade Luke to drop out of the mayoral race. Bobbie and Ruby pleaded with him to stop, but Scotty denied any involvement in the smear campaign. Finally, Ruby told Lee what was going on. Outraged, Lee fired Scotty, who left Port

In the wake of her broken romance with Dr. Noah Drake, Bobbie jumped into a stormy relationship with crafty real estate developer D.L. Brock. Against her better judgment, she made the ill-fated decision to marry him in late 1983.

Charles for a new job in Richmond. Scotty was gone, but too late to protect Bobbie. Jackie Templeton had overheard Scotty and Lee's conversation and arranged to have Bobbie's sordid story published. The bad publicity and Brock's rejection left Bobbie hurt and humiliated. But they eventually reconciled. All was forgiven as they made passionate love.

There was no love lost between Robert and Luke. Robert's marriage, and his opposition to Luke's candidacy, strained their friendship to the breaking point. An incredible era was over.

In May, Celia forged ahead with plans to marry Dr. Grant Putnam, though the groom nearly canceled the wedding because of her continued "interest" in Jimmy Lee. Just days before the nuptials, Grant presented Celia with an ultimatum: Get Jimmy Lee out of your life or the wedding's off! Forcing a meeting with Jimmy Lee, Celia made her feelings clear when she informed him that the affair was over.

"I'm in love with Grant!" she implored.

As the big day approached, Grant's behavior grew ever more curious. One day in the hospital med- icine room he met privately with Luke's physical therapist, Natalie Dearborn. As the pair whispered secrets, it became evident that they were spies. Enemy agents had infiltrated General Hospital! Natalie informed Grant that she was "Natasha," a "control" agent for the notorious international espionage organization, the DVX. Grant, Natasha and their DVX superior Gregory Malko had recently moved to Port Charles to steal the Prometheus Disc, a top secret high-tech energy source being developed by a brilliant scientist, Dr. Jerrold. Grant, the DVX mole, was under orders to cultivate a relationship with Dr. Jerrold in an attempt to gain his trust, then break the code to his secret project.

On Celia's wedding day, Jimmy Lee made a last-ditch plea for her love. Luring her to a country cabin, he tried to get her to admit that she loved him. When she refused, Jimmy Lee hid Celia's dirty clothes and walked out, leaving her locked inside the cabin. With her wedding moments away, Celia climbed through a window and, wearing only a blanket, flagged down a chicken truck to take her to the church on time. At the church,

Bridegroom-to-be Grant Putnam paid back Jimmy Lee Holt for kidnaping his bride-to-be, Celia, by knocking him out just minutes before their big wedding.

the guests gathered, the anxious groom waited, and finally the bride arrived—on the back of a truck! Grant, furious, accused her of being with Jimmy Lee. In front of the church he ran into Jimmy Lee and knocked him out. The wedding was off—or was it? Natalie ordered Grant to "change your mind" and, in the name of the DVX, Grant and Celia became husband and wife.

Over the summer of 1983, Celia grew suspicious of Grant's intentions. Why was he spending so much time in Dr. Jerrold's lab? Why did he have scars on his face? Were the marks from plastic surgery? Celia's questions concerned Natalie and Gregory and, rather than allow her to jeopardize their mission, they threatened to have her "eliminated." As the assignment progressed, a tormented Grant began to question his motives. He loved Celia—not the DVX! The turning point came in a showdown at the lab when Grant, paralyzed by an internal conflict, could not carry out his orders to kill Professor Jerrold. Just then, gunfire erupted and Professor Jerrold slumped to the floor, dying from a gunshot wound inflicted by DVX chief Gregory Malko. Gregory watched as Professor Jerrold died in Grant's arms, uttering, "Keep the disc safe…"

Under the threat of death, Grant carried out his orders to steal the valuable energy disc. In a wild chaotic scene, Luke got hold of the disc and was abducted, along with Holly and Celia, during an international exposition being held in Port Charles. Gregory killed Natalie, then threatened to murder the hostages unless a microfilm—containing the one-of-a-kind equation needed to create the Prometheus Disc—was turned over to him. At the same time, the WSB desperately needed the disc to power a top-secret satellite which was about to launch. As precious time ticked away, Grant learned that Gregory planned to release Celia and keep Luke and Holly until he could authenticate the microfilm. As planned, Celia was released into Scorpio's custody, while Holly and Luke, bound and gagged, were moved in baskets to the Gulistan Pavilion at the Expo. Robert became outraged by WSB Chief Ballantine's betrayal when he learned from Gregory that the microfilm was phony. Robert prepared to storm the Gulistan Pavilion to rescue the hostages while Grant, still working for the enemy though loyal to the good guys, surreptitiously substituted blanks in the guard's gun to subvert any killings. In a vicious fight, he knocked out Gregory and took off. Robert arrived and found Gregory, but where was Grant? At that very moment, Robert heard the rumblings of the satellite launching and realized that Grant was on their side!

In police custody, Grant Putnam held a press conference to confess his incredible story. As a DVX spy, he had been trained in an American village, given a new identity and ordered to carry out his mission. But Grant came to feel more "American" than DVX. In time, Grant named names and was released from jail. But reality hit when he and Celia encountered hostility at every turn. Grant was crushed when he learned he had been fired from his position at General Hospital. As if this weren't enough, he received word that the Board of Professional Medical Conduct was conducting an investigation into his activities. Now he was faced with the possibility of never practicing medicine again. Feeling like an outcast, he wanted to move but a devoted Celia gave him a pep talk, urging him to stay on in Port Charles.

Throughout the summer of 1983, Holly remained conflicted over her feelings for both her current husband, Robert, and her former love, Luke. Her lingering doubts were finally erased while she was held hostage in the Gulistan Pavilion. With death staring her in the face, Holly realized that the man she truly wanted to be with was Robert Scorpio. Luke was the odd man out.

In September, Bobbie discovered that she was pregnant with Brock's child. However, she couldn't tell him because the hardheaded D.L. Brock—who had a grown daughter, Terri—had made it abundantly clear that he didn't want any more children. To make matters worse, Bobbie soon learned that her pregnancy was in jeopardy because of her previous abortions. Bobbie, however, suffered a miscarriage.

Dr. Rick Webber faced a medical crisis of his own when he was diagnosed with a tumor on his heart. In a complicated surgical procedure, Monica saved Rick's life.

At home, Monica resisted Alan's efforts to bring his illegitimate son Jason into their home. Upon the death of Jason's guardian, Alice Grant, Alan pressed the issue. Alice, in a dying request, asked that Jason be turned over to Heather's care.

"Not Heather!" Alan declared.

"No, not Heather," agreed Monica.

Heather teamed up with Jimmy Lee to wage a campaign to gain custody of baby Jason and, of course, the child's million dollar trust fund.

"I know how to control the Quartermaines," Jimmy Lee told Heather, alluding to the unsigned

GREAT MOMENTS

Luke couldn't believe his eyes—Laura was alive! On the day he was inaugurated as the new mayor of Port Charles, he was stunned to find his long-missing wife on the lawn of his new mansion.

immediately overwhelmed with the realities of being mayor of Port Charles. When he learned that Laura's old apartment building was about to be demolished, Luke returned to take one last look. While on the premises, he fondly remembered the good times with Laura. She was still in his mind—and his heart. Heading to Wyndham's department store for his inaugural suit fitting, Luke felt a chill in the air. Again, he thought of Laura. A distance away, a woman in a trenchcoat hid behind sunglasses, watching Luke's every move. It was Laura!

Two years after she disappeared from the Port Charles waterfront, Laura Spencer returned as mysteriously as she had left. The force that separated Luke and Laura was not the Cassadine curse, but the Cassadine nephew, Stavros! He had abducted Laura (with Helena's approval) to avenge the destruction of his family at the Spencer hand. For nearly two years, Laura had been held captive on a remote island off the coast of Greece. After a while, Helena presented her with a newspaper informing Laura that her beloved Luke died in an avalanche. Now, months later, Helena had grown tired of her nephew's legacy of treachery. Learning of Luke's election victory, she allowed Laura to escape.

Stavros Cassadine, obsessed with Laura's beauty, was consumed with getting her back. Calling his henchman George, he ordered him to bring Laura back immediately. On inauguration day, Laura lurked in the background at the mayor's mansion. Tears flowed freely as the memories of her glorious wedding, held on the grounds of the estate, came flooding back. Luke, learning that Bobbie had miscarried her baby, visited her in the hospital, then returned to his new mansion. By now the reception was over and an eerie stillness had replaced the din of the ceremony. Pouring himself a glass of champagne, Luke's mind filled with precious memories of Laura and the wedding. Deep in thought, he walked out onto the balcony and noticed someone in the yard.

Could it be?

"Laura!" he shouted, running down the steps and onto the lawn.

Seeing Luke, Laura began to run away, only to catch sight of a Cassadine henchman, George. Turning back, she ran into Luke's arms. Luke could not believe his eyes! Overcome with exhilaration and euphoria, Luke asked Laura a thousand questions in a second. Laura interrupted to inform him that someone was following her and their lives were

divorce papers given to him by Crane Tolliver before his death.

When he went to retrieve the papers from their hiding place, however, Jimmy Lee was stunned to discover that they had been destroyed in a fire. Soon after, Monica realized her folly and consented to allow Alan to bring Jason into the house. Eventually she would come to love the boy as she loved her own son, Alan Jr.

With the Prometheus Disc crisis over, Luke plunged into his campaign for mayor. His candidacy received a boost when Robert made a public appearance on television saying that Luke would make a qualified mayor. In a heartfelt meeting on the docks, he and Robert renewed their pact of friendship. On election day, Luke won a stunning victory and was

It was a case of obsessive love gone haywire when, in a crazed attempt to avenge his honor, Stavros Cassadine nearly raped Laura at knife point in front of a tied-up Luke. In the nick of time, Luke broke free and knocked out Cassadine with the top of the bedpost.

in danger. Vowing to protect her, Luke took his beloved Laura inside. Gathering her strength, she explained to him how she had been hypnotized, then awoke in a boat and was taken to the Cassadine compound where she was held prisoner for all these months. After listening to the incredible tale, Luke still didn't understand why she was so afraid. Laura couldn't bring herself to reveal one missing fact: She had married Stavros when she heard Luke was dead. Before collapsing from exhaustion, she made Luke swear not to tell anyone she was in Port Charles. Meanwhile, learning that Laura was with Luke, Stavros swore to avenge his honor.

After a restless night, Laura awoke to find a devoted Luke sitting by her side. Canceling all his appointments, he brought Laura breakfast and listened as she broke the news of her marriage to Stavros to a stunned Luke. Taken aback momentarily, Luke vowed to free Laura from Stavros' grasp once and for all. Meanwhile, Stavros checked in at the International Hotel and engineered plans to reclaim his love. In the afternoon, Luke summoned Rick, Lesley, Robert and Tiffany to the mansion for a tearful and joyful reunion with Laura.

In the hospital, a depressed and secretive Bobbie called off her wedding to Brock after suffering the miscarriage. Upon her release, she received more devastating news when Dr. Mason informed her that

she should have a hysterectomy. Troubled by the cold facts, Bobbie put off the painful decision.

Several nights later, Stavros made his move. While Luke worked in his office at the mansion, Laura prepared for bed upstairs. Suddenly, the lights went out! Hearing Laura's screams, Luke raced out, but a henchman cut off his path. Upstairs, Laura froze at the sight of Stavros. She tried to break away but she couldn't get free of her pursuer. Lust and revenge in his eyes, Stavros prepared to rape Laura at knife point as Luke, his hands tied to the bedpost, watched in horror. With superhuman strength, he worked one hand free and used the top piece of the bedpost to issue a crushing blow to Stavros' head. Luke and Laura fled, with Stavros in pursuit. But this reign of terror quickly ended when a groggy Stavros fell down the stairs. Later, in the hospital ICU, the dying Cassadine expressed his lasting love to Laura—then placed a curse on the couple before expiring.

Luke and Laura, greatly relieved, were left to deal with life in the mayor's mansion. Quickly, they found that demands, pressures and lack of privacy were not to their liking. They just wanted to be together. Although their family and friends were disappointed when Luke resigned, they understood and wished the lovers well. Arm in arm, Luke and Laura departed Port Charles in pursuit of new adventures.

The Complete Stories 1983

*T*he new year began with the simple wedding of Bobbie Spencer and D.L. Brock. Just before the ceremony, Bobbie informed Ruby that she still hadn't told Brock she needed a hysterectomy. Lee pronounced Bobbie and Brock husband and wife, and Bobbie cringed slightly when her groom offered a toast to his bride.

"To Bobbie, who will make the best wife and *mother* ever!"

Claudia Phillips, raised in a wealthy family, had a difficult time adjusting to the fact that she had to live on her new husband Bryan's meager salary. Then she was dealt a crushing blow when her parents died in a car accident. Inheriting a fortune, the newlyweds were faced with the privileges—and problems—that come with enormous wealth.

Rick Webber brought a wealth of experience to his new position as Port Charles Health Commissioner. When an outbreak of botulism sent a score of patients to General Hospital, Dr. Webber traced the source of the outbreak to a sauce produced by Delice Gourmet, a food cannery owned by none other than D.L. Brock. Brock returned from his honeymoon to find Delice shut down. When he confronted Rick, Rick told him he couldn't reopen the plant until the outstanding cases of sauce were recalled. To compound his problems, several irate botulism patients sued Brock.

"Webber's trying to ruin me!" Brock angrily told Bobbie, who had always known Rick to be a kind and compassionate doctor—and told Brock so.

This difference of opinion led to a bitter quarrel—the first of many between the newlyweds.

When Brock stormed out, Bobbie collapsed and began to hemorrhage. She was admitted to General Hospital, where doctors performed an emergency hysterectomy. Discovering Bobbie's secret, Brock was livid! On the work front, he sought revenge on Rick Webber and he began to formulate a plan of attack when he met Rick's son, Mike, and learned that the Webbers had adopted the boy.

At home, Mike noticed that his older brother, Blackie, wasn't as much fun as he used to be. At the expense of his family ties and his relationship with his girlfriend Lou, Blackie poured every ounce of his energy into making his new band, "Blackie and the Riff Raff," a rock and roll success. With Amy Vining as lead singer, the Riff Raff found their fortunes skyrocketing when Tiffany hooked them up with her shady agent, Mario Pirello, who sent his hotshot associate Steffi Brand to check out the new musical group. The trendy, fashionable and well connected Ms. Brand liked what she saw—with one exception. "I'll make you a hit," she told Blackie. "But only if you fire that girl singer."

Steffi wanted Amy out and her man in. Blackie, hungry for success, brazenly gave Amy her walking papers. He was just as insolent in his treatment of Lou, and their once-tender relationship suffered.

As the new manager of The Riff Raff, Steffi attempted to pacify Blackie by informing him that she had a "surprise." With enormous fanfare, she produced a hot new male singer—with the unusual name of "Frisco" Jones. Blackie felt a twinge of jealousy. After all, he didn't want this charismatic new singer cutting into his turf. The unscrupulous Steffi assured him that he would still be the star. Within weeks, the band cut Blackie's song—and the newly released single was an instant smash. But when Steffi picked Frisco to go to New York for a radio interview, Blackie was upset. Later, when he caught Steffi and Frisco in an embrace, he grew suspicious. Steffi insisted that she and Frisco were "just friends," allaying his fears by coming on to Blackie sexually. With a hot kiss, Blackie's manager sent him off to write a new hit song—while she went off to bribe another local disk jockey. Blackie discovered that he couldn't create anything at the Webber house—the place was too noisy. So Blackie moved in with Frisco at the Port Charles Hotel and found he still couldn't come up with a tune. Feeling the pressure to produce a hit record, Blackie developed a case of writer's block.

He grew frustrated as he tried to compose tune after tune, but was unable to come up with another winner. While he was at the Port Charles Hotel, Josh Clayton, the bellboy, hounded Blackie to listen to a song he'd written. Blackie, a bit distracted, had his

Driven by an unquenchable desire to become a rock star, Blackie stole a song from aspiring songwriter Josh Clayton, a bellboy at the Port Charles Hotel. When the song became a hit, Josh pressured an unfeeling Blackie to give him the credit he was due for penning the tune.

tape player recording as he listened to Josh play his song, "Make Me Believe It." Afterward, Blackie told the bellboy/songwriter to "try again. It's not any good."

When Josh left, Blackie toyed with his keyboard and began subconsciously playing the melody from "Make Me Believe It." Frisco perked up when he heard the tune. "That's our next single!" he beamed. Relieved but guilt-ridden by his charade, Blackie turned *his* new tune over to Steffi and Pirelli, who agreed to finance a music video. But when Josh heard that Blackie was using his song, he attempted to get credit for his work—and he wasn't about to give up. Driven by his desire to become a star, Blackie Parrish had changed indeed. At home, the Webbers realized that an arrogant, mean and driven young man had replaced the old, fun-loving Blackie. At the same time, Rick and Lesley dealt with another problem. Her name was Ginny Blake.

D.L. Brock put his plan to destroy Rick Webber in motion as he poured through Port Charles High yearbooks, then mysteriously left for New York. Shortly after his return, Ginny Blake, an attractive middle-aged woman, surfaced at the Webbers, claiming to be Mike's mother. Jake assured the Webbers that the courts would not allow Ginny to take Mike away. Still, they were extremely upset over the prospect of putting their son through an ugly court battle. Meanwhile, Bobbie—dismayed that she couldn't give Brock a child—overheard

him on the phone with Ginny and began to suspect that he was having an affair. When she confronted him, Brock reassured his new wife she was the only one and suggested she look into adopting a child. But when she set up an appointment with an adoption agency, Brock refused to go. Meanwhile, Rick and Lesley attempted to get Ginny to give up reclaiming Mike. But by now, Ginny had secretly met and enchanted young Mike. Soon after, Ginny relieved the Webbers' concerns when she announced that she was leaving town. First she wanted to meet with Rick in her hotel room to give him a $25,000 check for Mike's college education. After Rick left, Ginny removed a roll of film from a hidden camera, then placed a phone call to tell the person on the other end that "the trap's been sprung and Webber's been caught."

The person on the other end of the phone was none other than D.L. Brock.

A storm of controversy erupted at General Hospital when Brock exposed Dr. Rick Webber as a "crook" who had taken a bribe from a Delice employee, Ginny Blake, to reopen the plant. Bobbie, suspicious of Brock's involvement, went to Lesley with the suspicion that Ginny was an actress possibly working for Brock. Agitated by Ginny's false accusations, Lesley pleaded for her to tell the truth. "Do it for Mike," she pleaded, but Ginny wouldn't budge.

Later, at the hospital, Brock ripped into Lesley about "harassing" Ginny. A distraught Lesley Webber took off for home, but she would never get there. On Friday, March 9th, Police Chief Burt Ramsey showed up at the Webbers' with grim news: Lesley's car had skidded off the road in an ice storm.

"I'm sorry, Rick. She's gone."

Rick reeled from the shock. His beloved Lesley was gone.

In the days after the tragedy, Rick was cleared when Bobbie went to Robert Scorpio with her information that Ginny was an actress. Robert coerced a confession out of Ginny and had Brock print a retraction in the newspaper. Rick could have sued, but decided to drop the matter for Mike's sake. Hurt by the tragic turn of events, Rick warned Ginny to stay away from Mike. But Ginny wasn't about to leave town. Sticking around in hope of establishing a relationship with her son, Ginny won a job as hostess of WLPC-TV's new show, *Teen Time*. Burning the candle at both ends, she ignored the chest pains that began to plague her. Finally, she had no choice

The Complete Stories 1984

but to undergo open-heart surgery. Mike still had no idea that this woman he had grown to care for was his real mother. But that was about to change when Amy blurted out the truth to a bitter Mike, who resented her intrusion into his life and refused to see her.

To protect his son, Rick began to entertain the idea of taking Mike and leaving Port Charles for good. The idea outraged and threatened Ginny, who vowed to fight Rick in court if he tried to take Mike away. She consulted her lawyer, who believed that, with Lesley dead, Ginny had a good chance of winning custody from Rick. When Jake confirmed this to Rick, he became increasingly worried that he would lose his beloved son. In desperation, Rick proposed his solution—a marriage of convenience to Ginny Blake. In time, the chill between Rick and his new wife thawed and then the impossible happened: They developed a deep affection for one another. Rick and Ginny's blossoming love would be put to the test when Derek Barrington came to town. Derek was Mike's real father!

Bobbie Brock grew increasingly distant from her husband, D.L. When he struck back by hitting her, she kicked him out. Yet, hoping to save their marriage, she allowed him to return and even mortgaged her house to save Delice from going under. Nevertheless, when Brock learned that Delice products weren't selling, he hired an arsonist to burn the place down. To complicate matrimonial matters, Brock's spoiled and snobby daughter, Terry, moved in with her dad. Her presence put an incredible strain on the Brock marriage. Soon Terry got into a huge fight with her father and she headed for a bar, where she proceeded to get herself arrested. Bobbie bailed her out, and slowly the two women bonded.

At Kelly's Diner, Rose accepted Jake's engagement ring, and the lovers decided to marry right away, but religion drove a wedge between them. Jake's rabbi refused to officiate unless Rose converted. A priest declined to conduct the ceremony unless the couple agreed to raise their children as Catholics. When Jake balked, Rose angrily returned the ring and left town to work with her stepson, Joe. In her absence, Ruby Anderson stepped in at Kelly's Diner, offering homespun advice—and the best damned chowder and chili in New York State!

Caught up with his pursuit of fame, Blackie hardly noticed the crisis that enveloped his family—the Webbers. Becoming ever more brash and pigheaded, Blackie was about to become embroiled in a crisis of his own. Lou had unearthed the tape which proved that Blackie was a song-stealer. Lou wondered what to do with the incriminating evidence, which proved that the boy she loved had plagiarized his hit song from bellboy Josh Clayton. Fueled by her jealousy of Blackie's affair with Steffi, Lou pushed her way past a cordon of security and groupies, hoping to confront him with the tape.

"I know you stole that song!" she screamed out, only to be pushed aside by Ginny Blake and her camera crew, who were on the scene to interview Blackie-the-star.

With Josh's assistance, Lou finally forced her way into Blackie's room where, in a fury, she played the tape. Steffi entered the room, listened, and, with Blackie, tried to convince Lou to give up the tape. Losing patience, Steffi lunged for the evidence. Backing away, Lou tripped and fell, hitting her head! Seeing that she was badly injured, a horrified Blackie rushed to her side, muttering "It's all my fault."

At General Hospital, Dr. Alan Quartermaine tried to save Lou's life, but his efforts were in vain. In despair, Blackie blamed himself, not Steffi, for Lou's tragic death. Adamantly refusing to defend himself against manslaughter charges, Blackie went to prison.

"I deserve to be punished," he said on his last day of freedom. Realizing that greed and unbridled ambition had led to his downfall as a musician and as a human being, Blackie was prepared to serve his sentence.

In an emotional farewell, he sobbed to Rick, "Thanks for teaching me how to be a man. Now let me go and do it."

Without her star attraction, Steffi scrambled to keep The Riff Raff alive. She knew exactly who could help her keep the cash flowing in—Frisco! After all, the handsome singer had been her ace in the hole all along. But Frisco had seen enough of the cutthroat music business. Steffi panicked when he informed her that he wanted "out of the business." In anger, she ordered him to get on a plane to New York, but he steadfastly refused. In desperation, Steffi informed her boss, Pirelli, who sent a couple of thugs to rough up Frisco Jones. They did their job too well. When the goons attacked Frisco, they struck him in the larynx. Dazed and beaten badly, he staggered into Kelly's Diner, unable to speak!

Across the Atlantic, a young man suffered from

a similar malady. Unable to speak or remember his past, he sat aimlessly in a British mental institution until the day he came across an article in an American publication that chronicled the story of Grant Putnam, spy—A.K.A. Andrei Chernin. The man's hands began to shake as he read the story. Memories came flooding back and he regained the ability to speak. This imprisoned man was the real Grant Putnam, whose identity had been usurped years earlier by the DVX! Over the opposition of one doctor, Campbell, who believed the patient to be psychotic and dangerous, he convinced hospital officials to discharge him. Despite Dr. Campbell's warnings, the real Grant was set free and Campbell was not allowed to share his fears with U.S. authorities.

Before departing England, the real Grant met with State Department officials. Masking his rage, he left for the United States—hell bent on destroying the man who had stolen his face and his identity. In Port Charles, Celia was stunned to meet the real Grant, who promised not to interfere in her life. Meanwhile, the impostor Grant and Celia cemented their love and, to avoid confusion, changed their last name to Andrews. The appearance of the real Grant Putnam was the latest blow in a string of failures for the turncoat-spy. After being given asylum, his license to practice medicine was revoked and he was forced to take a job on a construction site—with his arch-rival, Jimmy Lee Holt, as boss. Grant Andrews sank into a deep depression, made worse by Grant Putnam's out-of-the-blue appearance.

With steely inner determination and an outward smile, Grant Putnam waged a secret war on Grant Andrews by setting out to systematically destroy Celia and Grant's marriage. When Andrews struck up an innocent friendship with Tania Roskov, a strikingly beautiful Russian emigre, Putnam planted evidence to make it seem that they were having an affair. At the same time, he planted a nightgown, exactly like one owned by Celia, in his home, and made sure that the impostor, Grant Andrews, saw it. Their confidence in each other eroded, Andrews and Celia began to have trouble in the bedroom and both anguished privately that they had "lost the spark" in their marriage. Putnam was unstoppable in his pursuit of destruction. Dr. Campbell, from the British mental institution, was the only one who knew the depths of Putnam's evil. But he would never share his fears with anyone because, when Campbell came to the United States, Grant Putnam

strangled him to death and dumped the body in the Port Charles River!

Stepping up his surreptitious scheme, Putnam continued to win Celia's confidence. They formed an attachment while, behind the scenes, Putnam schemed to make Celia believe that her husband was trying to kill her! When an explosion ripped through a boat that she was supposed to be on, Grant Andrew's footprints—courtesy of Putnam— were found at the scene. The police charged him with the attempted murder of his own wife.

"Someone's framing me," he told Celia and his lawyer, Jake Meyer.

Falsely convicted of attempting to murder his wife Celia, Grant Andrews was sentenced to 15 years in prison. His incarceration was made more tolerable by frequent visits from friends like Tania Roskov, who loved Grant from afar.

Celia, conflicted, turned to Jimmy Lee, who offered a shoulder to cry on and his everlasting help. Ultimately, Celia's damaging courtroom testimony was a key factor in the jury's decision to find Grant Andrews guilty of attempted murder. The sentence: 15 years in prison.

With Grant Andrews out of the way, the demented Grant Putnam made a play for Celia's affections. He quickly discovered that he had some competition—Jimmy Lee Holt. Tortured by the testimony that sent her husband to jail, Celia got drunk at the Bucket of Blood and spent the night in Jimmy Lee's bed.

Plagued by doubts, Celia knew in her heart that her husband was innocent. She began to investigate and unearthed clues leading her to believe in Grant Putnam's guilt. Playing detective, she traveled to England to tell the sanitarium head, Dr. Borden, of her suspicions. They agreed to reexamine Putnam's records, but Grant, who followed Celia to England, stole them. When she returned to her hotel, Putnam tried to kill her—but was interrupted by room service. Dr. Borden told Celia to return to the States while he searched the missing Dr. Campbell's fishing shack for notes. At the airport, Putnam again tried to murder Celia, but was foiled when the airline called her plane for boarding.

Safely back in Port Charles, Celia kept Grant Putnam at bay while she secretly worked with Robert Scorpio to uncover more evidence to nail Putnam. When she returned to the gatehouse, Celia got the proof she needed when Dr. Borden phoned from England to say that he'd found a tape Dr. Campbell had sent to himself indicating that Putnam killed him. Her heart beating with anticipation, Celia went to meet Borden at her lakeside cabin, only to encounter Putnam standing over the body of Borden. She knew she would be next.

"I want to love you," he threatened. Grabbing Celia, he was just about to make his move when Robert Scorpio burst in and overpowered the madman.

Her ordeal over, Celia and Grant Andrews— released from prison and reinstated as a doctor— were reunited—with an infatuated Jimmy Lee lurking in the background. Tania, heartbroken by Grant and Celia's reconciliation, found comfort with Frisco Jones, the singer who had been mooning over her for months.

Frisco made a rapid recovery from his serious throat injury, thanks to Tania, who served as his speech therapist and friend. Frisco secretly hoped that they would graduate to lovers and warmly welcomed her visits. But he grew sullen when his brother, Tony, a new neurology resident, walked into his hospital room. The rest of the staff found Dr. Tony Jones to be a very affable fellow, but it was clear that Frisco harbored a grudge against his

Singer Frisco Jones recovered from a career-threatening throat injury with the help of his speech therapist and girlfriend, Tania Roskov. When they broke up, Tania dated and later married Frisco's older brother, Tony.

older brother. Even though Tania urged him to patch things up, Frisco wasn't ready to bury the hatchet. When Tony arranged to have their father call his estranged son, Frisco exploded in anger.

"Why do you despise him so much?" Tania asked.

Frisco felt he had good reason. Years earlier in San Francisco, Tony and Frisco's mother had fallen ill and a nurse, Rita, was brought in to care for her. Rita was nowhere to be found when Mrs. Jones died, however, because she was making love to Tony at the time! Later, Mr. Jones married Rita and the Jones family remained hopelessly divided. Until now. With Tania's intervention, Tony and Frisco reconciled, and the doctors discharged Frisco. In time, he would sing again, but not for Steffi or her boss Pirelli. Their names were mud in Port Charles! Taking Tony's advice, Frisco pursued Tania romantically, and though she still pined away for Grant Andrews, she agreed to move in with Frisco.

Several new arrivals moved to Port Charles and succeeded to agitate the shaky Quartermaine clan. One was Monica's cousin, Lorena Sharpe, who moved in on the Quartermaines and, using her endless supply of charm and persuasive powers, managed to get the family to invest in her failing chain of Avalon health spas. Another unwelcome arrival was Jimmy Lee's mother, Beatrice LeSeur, a clever and conniving opportunist who specialized in blackmail. Together with her vengeful son, Beatrice proceeded to blackmail the Quartermaines. She knew that Lila and Edward weren't legally married—which meant that the rest of the Quartermaine clan were all illegitimate—and Beatrice claimed to have the necessary documents to prove it. Worse, she planned to make this blockbuster news public, humiliating the family. Beatrice had to be stopped!

While blackmailing the Quartermaines, Beatrice LeSeur also gathered incriminating evidence against other prominent Port Charles socialites, including Amanda Barrington and Sylvia Whitby. The shady Ms. LeSeur was not the only blackmailer in Port Charles. Amanda and Sylvia had fallen victim to the blackmailing tactics of Leo Russell, a studly masseur at the Avalon Spa. Sleazeball Leo seduced and charmed his victims on the massage table, then used a hidden camera to catch them in an assortment of compromising positions. Holly Scorpio—who had turned private detective against Robert's wishes—caught wind of Leo's lovefest and tried to catch him in the act. But she got caught in an incriminating position herself. When Beatrice got her greedy hands on Leo's sinful photo of Mrs. Scorpio, Holly agreed to pay her $25,000 to keep quiet. Armed with evidence against a host of victims, Beatrice was ready to extort a fortune. But on the night of the annual charity ball, Beatrice dropped dead!

Edward spent a night in jail after confessing to Beatrice's murder. Eventually, he was released when Scorpio discovered that Edward was only protecting his beloved Lila. But Lila didn't kill Beatrice! Neither did Alan nor Monica. Or Holly. Amanda, Sylvia and Leo weren't the culprits—though all or most of them had slipped knockout drugs in Beatrice's beverage at the ball. Using his masterful investigative skills, Scorpio studied the evidence and deduced that no one had done her in! With Holly's help, Robert staged a dramatic recreation of the night of the murder in which he proved to all that Beatrice's death was caused by her accidental intake of Lila's heart medication coupled with the other drugs in her system. As a result, the blackmailing Beatrice overdosed and died. His theory was backed up by Ginny Webber's TV camera, which captured the victim accidentally consuming her deadly drink. With the case closed, a lot of people collectively breathed sighs of relief.

GREAT MOMENTS

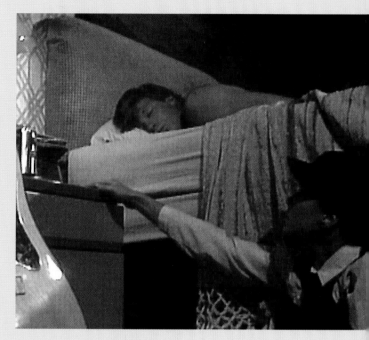

Frisco Jones might never have met his future wife Felicia if it hadn't been for a ring that he bought at an art fair. Little did he know that it was part of an Aztec treasure that Felicia wanted back. Disguised as a boy, she sneaked into Frisco's bedroom—and got caught!

Frisco sighed with pleasure upon moving in with his girlfriend, Tania. But their romance was over almost before it even began. Every time they began to make love, her thoughts turned to her lost love, Grant Andrews, prompting a miffed Frisco to walk out of her life. He wouldn't be lonely for long. A new young woman was about to become the lady of his heart. Her name was Felicia Cummings, and Frisco might never have met her if it hadn't been for a ring that he bought at a charity ball. He thought it was just a piece of costume jewelry, but little did he know that it was part of an Aztec treasure Felicia wanted back.

One night in the summer of '84, disguised as a boy, she sneaked into Frisco's bedroom and hid under his bed while trying to retrieve the ring. How about that—his future wife under his bed! Awakening with a start, seeing a hand reaching out from under his bed, he grabbed it. The intruder escaped—with

Frisco in hot pursuit. Racing out into the hall, he tackled him—but quickly found out it was a *her* when the boy's cap fell off revealing a mane of long, silky blond hair. The intruder was a woman!

"You're in my apartment and you're gonna tell me why! Got it? Or I'm calling the police!" shouted Frisco.

"Look, I don't have to explain myself to you," retorted Felicia. "The ring is mine and I wanted to get it back."

"Well, there are easier ways—like asking me for it!"

"Give it to me, damn it! It's mine!"

Seizing the moment, she grabbed the ring and fled again, this time falling and injuring her ankle. As she cried out in pain, Frisco scooped up the injured girl and took her to General Hospital. Seeing some thugs lurking in the hall made it abundantly clear to him that she was in serious danger. To protect her from harm, Frisco spirited Felicia out of the hospital to a vacant apartment. Hostile and defensive, the scared girl refused to reveal her secret, and that irritated him. So did her ill manners. When she criticized his cooking, that was the last straw. Frisco stormed out, but returned much later with carry-out food.

"Truce?" he offered.

Felicia grudgingly nodded her approval.

Frisco continued to hide his helpless female friend from the thugs who pursued her. During their captivity, the pair engaged in some lively arguments, but they also shared a kiss! Still, the war was on—especially when Felicia continued to make outrageous demands on her friendly savior.

"Who do you think you are, a princess?" he asked.

The answer was yes! Felicia confided that she was an Aztec princess. Not believing her tale, Frisco laughed, prompting Felicia to toss her crutches at him. No doubt about it—Frisco Jones and Felicia Cummings were feisty, fighting—and falling in love! At the same time, Tania tried to win him back but suddenly he had no time for her. Dismayed by the rejection, Tania turned to his brother, Tony.

Frisco frantically tried to keep Felicia out of the public eye. But someone desperately wanted to get their hands on her and that ring—which was part of an Aztec treasure. Coupled with a royal scepter, it was the key to a hidden treasure. Felicia finally confessed the whole truth to Frisco when she explained that her great-grandmother had shown the ring to her on her deathbed. When thieves tried to break in, the elderly woman pressed the ring into Felicia's hand and urged her to take it away. On her way to Port Charles she lost it, only to discover Frisco buying it. So when she slunk under Frisco's bed, she was just trying to get back what was rightfully hers. Someone else wanted it too!

That someone turned out to be Peter Harrell, Felicia's ex-fiancé. Peter had the scepter in his possession. To unlock the mystery of the legendary treasure, he desperately wanted the ring! Meanwhile, Robert Scorpio received a frantic phone call from his old pal, Luke Spencer, who was on the run in Mexico—framed for a murder he didn't commit. Robert rushed down to Mexico, arranging to meet Luke at the home of the former Director of WSB, Sean Donely. Suave and smooth, Sean Donely lived a seemingly peaceful life in a plush villa in Mexico City with his exotic mistress, Cruz. But unbeknownst to Robert, Donely, an expert on Aztec culture, was in hot pursuit of the elusive treasure. He would stop at nothing to keep all other fortune hunters from getting their paws on it.

Together again, Luke and Robert displayed that same lust for action they shared on that tropical island years earlier. Holly joined the buddies after learning Felicia's story and realized the two tales had much in common. Luke enlisted Robert's aid to clear himself of a phony murder charge. Luke explained that he had been sitting with Peter Harrell on the veranda of a Texas Hacienda—owned by Maria, Felicia's grandmother—when all of a sudden a bunch of men on horseback raided the place. They took a valuable scepter and, while chasing it down, Luke was knocked out. When he awoke, he had a bloody knife in his hand! The scepter was gone—and the culprits had framed Luke for a murder! Since then, Luke had learned that the missing scepter was part of an Aztec treasure map. What he didn't know was that his "friend" Peter, who secretly had the scepter, had framed him.

Robert welcomed the challenge to save Luke's hide and regain the scepter. Scorpio was ecstatic at the prospect of an adventure, but Holly felt a bit excluded, especially next to Donely's exotic mistress Cruz. Soon, Cruz left Donely's villa ostensibly to care for her ailing mother, but she was actually teaming up with Sean's enemy, Peter Harrell. The stage was set for adventure!

The dynamic duo—together again! Framed for a murder he didn't commit, Luke Spencer called his old buddy Robert Scorpio to Mexico to help bail him out of yet another mess.

With Peter in eager anticipation, Donely fit the scepter into a slot and the door swung open. Inside the chamber, he used the ring to open a vault—revealing a wealth of dazzling treasure! Then he carefully closed the vault and went on to double-cross Peter! Just as Sean pulled his gun, Luke and Robert appeared and Peter escaped with Luke giving chase. When Peter fell to his death over a waterfall, a lying Sean Donely gave Felicia back her ring. He told everyone that he hadn't found any treasure. What was he up to?

Eventually, Luke was cleared of the murder charge and reunited with Laura at the hacienda, accompanied by Felicia, Frisco, Holly, Robert and Donely. Alone with his wife after weeks on the run, he and Laura shared a night of passion, then Laura shared a secret—she was pregnant! While Luke and Laura eagerly anticipated the birth of their first child at their new ranch, Donely entertained the Scorpios, Frisco, Felicia and Maria at his villa. Unknown to his so-called friends, the double-dealing Donely had big plans to slowly liquidate his hidden treasure through a Port Charles shipping company which his henchman, Jack Slater (alias Matt Hines) acquired for him. Scorpio was excited at the prospect of Donely moving to Port Charles, but not Holly. Mrs. Scorpio was wary of the close bond between the two former WSB buddies—and rightly so!

Back in Port Charles, Felicia and Frisco were engaged in a series of madcap adventures of their own as they attempted to hide the ring and elude their pursuers. In Texas, Felicia's grandmother, Maria, anxiously waited for word from her missing loved one, as did her houseguest, Laura Spencer, who feared for Luke's safety. Frisco followed Felicia south of the border, where Peter fooled her into giving up her ring. Eventually, Peter and Sean teamed up and all parties ventured into the jungle heading for the site of the treasure.

While her husband Luke romped through Mexico in pursuit of an Aztec treasure, Laura Spencer stayed at the Texas hacienda owned and operated by Felicia's grandmother, Maria.

*19*85 began with the arrival of Holly's cousin, Algernon, who showed up in Port Charles in an obvious state of distress. The handsome young man had fled Paris after discovering someone had planted the recently stolen Cassadine brooch on him. Robert immediately became alarmed when Algernon claimed that he came to Port Charles because Holly had sent him an airline ticket. Stunned, Holly denied anything of the sort.

Perplexed by the mystery, Scorpio consulted with Sean Donely, who suggested that they smuggle the brooch back to the Cassadines. But Sean was being less than honest with his "friend." It seemed that Donely had masterminded the entire scheme to provide a distraction in Port Charles while he smuggled the Aztec treasure through town. Petros Cassadine, the black sheep of the Cassadine clan, arrived in Port Charles and the brooch was prompt-

The 1985 arrival of the mysterious Anna Devane prompted her former husband, Robert Scorpio, to flashback to their torrid romance in Italy several years earlier.

ly returned. Both Scorpio and Petros were anxious to learn who set them up. Petros promptly left town issuing threats of vengeance.

As a result of the Cassadine visit, Scorpio and WSB chief Ballantine were convinced that a WSB agent should be present in Port Charles and they persuaded Donely to accept the position. But Donely had clearly planned this maneuver all along to give himself an irreproachable cover during the transport of the rare artifacts and jewels.

Meanwhile, Donely did his best to ingratiate himself to Felicia. Warning his accomplice, Jack Slater, to stay out of sight, Donely sent Felicia a copy of a valuable Aztec painting. Donely's attention made Frisco furious. So furious, in fact, that he broke the painting in a rage over Felicia's obsession with her heritage and Donely's potentially compromising generosity. The air between Frisco and Felicia was thick with tension as the lovers used various ploys to make each other jealous. Felicia took a job and a room at Kelly's, while Frisco tried to impress Felicia by agreeing to star in a new syndicated TV show. The sudden news of his father's death altered Frisco's plans. Upon hearing about it, Frisco bolted from Tony. "I don't care if he's dead!" he cried. After wandering all night, Frisco returned and, with Felicia's help, he eventually came to grips with the emotional strain of losing a loved one.

Despite their closeness, Frisco resented Felicia's friendship with Donely and her obsession with her Aztec heritage. The only thing the pair could agree on was their happiness over Tony and Tania's February wedding in the hospital chapel. Courtesy of Frisco and Felicia, the newlyweds honeymooned at Maria's Texas hacienda. Frisco and Felicia planned to visit them en route to Mexico, where Frisco agreed to help Felicia open the crypt containing the treasure. Ever wary, Donely got to the treasure first and removed it just before Felicia and Frisco reached the crypt. Peter Harrell, alive and well, vowed revenge on his old friend Sean for arranging the heist.

Back in Port Charles, Tony and Tania received wonderful news: They were going to have a baby. Frisco and Felicia, their devotion renewed, made love for the first time. As they contemplated moving in together, the lovers agreed that the worst was behind them. Little did they know that Peter Harrell was about to return to Port Charles and turn their lives upside down. Soon after arriving in town, Peter trailed Felicia to Donely's warehouse, where he escaped an altercation with Slater with a knife wound. Bleeding and hurt, Peter placed a call to Felicia and urged her to meet him at a deserted railroad car. At first reluctant, Felicia agreed to go after Peter enticed her with news that the Aztec treasure existed—and could be hers.

Felicia entered the dark railroad car and upon seeing the weak and wounded Peter, she realized he needed immediate medical help and called Tony. While treating Peter, Tony learned an incredible secret when his patient confided that "Sean Donely has the treasure." But Tony wouldn't reveal the news to anyone because Jack Slater arrived on the scene and shot Tony in the head and heart! Peter slipped away and headed for Brazil while the ambulance meant for him picked up Tony and whisked him away to General Hospital. After delicate brain surgery, Tony slipped into a coma.

Frisco blamed Felicia for his brother's tragedy.

"If you hadn't run to Peter, this never would have happened!" he told her as he bitterly shunned her attempts to apologize.

Donely, desperately trying to cover his tracks, ordered Slater to leave town. Before leaving, Slater stole a bag of precious jewels from Donely's safe. He tried to fence them with a charming new arrival who showed a keen interest in Donely's role in the heist. Her name was Anna Devane.

It was obvious from Anna's first tension-filled run-in with Robert Scorpio in New York that the pair shared a past. While Robert was away in New York, Anna Devane headed for Port Charles, where she ingratiated herself to Holly by pretending to be a down-on-her-luck friend of Nanny McTavish.

Normally flashy and elegant, Anna now wore drab clothes and her flowing hair cascaded forward, obscuring the left side of her face. While befriending Holly, Anna secretly obtained information about Mrs. Scorpio's past and snooped around Robert's WSB communication room. What was she up to? The two women grew closer as Anna revealed that she had led a lonely life since the end of her relationship with "the love of my life." Unbeknownst to Holly, that man was Robert Scorpio. Scorpio returned from New York and was shocked to find Anna in his home.

"Get out!" he insisted in no uncertain terms.

As he ordered her to leave, Anna, distraught, fainted on the spot. Robert and Holly raced to her side and discovered that this beautiful woman's long hair had been obscuring a hideous scar on one side of her beautiful face. Robert carried the fallen Anna to the guest room and demanded to know what she was up to. Revealing a bit more of her past with Robert, Anna told him that "the real scar is on my soul." Without letting Holly in on his private pain, Robert began to relive the memories of his past with Anna—and what a past it was.

Many years earlier, Robert Scorpio and Anna Devane had been partners in the WSB. Falling deeply in love, they fled to Italy and got married in a beautiful outdoor village ceremony. The newlyweds decided to resign from the WSB, but not before Sean Donely enlisted Scorpio's help in uncovering a treacherous WSB double agent. The double agent turned out to be Anna, whose face was badly scarred in an explosion! Scorpio was distraught to learn that his new wife was a fraud, but his love prevented him from revealing Anna's duplicity to Sean, who mistakenly executed an innocent agent. Anguished and bitter, Scorpio made Anna promise she would get a divorce and stay out of his life.

Now, years later, she was back. And back in Sean Donely's life, too. Anna became Donely's secretary as a cover for a partnership they formed to fence the Aztec treasure. Robert grew suspicious of their motives, then all three were suspicious when the treasure turned up missing again. Where could it be? Robert suspected Sean. Sean suspected Robert. And Anna suspected them both. Putting aside their differences, Robert teamed up with Anna to find the treasure and their close relationship made Holly jealous. She had to notice that Robert and Anna had a mysterious chemistry that they could not deny. Holly's curiosity piqued when Robert evaded her probing questions.

Early in 1985, Bobbie questioned her own marriage to D.L. Brock, who had become even more violent and abusive in the new year. Bobbie realized that Brock was unbalanced when he accused her—in public—of having an affair with Dr. Rick Webber. Ginny Webber was also subjected to Brock's wrath when he tormented her about the time she spent in jail for smuggling drugs.

"I'll ruin you!" he threatened in a rage.

Brock's threats filled the once-fiery Ginny with despair, especially as her love for Rick grew stronger. Somehow, she had to stop him.

After one last blowup, Bobbie and Terry realized they had to get away from Brock, who had turned into a maniac. He arrived at their penthouse just as Terry and Bobbie packed some clothes to move out. A bitter argument resulted and Brock brandished a gun! As Terry ran, he knocked Bobbie out and she fell unconscious behind a sofa. Ginny arrived on the scene intending to threaten Brock with a fake gun. But Brock surprised her by pulling out his real gun! Brock and Ginny struggled and Brock's own gun went off—killing him!

The police arrested and charged Bobbie with murder. Ruby, Rick, Dan, Jessie and others gave her moral support as Jake Meyer struggled to defend her against the charges. Eventually Robert Scorpio tracked down the real killer, Ginny, and scared her into telling the truth. In the aftermath, Rick couldn't forgive his wife for her behavior toward Bobbie, but promised to stand by her "for Mike's sake." In her distress, Ginny turned to Derek for solace, who offered her a shoulder to cry on—and a bed to make love in. As Ginny's trial approached, Jake worried that Bobbie would seek revenge on Ginny. In fact, Bobbie's upcoming testimony was the talk of the town. What would she say under oath? To everyone's surprise, Bobbie did the unexpected and exonerated Ginny. She told a stunned courtroom that Brock had been in a homicidal rage on the night of his death. Thanks to Bobbie's courtroom admission, Ginny Webber was set free. With her marriage to Rick crumbling, Ginny feared that conceiving a child might be the only thing that would enable her to keep a hold on Rick. To further damage her relationship with Rick, Derek Barrington arranged for Rick to discover the shocking truth that Derek was Mike's real father. Rick berated Ginny for her deceit and contacted Jake Meyer about the possibility of getting sole custody of Mike. Eventually, he reconciled with Ginny who became pregnant with Rick's baby. Late in the year, Ginny gave birth to a son, Rick Jr. After Mike discovered that Derek was his real father, the boy moved with him and his new wife, Lorena Sharpe, to Omaha. Ginny, devastated by the loss of her son, poured her attention into her work and later moved with Rick and Rick Jr. to New York.

Though busy with his law practice, Jake Meyer couldn't get Bobbie Brock out of his mind. Released from jail, she continued to see Jake, but a romance was out of the question. Bobbie was determined to become a self-sufficient woman, free from the "heartaches of men." The two were drawn together when they bought and renovated a brownstone on Elm Street. As the exciting project neared completion, they began to assemble tenants for their new dwelling. Two of their tenants were Bobbie's step-daughter, Terry Brock and young Dr. Kevin O'Connor. When they bumped into each other at the brownstone, the smiles vanished from Terry and Kevin's faces. They knew each other! Kevin and Terry were both from the same hometown—Laurelton, and they were obviously more than just passing acquaintances. These two youngsters shared a secret past.

At General Hospital, Dr. Tony Jones finally regained consciousness, but remembered little about his past—including the fact that he was married to Tania. Recovering from the coma, he uttered a single word—"Donely"—in Robert's presence. The stress of the past few months proved too much to bear for Tania. One day, Felicia returned to the brownstone and found her sister-in-law lying in a pool of blood. Tania had miscarried the baby! Despite the tragedy, Tania had one reason to be grateful when Tony got his memory back. He remembered his love for her, but recalled nothing about the shooting. To make matters worse, Tony's injuries left him paralyzed. Felicia and medical student Kevin O'Connor found a device that could stimulate Tony's muscles. Frisco, still estranged from Felicia, became a trifle jealous of her close friendship with Kevin.

The missing treasure again brought Frisco and Felicia back together for another hair-raising adventure. While continuing to deny their love, they teamed up to sneak into Donely's penthouse to search for the treasure, but hid when Scorpio and Anna arrived moments later to crack the safe. Donely caught his old friends in the act and, after they left, Frisco and Felicia removed the valuable jewels from the safe. Scorpio obtained a search warrant for Donely's penthouse but, to Donely's shock, the jewels were no longer in the safe. Scorpio and Anna continued to suspect that Donely was holding out on them while Holly grew angry with Robert for holding out on her. After discovering Robert and Anna were former WSB partners, Holly demanded the truth. Holly thought the only thing Robert was concealing was his guilt over Anna's scar. She was not prepared when he revealed that Anna was his wife. Holly was outraged, storming out of their penthouse and heading for London, determined to stay away from Robert.

"Decide who you really love!" she declared before leaving town.

The whereabouts of the Aztec treasure remained a mystery for months. Everyone wanted it. Jack Slater died in pursuit of it when he tried to kill Tony Jones and was gunned down by Sean Donely, who was now secretly in cahoots with Peter Harrell's brother, Prescott. Only one man knew where the treasure was, because he had stolen it and hidden the valuables in the basement of the newly refurbished brownstone owned by Bobbie Brock and her partner, Jake Meyer. The culprit was none other than Grant Andrews!

Grant had snatched the treasure in a desperate move to win back his ex-wife, Celia. Early in 1985, their marriage went sour when Celia gave in to temptation and made love with Jimmy Lee in New York. Soon after their divorce, Celia accepted Jimmy Lee's proposal and they made glorious plans to marry in a Gay Nineties-style wedding to be held aboard a train in a specially outfitted pullman car. Sean—now in cahoots with Grant and Prescott—agreed to help Grant transport the treasure on Jimmy Lee and Celia's wedding train. News of the wedding outraged Grant at first. Soon he came to realize that this affair could be the perfect cover for him to get the treasure to its final destination, a medical ship. But the double-crossing Donely actually intended to use a second pullman to transport the treasure north to Canada, where he hoped to sell the gold and jewels to a potential buyer—a cold-blooded man of Chinese descent, Mr. Wu. When Grant discovered that Sean duped him, he became anxious to redeem himself by teaming up with Scorpio, Anna, Frisco and Felicia to bring Sean to justice.

Donely's reign of deception came to an end in Canada, where he kidnaped Holly, who had returned to the United States and overheard his plans to transport the treasure. In hot pursuit of his former friend, Robert tracked down the treasure, which was hidden under a tarpaulin in a chalet in the mountains. He then set out after Sean, and the two met up in a tramway precariously suspended by a cable high in the mountains. With Anna watching from below, Robert and Sean fought a bitter fight for their lives. As the tram cars doors flew open, Robert lost his balance and fell out of the car—apparently to his death! Sean, exhausted, was devastated at the thought that he had killed his best friend. To complete the transfer of the treasure, Sean headed in the tram to meet Mr. Wu. Instead, he was greeted by Wu's assistant, Mr. Yang—who was actually Robert, very much alive, in disguise!

Scorpio ripped off his rubber mask, then handcuffed Donely who was both shocked at the turn of events and relieved to learn that Robert had escaped death by clinging to the bottom of the tram. With the danger past, Frisco and Felicia journeyed to Texas, where they returned the cache of rare jewels and artifacts to Maria. Grant headed to Egypt to oversee a medical supply ship. The mystery of the Aztec Treasure was finally over! But another exciting and baffling adventure—centered in Port Charles' Asian Quarter—was about to begin.

The New York police returned part of the treasure—two stolen jade buddhas—to Mr. Wu, who was forced to give them to their rightful owner, a wise old Chinese gentleman known simply as "The Ancient One." The Ancient One explained to Mr. Wu that the real value of the buddhas was the black pearls contained within. The Ancient One intended to sell the pearls to obtain money for the final payment on a Port Charles cannery for his Asian people who were oppressed by an unfair labor system. But the pearls were missing! Unbeknownst to The Ancient One, the sinister Mr. Wu was actually the oppressor of the Asian population of Port Charles. Wu intended to prevent the Asians from escaping his oppression by depriving them of the buddhas. He had arranged for them to be stolen, but at the time was unaware of the tremendous value of the pearls. Realizing their worth, Wu assumed Scorpio and Anna must have taken the pearls and he instructed his grandson Kim to get them back.

After a painful summer marked by lies and deceit, the newly reunited Robert and Holly Scorpio faced a brilliant future. With their marriage on solid ground at last, the Scorpios stunned their friends in September by announcing plans to move to Australia. In preparation for the move "down under," Robert resigned as police commissioner and Holly and Anna mended their fences and enjoyed an amicable parting before Holly left for Australia, to be joined by Robert after he tied up his final affairs in Port Charles. Anna, too, was about to bid farewell to Port Charles. After revealing that her disfiguring scar was actually a fake—worn as a bizarre form of penance for her past sins—Anna flew off, but not before offering Felicia some words of wisdom.

"If you love a man, never lie to him."

Felicia took the advice to heart as she wished Anna a fond farewell.

That same day, Robert Scorpio returned home to his apartment only to encounter an unexpected intruder. Lo and behold, Robert's visitor was a pint-sized little girl.

"My name is Robin!" she announced with a toothless smile!

Who was this cute little girl who had landed so unexpectedly on his doorstep? Questioning her, Robert learned that she lived in New York with her grandma, whose last name was Soltini. Robin told Scorpio that she had been picked up at camp by an Asian chauffeur and told to wait at Robert's house until her grandmother picked her up. The cuddly kid charmed Robert, but he feared that there was more to the puzzling situation. Leaving little Robin in Frisco and Felicia's care, Scorpio headed for New York to find Robin's grandmother. Meanwhile, Anna Devane arrived home to her New York apartment and found it ransacked—and an elderly woman, Filomena, tied up. Filomena was Robin's grandmother! Robin had a mother, too, and her name was Anna Devane! More than anything, Anna did not want anyone, including Robin, to know the truth. So Robin knew Anna only as "Luv," a woman who cared for her.

With Robert away, Frisco and Felicia enjoyed playing surrogate parents to Robin. But their fun quickly ended when, while walking on the water-front, an Asian man attempted to grab a doll from Robin's arms. An enraged Wu, fearing that Frisco could identify his grandson Kim as the thief, ordered Frisco's execution. Wu's henchman poisoned Frisco's drink, but in a twist of fate, Frisco's pal, Josh, sipped the drink instead and fell to the floor—dead! Death, danger and a baby doll. What did it all mean?

After fruitlessly searching for clues to Robin's identity, Robert Scorpio returned home with Anna—determined to break the news that he was Robin's father—hot on his trail. Back in Port Charles, Robert took one look at Robin and Anna together and realized that they were mother and daughter. Robert's instincts shifted into high gear as it dawned on him that this beautiful little girl was

Frisco Jones got his first taste of police work when he went undercover in Port Charles' Asian Quarter. Scorpio arranged for him to be charged with a crime he didn't commit. On the run from the law, the fugitive Frisco sought refuge in the Asian underworld, where he helped the authorities capture a crime lord.

his very own daughter. Determined to keep his loved ones safe, he postponed his Australia trip to find out why Robin was in danger.

At General Hospital, Frisco and Felicia became acquainted with an Asian intern, Dr. Yang Se-Chung, whom friends knew as "Yank." Yank was a young man on an urgent mission—to find his fugitive brother, Tey. When Robin saw Yank for the first time, she was certain that he was the man she saw hiding in the bushes at her camp. Yank knew he wasn't the guilty party, but he suspected that it could have been Tey.

Meanwhile, the authorities released Sean after he received a well-timed pardon from the governor of New York. Robert, skeptical of Sean's innocence, had no choice but to accept it because the WSB backed him up. Free at last, Sean went to work with Wu to find the pearls. Frisco joined in the dangerous game. At the hospital, Yank met Wu's beautiful grand-daughter, Jade, and they became attracted to each other. Jade introduced Frisco to her brother, Kim, who was instantly recognized as the culprit who had tried to take Robin's doll—which was now missing again, having been stolen by an Asian delivery woman. Why did everyone want a simple little doll?

Tey arranged to see his brother, Yank. But just before their meeting, a hit-and-run driver ran down Tey. Scorpio needed someone to go undercover in the Asian underworld, and Tey's death provided him with the opportunity to choose Frisco. Together, he and Frisco concocted a plan to incriminate Frisco as the driver of the car. Eager to solve Josh's murder, Frisco volunteered to take the rap although he knew it would destroy his peaceful life. To successfully infiltrate the Asian underworld, he would have to turn his back on his friends and loved ones—including Felicia—and go on the run in the Asian Quarter. At first, a stunned Felicia refused to believe that the man she loved had turned to a cold, hard life of crime. It pained him to keep his true motives secret from Felicia. Still, to keep her safe, he knew he had to let her go. Tony, too, was skeptical of his brother's moral slippage. He confronted Frisco.

"Where is my kid brother? Where?" Tony demanded to know.

"He smartened up, that's what he did."

"I don't believe you, Frisco."

"Tony, you're half a man. You understand me, you're half a man! You can't run, you can't do anything. You're barely out of a wheelchair. And that's the bottom line."

With Frisco's undercover help, Robert managed to put all the pieces together—and realized that Robin was the common bond in the mysterious disappearance of the black pearls. Meanwhile, Robin was shocked to overhear Anna and Robert admit that they were her parents. Feeling hurt and rejected, she ran away! While hiding at General Hospital, she recovered her lost doll and met up with The Ancient One in the Asian Quarter. The Ancient One, in his wise and soft-spoken way, told Robin that he may have destroyed his people's dream by losing the pearls. Robin knew where they were—in her doll's eyes! Weeks earlier, she had replaced her dolls eyes with the pearls belonging to the priceless jade buddhas. The Ancient One gave the pearls to a kindly Asian woman, Olin, for safekeeping. He then convinced Robin to give him some information that would help him get her home. But when Robin and The Ancient One went to meet Buzz and Anna, they were abducted by Kim, a member of the rival faction, who wanted the priceless pearls for themselves.

Scorpio and Anna grew frantic when Kim's men kidnaped Robin and The Ancient One. They set up headquarters in the Bamboo Bar, unaware that Robin and The Ancient One were concealed behind the bar in a secret room. Frisco asked Olin to surrender the black pearls as ransom, but both knew it was a decision the Asian community must make on their own.

Little Robin Scorpio was in for a happy surprise when she discovered that her dear friends "Luv" and Robert were, in reality, her parents.

GREAT MOMENTS

In November 1985, Anna Devane's prayers were answered when daughter Robin was safely returned after having been kidnaped by evil forces in Port Charles' Asian Quarter. Upon seeing Anna, little Robin raced into her waiting arms.

suade mayor-elect Morgan to make Burt Ramsey the new police commissioner. But the mayor believed that he needed someone with an international background for the post. Robert modified his proposal and suggested that the job of police commissioner be split into two "co-chiefs"—Ramsey *and* Anna Devane. With a final farewell, Robert Scorpio left to join Holly in Australia, but not before making a tender promise to Robin that she would be well cared for by her surrogate "fathers" Buzz, Sean and Frisco. Goodbye, Scorpio—we'll see you again!

At the renovated brownstone, Bobbie and Jake enjoyed playing landlord to a group of young people, including Frisco and Felicia. The brownstone gang got along splendidly—except two tenants—Dr. Kevin O'Connor and Terry Brock. A chill filled the air whenever these two kids were in the room. Realizing that their tension was troubling their fellow tenants, Terry and Kevin made a pact to forget their secret past. But Terry's jitters soon came rushing back and she began to drink heavily. Bobbie and Jake soon realized that Terry's problem had a psychological basis. Questioning Kevin, they learned that Terry was involved in a long-ago scandal in their hometown of Laurelton. Bobbie and Jake tried to provide Terry with a sense of family and, as a result, her mood began to improve. That is, until Kevin told her that his brother, Patrick, was coming to town.

Just in time for Thanksgiving, Robert teamed up with Anna to rescue The Ancient One and Robin. Seeing Anna, Robin raced into her arms. The Ancient One exchanged the pearls for cash and the Asian community celebrated the purchase of the cannery.

With Robin safe, Frisco joined with Sean and Yank to destroy Wu's evil empire, which he financed by operating an illegal drug-selling operation. Yank killed Wu's vengeful grandson, Kim, who planned to blow up the cannery, but Frisco defused the dynamite before an explosion destroyed the building, killing hundreds of celebrants. Jade, devastated to learn that her lover, Yank, had killed her brother, suddenly went blind! Tony persuaded Scorpio to allow Wu, who was about to be carted off to prison, to confess his wrongdoing to Jade. Free of shame and guilt, Jade recovered from her traumatic blindness.

With his mission over and his loved ones safe, Robert Scorpio made final preparations to leave for Australia. Just before his departure, he tried to per-

Jade Soong suffered a case of traumatic blindness when she discovered the depth of her grandfather, Mr. Wu's, depravity. With her friend Felicia's support, Jade recovered and entered General Hospital's student nursing program.

An air of mystery surrounded two of General Hospital's newest staff members, Drs. Kevin and Patrick O'Connor. The brothers shared a cryptic connection to Terry Brock, who was troubled by their presence in Port Charles.

"No, not Patrick..." said Terry, shuddering with fear.

From the day that handsome Dr. Patrick O'Connor arrived at General Hospital, Terry was hostile to him. Excessive drinking and bad dreams prompted Jake and Bobbie to go to Terry's hometown of Laurelton. Pretending to be lovers, Jake and Bobbie set out to investigate Terry. But the information wasn't so easy to ascertain because everyone, including Terry's own grandmother, Jennifer Talbot, was exceedingly uncooperative. What could the people of Laurelton possibly be hiding?

Back in Port Charles, Terry grew closer to Kevin. Working as a paralegal, she announced to Jake and Bobbie that she planned to attend law school. But Patrick warned her against it.

"Bad move, Terry," he chided, telling her that a law school ethics committee could rake up her past.

When he wasn't harassing Terry, Patrick was warning his brother to "stay away" from Terry Brock.

In late fall, Terry's grandmother, Jennifer Talbot, arrived in Port Charles, accompanied by her affable lawyer, Ted Holmes. Terry and her grandmother reconciled their longstanding differences quickly, which only made Bobbie more suspicious of Jennifer. Soon after her grandmother's arrival, more bad dreams plagued Terry. In a daze, she wandered into Kevin's bed and later Bobbie caught the troubled girl sleepwalking while holding a knife in her hand. Days later, a loud scream echoed through the halls of the Brownstone, sending the residents rushing into the living room. To everyone's horror, Terry stood over the body of a young man with a knife in his back! Bobbie's shock was greatest of all, because she had seen the knife before—in a sleepwalking Terry's hand.

As for those quibbling Quartermaines, Alan and Monica, the more things changed, the more they remained the same. Throughout 1985 their turbulent marriage was in danger of falling apart yet again. Ever insecure, Alan became jealous of Monica's infatuation with Dr. Buzz Stryker, a charismatic new arrival whose unorthodox medical methods made him the talk of General Hospital. Buzz spurned Monica's subtle advances, assuring her that their relationship must be "purely professional." Monica and Alan made the effort to get their marriage back on track, but soon Alan, determined to "live life to the fullest," had a fling with a young nurse. Monica warned her wayward hubby to stop fooling around! But she soon became diverted from Alan's affairs by her own connection to Sean Donely, who had been admitted to General Hospital suffering from symptoms of a heart attack. Donely wasn't sick at all; however, this was just the latest in his long string of clever deceptions. It seemed that Sean had simulated his heart condition by secretly taking a medication that produced symptoms of heart failure. He thought he could fool everyone—but he couldn't pull the wool over Monica's eyes. Monica quickly figured out Sean's deception and he begged her not to report him. She agreed to keep mum, and the gleam in her eye indicated that the acerbic Dr. Q. was falling for her con-artist patient!

1986

The mysterious murder inside the brownstone sent shock waves through Port Charles. Who could have committed such a heinous act of violence? Who was the unfortunate victim? The brownstone had been securely locked at the time of the crime. Chief Anna Devane began her investigation by making the building's residents her prime suspects. Jake insisted that Bobbie tell the authorities that she had seen a sleepwalking Terry carrying the very same knife that someone had plunged into the victim's back.

Co-Police Chief Burt Ramsey discovered a glass eye in the dead man's pocket. When Anna confronted the brownstone residents with the evidence, the O'Connor boys—Kevin and Patrick—admitted that their uncle Earl Moody had a glass eye. Earl Moody had disappeared three years earlier on the night of Laurelton's annual Valentine's Day Dance. The mystery deepened when the identity of the corpse was revealed. It was Kevin and Patrick's cousin, Neil Johnson, a man they hadn't seen in years.

The mystery grew more confounding when Anna Devane discovered the strangled corpse of Earl Moody in a fresh grave. She suspected a connection between Earl's death and the more recent death of Neil Johnson. Meanwhile, Terry took sodium pentothal to get to the root of her problems. Under the influence of the truth serum, Terry revealed that she had been banished from Laurelton three years ago because of an incident involving a boy. As Terry got closer to the truth, her worried grandmother, Jennifer, dissuaded her from continuing therapy. Throughout the early days of January, Jennifer and her lawyer, Ted Holmes, lurked in every corner of the brownstone. They suspiciously engaged in constant telephone communication with Laurelton's Sheriff Broder. For comfort during this stressful period, Terry turned to Kevin, who proposed marriage. Hoping to rid herself of a painful past, Terry accepted and eagerly made plans for the wedding.

In his will, the late Earl Moody left his entire estate to eldest nephew, Neil. Because of the death of Neil, Patrick inherited every penny of Moody's money. The news left Jennifer aghast and Kevin visibly upset. Both wondered how Patrick—Laurelton's black sheep—could have suddenly become a rich man. Could he have killed Uncle Earl? As a result, Patrick O'Connor became the prime suspect in the murder case. At the same time, Anna was curious to discover a picture of Terry on a bottle of Purity Water—Laurelton's town industry. To complicate matters, a Purity Water Company pendant found on Neil Johnson's body had been lifted from the body by an unknown person who filed off the initials. Whoever did that must be the murderer.

"What's going on here?" a perplexed Anna wondered as she set out to solve the mystery of the multiple murders.

Terry received a chilly greeting from the people of Laurelton when she returned home for her wedding to Kevin. As she made final preparations for the affair, Terry began to suffer flashbacks of the night of the annual Valentine Dance. She tried in vain to suppress the painful memories. On the way to the wedding in a limousine, the haunting flashbacks began to occupy Terry's every thought. When she spied a sleazy hotel, she suddenly remembered running from that very spot years ago. Ordering the car to stop, Terry insisted upon walking to the wedding. As she wandered through the streets of her hometown, Terry began having bizarre flashbacks. She remembered running naked through the streets of Laurelton while the shocked townsfolk looked on. Tormented by her memories, Terry was unable to make love to her new husband on their wedding night. As Kevin kissed and seduced Terry, memories of Patrick seducing her in a sleazy motel room came flooding back.

"I'm a patient guy!" Kevin told his new bride as they drifted off to sleep without consummating their marriage.

Frisco Jones was anxious to do some private sleuthing on the brownstone murder, but his studies at the Port Charles Police Academy kept him busy. His Asian Quarter escapade had whetted Frisco's appetite for adventure. Joining the Port Charles Police Department seemed the perfect career choice for the adventurous young man. Little did he know that the adventures would begin so soon! While out on police academy maneuvers, Frisco and his blonde, curvaceous partner, Samantha "Sam" Welles, discovered a corpse. This time, the dead body was Jennifer Talbot!

The discovery of Jennifer's body struck fear in the hearts of the brownstone residents, who worried that the murderer had struck again! An air embolism killed Jennifer, and when two hypodermic needles were found missing from Patrick's medical bag, he came under Anna's suspicion. But tire tracks near the scene of the crime didn't match Patrick's car. A bartender from a nearby pub identified Kevin as the young man he saw with Jennifer at the airport on the morning of the murder. After Jennifer's will revealed that half her estate had been left to Kevin, Anna arrested Kevin O'Connor for murder.

Jake took on Kevin's defense and Frisco and Felicia helped Anna in verifying Kevin's story that he had attended an early morning class and then went to the medical reference library. Kevin claimed that only one person could verify his claim—a mousy librarian by the name of Lucy Coe. Both the prosecution and the defense realized that Lucy held the key to the case, but she was nowhere to be found. As Kevin languished in jail, Miss Coe was away on vacation!

"Don't worry," he assured his worried friends. "Lucy Coe will verify my alibi."

As the trial began however, the elusive Lucy could not be found. Both the defense attorney, Jake Meyer, and the District Attorney, Brett Madison, searched for this witness, hoping she could be the key to the case. Finally, Miss Coe returned to town and took the stand with her hair pulled back into a tight, matronly bun. With control and confidence, she delivered damning testimony in which she denied seeing Kevin in the library on the morning of Jennifer Talbot's murder!

"That's a lie!" screamed Kevin, rising from his seat to attack the witness.

Jake, unable to shake Lucy, instructed Frisco to investigate Lucy Coe. "Get me some dirt!" he ordered the fledgling cop.

What dirt could Frisco possibly unearth? Lucy appeared to be a shy and retiring old maid. But Frisco found something interesting when he discovered a series of Lucy's sexy love poems to Kevin, one of which he stole and brought back to Jake. Upon seeing the erotic poems, Jake realized he might have found the key to solving the case.

Back in court, Jake warned Kevin that if he was keeping any secrets about Lucy, he'd better tell them now. Jake intended to tear her apart when he recalled her to the stand. Sitting in the witness box, Lucy listened as Jake pulled out a sheet of lilac-scented paper and began to recite Lucy's love poem. Horrified, the lovelorn librarian's composure crumbled as she told the packed courtroom that she'd "lied about everything!" She wanted to get even with Kevin for marrying Terry.

"He never looked at me! He hurt me and I wanted to make him pay!" cried Lucy.

Finally, she admitted the "truth"—that Kevin was in the library on the morning of the murder. Her testimony saved Kevin, who breathed a huge sigh of relief when the jury returned a verdict of "not guilty." Charged with perjury, the courts gave Lucy a sentence that involved long hours of community service. With her fifteen minutes of fame behind her, it was time for the prim and proper Miss Coe to fade back into obscurity, right? Wrong!

One day, she came home to her neat-as-a-pin cottage and let her hair down. In an amazing transformation from spinster to sexpot, Lucy whipped off her cardigan and tailored blouse, then slithered into a pair of black lace stockings, spike-heeled shoes and a slinky slip of an outfit. She awaited the arrival of her mystery man. The doorbell rang, and Lucy planted a white-hot kiss on the lips of her suitor—Kevin!

Kevin and Lucy had been having an ongoing affair. Amazingly, her courtroom switcheroo was actually part of an elaborate ruse designed to set Kevin free. Now Lucy wanted him more than ever. Terry was now the only impediment to their togetherness. Kevin knew how to solve that problem. He planned to do away with his wife on their upcoming second honeymoon!

With the trial over, Terry O'Connor enjoyed a new lease on life—until the haunting flashbacks abruptly returned. At Laurelton's town hall, Terry recollected seeing Kevin strangling Moody. Kevin convinced his wife that the disturbingly deadly images were simply hallucinations, brought on by the stress of the past weeks. Exuding charm and sympathy, Kevin persuaded Terry to leave town with him. But Kevin didn't plan to return with Terry because he planned to kill her on their honeymoon.

With Anna hot on his trail, Kevin took Terry from Laurelton to Atlanta, then on to Catalina Island. Pretending to be the ideal husband, Kevin began to

Dr. Kevin O'Connor's reign of terror came to a spellbinding conclusion on a cliff in this scene shot on location on Catalina Island.

drug Terry. He succeeded in gaslighting her into signing a confession that she was the one who killed Moody. As the next part of his plan, Kevin called his brother, Patrick, and told him to come to San Diego. Upon his arrival, Patrick was shocked to hear from Kevin that Terry was a murderess! Anna and Jake, still suspecting Kevin, left for Los Angeles, followed by Frisco, who had found Lucy's sexy stockings and coerced "the truth" out of her.

On Catalina, Frisco spotted Kevin and Terry, both in scuba gear, wading out into the Pacific Ocean, and followed them into the water. Underwater, Kevin spotted Frisco! Hiding behind a piece of coral, he waited until Frisco turned his back and jumped him. In one fell swoop, Kevin conked him over the head and tore off his breathing apparatus. Terry didn't see her husband strike the potentially deadly blow to Frisco's skull. Terry and Kevin returned to their hotel, but not before Kevin, in another attempt to gaslight Terry, ripped his scuba belt to make it appear that Terry tried to kill him in the water. After regaining consciousness, Frisco swam groggily ashore and was rushed to the hospital with a severe concussion. Meanwhile, Anna and Jake arrived on Catalina to search for Frisco, Terry and Kevin. They were relieved to find Frisco hospitalized but unable to communicate. Their worst fears about Kevin were confirmed when they found a scrawled message at the Catalina hotel:

"I am a murderer. Help me."

The eerie words, written by Terry, were a strong indication that Kevin's gaslighting was working. Ultimately, he didn't want to have to murder Terry in cold blood because, if his plan succeeded, she would kill herself.

Kevin stepped up his plan to drive Terry over the edge when, after fleeing their hotel, he staged yet another incident to make it seem that his wife was trying to kill him. Finally, when Terry was about to collapse from fear, drugs and exhaustion, Kevin handed her a gun, hoping she would commit suicide. But to his shock, she turned the weapon on him. Terry was fully aware of what her evil husband had been trying to do to her, and threatened to kill him. As Anna and Jake arrived on the scene, a frenzied Terry fired the gun until she ran out of bullets. Grabbing and reloading the pistol, Kevin chased after her, scurrying away to the edge of a nearby cliff. With jagged rocks and raging waters below them, Kevin went in for the kill, pushing Terry over the side of the cliff. Miraculously, she caught hold of a drain pipe and held on for dear life! Racing to Terry's aid, Jake seized Kevin and a vicious struggle followed. Then, out of the blue, Terry appeared behind Kevin and struck him with a boulder, sending him sprawling over the edge of the cliff!

Kevin was dead—killed by Terry's own hand! But Jake persuaded her to let him take the responsibility for this, since he made the mistake of getting Kevin off on the murder rap. Patrick, agonized by the death of his beloved brother, had a hard time believing that Kevin was a killer, but Lucy Coe's confession made

It was a long time in coming, but Frisco and Felicia finally tied the knot in a hastily arranged June wedding. Frisco's bride-to-be nearly canceled the affair when she decided she wasn't cut out to be the wife of a cop.

him realize that his brother was nothing more than scum! Patrick and Terry confronted the Laurelton group about the cover-up, but promised not to make the scandal public and ruin the Purity Water company.

Lucy Coe planned to get rich quick by writing a tell-all book about her sensational relationship with the murderous Kevin O'Connor. Still looking for love, Lucy ingratiated herself to Patrick O'Connor, who was confused and troubled by his late brother's string of cold-blooded murders. Like many others who failed to see Lucy's true colors, Patrick believed that she was sincere in her desire to atone for her past mistakes. Little did they know that Lucy was just beginning to spin manipulative webs around the people of Port Charles.

In June, the town readied itself for the wedding of the year! But the marriage of Frisco and Felicia was promptly called off by the bride after an incident in which Frisco was nearly shot and killed.

"I'm just not cut out to be a policeman's wife," cried Felicia as she canceled the impending nuptials.

At the last minute, she reconsidered. Bobbie and Ruby rushed to restore the canceled preparations, rounded up the guests and located the minister. The wedding was on again! In a joyous brownstone wedding, Frisco Jones married the "lady of my heart," Felicia Cummings.

Anna Devane could only wish for such a loving man to enter her life. With her police work and her daughter taking up her time, Anna simply had no room for a man in her life. But that situation changed on the night of the annual policeman's ball. After receiving a commendation for solving the Laurelton murders, Anna caught the eye of an attractive stranger across the room. The lonely co-police chief was even more intrigued when the handsome gent sent her a sprig of heather. After encountering Duke Lavery, Anna's life would never be the same again.

With his lilting Scottish brogue and darkly handsome looks, Duke looked every inch like an upstanding citizen, and not the mobster that he actually was! To Anna and the rest of Port Charles, Duke appeared to be a hardworking nightclub owner and local businessman. He was running for president of the Dockworker's Union to bring fair labor practices to the Port Charles waterfront. Unbeknownst to Anna, the suave Mr. Lavery was deeply involved in the planning of an elaborate money-laundering operation headed by a never-seen underworld chief, "Mr. Big." As Duke fell in love with Anna, he slowly began to deeply regret his mob ties. Duke cared deeply for Anna and her daughter, Robin. He would never allow any harm to come to them. He wanted out of the rackets! Yet Duke was in too deep.

After defeating Jimmy Lee Holt in the union election, Duke shared his joy with Anna as they made passionate love for the first time. Secretly, Duke yearned for the day he would be free of his underworld connections but, until then, he knew his loved ones could be in jeopardy. Knowing that Anna was in danger, Duke coldly backed away from the budding romance. The arrival of Mr. Big's right-hand man, Damon Grenville, meant that Duke would have to step up the plans to put their money laundering scheme, dubbed "Operation Tumble Dry," into effect. Damon immediately put the squeeze on Duke. "There's a cop nosing around and I want him taken care of," ordered Damon. Duke stiffened, knowing that the cop in question was Frisco Jones.

Acting with care so as not to reveal his true colors, Duke maneuvered to prevent a hitman from killing Frisco. Then he promised Damon that he would be responsible for keeping the pasty Jones boy —and his snooping wife, Felicia, whom Duke had hired as a bookkeeper—under control while they carried out "Operation Tumble Dry." The best way to get Frisco and Felicia out of the way was to frame them for crimes they did not commit. Duke and his maitre d'/accomplice, Angel, planted an ermine coat that Felicia had admired and a box of money in the Jones' apartment. When the bank discovered an error in Duke's account, Anna was called in to investigate a possible theft by Felicia. Frisco got word of all this first from Sam and went home to confront Felicia. They concluded that someone had framed her, but who knew why? To keep Felicia out of jail, Frisco needed answers—fast! Answering a frantic call from his waterfront informant, Tessie, to meet her in New York, Frisco and Felicia grabbed the fur coat and the box of money, then fled town on a motorcycle. Also in their possession was a computer printout—in code— detailing "Operation Tumble Dry." On the run, Frisco

and Felicia hoped to break the code and expose the waterfront mob activities.

As Anna investigated Frisco and Felicia's disappearance, she feared Duke may have had something to do with it.

"Trust me," he implored to a wary Anna.

Meanwhile, Robin overheard a conversation in

In June 1986, dashing rogue Duke Lavery tangoed into Anna Devane's life. At first she doubted the sincerity of the mysterious Scotsman, who kept many secrets.

the park between Damon and a cohort in which they threatened to kill Anna. In fear, Robin knew she had to place a long-distance call to the one man who could save Anna's life—her father, Robert Scorpio!

On the run and disguised as a pair of kindly senior citizens, Frisco and Felicia fled to Atlantic City, where they attempted to put together the keys to enable them to crack the code. In the process, they befriended an old woman, Edna, who was actually a mob hitwoman! Edna waited for the right moment to kill her prey, but an unexpected hero thwarted her "hit." The heroic citizen was none other than Robert Scorpio, back from Australia in the nick of time! After rescuing Frisco and Felicia, Robert headed for Port Charles.

Frisco and Felicia's trail of clues next took them to a circus, where they came across a treasure chest full of money that was about to be transported as the next phase of "Operation Tumble Dry." Following the chest back to Port Charles, the fugitive couple were finally caught and arrested.

On the home front, Tony and Tania Jones anticipated the birth of their child. But Tony had to admit that he was bitter toward his brother for putting them through these weeks of anguish. Bryan and Claudia, who had been estranged for months, observed Tony and Tania's happiness and wondered if they should give their own marriage another chance. Celia and Jimmy Lee's marriage began to collapse when Jimmy Lee made a series of bad business deals that caused him to squander his personal fortune. Celia—who had always been wealthy—wasn't comfortable with the idea of living on a budget. Using her own money, she surprised her mate while he was away on a business trip—only to find him in bed with another woman! It didn't matter that Jimmy Lee was doing "research" for the Quartermaines. Celia wanted a divorce!

The Quartermaines encouraged Monica to charm business secrets out of Sean Donely, who was now a free man thanks to a pardon from the governor. Sean and Monica embarked upon a sexy affair, then realized they had fallen in love. Soon they became partners in both the bedroom and the boardroom as they united to bring down the Quartermaine empire through a series of backstabbing business deals. The Quartermaines were broke! Sean had all their money, which he kept in a Swiss bank account where no one, not even Monica, could get their hands on it.

Swingin' Jimmy Lee Holt abandoned the high life and got back to basics when he married Charity Gatlin, a sweet woman who ran a general store in the rural town of Pautuck.

To add insult to injury, Monica kicked the Quartermaines out of the mansion and instituted divorce proceedings against Alan. With no money and nowhere to turn, Edward, Lila and Alan were forced to move into rooms above Kelly's Diner. They were down, but not out! Lila rolled up her sleeves and with the help of her faithful maid, Stella, she began selling a secret family relish, which they dubbed "Pickle-lila." The tasty concoction earned Lila a fortune of her own! Alan cleverly concocted another strategy designed to regain the family fortune. Convinced that Sean had their money, Alan masterminded a plan to make Sean look guilty of murdering him for the insurance money. According to the carefully crafted scheme, Alan would simply drop out of sight and later return, claiming to have had amnesia. By then, the Quartermaines would have strongarmed Sean into relinquishing the money he bamboozled from them in exchange for his freedom.

The Quartermaine stratagem worked like a charm when news reached Port Charles that a plane piloted by Alan had crashed. He was presumed dead. Edward was one of a select few who knew his son was very much alive!

Alan assumed a new identity in Pautuck, a small town in upstate New York. Calling himself "Simon," he eagerly went to work in a general store operated by a down home gal, Charity Gatlin. Trading in his hospital robe for a flannel shirt and jeans, Alan began to appreciate the charms of country life and was reluctant to ever return to the dog-eat-dog world of big business that he left behind in Port Charles. Edward, too, proved he had a trick up his sleeve when he brought Tiffany Hill back to Port Charles, where he planned to use her to drive a wedge between Sean and Monica. In exchange for her participation in the elaborate ploy, Tiffany demanded that Edward buy WLPC-TV and give it to her, and that's not all! She wanted 40% of the Quartermaine fortune.

As planned by the scheming Quartermaines, Sean became Anna's prime suspect in the apparent murder of Alan Quartermaine. Fearing that he would be confined to prison, Sean began avoiding Monica and seeing more of Tiffany. Upon seeing Sean and Tiffany in public, Monica became so livid that she poured a pitcher of ice water over their heads. While Monica tried to cool down, the investigation into Alan's death heated up—and the police eventually charged Sean with murder! That's when Edward went in for the kill! Putting the screws to Donely, Edward offered up a deal: "Return my fortune and I'll give you information that will clear you of Alan's murder."

Faced with no alternative, Sean gave in to Edward Quartermaine's demands and signed away the millions in his Swiss bank account in exchange for freedom. In court, Edward made the "stunning" announcement that his son was alive! Alan returned from Pautuck—and amazingly, a blow to the head had him believing he really was Simon.

Monica set out to prove Alan was faking. In the process, she fell back in love with her husband! In a strange turnabout, Jimmy Lee fell in love with Charity Gatlin and decided to settle down in peaceful little Pautuck. At a farewell party, Edward and Jimmy Lee shared a tender parting scene, while Alan and Monica got tipsy and shared an evening together.

Meanwhile, Duke Lavery agonized over his fateful decision to leave the mob. As the days turned into months, Duke decided that he couldn't wait for the mob bosses to fulfill their promise to let him leave the organization. Trapped in their web, Duke decided to sacrifice himself to save himself. Knowing it could mean his certain death, he prepared a package of evidence against the mob and sent it to Burt Ramsey. Then he planned to skip town. But before he could sneak away, the dastardly Damon unceremoniously stopped Duke, calling him a traitor and warning that unless he cooperated fully with the mob, Anna and Robin would suffer. At the same time, Damon ordered Duke to marry Anna. Touched by Duke's proposal, Anna accepted, unaware that it was against his will.

In the fall of 1986, the identity of the enigmatic Mr. Big was revealed, and his identity proved to be a shocker—Co-Police Chief Burt Ramsey! Burt? How could kindly Burt Ramsey possibly be the mob master of Port Charles? In conversations with Damon, Ramsey revealed that years earlier he had turned to a life of corruption out of bitterness for his being forced to share Police Commissioner duties with Anna Devane.

"A woman! That was it, I couldn't take it anymore. You made me do it! Don't you see? Ha, you win again, Scorpio, you win again!" uttered a demented Ramsey as he carried out his private war.

Home at last, Scorpio accused Duke Lavery of being involved in the money laundering scheme and accessed Duke's computer files. Anna defended Duke at first but, after Frisco accused him of being up to no good, Anna reluctantly broke their engagement. Frisco and Felicia were released on bail but, at Ramsey's urging, Frisco was promptly kicked off the police force. He was bitter at his superiors, especially Anna, for not believing that he and Felicia had no other choice but to go on the run. Once again, he went undercover. Convincing Duke that he had turned against the police, he got a job at Duke's club. Scorpio, pleased that Frisco was working undercover for him at the club, turned his attentions to Duke's past. He became curious when he investigated a missing month in Duke's life when he claimed to have been in Scotland. Duke's missing month appeared to be connected to a place called "L'Orleans." Robert reported his findings to Anna, who confronted Duke during a romantic getaway.

"I'm sorry, Anna. That must remain my secret," he firmly told her.

L'Orleans…what could it mean?

Determined to extricate himself from the mob, Duke paid a visit to Mr. Big's boss, Angus McKay, who was second-in-command to the head honcho, Pilgrim. Angus, a fellow Scotsman, gave Duke his solemn promise and a ring as a symbol that Duke would be free of all involvement in the mob by December 1st. After six weeks, Angus swore that Duke would be free to marry Anna. The two men shared a strange closeness and rapport as they spoke of their beloved homeland, Scotland. Duke left Angus feeling buoyant and hopeful at last!

Assured of a safe future, Duke Lavery asked Anna Devane to marry him—and this time he meant it with all his heart. But when Damon orchestrated a bombing of Anna's house, an anguished Duke decided that he must tell the police all he knew about the mob in order to protect Anna and Robin. He tried to tell Anna first, but she was preoccupied with wedding plans. Instead, Duke revealed all to Burt Ramsey, unaware that he was the notorious Mr. Big! Afterward, Duke overheard Ramsey order a hit on Duke, and confronted him. In the ensuing struggle, Duke shot and critically injured Ramsey. Anna was devastated when she arrived at the scene of Ramsey's shooting, only to be shown by her police force that the man in custody for the shooting was none other than Duke—who had been found standing over the chief holding Ramsey's gun! Anna was stunned, at first refusing to believe Duke's allegations against Ramsey. Robert, on the other hand, wasn't sure, especially after catching the recuperating Ramsey in a lie. With his thirst for adventure fully restored, Robert convinced Anna and Frisco to join him in a secret mission to expose Burt Ramsey and bring down the Port Charles mob.

Duke was sent up the river—but not for long. Mobster Angus McKay arranged for Duke's escape so that the "organization" could rub him out once and for all. Scorpio managed to intercept Duke during the jailbreak, and in an elaborate ruse to fool Burt Ramsey, he planned to "shoot" and "kill" Duke. But Burt jumped the gun, shooting Duke first. The "injured" Duke was rushed to General Hospital, where Frisco had arranged with his brother, Dr. Tony Jones, to pronounce the patient dead. Duke was actually very much alive, however, since Scorpio had the forethought to fill Ramsey's guns with blanks!

With Duke seemingly dead, Ramsey implemented the final stage of his money laundering scheme. Scorpio, Sean and Anna schemed to intercept the final drop of laundered money to be delivered to the Dockworker's Savings and Loan during Ramsey's retirement luncheon. But the plan went awry. Hitmen pursued Scorpio and Duke prevented Anna from rushing to aid Robert. The hitmen arrived, took aim at Robert and fired—but Duke heroically stepped into the line of fire and took a bullet intended for his rival.

In the aftermath, it was Scorpio's duty to confront and arrest his long-time friend, Burt Ramsey.

Grabbing Ramsey by the neck, Robert let out his venom.

"Why did you do it!" he demanded.

"I'll tell you why, Robert Scorpio! Because of you—I was tired of playing second-fiddle to Superman," Ramsey retorted, scowling as he was dragged off to a mental institution.

Frisco and Felicia reopened Duke's club and moved into a luxurious penthouse. Anna tried to bolster Duke's spirits when, paralyzed from the waist down, he was given a fifty-fifty chance of walking again.

As 1986 drew to a close, several couples celebrated their good fortunes. Of everyone, Tony and Tania Jones had to be the happiest twosome in Port Charles. After Tania went into premature labor, Bobbie and her fiancé, Jake, rushed to her side to assist in the delivery of a beautiful baby girl. In appreciation, the Jones named their newborn daughter Barbara Jean, or "BJ" for short! Bobbie, witnessing Jake's excitement over BJ's birth, became distressed by the realization that she would never be able to bear him a child. Confiding her feelings to the man she loved, Bobbie set out to find the right woman to serve as a surrogate mother to have Jake's baby. Learning of Bobbie's plight, Lucy Coe's ears perked up! Oh, that Lucy—what could she possibly have on her mind now?

With intensive physical therapy, Duke Lavery rebounded from his paralysis and got back on his feet. Grateful to receive a light prison sentence, he didn't know how he would pay back the heavy fine he had been assessed for his illegal mob activities. Sentenced to the same prison as mobster Angus McKay, a stoic Duke didn't fear life behind bars. But he shuddered with trepidation whenever his thoughts turned to Anna and Robin's safety. He knew of only one way to keep them safe from harm—and the secret of L'Orleans was his ace in the hole. Scorpio agreed that the only way to ensure Anna and Robin's well being was to use the secret of L'Orleans as leverage with his fellow prisoner, Scotsman Angus McKay.

What was this devastating secret? And what was the unusual tie between Duke and Angus? More of Duke Lavery's undisclosed past came to light when it became known that Angus McKay was actually his father! In early January, a young nun, Sister

Camellia, arrived in Port Charles. After studying newspaper articles about Duke's recent difficulties, she headed to prison where viewers learned her true identity. The pretty but troubled young nun was the daughter of Angus and the half-sister of Duke. In happier times, she had met and fallen in love with Duke, unaware that they were related. The mystery deepened when it became apparent that Sister Camellia was deeply troubled by a night in her past. It was a night she spent in Canada. In a town called L'Orleans.

Back in a town called Port Charles, Dr. Steve Hardy was overjoyed to receive a letter from his son Tommy—who was now a full-fledged doctor: Tom Hardy! Energetic and upbeat, Tom arrived at General Hospital in the spring of 1987 and immediately impressed staff and patients alike with his dedication to healing.

Lucy Coe was equally dedicated to causing trouble! Early in 1987, it was Lucy who was in big trouble when she was unjustly charged with the murders of Laurelton's Sheriff Broder and lawyer Ted Holmes. Everyone, and most especially Bobbie, believed that Lucy was a cold-blooded murderess. In a bitter blow up, her new husband, Jake Meyer, maintained that Lucy was innocent until proven guilty. Not one to sit back and let the legal process take its course, Lucy jumped bail and headed for Laurelton in an effort to find some evidence to clear herself. Jake, who had taken Lucy's case, gave chase and found her in a desperate state. In a night bound to have cataclysmic ramifications, Lucy hysterically pleaded her innocence. She needed a lawyer and, more than anything, she needed a friend. Jake comforted Lucy and, in an emotional moment charged with pity and passion, he made love to her.

Back in Port Charles, Jake eventually got the charges against Lucy dropped—but she had a surprise in store... Jake, deeply regretting his night of passion with Lucy, patched things up with Bobbie. He joined her in another search for a surrogate mother when the young woman originally selected to have Jake's child, Gretchen, backed out of the arrangement. As Jake would soon learn, he wouldn't need to

Sister Camellia had a mysterious connection to Duke Lavery. Duke's former lover, Camellia suffered from nightmares about a long-ago night in Canada the events of which she could not recall.

look very far for a woman to have his baby— because Lucy was pregnant with his child!

Word of Lucy Coe's pregnancy spread quickly through General Hospital. Gossip queen Amy Vining blabbed the news to Bobbie, who nonchalantly passed it on to Jake. Rocked by the revelation, Jake broke down and told Bobbie the truth: He could be the father of Lucy's baby! With Ruby's help, a humiliated Bobbie was able to forgive him, though his adulterous affair had caused irreparable damage to their marriage. Lucy insisted that she didn't want to break up Bobbie and Jake's marriage, but that Lucy was scheming up a storm! When Bobbie and Jake asked her to bear Jake's child and let them adopt it, Lucy kept them hanging when she hesitated to give them an answer. Eventually, she agreed to bear Jake's child and, to Bobbie's shock, she refused to take any money in return. Unpredictable as always, Lucy had already found another cause to occupy her nervous energy. A new man had entered her life. He had everything Lucy craved—respectability, class and money. And he was ripe for Lucy's machinations because he had just lost his wife in a terrible accident. Lucy had found just the man to ensnare in her web. The spider woman's victim was none other than Dr. Tony Jones.

For many, St. Patrick's Day is a day to celebrate life. But for Tony Jones, March 17th would always be a day to mourn, a day to reflect on what might have been. On March 17, 1987, Tania Jones went shopping with Felicia for a birthday present for Tony and was struck down by a hit-and-run driver. Despite heroic efforts by Dr. Buzz Stryker and the rest of the General Hospital staff to save her life, Tania died in Tony's arms. In the numbing days after the tragedy, Tom Hardy helped Tony handle his grief and Tania was remembered by all who loved her in a beautiful memorial service. Frisco was determined to find Tania's killer. Tony, throwing himself into his work, was determined to be a loving father to his infant daughter, BJ. And Lucy Coe was determined to worm her way into the Jones family unit!

A sweet but suicidal teenage boy, Corey Blythe, was being treated by Tom Hardy, who determined that Corey's problem was neurological and decided to operate. At the same time, Frisco's search yielded information that Corey was the owner of the hit-and-run vehicle that killed Tanya. Tom Hardy also suspected that Corey was the driver and, as the operation was set to begin, he confided to Steve that Tony might end up operating on his wife's killer.

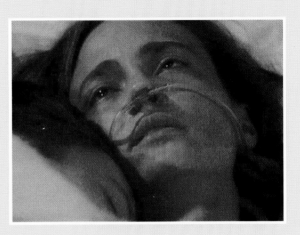

Tania Jones had been shopping for a birthday present for her husband Tony when she was suddenly struck down by a hit-and-run driver in March 1987. Rushed to General Hospital, a dying Tania shared a final farewell with a grief-stricken Tony.

Steve agreed that Tony must be told prior to the surgery, but Tom was unable to get to Tony in time. A reporter leaked the information and, in the middle of the delicate surgery, Tony heard a radio news bulletin detailing the facts. Tony, stunned, acted as a dedicated professional and saved Corey's life, despite his own personal trauma.

In prison, Angus McKay proved that he would do anything to protect his daughter when he was confronted by a vengeful fellow inmate, Jonathan. Jonathan was out for blood over the death of his cousin, Evan Jerome, four years earlier. Angus admitted that his people had killed Evan Jerome because he had raped Camellia, who remembered nothing of that deadly night. Angus and Duke hid and buried Evan's body in the garden because, if the Jerome family had learned that a McKay murdered their son, it would have sparked a mob war. That was the "secret" of L'Orleans!

After four years of strife, Angus McKay, elderly and imprisoned, desperately wanted to end the vendetta between the warring McKay and Jerome families. To call a halt to the mob war, Angus chose to make the ultimate sacrifice. To pay back the Jerome family, he drank poison and died! With his dying breath, Angus begged Duke to protect the secret of

L'Orleans and look after Camellia. Anna investigated Angus' death, but Duke kept his lips sealed. "Let the matter rest, my darling," he told the perplexed police chief. Anna wondered if Duke or Camellia knew more than they were letting on, but against her better judgment she backed off from further investigation. Weeks later, Duke was paroled. Finally free, he returned to the club and set out to raise the necessary funds to pay his heavy fine. When his debt was paid back, Duke would be free to marry Anna Devane. Accompanying Duke to L'Orleans for Angus' funeral, Anna's intuition went into overdrive. She began to realize that there may have been far more in Duke and Camellia's past than just a sibling relationship. Though Duke vehemently denied it, the revelation that he was Camellia's brother drove Camellia to commit a murder she could not recall! Now, four years later, Camellia was determined to find out what happened on that fateful night—although Duke warned her that it could destroy them both.

As she explored her past, Camellia discovered another horrifying twist when an elderly seer informed her that Angus wasn't her real father after all—nor was Duke her brother. Once she learned that she and Duke weren't siblings, Sister Camellia abandoned her vocation and set out to win the man she loved away from Anna. Camellia raced to Duke and tried to convince him that because they weren't related, they could now resume their love affair.

"Now we can be together—at last!" she exclaimed to Duke, who didn't share Camellia's enthusiasm for resurrecting their relationship.

Duke insisted that Anna was the only woman for him and demanded that Camellia stay out of his life before the larger secret of L'Orleans came to light.

"You'll destroy yourself, don't you see!?" Duke warned her.

But Camellia was committed to her quest. She wasn't going anywhere! Camellia accepted a nursing position at General Hospital. Then she secretly contacted a sleazy investigative reporter, Mark Carlin, in an effort to ruin Anna by exposing her failure to properly investigate Angus McKay's death. Carlin unearthed much more! Digging into Duke and Camellia's past, he discovered the secret of L'Orleans and exposed it—on Duke and Anna's wedding day!

On May 1st, 1987, Anna blissfully walked down the aisle to meet and marry the man she loved. Yet both bride and groom were unaware that reporter Mark Carlin was in the process of breaking the

story of the year! "POLICE CHIEF TO MARRY MAN WHO COVERED UP MURDER," screamed the headlines of the paper on the day of the wedding at Duke's Club. Across town at General Hospital, Camellia received in the mail a candlestick that brought back a deluge of memories. Terrified, she finally recalled the horrible truth that she had used that very candlestick to murder Evan!

Back at the club, the wedding was just underway when a hoard of reporters, spurred on by Carlin's published allegations, burst through the doors to confront the bride and groom, verbally attacking Anna and accusing her of covering up her fiancé's crimes! In shock, Anna turned to Duke who had no choice but to admit that he had concealed Camellia's crime. For Anna, embarrassed and stunned, this was the ultimate betrayal. Lie after lie had destroyed Duke's credibility. Anna wanted him out of her life forever! As for Camellia, Dr. Tom Hardy helped the troubled young woman to comprehend that she was not a cold-blooded killer but a woman who fought back while being raped. Deeply regretting her contact with Carlin, a tormented Camellia apologized to Duke for exposing the secret of L'Orleans and for ruining the lives of so many people, including Anna, who resigned because of her failure to properly investigate Angus McKay's death.

Duke and Camellia were extradited to Canada, where they were ultimately acquitted of any wrongdoing in the death of Evan Jerome. Camellia eventually left for a new beginning far from Port Charles.

Disheartened by Duke's betrayal, Anna made an announcement to her friends.

"I'm taking control of my life!" she resolved.

Duke tried in vain to win back his lady love, but Anna was determined to get on with her new life, a new career—and an old husband! In the spring of 1987, Anna decided to start her own PI agency. She was delighted to have her ex-husband Robert Scorpio return to Port Charles to be her partner. Robert came back with shocking news: Holly was dead! Just like Anna, Robert had been the victim of a betrayal because the plane crash that killed his wife also killed her secret lover! Hiding his grief, Robert explained that he returned to the United States on a mission to prevent the assassination of WSB agents by the DVX. Chief Ballantine was already dead. And Holly had been killed in a plot intended to eliminate Scorpio! Now the DVX was about to strike again. Devane and Scorpio were back in business.

Sean Donely was embroiled in a stratagem of his own involving the newly arrived Dr. Greta Ingstrom. Greta, a brilliant and beautiful geneticist, was secretly engaged in formulating a top-secret antidote to a lethal germ warfare virus called MOX 36, which was a powerful weapon in the DVX's cold war arsenal. She conducted her humanitarian research for Helix Technogen Industries, or HTI, a financially troubled research firm that the WSB had contracted. Sean successfully attempted a hostile takeover of HTI. Monica and Edward Quartermaine participated in the takeover bid, along with a down-on-his-luck Wall Street genius named Von Schuler. In the process of taking over HTI, Sean became attracted to the enchanting Greta, much to Tiffany's chagrin. Sean was forced to employ his WSB training to keep the MOX 36 antidote from falling into the hands of the evil DVX, who wanted to stop its development and preserve their viral weapon. In time, DVX moles who infiltrated HTI chased Greta to Niagra Falls, where she was rescued by Sean and Frisco, but not before being critically stabbed.

While Greta lay recuperating in ICU, yet another DVX agent took the staff of General Hospital hostage in the cafeteria after a failed attempt to reach Greta and kill her. Before being subdued, the spy managed to scratch Bobbie with a syringe tainted with the deadly MOX 36. The doctors at GH called upon Greta to develop a batch of her untested antidote. Greta saved Bobbie's life, but she was left without any feeling in her legs. Bobbie was paralyzed!

The arrival of Dusty Walker, a baby-faced drifter in his early twenties, at the brownstone, gave Terry's spirits a boost. Like Terry, Dusty was a singer. The two struck up an instant accord and decided to team up as a singing duo, with Tiffany Hill as their manager. Patrick was jealous of Terry's budding relationship with Dusty, and rightly so because Dusty was personable, talented—a future star. What no one knew, not even Dusty himself, was that he was under the control of terrorists! Dusty's mentor, the beguiling ex-DVX operative, Elena Cosgrove, had commanded him to kill top WSB agents through posthypnotic suggestion. Elena was the ringleader of a fanatical terrorist group comprised of former WSB and DVX agents bent on securing "world peace" by wiping out both organizations! The key to Elena's masterful plot was a hauntingly melodic song, "40 Million Stars," which contained secret rhythmic and lyrical codes instructing Dusty who and when to kill!

Much to Duke's chagrin, Robert and Anna teamed up to attempt to thwart Elena's deadly plot. During their vigilant investigation, Robert's long-dormant feelings for his ex-wife began to surface. In a moment fraught with sexual tension, Robert confessed his inner turmoil to Anna, who urged him to concentrate on their mission to save the WSB agents. Privately, Robert's heartfelt confession stirred Anna's emotions. After all, she still deeply loved Duke and had only recently warmed to his overtures to "begin again." After a tumultuous summer in which she was torn between her two men, Anna removed herself from any involvement with either Duke or Robert.

At historic Mt. Rushmore, the maniacal Elena programmed Dusty to plant a bomb on a train which was due to pass by an early-warning system for nuclear weapons. Terry, confused by Dusty's bizarre behavior, tried to prevent him from walking out on her, but Dusty was clearly under the control of Elena. Robert and Anna pursued Dusty to the train, but Robert urged Anna to stay behind. "It's too dangerous," he implored.

But Anna was not one to be left behind! On horseback, Anna caught up to the moving train and daringly leaped aboard. She then aided Robert in setting the timer on the bomb ahead to prevent it from destroying the early warning system. Before the train exploded, Robert leaped to safety, but not Anna— her foot was caught!! Duke, who had been prevented from accompanying them, hovered from a helicopter and freed the woman he loved from certain doom.

In the aftermath of the Mt. Rushmore adventure, Elena escaped and the authorities arrested Dusty. At the trial, with Jake as his attorney, Dusty took the stand in his own defense and submitted to mind-control in front of the stunned onlookers. Seeing firsthand evidence that he was an innocent victim in Elena's lethal scheme, the judge decided in favor of the defense and he went free. Bobbie urged Terry to stand by her man, but Dusty, tormented by the catastrophic events, prepared to leave town. Before departing, he led the government agents to Elena, who committed suicide before she could be brought to justice. Despondent over Dusty's departure, Terry lost her voice. Dr. Tom Hardy treated her with care and compassion. By now Tom had a problem of his own—his former fiancée, Simone, had arrived in Port Charles.

Tom and Dr. Simone Ravelle, an enchantingly beautiful black woman, had met the previous year when both were interns at Bellevue Hospital in New

York. When their friendship turned to love, an agonized Simone decided to cool the relationship because her wealthy parents didn't approve of her involvement with Tom. Their disapproval had less to do with Tom's paltry bank account than it did with the color of his skin, for the Ravelles felt that today's world was not yet ready for an interracial couple. Heartbroken, Tom moved home to Port Charles. Simone quickly followed when Steve Hardy decided to bolster his depleted staff. Buzz Stryker left to work with Vietnam vets and Yank and Jade recently departed for Asia.

Steve hired Simone as his new resident—unaware of her connection to his son. Working closely together, Tom and Simone pledged to remain "just friends," but it was apparent to everyone who witnessed their incredible chemistry that these two kids were in love! Soon after joining the staff, Simone became attached to a patient, Andy Matthews, a football hero whom doctors had diagnosed with a deadly form of cancer. As Andy grew weaker, Simone observed his lack of will to live and decided to give him motivation to undergo therapy for his cancer. She promised to marry him! Not wanting to lose the woman he adored, Tom convinced Simone that marrying Andy was wrong. Yet before she could tell Andy she couldn't become his wife, he collapsed and died. In the wake of the tragedy, Tom and Simone found their way back together.

A forlorn Robert Scorpio quietly observed Duke and Anna's renewed happiness. He watched with sadness as they zealously set an autumn date for a glorious Scottish wedding. They invited all of Port Charles to attend the nuptials, which featured bagpipe players, Scottish dancers, a kilt-wearing bridegroom and a dazzling bride, whom her loving ex-husband, Robert, walked down the aisle. The only person who felt even the remotest bit of melancholy was Felicia, who was sad because her own husband, Frisco, was unable to attend. Despite her reservations, he had decided to abandon his local police work to join the WSB. On his last day in Port Charles, Frisco bade farewell to all his friends. In a tearful airport scene, he handed Felicia an engraved locket in the shape of a heart. With a heartfelt promise to return, Frisco Jones departed Port Charles for new horizons.

After the death of his beloved wife, Tania, Frisco's brother Tony Jones was vulnerable and lonely, the perfect candidate to become ensnared in Lucy Coe's trap. Lucy became BJ's new nanny and began preying on Tony's sympathies. Soon after moving into Tony's home, Lucy was about to suffer a terrible tragedy of her own. Rushed to General Hospital with severe abdominal pains, Lucy miscarried her baby. Jake took the loss of his child with great difficulty.

"Thank God we still have each other," he told Bobbie tearfully, as they abandoned their surrogacy plans and began exploring the possibility of adopting a child.

Lucy stepped up her quest to snare Tony. Within days of her miscarriage, she was back in the Jones household, using her now-trim body to entice Tony, who couldn't help but notice Lucy's stunning shape.

As the days passed, Tony tried in vain to fight his temptation. One night, he gave in to his lust and kissed her passionately.

"I'm…I'm so sorry!" he apologized, retreating upstairs.

Oozing sex appeal, Lucy was unstoppable. On yet another steamy night, craving her artful form, Tony kissed Lucy again. Finally, he couldn't contain his lust another second. After an arousing game of Scrabble, Tony carried Lucy off to bed for the first time. Despite the stern warnings of his wary friends, Dr. Jones took the sexy Miss Coe as his wife in a hastily arranged ceremony. The spare wedding didn't faze Lucy—she had triumphantly nabbed her prey! Now Lucy Jones was determined to take her new place as the dutiful, benevolent wife of a prominent Port Charles doctor. Lucy's wacky and tacky Aunt Charlene sashayed into town, intending to share her niece's good fortune. Charlene, a southern belle with dubious credentials, insinuated herself into the Jones' household as the housekeeper without telling Tony that Lucy was kin.

"You're nothing but a whore!" bellowed a livid Bobbie to Lucy upon hearing of her marriage to Tony.

At the time, Bobbie was on the long road back from paralysis. She was helped through therapy by a marvelously optimistic paraplegic, Martha McKee, who was suffering from pneumonia. When Martha took a turn for the worse and needed to convalesce in Colorado, Bobbie and Jake became guardians of her two children, teenager Melissa and ten-year-old Skeeter. As Bobbie's limbs grew stronger, she felt up to the task of raising the McKee children. Melissa posed the biggest problem when she rebelled against Bobbie's house rules, spurned her boyfriend Corey Blythe and began hanging out with a bad crowd.

Hoping to share in Lucy's good fortune, Aunt Charlene finagled a job as the Jones family housekeeper.

One wild night, the rowdy teenagers ended up robbing Kelly's and injuring Ruby. In fear, Melissa and her friend, Lori, ran away. Taking a bus to Miami, they became instant prey to a pimp, Al, who forced the girls to enter the seedy world of prostitution. Corey and another of Melissa's suitors, Greg, rushed to Florida and phoned Bobbie. She decided to fly to Miami herself—without telling Jake where she was going—because she feared she might have to resort to an unorthodox method to rescue the young people.

Posing as a high-class call girl, Bobbie re-entered a world that was all too familiar to her from her own teenage years. Working for Al, Bobbie delayed her "john" with a slow striptease. Then, to avoid sleeping with him, she phoned the police to alert them to Al's illegal activities. But the plan backfired. The local vice squad caught Bobbie and threw her in jail. Finding out about Bobbie's ruse, Al arranged for the story of her prostitution rap to be published in the papers. A local lawyer took note of Bobbie's photo in the papers and showed up at the jail to bail her out. Bobbie gasped upon seeing her savior—because it was none other than Scotty Baldwin!

Scotty's help so relieved Bobbie that she decided to forgive him his past transgressions. With Melissa and Lori in tow, Bobbie headed back to Port Charles, unaware of the wrath she was about to encounter. A shocked Jake learned of Bobbie's sordid exploits not from his wife, but from the front page of the *Port Charles Herald*. And his worst fears were realized when the courts took away Skeeter and Melissa. Of course, Jake was livid with his wife. Thank goodness for Scotty Baldwin. He offered Bobbie solace and a helping hand when she needed it most. Nearly a decade after they first met, Scotty and Bobbie were closer than ever.

As 1987 drew to a close, Edward Quartermaine received word that his dying cousin Herbert planned to finish out his final days with his Port Charles relatives. Edward was less than thrilled to have his cousin visit. Still, he agreed to renovate the east wing of their mansion, especially after Herbert hinted that he would combine his fortune with Edward's. At the same time, a beautiful and mysterious woman showed up at Robert Scorpio's office, demanding his help in saving a friend whose life was in danger. The mystery woman fled when Robert called the police.

Edward wasn't the only one who wanted to get his hands on cousin Herbert's money. It seemed that his fortune was the object of everyone's desire. His son, Quentin, and Quentin's new wife, Betsy, were among those who wanted a share of the other Quartermaine fortune. Robert was shocked to discover that Herbert's secretary/companion, Autumn Clayton, turned out to be the same woman who begged him for help. Scorpio was attracted by the auburn-haired temptress, whose dark and exotic appearance reminded him of Holly. Still, he was suspicious of her intentions and became intrigued

Edward Quartermaine suspected that Autumn Clayton had something to do with the foul-play death of his cousin Herbert.

when, as she predicted, Herbert suddenly took ill and died.

Robert's suspicion of foul play was confirmed when a medicine bottle containing traces of poison was found in Edward's bedroom—with Alan's fingerprints on it! Even Monica distrusted her own husband because Alan and Edward had the perfect motive to kill Herbert before he could write them out of his will. But the very day that Herbert's body was supposedly cremated, he turned up alive and hiding in a secret room, having faked his own death! Autumn was the only one who was privy to Herbert's plan to test the loyalty of his relatives. Over the last weeks of the year, Herbert snooped on all his relatives from peepholes, observing their irreverence to his death. Consequently, he wrote a new will before telling Autumn that he would reveal himself alive in front of all the Quartermaines. Robert became mystified when he found a new will naming Autumn the sole beneficiary. Then a mysterious person found Herbert in his hiding place and killed him—this time for real! All the clues pointed to Autumn, who was wrongfully charged with murder. Robert succeeded in smoking out the real killer, who turned out to be Herbert's daughter-in-law, Betsy.

Thanks to Scorpio's sleuthing, Autumn Clayton was found innocent. All the fortunes in the world couldn't buy Autumn what she really wanted: the love of Robert Scorpio. But Robert still had not gotten over Holly's death.

Just before the new year, Autumn came to the sorrowful conclusion that Robert would never be able to fall in love with her. The newly rich woman kept Alan and Quentin on pins and needles, hoping they could recoup some of the money Herbert left her. But before any money changed hands, Autumn's former lover Olivier Montand showed up and persuaded her to leave town with him. Bidding a sad farewell to Robert, Autumn departed, leaving the Quartermaines high and dry.

Robert was momentarily crushed by Autumn's hasty exit. Soon, other pressing matters would occupy his time. Far from Port Charles, British doctors released a patient from a mental institution, believing he was no longer a threat to society. The man immediately sent Robert Scorpio a letter which he found curious, but not alarming. It read: "THE SNOWMAN WATCHES EVERYTHING YOU DO."

Robert should have taken heed. Someone was about to settle an old score!

*A*complex man like Robert Scorpio makes few friends and lots of enemies. In the winter of 1988, one of those hateful souls was on a mission to destroy his old enemy: Grant Putnam, who was about to exact his plan of revenge against Robert Scorpio by kidnaping his daughter, Robin!

Grant made his move while Robin was at home with Filomena. But the plan misfired when Anna arrived home and confronted the intruder, who kidnaped her instead! Grant struck and killed Filomena, and left without taking Robin, who was totally immobilized by the tragedy. Unable to tell anyone what happened, Robin clutched a ring Grant dropped during the struggle. Grant didn't care—he had Anna. Taking her to the cellar of a rented bungalow, he threw his victim into a specially constructed chain-link prison guarded by a vicious Doberman. The dog was appropriately named Satan.

With the help of Sean Donely and Police Chief Guy Lewis, Scorpio checked out every possible lead in connection with Anna's disappearance. He put Anna's abduction above all the other cases on the police blotter and excluded Duke from the investigation. As a result, the two men nearly came to blows, especially after Duke overheard Robert say that he was determined to find Anna because he "loved" her.

"She's still my wife," warned Duke, who turned desperately for help to the one person who had the contacts to get to the bottom of Anna's perplexing disappearance—underworld chieftain Victor Jerome! For Anna's sake, Duke struck up an unholy alliance with his former rival, which required that Duke reluctantly rejoin the mob! In exchange for Victor's assistance, Duke allowed the mob boss to store untaxed liquor in the basement of his club. Duke was desperate because he wanted to find Anna before Robert did. Meanwhile, Robin concealed Grant's ring under her hospital room bed, but it was lost when an orderly changed the sheets.

Throughout the early days of the ordeal, Felicia remained by Robin's side and began to break through to her. Meanwhile, Anna, a trained WSB agent, tried everything in her power to escape her clever jailer, but she had to contend with the addi-

tional impediment of the vicious guard dog, Satan. In one desperate attempt to get free, Anna resorted to seducing Grant, then stabbing him with a makeshift weapon. Grant contracted an infection from this wound and became delirious with fever! In pain and bewilderment, he wandered away from the bungalow and nearly collapsed on the waterfront. He was found by Dr. Patrick O'Connor, who admitted the sick man to General Hospital and treated him for pneumonia. Within the hospital walls, Grant tried to get to Robin, but she was too well guarded. Back at

Released from a British mental institution, the still-maniacal Grant Putnam kidnaped and taunted Anna Lavery, whom he kept locked away in a cage guarded by an attack dog named Satan.

the bungalow, Anna broke the lock on her cage, but couldn't leave the cellar because a ravenous Satan was still standing guard. Ever resourceful, Anna came up with a plan to link a wire to the fence so that she could stun Satan with a jolt of electricity.

Meanwhile, the rift between Robert and Duke continued to widen despite Sean's efforts to get them to work together. Robert finally got the break he needed when Felicia mentioned Grant Putnam's file.

"That's it!" he shouted, now setting his sights on finding his old rival—unaware that the lunatic was lying in General Hospital!

After undergoing surgery, groggy but determined, Grant switched ID bracelets with another patient and escaped from General Hospital. He set out for the bungalow where Anna's electrical engineering had managed to stun Satan. She was just about to flee her makeshift prison when he arrived home to thwart her escape!

Putting together the clues, Duke and Robert independently located Grant Putnam's hiding place and rushed to the scene. Ever wary, Robert suspected a trap, but a hotheaded Duke rushed inside with Robert in hot pursuit. Just then, the bungalow exploded! Fortunately, the men were able to get out in time. Grant and Anna were already on their way to a desolate area of the Adirondack Mountains, where Anna made a daring escape from her captor. Hoping to make her way to safety through the freezing weather and treacherous terrain, Anna set out into the woods, only to become hopelessly lost.

Using information provided by Victor Jerome's son, Julian, Duke headed into the snow-covered mountains, but lost his chance to save Anna when his jeep broke down. In a final snowmobile chase, Robert caught up to Grant. In a heart-stopping climax, he rescued the evil killer just as he was about to plummet from a cliff. After subduing Grant, Robert turned to Anna, who raced into his comforting arms, her ordeal finally over! Just then, Duke arrived on the scene and stood in stunned silence as he witnessed the sight of his wife in her ex-husband's arms.

Bobbie and Jake's marriage continued to unravel, and Scotty Baldwin's presence in the brownstone didn't help relations between the Meyers. Their union was dealt another blow when the adoption agency removed their name from the list of prospective parents because of Bobbie's prostitution skirmish in Florida late in 1987. The agency's

decision devastated Bobbie, whose yearning for a child had developed into an obsession, and ultimately drove Jake over the edge. Pushed to the breaking point, Jake considered leaving Port Charles for a time to help Uruguayan flood victims. When Bobbie refused to go with him, he left anyway—without even saying goodbye to his wife. Jake's departure crushed Bobbie—but never fear—Scotty was there to take care of her.

"You can always rely on me, Bobbie," he purred.

To a distraught Bobbie, Scotty had good intentions, but try telling that to Ruby and Terry. They refused to believe that Scotty Baldwin was anything but a two-bit shyster and con artist. Port Charles' old guard—Steve, Audrey and Jessie—weren't sure what to think about young Mr. Baldwin's apparent "new leaf."

Scotty skillfully stepped in and offered to take over Jake's practice. Was this a new Scotty Baldwin? Apparently not! The real Scotty Baldwin was as sleazy as ever! While working as the hospital's counsel, he used his position to pilfer funds from the Tania Jones Daycare Center bank account. At the brownstone, Scotty intercepted a letter from Jake to Bobbie and discreetly removed the last page in which Jake offered an explanation for his actions and expressed his love to Bobbie. Scotty made sure that Bobbie never saw that part of the letter. In Jake's next letter, he asked Bobbie to come to Uruguay and join him. Again Scotty intercepted the note and continued to feed Bobbie's resentment toward her husband. Next, he allowed her to receive one of Jake's letters, but this one had an angry, bitter tone. Finally, Jake called Bobbie and coldly told her of his intentions to remain in Uruguay for two years. Scotty, of course, was there to comfort a devastated Bobbie. Putting the final nail in the marital coffin, he maneuvered to keep Bobbie from receiving flowers from Jake. He then sent and made sure she saw a photo in a newsletter that had Jake with his arm around a pretty volunteer.

"I'm divorcing Jake!"

Scotty managed to hold back a sly smile as Bobbie broke the news of the dissolution of her marriage. Within days, Scotty had Bobbie just where he wanted her—in his bed! When Ruby found Scotty and Bobbie together, she let it be known plainly that she did not approve! Four months passed before Bobbie wised up to Scotty's dirty

A decade after they first met, Scotty and Bobbie got back together for a short time in 1988. Young Mr. Baldwin used every trick in his oily repertoire to sabotage Bobbie Meyer's already troubled marriage to Jake.

tricks. When she did, she tossed him out of the brownstone and out of her life!

After dumping Scotty, Bobbie sought out an "interesting" man that she met in, of all places, a bar. The handsome gent was everything that Scotty wasn't—sophisticated, suave, successful—and married! Trapped in a loveless marriage, Gregory Howard enjoyed his stool-side chats with Bobbie, and she found him comforting and fun to be with. After weeks of "chatting," Gregory finally persuaded Bobbie to go away with him for the weekend, but their plans fell through when a political party drafted Gregory to run for the state assembly. The news crushed Bobbie, who realized that his politics would prevent her from finding happiness with her new man. Once again, Bobbie, her heart breaking, was alone.

Determined to become the queen of Port Charles society, Lucy Coe Jones spent the winter of 1988 sashaying her way through power lunches and charity meetings. Among her many goals, Lucy desperately wanted to head the new Tania Jones Daycare Center. She wasn't happy having a "simple surgeon" for a husband, so she nagged Tony to get a promotion. The only person Lucy couldn't fool was her Aunt Charlene, who saw through every one of Lucy's games. Tony still had no idea that Lucy and Charlene were kin until the day that he came home and found a young man named Colton Shore in his house. Colton, a tall, blond, all-American ex-Marine with an air of spirituality, innocently introduced himself to Tony as Charlene's son and Lucy's cousin. Lucy's cousin? If Colton was Lucy's cousin, that meant that Charlene was her aunt! Tony fumed at his wife for this deception.

"I thought I could trust you, but this proves we don't have a marriage!" he spouted.

With Colton's help, the Joneses eventually reconciled, and Tony even encouraged Lucy to pursue her own career. Maybe she could even get a place on the hospital board. Hearing this, Bobbie warned Lucy she would try to stop her at any cost!

Lucy's pursuit of an esteemed position on the General Hospital board put her in contact with Scotty Baldwin, the hospital counsel. Lucy and Scotty proved to be a match made in hell! Both driven by greed and ambition, it was only a matter of time before they were in each other's arms. At first, Lucy slapped Scotty for kissing her, refusing to believe his admonition that they were "meant for each other." At home, Lucy and Tony's marriage eroded to the point that Tony wanted out! The last straw came when he overheard his wife making nasty remarks about Tony's "late" brother, Frisco.

"This marriage is over," he calmly informed

ISSUES

General Hospital *has a long history of dealing frankly with socially relevant issues. In 1968, Dr. Steve Hardy threatened to resign if the hospital board vetoed his appointment of Dr. Tracy Adams, a black woman, to the hospital staff.*

Two decades later, General Hospital *didn't back away from showing the obstacles encountered by an interracial couple—Dr. Hardy's son Tom and his fiancée, Dr. Simone Ravelle. After they married, Tom and Simone continued to withstand challenges to their happiness. Above, Tom lost his temper and physically attacked a patient who made insulting racial slurs about his wife. Tom's inappropriate behavior, which resulted in his suspension, forced the young doctor to examine his own prejudices regarding race.*

General Hospital *was the first of ABC's daytime dramas to incorporate Asian characters into the storyline. A 1974 story involving a visiting troupe of dancers from Communist China performing in Port Charles led to a forbidden romance between G.H.'s Dr. Henry Pinkham and ballerina Mai-Lin. Again in 1985, a long-term story involved the residents of Port Charles' Asian Quarter.*

Lucy, telling her that he wanted her out of the house immediately.

Still, Lucy wasn't about to give up on Tony! Soon she forced Charlene to allow her to babysit for BJ, hoping she could make one last pitch to convince Tony not to divorce her. But when Lucy was distracted, BJ swallowed a bottle of toxic nail polish remover. In a panic, Lucy rushed the little girl to General Hospital. Tony, Bobbie and Lucy held a vigil at BJ's bedside. When she pulled through, Simone cited Lucy's quick thinking as crucial in saving BJ's life. Tony softened slightly, giving Lucy hope that a reconciliation was at hand! But any hope of resurrecting the marriage ended when Tony threw Lucy's luggage out of the house.

Tom and Simone's relationship fared much better than Lucy and Tony's ill-fated pairing. Thanks to a well-timed snowstorm that stranded them in a mountain cabin, Tom Hardy and Simone Ravelle were able to patch up their differences. Alone together in front of a roaring fire, their animosities melted as Tom proposed and Simone accepted. Audrey and Steve were thrilled and anxious to make wedding plans. Simone feared that she couldn't expect the same positive reaction from her own parents. Audrey ignored Steve's advice to stay out of the matter and invited Mr. and Mrs. Ravelle, Simone's wealthy parents, to dinner. After a tentative start, the evening, reminiscent of "Guess Who's Coming to Dinner," proved to be a delicious hit for everyone. The Ravelles gave Simone and Tom their blessing, and the wedding was on! Steve Hardy, who had been wheelchair-bound due to a ruptured disk in his back, was determined to walk into his son's wedding under his own power. Dr. Tony Jones performed surgery on Steve, whose dream was fulfilled when he walked down the aisle at Tom and Simone's wedding.

After their marriage, Tom and Simone's troubles didn't simply disappear. The outside pressures of an interracial marriage quickly became apparent when Tom lost his temper and punched out a prejudiced patient who uttered a racial slur against his now-pregnant wife. As a result, Dr. Steve Hardy was forced to suspend his son, and Simone, who miscarried her baby during this stressful time, left on a world cruise with her mother. During her absence, Tom fended off the advances of an obsessed patient, Louise Knotts, and reconciled with Simone upon her return to Port Charles.

Unfazed by his cousin Lucy's shenanigans, Colton Shore took a room at Kelly's and instantly became a waterfront hero when he saved Sean Donely's life by lifting a huge crate that had accidentally fallen upon him. After freeing Sean—who escaped the potentially fatal mishap with a separated shoulder—Colton was spotted by WLPC-TV's Tiffany Hill. Tiffany was so convinced that the handsome newcomer had star quality that she gave him his own inspirational TV program, The Colton Connection. Settling into his new life in Port Charles, Colton met and became instantly enamored with Felicia Jones, who was anguished by the news that her husband Frisco was missing and presumed dead.

Felicia refused to accept the news that her beloved Frisco was gone. Colton offered his friendship and, as the news sunk in, Felicia truly needed a friend. Thank goodness for Colton and Sean, who agreed with Felicia that the WSB knew much more about Frisco than they were saying.

As Felicia and Sean gathered information about Frisco's last days, Colton grew increasingly concerned. He warned her against going off to Quebec —Frisco's last known address—because obviously whatever Frisco was involved in could prove very dangerous. Terry and Bobbie tried to cheer up Felicia, who had received Frisco's wedding ring from the WSB. This was a sure sign that he really was gone. As her wedding anniversary approached, Felicia opened a package and was shocked to discover a music box sent weeks earlier by Frisco to commemorate their special day. Initially, she grasped at the hope he could still be alive, but a compassionate Colton convinced her that Frisco must have sent it prior to his death. Felicia finally grieved for the man she loved and, as she did, a fire broke out at the brownstone! She exited to safety along with Terry and Bobbie. But realizing she'd forgotten the music box, Felicia raced back into the inferno to retrieve it. Inside the smoky building, she fell and passed out! Would Colton realize her absence in time to save her? Yes! Racing into the burning brownstone, Colton once again proved himself a hero when he pulled Felicia to safety.

Felicia finally faced the fact that the man she loved was gone. But Frisco's legacy of danger lived on! An international terrorist group, led by double agent Collette Francois, was on its way to Port Charles in search of Felicia's music box—or more

Dr. Tom Hardy felt insurmountably guilty when his wife Simone suffered a tragic miscarriage in March 1988. Simone was injured while trying to break up a scuffle between Tom and a racist patient in the halls of General Hospital.

specifically, its knob, which contained a microchip with invaluable information that Frisco had gathered on the evil group's secret activities. The knob was designed to be opened only with Frisco's wedding ring. Sean realized that Felicia was wearing the ring around her neck and could be in dire danger! He called her to alert her to be careful of the ring—but Collette overheard his message on the tapped phone line. Sean explained to Felicia and Colton all about the knob and the ring, but they had no idea where the knob could be! What they did know was that someone appeared to be following their every move!

The action came to a head at the annual Port Charles Art Festival, where terrorists planned to set off a bomb. But their plans went awry and the leader, Collette, was critically injured! Felicia begged Tony to save her so that they could finally know the truth about what happened to Frisco and where he was buried. Finding the knob—which was glued to a collage displayed at the Arts Festival—

Colton Shore accompanied Felicia and Tony Jones to Quebec where they said their final goodbyes at Frisco's grave.

Colton and Felicia later used Frisco's wedding ring to unlock the microchip. They learned that Frisco completed a masterful mission to expose the identities of an international terrorist group. But there was also a mysterious message from Frisco that Felicia should "Beware of Sanctuary." What could it mean? Perhaps the cryptic message could be answered by Colton, who was suddenly plagued by a series of disturbing flashes of memory. Horrible searing memories which he kept hidden from Felicia as they journeyed back to Quebec, found Frisco's grave and vowed to put the past behind them. In the course of this journey, Felicia and Colton fell in love.

Felicia returned from Quebec, having finally put her memories of Frisco to rest. But Sean reminded her to heed Frisco's warning: "Beware of Sanctuary." Meanwhile, Colton continued to be plagued by troubling thoughts that he couldn't quite identify, and

flashbacks of a beautiful woman from his past. One night, as Colton dozed in Felicia's arms after a romantic dinner, he whispered the name "Arielle" and that he "loved" her. Felicia was shocked to hear mention of a woman from Colton's past just as their own relationship had begun to move forward.

At Felicia's urging, Colton underwent hypnotherapy with Dr. Tom Hardy, who used hypnosis to dig deeply into Colton's psyche. Tom helped Colton recall his affair with a beautiful girl named Arielle. Later, Colton had a very disturbing session with Tom during which he learned that Arielle's friends were really terrorists who had brainwashed Colton to kill Frisco! Arielle was aware of the deception and tried to stop Colton, but, like a robot, he was unstoppable. Colton was horrified to realize that he was the one who killed Frisco. Tom tried desperately to calm him, but Colton was overwhelmed with guilt. "I killed him. I killed Frisco!" he cried, fearing that Felicia would be devastated if she ever learned the horrible truth.

Unbeknownst to Colton, Felicia had overheard his confession and, in a state of shock, obtained a gun to avenge Frisco's death. With fierce determination, she scowled at Colton as she pulled the gun and aimed it at his chest. "Do it! Shoot me. I deserve to die!" Colton cried out. But even with her finger poised on the trigger, she couldn't do it. As she backed down, Robert and Tom came rushing in and averted a tragedy.

The news stunned the entire town of Port Charles. How could Colton have been arrested for murder? Tom visited a dejected Colton in jail and tried to convince him that Frisco's death wasn't his fault. Still, Colton insisted that he must pay for his crime. As his sentencing drew near, fate intervened in the form of Sean Donely. Sean brought Arielle's brother, Etienne Gastineau (also known as Ted Ripley) to town to confess that he witnessed terrorists—not Colton—murder Frisco. Colton was innocent! But he still faced charges of conspiracy until he gave Tom permission to come forward with the hypnosis tapes verifying the fact that he had been brainwashed.

Colton was free! Before leaving town, Gastineau tried to convince Colton that his sister, Arielle, meant him no harm. Still, Colton insisted angrily that he wanted nothing to do with her "wherever she is." In the weeks after his acquittal, Colton quit his TV show and, determined to make a new start, became partners in a marine repair shop. In a strange twist of fate,

Arielle was now sailing into Port Charles on a yacht, the Aphrodite, with her husband, Larry Ashton. Colton became the ship's mechanic. Having lost Felicia—who left for a round-the-world cruise with her grandmother, Maria—Colton was about to cross paths with his long lost love.

At General Hospital, the position of assistant Chief of Staff became available, and both Alan and Monica wanted it. In a heated contest, Monica won the job! Alan publicly offered his congratulations, but privately he seethed and plotted to sabotage Monica's new position. Alan set out to make Monica, her family and the hospital staff believe that she was unable to balance her new administrative job with her surgical and maternal duties. When an exhausted Monica overslept, Alan did not wake her. When their young AJ felt ignored, Alan encouraged him to run away. As a result of Alan's discreet tactics, Monica nearly suffered a nervous breakdown.

Throwing up her hands, Monica "surrendered" her juggling act and quickly quit her new post. In desperate need of a break, she headed for the Green Meadows Spa for some well-needed rest and relaxation. At the spa, Monica got R&R and then some—courtesy of a virile, young tennis pro, Ward, who aspired to give her more than lessons on the court. Monica resisted his flirtatious overtures at first, but couldn't help but notice his lithe, athletic form. She was taken aback, however, when he joined her for a dip in the hot tub! Fearing that she couldn't contain her sexual appetite another second, Monica decided to leave the spa. But when she found out that Alan had left town to seek out his missing nephew, Ned, Monica stayed one last night and made love with young Ward. She tried to leave without saying goodbye, but he vowed to see her again.

Monica returned home from the Green Meadows Spa, but she missed her young stud. Meanwhile, Alan announced that he had found Tracy's son, Ned, and was bringing him home. Monica couldn't believe her eyes when she saw that her nephew, Ned, and her lover, Ward, were one and the same! Monica tried gamely to hide her utter shock and, in their first moment alone, she accused Ned of being aware that she was his aunt when he seduced her at the spa. He steadfastly denied it— then attempted to seduce her again!

"I want you out of this house!" she bellowed, hoping to get rid of him before Alan found out about their affair.

Bridegroom Sean Donely couldn't hold back the snickers upon hearing his bride's real name for the very first time during their wedding ceremony.

MINISTER
"Elsie Mae Crumholtz, will you take"

SEAN
"Who? Who?"

PRIEST
"Ah, Elsie Mae Crumholtz. Isn't that correct?"

TIFFANY
"Yes. Will you just get on with it please!"

Meanwhile, Larry Ashton showed up at the Quartermaines and revealed himself as Ned's father. Ned bitterly rejected him, however, claiming that his father had neglected him for years. Ashton entreated Monica to help him reconcile with his son. Over the next several tension-filled weeks, Monica sensed that Ned was slightly attracted to his stepmother, Arielle, and she couldn't help but be jealous. Nevertheless, she encouraged Ned to make peace with Ashton.

Monica tried to ward off Ned's advances, but her libido was put to the test when she was forced to make a house call during a snowstorm. Alan insisted that Ned accompany his aunt for her own safety—and they ended up stranded together. Libidinous Ned would have liked to take advantage of the opportunity to resume their affair, but Monica would have none of it. Though sorely tempted, she spurned his advances. Returning home, Monica felt a sense of relief and freedom knowing that she had finally gotten naughty Ned out of her system.

Sean and Tiffany made it to the altar—barely. After a wedding day tiff with her groom, Tiffany had to be dragged—kicking and screaming—to the church! Robert Scorpio's love life fared much better. Encouraged by Tiffany to date Cheryl—to keep her away from Sean—Robert was captivated by the brainy and beautiful blonde, who was gravely ill with failing kidneys that forced her to undergo daily dialysis. After a tentative courtship, they fell in love.

Duke and Anna Lavery weren't so lucky in love. Their union suffered when Duke, unwillingly sucked back into the mob during the Grant Putnam escapade, struggled to keep his underworld involvement a closely guarded secret from his wife. But at what cost? Duke's strange behavior and frequent absences mystified Anna. Duke wanted out, but not before fulfilling his obligation to his boss, Victor Jerome, who assuaged Duke with a solemn promise to legitimize his organization. Victor's son, Julian, joined with his father in a quest to clean up the mob, but first they had to squelch the competing Carter family. To prevent the Carter/Jerome rivalry from erupting into an all-out war, Victor ordered Duke to meet the Carters in New York, but the meeting was a trap. Duke was set up by a faction within Victor's mob who were opposed to Julian and Duke's efforts to legitimize the mob. Shots were fired, and Julian Jerome took a bullet meant for Duke. On his deathbed, Julian made a last request of Duke, asking him to help his father clean up the family business. Back in Port Charles, a grieving Victor intended to hold Duke to his promise!

Meanwhile, Victor's brassy blonde daughter, Olivia, showed a strong attraction to Duke as they worked closely together to make Julian's dreams of a legitimate mob a reality. Secretly, Olivia was obsessed with ruling the mob. Only a select few knew that it was Olivia who ruthlessly ordered the hit on her brother, Julian. Now, she was just as driven to get her claws into Duke Lavery, and she would stop at nothing to achieve her goal! While carrying out his mob duties, Duke grew terribly concerned that his continuing association with gangsters would destroy his happiness with Anna. And he was right. When Anna discovered the depth of Duke's deception, she walked out, shattered. And there was Olivia, just waiting to pick up the pieces. One night she used her feminine wiles, and a quart of vodka, to lure Duke into her bed. The morning after, he was stunned to discover that he had slept with the mob princess. Then she claimed that she was pregnant with his child. Mortified and guilt-ridden, he confessed all to Anna, who ultimately forgave him. Their love renewed, she was overjoyed by the news that she was pregnant with Duke's child. Together they united, stronger than ever, and set out to destroy the mob.

Though Robert and Cheryl's romance continued to blossom, Cheryl worried privately that her new lover would discover her past affiliation with the Jerome family. Years earlier, Cheryl Stansbury's first love had been Victor's son, Julian, whom she had never really gotten over. One day, while paying a visit to his grave, Cheryl received the shock of her life when she encountered Julian—alive! In shock, she listened as he explained how his father arranged for him to go into hiding when his life was threatened by the Carter family. Cheryl couldn't bring herself to tell him what she had discovered: that Julian's own sister, Olivia, was behind his "death."

Unbeknownst to anyone, Victor planned to shock everyone at his upcoming birthday party by revealing Julian. Olivia—whose "pregnancy" turned out to be merely a false alarm—focused her venom on Duke and Anna. In a sick case of fatal attraction, she sent a poisonous snake to Mrs. Lavery and even kidnaped Robin for a day. Finally, when she realized that Duke was a "lost cause," Olivia decided to kill him so that he would no longer be an obstacle in her path to gaining control of the mob. But Anna became her unintended victim when she was caught in a booby-trapped elevator rigged to crash. Anna was rushed to General Hospital, where the fall cost her the life of her unborn baby.

Considering her brutal behavior, it was just a matter of time before someone became furious enough to do away with Olivia Jerome. Anna and Duke certainly had motives, as did Julian, Victor and Victor's loyal mistress, Dimitra, who made no secret of her disdain for the mob princess. Cheryl Stansbury clearly had reason to want Olivia dead, especially when she threatened to expose Cheryl's long-ago affair with Julian Jerome. On the night of a combined mob summit and birthday party for Victor Jerome, Olivia was unceremoniously gunned down in her hotel suite. When the police arrived, they discovered Anna holding a gun, standing over Olivia's fallen body. While Olivia lay comatose in General Hospital, Anna was charged with attempted murder. Scotty Baldwin, the new assistant District Attorney, belligerently pushed to convict her, while Anna's attorney, the newly returned Jake Meyer, worked feverishly to set her free. Anna's case looked dismal until the day that the real killer— Dimitra's son and Olivia's one-time henchman, Dino —interrupted the proceedings. In a bizarre, seemingly unexplainable development, Dino, posing as a photographer, detonated a bomb, then abducted Cheryl—whose testimony could exonerate Anna— and held her hostage in a stairwell! Robert saved Cheryl, with some help from Sean and Officer Samantha Welles, and the story behind Dino's attempt to kill Olivia was revealed. Dino was, much to everyone's shock, the illegitimate child of Dimitra and Victor. Dimitra had never told him about his other son, but hoped that once Olivia was out of the way, he would surrender the mob to Dino so that they could retire to Florida. Dimitra plotted the shooting because she wanted her son, not Olivia, to inherit Victor's syndicate.

With the crime solved, the charges against Anna Lavery were dismissed and, shortly thereafter, Olivia regained consciousness and "acting" child-like, she was shipped to a sanitarium.

At the trial's conclusion, Jake Meyer tried to reconcile with Bobbie, who was too hurt and confused to resume their marriage. So he returned to Uruguay, leaving her with a tough choice: divorce papers or a plane ticket to join him. After agonizing over Jake's ultimatum, she chose to get on with her life—alone. But was she truly alone? Lucy panicked when she perceived that Bobbie was going after her estranged husband, Tony. Though both would deny it, Tony and Bobbie had grown closer over the course of the year. He even changed his will to appoint Bobbie as guardian of both BJ and her trust fund. Scott suggested that Lucy forget about Tony.

"How about me?" he asked.

Lucy and Scotty? Hah! Lucy couldn't care less about her lousy lawyer!

Anna enjoyed a joyous reunion with her daughter, Robin, who had spent much of the year in Europe. But when she and Duke were plagued by the press to tell their side of the mob story, the Laverys decided to go off to their cabin for some privacy. Robert tried to cover the hurt he felt over Cheryl's betrayal. Julian tried to persuade Cheryl to run away with him, but she still clung to the hope that Robert might forgive her. When he refused to rekindle their ill-fated romance, Cheryl Stansbury left Port Charles and moved to New York City.

A spunky new woman was about to enter Robert Scorpio's adventurously romantic world. Seeking some solitude of his own, he rented the perfect cottage in the woods. One night, he was rudely awakened from a sound sleep by a beautiful woman with long, flowing blonde hair, pounding a concerto out on the cottage's grand piano. The woman was startled when a sleepy-eyed man appeared in front of her.

"Get out of my house or I'll call the police!" she ordered. "I am the police!" Robert answered!

And so began the tempestuous courtship of the police commissioner and the concert pianist. Katherine Delafield was a renowned—and quite wealthy—pianist and yes, this was indeed her cottage, too. Somehow it had been inadvertently rented to both of them, and neither was about to give up their new digs. Sparks flew as the two hot-headed combatants haggled over who should live there, but they finally agreed that Katherine could use it to practice the piano during the day while Robert was at work. That plan went awry, however, when Robert contracted the flu and was forced to occupy the cottage at the same time Katherine practiced. She pampered him with soup—but only so that he'd get well and leave her in peace. Though they fought like cats and dogs, it was clear to everyone that Robert and Katherine were falling in love!

The Quartermaines didn't exactly welcome Ned's father, Lord Larry Ashton, back into the family fold—especially when he successfully hit them up for money. Deeply in debt, Larry docked his yacht in Port Charles Harbor and set out on a mission to get rich again. Lord Ashton knew just how to regain his fortune. Using an ancient dragon bone as a key, he hoped to locate a long-lost Chinese civilization. Ashton wasn't alone in his quest because several other newcomers were equally driven to get their hands on the precious bone. Among them were Ashton's former lover, the exotic Yasmine Bernoudi, and a mysterious, bearded drifter named Charlie Prince, who took a room at Kelly's and persuaded Colton to give him a job repairing the yacht. The nefarious Domino, a cold-blooded international criminal, using the phony identity of bon vivant Nicholas Van Buren, also came to Port Charles in pursuit of the Dragon Bone. Finally, an enigmatic WSB agent, Darius, was also interested in the quest. In order to find the lost civilization, the rivals needed to acquire three objects—the Dragon Bone, a precious emerald and a map that would lead them to the spot.

Also aboard the Aphrodite was Lady Ashton, who just happened to be Colton Shore's former lover, Arielle. All the time Colton repaired the yacht, he never came face to face with his former flame—until a party at the Quartermaines which Charlene persuaded her son to attend with her. Seeing Arielle across the room, Colton fled. When Colton's shrink, Tom Hardy, learned that Lady Ashton's name was Arielle, he wondered if she was the same woman Colton once knew. "One and the same," answered a troubled Colton, who explained that he still blamed Arielle for involving him with the terrorists and now he "didn't want anything to do with her." Still, their paths continued to cross and a stern Larry Ashton noticed that Colton and the Lady were more than friends.

At the WSB's urging, Sean Donely began spying on the quest participants, and he enlisted Colton Shore to assist in the secret investigation. Both Sean and Colton took a keen interest in Arielle, whose strange behavior forced them to ask the question—whose side was she on? Questioning Arielle's motives, Colton challenged her in a confrontation fraught with sexual tension. Alone with Colton, Arielle confessed that she still loved him. Holding her in his arms, he admitted that he too still had feelings for her. He pledged to protect her from whatever danger there was in connection with Ashton and the Dragon Bone quest. Unbeknownst to them, Felicia had decided to return to Port Charles to resume her relationship with Colton. Arriving at Colton's room, Felicia was stunned to overhear him with another woman.

"I will never leave you again," he promised Arielle as Felicia listened to his every word.

Eventually, Colton and Felicia met face to face and cleared the air. Realizing that Felicia was his top priority, Colton informed the WSB that he was no longer available to do their bidding. Colton tried, as gently as possible, to inform Arielle that he loved Felicia, but the beautiful Greek temptress simply could not accept his explanation. Arielle wanted revenge! Scorned by Colton, Arielle contacted her Uncle Nicholas—really the powerful Domino—and agreed to cooperate in his quest to find the Dragon Bone.

Soon Ned Ashton received a letter from his mother, Tracy, who revealed her plans to visit Port Charles. She instructed her son to be her spy in the Quartermaine household. But Ned didn't want to be involved in his mother's scheme and confided his reluctance to his new girlfriend, student nurse Dawn Winthrop. Dawn and Ned's relationship began weeks earlier—with a bang—when Dawn's car collided with Ned's motorcycle. Monica tried to encourage the romance—in an attempt to squelch Alan's suspicion that she and Ned were romantically involved—but naughty Ned needed little prompting. He was instantly attracted to the pretty fair-haired girl who kept a deep, dark secret bottled beneath her festive facade. When Ned learned that Dawn was reluctant to celebrate her birthday, he and Monica arranged a surprise party for her. Meanwhile, the reason behind Dawn's reluctance became clear: Her adopted mother had recently died and Dawn had come to Port Charles seeking to reunite with her real mother—Monica!

Monica was thrilled when she finally discovered the truth that, after all these years, the beautiful daughter she'd given up for adoption had come back to her. Ned was equally delighted. In fact, he was so thrilled that he bought Dawn a present—Spoon Island—an oasis off the coast of Port Charles. The island and its centerpiece, a spooky old house called Windemere, strangely captivated both Dawn and Ned.

At the Quartermaines, the abrupt return of Tracy Quartermaine broke the sound of silence. With considerable fanfare—and a ton of luggage—Lila and Edward's wayward daughter sashayed back into Port Charles and received a warm welcome from her mother. She received a less than enthusiastic greeting from Monica, Alan and her ex-husband, Ashton. As for Edward, the family patriarch took to his bed to avoid the daughter who, nearly a decade earlier, had left him to die from an apparent heart attack. Soon after her arrival, Tracy was courted by Nicholas Van Buren, who was really the evil Domino. Tracy, ever crafty, revealed to Ashton her knowledge that he was not the real Ashton heir. She knew the truth that he was a bastard! Ashton

shuddered when Tracy looked him square in the eye and threatened to expose him unless he promised to give Ned and her a share of the profits culled from the Dragon Bone quest. But there were to be no profits! Ashton's carefully laid plans fizzled and, eventually, the Dragon Bone disappeared—Scorpio's dog, Friday, buried it—and Sean thwarted the elusive Domino's plans to get his hands on it. Sadly, Lord Larry gave up his quest, but the question remained: Who was the legitimate Ashton heir? Charlie Prince, the bearded drifter, eventually proved he was the real Lord Ashton and, after staking his claim to the title, he moved to England to take over the family estate.

Inside the Quartermaine mansion Edward became so fed up over Alan and Tracy's continual bickering that he decided to get even with his greedy kids. Edward plotted to perform an elaborate practical joke to torment his children. With Ned's knowledge, Edward changed his will—leaving everything to his grandson. Then the senior Quartermaine departed on a fishing vacation to Bermuda—from which he did not return. Edward's plane disappeared over the Bermuda Triangle! The

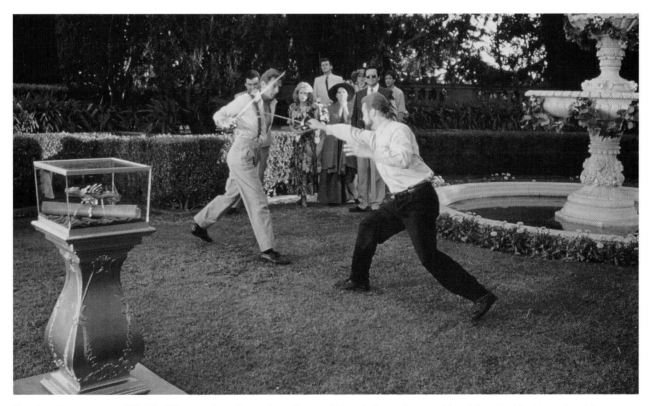

For the denouement of 1989's "Dragon Bone" storyline, *General Hospital* taped a swashbuckling duel between Lord Larry Ashton and his half-brother Charlie Prince on the grounds of the historic Greystone mansion in Beverly Hills. The site often doubles as the Quartermaine mansion.

Classical pianist Katherine Delafield got along much better with Robin Scorpio than she did with her irascible father, Robert.

family grieved the loss of their beloved patriarch, but fumed when they learned that Ned had inherited the bulk of his estate.

Ned became even wealthier when Charlie Prince, just before leaving for England, returned the Quartermaine investment in the quest to Alan, but gave Edward's share to Ned. Alan tried to rally support from the ELQ board members to prevent Ned from becoming the major stockholder, but Ned met with the board also and challenged Alan to a contest: Whoever made the best investments with their two million dollars would run ELQ. May the best Quartermaine win! Alan and his nephew, Ned, waged a nasty war to decide who was fit to rule. Monica was supportive of Ned's challenge, which built a deeper rift between Monica and Alan. Lila remained calm as she talked to Edward's portrait—which talked back! Edward was gone, but his ghost lurked in the Quartermaine mansion, observing and commenting on his wacky clan of greedy ingrates.

Tormented by their fears of what Colton couldn't recall from his past, Felicia and Colton agreed to seek Tom's help. To add further anguish to Felicia and Colton's tempestuous romance, a vengeful Arielle informed them that she was Colton's wife, having married him during their terrorist days. Under hypnosis, Colton recalled that Nicholas Van Buren was at his wedding, confronted him and

learned that Nicholas was Arielle's uncle. Colton wondered what other possible secrets this strange man might be hiding.

After obtaining a divorce from Arielle, Colton and Felicia decided to get married before anything else got in their way. Meanwhile, in a Middle East prison, an unknown man awaited his execution. Guards threatened the prisoner with death unless he revealed his contacts. This tortured man, who was somehow connected to the infamous Domino, eventually escaped his captors and headed on a long and arduous journey to Port Charles. Who could it be?

Where was Robert Scorpio while his friends and enemies were chasing dragon bones? Port Charles' resident super-sleuth was otherwise engaged throughout the winter and spring of 1989 because someone was trying to kill his new "roommate," classical pianist Katherine Delafield. Sharing the same cottage, Robert and Kate got to know each other better when the talented musician gave private piano lessons to little Robin. His relationship with Kate was fraught with sexual tension, especially when they spent an entire weekend snowed in in the cottage together. Alone with Robert, the intensely private Miss Delafield finally began to let down her guard. Kate intrigued Scorpio when she alluded vaguely to a long-distance lover whom she rarely saw. It was this man, dull and dreary archeologist Paul Devore, who showed up at the cottage to rescue the snowbound Kate. The two men, Robert and Paul, eyed one another warily within the confines of the cottage. Robert's nose was a little out of joint, and Paul was clearly jealous of his Australian competition. Once alone, Paul asked Kate to marry him and, much to Robert's regret, she accepted! They planned an engagement party at which Robert covered his true feelings. Yet Anna sensed that her ex-husband cared more for Kate than he was letting on. At the party, an unknown individual slipped poison into a glass of champagne intended for Kate. Who would want to kill Kate Delafield?

Over the next several weeks, someone made several more attempts on Kate's life, forcing Robert Scorpio to investigate. Why was Kate a target for murder? Could the killer be Kate's mentor, Claude Donnet? Donnet claimed to be a recovered alcoholic, but in private he was apparently a troubled man who continued to hit the bottle. Despite the threats on her life, Kate defied danger and continued to live her life as usual—which infuriated Robert.

"Blast it, woman, don't you see? Someone wants you dead!" he told her.

When Kate staunchly refused to heed Scorpio's warning, he took action. Learning that she had several unpaid traffic tickets, Robert issued a warrant for her arrest. "You'll be safer here," he advised, locking an irate Kate in a jail cell. After her release, Kate's car was discovered—burned and demolished—on an icy mountain road. Anna and Sean accompanied Robert to the crash site, where Robert grieved Kate's apparent death.

"This was no accident—it was murder!" he insisted.

Anna, fearing that Robert couldn't see the facts straight because of his personal feelings for Kate, agreed to help him investigate.

Filled with sorrow, friends gathered at a memorial service for Kate. Her fiancé, Paul, grieved in public. But alone with Kate's distant cousin Althea Carruthers, he revealed his murderous scheme to kill off members of the Delafield family to gain control of the family fortune. Sean and Anna uncovered the suspicious deaths of Kate's relatives while Robert read Kate's diary, which had been given to him by her kindly Irish maid, Mary Finnegan. Reading her private thoughts, Robert was amused and saddened to find out that despite her facade of contempt, Kate really cared about him. More than ever, he missed her. Returning to the cottage, Robert was in for a stunning but welcome surprise when he opened the door to find Kate inside waiting for him. She explained how she escaped the car crash and finally agreed with Robert that someone was trying to kill her. With danger in the air, the sexual tension sizzled between them in the confines of the cottage. One night, Robert wined and dined Kate and the overwhelming tension shattered when they shared their first kiss. There was no denying it now—they were in love!

On her way to a concert tour, Kate arrived in Los Angeles to tell Paul that she couldn't marry him because she loved Robert. Hearing the news, something inside Paul snapped! While feigning understanding and compassion, he plotted a way for Kate and him to be together always—in death! He locked her in a storage room at a deserted restaurant overlooking the ocean, then transformed it into an Egyptian tomb. At the same time, Robert finally came up with a lost letter which implicated Paul, then discovered that Kate never went on her concert tour as promised. To his shock, Robert discovered that his fair Kate was in Los Angeles with the man who killed her family! Robert and Sean flew to Los Angeles, where Paul was in the midst of an eerie Egyptian burial ritual. Kate feared that her end was near as she realized there was little hope of talking any sense into this demented man who had trapped her in this tomb-like storage room. Paul locked Kate in an ancient, airtight sarcophagus just as Robert and Sean arrived at the deserted restaurant. Robert chased Paul up a nearby tower, demanding to know where he had hidden Kate. But Paul refused to tell and then leapt to his death! Looking back, Robert saw smoke coming from the restaurant and raced to rescue Kate from the burning room. But the local doctors feared that she might have suffered brain damage from lack of air. A distraught Robert held a bedside vigil, regretting that he never told her how much she meant to him when she could hear. To his amazement, Kate regained consciousness and assured Robert there was never any doubt that she would be all right.

"I'm a close personal friend of the police commissioner!" she quipped.

Robert and Katherine returned to Port Charles, where their courtship flourished, but the virginal Ms. Delafield resisted Robert's attempts at lovemaking. Months later, Katherine finally decided that she was ready to make love, but Anna ruined their plans when she brought Robin to visit her father. Robert and Katherine's next attempt at lovemaking was interrupted by the untimely arrival of Katherine's wacky Aunt Iona, who seemed to be scatterbrained, fun and carefree, but in reality, the elegant old woman was a shrewd manufacturer of counterfeit money!

Anna and Duke prayed that their months of crisis were over. His demented suitor, Olivia Jerome, had been committed to a sanitarium and his turbulent life was seemingly free of strife for the first time since his arrival in Port Charles. Then one day an upset Anna learned that Duke had been called to New York City to give a deposition in the trial of the mobsters, who included Victor Jerome. Was the Lavery nightmare starting again? The Laverys tried to blot out their fears. Still, their worries returned in full force when Duke returned from giving his deposition against the mob and found an ominous warning—a dead canary. As Duke prepared to testify against them, Anna realized that her family might be better off if they entered the witness relocation program.

"Will our lives ever be normal again?" Anna asked Duke tearfully.

He couldn't offer a positive answer.

The Laverys' concern was magnified when they observed little Robin growing up into a young lady. What kind of life would she have under the witness protection program? Should she stay with Robert? The decision was Robin's, and she chose to go away with Anna and Duke. Although Robert understood his daughter's reasons, it pained him greatly to face losing his daughter. After Duke testified against the mobsters the dreaded day finally arrived. Sean and Robert escorted Anna and Robin to the site where they were to meet with Duke and the witness protection marshals. But Duke fell right into a trap engineered by none other than Victor Jerome! Fearing that Anna and Robin were in danger, Duke ran into an abandoned warehouse. Anna, Robert, Sean and Robin arrived just as the warehouse exploded into flames with Duke trapped inside. Duke was gone—or so it seemed.

The elusive Mr. Lavery wasn't dead at all. He was safely tucked away in an underground bunker where Federal marshals convinced him that the only way for him to protect Anna and Robin was to leave Port Charles, assume a new identity and allow everyone—the mob and his wife included—to believe that he had perished in the explosion. Duke, torn because of his love for Anna, finally agreed to leave Anna forever. Knowing that his wife would never believe that he had died unless there was some proof, Duke removed his wedding band for the first time, kissed it and cried.

"Goodbye," he whispered, throwing the ring into the flames of the burning warehouse. Resigned to his fate, Duke allowed the marshalls to whisk him away to his new life.

At General Hospital, Tom and Simone Hardy's marriage reached a crisis point when their pent up anger and jealousies exploded. Simone resented Tom's friendship with a patient, Louise Knotts, and his constant efforts to make everything a racial battle that must be fought. Tom resented how Simone left him for months after her miscarriage and her budding friendship with a handsome black surgeon, Dr. Harrison Davis. After one particularly bitter fight, Tom packed his bags and moved home with Steve and Audrey.

In the painful weeks after their separation, Tom continued to suspect that Harrison and Simone were becoming more than friends. In reality, Simone continually put off Harrison's advances and insisted to Tom that she wanted their marriage to work as much as he did. But everything changed on the night that Harrison lost a patient during surgery at General Hospital. Simone comforted her dejected friend, urging him to remember that the patient's death was not his fault. For one fleeting moment, Simone's comfort turned to passion and she made love to Harrison for the first time. The next day, Tom convinced Simone to give their marriage another chance and they, too, made love. In short time, an alarmed Simone discovered that she was pregnant! Months later, when an agonized Simone gave birth to Tom Jr. she confided her burning question to Audrey: Who was the father of her son?

As Colton and Felicia's wedding day neared, an escaped prisoner headed closer and closer to Port Charles. Colton and Felicia decided to ignore the taboo of sleeping together on the eve of their wedding, but they awakened to a bad omen: ominous thunder showers. And their wedding was to be held in the park! Despite the typical pre-wedding chaos and the threat of rain, everyone showed up in the

In the catacombs, Frisco tried to revive Felicia after she fainted from the shock of seeing the husband she had given up for dead.

park to witness the marriage of Felicia Cummings Jones and Colton Shore. Meanwhile, the escaped prisoner arrived in Port Charles and headed straight for Felicia's apartment, where he became alarmed that a wedding was about to take place. Was his wife about to marry another man? For the first time, viewers saw that the haggard ex-prisoner was Frisco Jones! In a panic, he rushed to the park and arrived just in time to see Felicia say her vows. Frisco's ultimate shock came when he realized that the groom was "Sanctuary," the man who tried to kill him!

Frisco tried to get to Felicia, but he was stopped by two armed guards sent by his enemy, Domino, to kill him. By the time Frisco escaped from the guards the newlyweds were en route to the Lavery cottage to spend their honeymoon. A dejected Frisco lurked in Port Charles, trying not only to evade the guards but to find out how his friends could have left him to die in prison and let Felicia marry a terrorist. He unleashed his fury on Sean and then hid out in the catacombs, where he met a young throwaway girl, Mouse. Finally, Frisco decided that his only recourse was to leave town so that Felicia wouldn't be endangered by Domino. Meanwhile, Felicia and Colton's honeymoon got off to a rocky start when Felicia admitted that she couldn't help but think about her dead husband because it was Frisco's birthday and their anniversary. Colton, very understanding, agreed to return to Port Charles earlier than expected. While Sean and Robert sought out Felicia to break the news to her about Frisco, they were too late. On the docks, Felicia came face to face with her "dead" husband—and fainted from the shock. Frisco scooped the lady of his heart tenderly into his arms and carried her off to the catacombs.

Once the shock wore off, Felicia lashed out at Frisco for not trying to contact her. He calmly tried to reason with her by explaining that he couldn't risk endangering her, nor could she go on thinking that he would come back to her.

"I'm married now to a man I love very much," she told him defiantly.

In truth, Felicia didn't know what she would do, but she knew she needed time alone—to think. Colton was in anguish. "After all we've gone through to be together, how could this be happening?" he asked in amazement. Felicia tried to assuage his concerns, but her conflict was evident. Which man did she love? Or did Felicia love both of her husbands? She confided her dilemma to Anna, who

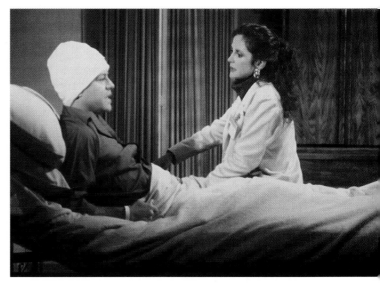

Two brain surgeries left Dr. Tony Jones with severe damage to the optic nerve, and it was uncertain whether or not he would ever recover his sight.

clearly could offer no simple answer. Charlene insisted on throwing a welcome home party for the newlyweds, who were forced to keep up the charade that they were happy despite Frisco's return. After days of agony, Felicia finally made a decision, telling him that while she would always love and care for him, "Colton is my husband now and I intend to stay with him."

With much sadness, Felicia and Frisco made plans to divorce.

Rebuffed by Felicia, Frisco muted his sorrows by devoting every ounce of his energy to putting an end to the threat of Domino, who was orchestrating a sinister plot to overthrow a South American country as the first step in his master plan to take over the world. In the peaceful burg of Port Charles, Frisco shared a warm reunion with his brother, Tony Jones, who was in the middle of a horrible year marred by messy marital troubles. Lucy was driving Tony crazy. In the center of the turmoil, Tony began to suffer terrifying dizzy spells and blurred vision. Tests determined that he needed brain surgery, which he delayed—until it was too late. After a stressful argument with Lucy, Tony collapsed. Bobbie found her fallen friend and rushed him to General Hospital for emergency surgery. Since Lucy was nowhere to be found, Bobbie authorized the surgery, which outraged Lucy, who declared all-out war on Bobbie Meyer! If Tony died, Bobbie would gain control of BJ's trust fund—and Lucy wanted desperately to control the purse strings.

Much to the relief of his loved ones, Tony made

Felicia first encountered Decker Moss while the young con man was working in a small town in Ohio. After developing amnesia, Felicia donned a wild wig and outrageous outfits, and she assumed the identity of Decker's girlfriend, Phoebe.

it through surgery. But the delicate operation had left him blind! Over the course of the spring and summer, Bobbie grew closer than ever to the Jones family, as she lovingly assisted Tony in the care of his infant daughter, BJ. Afraid to declare her love, a jealous Bobbie sat back and watched Tony date his therapist, Valerie Freeman. Bobbie poured her energies into adopting the child she had always wanted. But her devotion to Tony during his illness prevented her from filling out her adoption papers on time. Later, an adoption was arranged, but Bobbie was devastated when the birth mother, Molly, backed out at the last second. Desperate, Bobbie contacted an illegal baby broker who arranged for her to obtain the child she always wanted. Unbeknownst to anyone, Bobbie's newly adopted baby belonged to Tiffany's sister and Robert's former girlfriend— Cheryl Stansbury. Cheryl had given birth to the child and, upon emerging from the anesthesia, she was told that her baby had died. But unknown by anyone, Cheryl's shady doctor had handed the baby over to a baby broker, Clayton, who sold the baby to Bobbie. In New York, Cheryl grieved the loss, then headed to Port Charles, where an unsuspecting Bobbie had joyfully named the miracle baby boy Lucas, after her own brother, Luke.

Meanwhile, another miracle was about to occur on the Port Charles docks. While walking on the waterfront, Tony Jones regained his eyesight just in time to push Bobbie and BJ out of the way of an oncoming forklift. Only Frisco and she knew that he could see again, because Tony wanted to keep the news secret so he could help Frisco in his kamikaze pursuit of Domino. At the same time, Domino pursued the pesky Frisco and planned to eliminate him once and for all using a brainwashing technique applied by Serge, an ice cream vendor. Serge would trigger Colton's urge to kill Frisco by ringing the bells on his ice cream cart! But the forces of justice were making progress in cracking down on the deadly Domino. Robert and Anna found the map which led them at last to comprehend the magnitude of Domino's plans. With Sean's help, Anna risked an exploratory mission to Domino's tanker, the *Sparrow,* looking for munitions on board. Unaware of the visit by Sean and Anna, he rigged a time bomb to explode on the ship. Learning too late that his friends were on board, Frisco watched from the shore in horror as the boat exploded into flames, leaving the lives of Sean and Anna hanging in the balance. Fortunately, Frisco's friends managed to escape the blast. But the explosion infuriated Domino, who sped up his plan to program Colton to kill Frisco.

Colton was livid when Felicia couldn't make love to him because she was so upset over Frisco's latest escapade, which had landed him in jail.

Bobbie's friends shared in a special moment when her newly adopted son Lucas was christened. Cheryl Stansbury was actually the boy's mother.

Colton angrily forbid Felicia to see Frisco, but she defiantly visited him in jail on the day their final divorce papers arrived. To Felicia's surprise, Frisco refused to sign the papers. Instead, he professed his love! Torn by his heartfelt confession, Felicia decided to postpone the divorce until later. Hearing the news, a programmed Colton violently tore up the docks and pumped a round of ammunition into a life-size dummy of Frisco. Soon it would be time to fire his Uzi at the real thing!

In late summer, Colton informed Domino that he was ready to carry out the assassination of Frisco Jones. In a trance-like state, Colton directed his intended victim to a waterfront warehouse which had been modified to resemble a Greek sanctuary. As Frisco entered, the door slammed shut. Domino, watching from the shadows, rang the bells to trigger Colton's brainwashing. In a stunning twist, Colton raised his gun and, instead of firing at Frisco, he turned the gun on Domino! Instantly, Domino realized that his reprogramming had failed! So he raised his own gun and shot Frisco himself! Tony—who had been kidnaped by Domino's men when he discovered the secret of the bells—managed to escape from his captors and arrived on the scene with Felicia, who assumed the worst when she saw Colton, gun in hand, standing over the wounded Frisco. Rushing to her fallen husband's side, Felicia cradled him in her arms, begging him to live.

Tony performed delicate surgery on Frisco and in spite of his many months away from the O.R., he performed with the skill necessary to save his brother's life. Domino was arrested and, after a speedy recovery, Frisco hoped to restart his marriage to Felicia, but she had other ideas. Both Frisco and Colton were stunned when Felicia signed the papers to divorce Frisco but refused to marry Colton. Felicia decided to spend time thinking in Texas with Maria. Colton said his goodbyes to Felicia, unaware that Frisco had taken off and planned on meeting her train when it stopped in a small town in Ohio. Incensed, Felicia refused to get back on the train with Frisco on it. Desperate to hang on to her, Frisco made Felicia believe that his gunshot wound had reopened. She agreed to nurse him back to health as they settled into a motel near the Hat Trick, a seedy bar where a hip young bartender named Decker Moss served up drinks with the help of his flamboyantly tacky female friend, Phoebe Dawson. Decker shared more than a passing

GREAT MOMENTS

In 1989, Tony Jones stunned Bobbie Meyer with a proposal…

BOBBIE
"Tony, what is this? What's it for?"

TONY
"What it is is a ring. And what it's for, it's to become engaged. That's what it is and it has a special wish from me that you accept it."

BOBBIE
"Oh Tony. You're my best friend!"

TONY
"Friends can become lovers. It's happened. I love you, and it is a love different from any love I've ever had, and good and strong and beyond friendship. Will you marry me?"

BOBBIE
"I'd love to marry you."

Dr. Harrison Davis and attorney Scott Baldwin wondered whether Olivia Jerome, mob princess, was really suffering from selective amnesia—or was she simply performing a slick con job?

acquaintance with Felicia because this tough-talking con artist just happened to be Colton Shore's half-brother!

Felicia cared for the "injured" Frisco—until she discovered he was faking. Feeling angry and betrayed, she hit the road. Walking along a dirt road she was run down by a motorcycle driven by Decker and Phoebe. Petrified, they took the unconscious Felicia to an abandoned chicken coop. Phoebe watched as Decker tenderly nursed the pretty blonde victim. And this infuriated Phoebe so much that she bolted. Meanwhile, Felicia shocked Decker when she regained consciousness and claimed to be Phoebe! Suffering from amnesia, Felicia dressed in Phoebe's clothes and took off with Decker on a wild spree of con games. They eventually landed in Atlantic City, where Felicia/Phoebe bought a cameo with the face of Andrew Jackson emblazoned on it from a man named Jimmy O'Herlihy, whom she met at a craps table. Little did she know, but Felicia had just gotten her hands on an invaluable key to an illegal counterfeiting ring run by Katherine Delafield's not-so-wacky Aunt Iona!

Back in Port Charles, Bobbie's friends shared her joy as baby Lucas was christened at the brownstone. A teary Cheryl Stansbury sadly looked on, unaware that Bobbie's precious new baby was actually hers.

After a whirlwind courtship, Tony surprised Bobbie with a very special wedding in Puerto Rico. Terry, Frisco, BJ and Lucas looked on as Bobbie Spencer Brock Meyers added "Jones" to her long list of names. There was another surprise in store for the visitors from Port Charles. Felicia was staying in the same Puerto Rican hotel with Decker. Meanwhile, Colton heard that a woman matching Felicia's description had been sighted in Puerto Rico and he caught the next plane to the Caribbean. Rushing into the hotel, Colton confronted Frisco. Then to their mutual shock, Felicia stepped out of the shadows and revealed herself to them for the first time! Her memory had recently returned but she chose to keep the news secret to prevent her from having to make a decision between the two men. After months of uncertainty, Felicia still could not make up her mind.

Lucy raged when she heard about Bobbie and Tony's wedding. Soon, the former Mrs. Jones' attention was diverted when she began receiving expensive gifts from an anonymous admirer. Having lost Tony, Lucy moved in with Scotty Baldwin. She knew the diamond bracelets and necklaces couldn't have come from him because as Lucy admitted, "Scotty's too cheap!" Besides, someone was being equally benevolent to Scotty, having anonymously paid his rent for an entire year. Who would do such a generous thing? The mysterious benefactor turned out to be imprisoned mobster Victor Jerome. Victor was attempting to bribe assistant DA Baldwin into dropping his case against Olivia, whom Scotty believed was faking amnesia. Figuring out that Victor was his patron, Scotty informed the chieftain that he wouldn't be bribed into dropping his case against Olivia. "I'm going to put your daughter behind bars!" taunted Scott as he returned the money and jewels.

Defying Victor Jerome, Scott fought to have Olivia declared competent to stand trial, but the testimony of Bobbie, Harrison and Tom all worked against him. To Scotty's disappointment, Olivia was declared incompetent to stand trial and was set free. Leaving the sanitarium, Olivia smiled with satisfaction, knowing that she had masterfully pulled off the scam of a lifetime. She was now a free woman—but not for long. Anna was more determined than ever to make Olivia pay for having killed her unborn child. One night she trapped Olivia in the elevator of Duke's club and forced her to make a taped confession of her guilt. A triumphant Anna watched with delight as Olivia Jerome entered a guilty plea and was shipped off to Pine Circle Sanitarium. Though she would escape captivity on several occasions over the course of 1989, Olivia Jerome's long reign of terror against Anna was finally, unmistakably over!

To get over the loss of Tony Jones, Lucy entered into a steamy affair with Scotty Baldwin. But not for long. Soon the two-timing Lucy began romantically pursuing Dr. Alan Quartermaine, who was going through yet another mid-life crisis. At the same time, she was thrilled to receive flowers and notes from a secret admirer. Lucy, believing the admirer to be Alan, sent an encouraging note in return. Soon, she received more flowers and a note telling her to rendezvous at the Quartermaine boathouse. Lucy was shocked when she arrived to discover not Alan, but Victor Jerome, fresh from a jailbreak. "I love you!" he pined. "Run away with me." Flabbergasted, Lucy rejected his outpouring of affection, prompting Victor to swallow the engraved heart-shaped pendant he had made especially for her. Suddenly, the mobster began gasping for air. He was choking! Lucy ran to get Alan, and they returned too late. Victor Jerome was dead!

Lucy and Alan stared in horror at Victor's dead body. In a panic, Lucy convinced Alan not to call the police. Instead, she persuaded him to try getting the engraved locket ("Victor and Lucy Forever") from the dead man's throat. After several unsuccessful attempts, Alan dragged the body off to the Quartermaine family freezer while Lucy secretly pocketed Victor's stash of diamonds. The next day a guilt-ridden Alan phoned Lucy to inform her he would be turning Victor's body over to the police. Fearing incrimination in the death, Lucy lured Alan to a motel, where she seduced him into helping her

GREAT MOMENTS

When Lucy rejected his declaration of love, obsessed mobster Victor Jerome proceeded to swallow and choke on a heart-shaped pendant bearing their engraved names. Lucy rushed to get help from Dr. Alan Quartermaine, but he arrived on the scene too late. Victor was dead.

dump the body in the lake! As they dragged the corpse to the water, Victor's valet, Emil, looked on from the shadows. Back at home, Alan's nervous behavior fed Monica's suspicions that he was having an affair with Lucy. At the same time, Scott was feeling the strain on his volatile relationship with Lucy.

Like loose Lucy, Felicia had one man too many! At Halloween, she attended a costume gala at Windemere—the house on Spoon Island—with both Colton and Frisco, but tried to spend as little time as possible with either since both men were beginning to believe she was faking her amnesia. A carefree scavenger hunt turned into a nightmare for Felicia when counterfeiter Jimmy O'Herlihy, costumed as the headless horseman, began stalking her in order to obtain the cameo which she wore around her neck. Felicia's true love for Frisco was revealed when, faced with danger, she instinctively called out his name for help. "Frisco!" she cried, racing into his open arms. He kissed her soundly as Colton, crushed, watched nearby. During the scavenger hunt, Anna was horrified when Robin and her friend Rowdy stumbled upon Victor Jerome's dead body, which had washed up on shore. Meanwhile, Lucy and Alan shared a sexual rendezvous aboard the Aphrodite, and were almost caught by Monica. Did this stop them? Heavens, no. Lucy and Alan's lusty affair was just beginning!

Robert Scorpio began to suspect foul play when WSB agent Tucker died of an apparent heart attack while investigating a Port Charles counterfeit ring. Soon after, Scorpio's friend, Tangeneva, an Australian aborigine, made his way to Port Charles, where he had a warm reunion with Robert. Tangeneva sent shivers down his friend's spine when he made a shockingly ominous prediction: "Before the year is over, Robert Scorpio will die at the hands of a blonde."

Scorpio ignored the warning as he set out to pick up Tucker's trail and solve the counterfeiting mystery. Eventually, he enraged Katherine by arresting her kindly Aunt Iona, who was indeed involved in some homemade counterfeiting, but she wasn't part of the huge counterfeiting ring. That notorious enterprise, Scorpio discovered, was being operated by Tracy Quartermaine's new lover, David McAllister, and his assistant, blond-haired Jimmy O'Herlihy. The investigation took a deadly turn when McAllister was found with a bullet lodged in his brain and rushed to General Hospital, the victim of an apparent suicide. But after questioning witnesses and discovering a million dollars in missing bonds, Robert and Frisco arrested David's lover, Tracy Quartermaine, on charges of attempted murder. Meanwhile, it had been determined that the heart of the brain-dead David was a perfect match for Katherine's Aunt Iona, who was in General Hospital in desperate need of a heart transplant. Upon hearing this information, Jimmy O'Herlihy began to inwardly sweat knowing that if the heart failed, pathologists might detect the poison he planted in David's after-shave. Jimmy was the culprit who murdered WSB agent Tucker and attempted to kill McAllister. Next, the blond-haired killer set his sights on Robert Scorpio. Was Tangeneva's prediction about to come true?

On New Year's Eve Robert made the startling discovery that WSB agent Tucker wore the same after-shave as David McAllister. On the phone, Robert filled Kate in on his progress with the investigation. Jimmy, who had been listening on the extension phone, decided things were getting too close for comfort and proceeded to poison Robert's after-shave. As Robert prepared for a New Year's Eve murder mystery party at the Windemere Mansion, he poured his after-shave in his hand and noticed the smell of witch hazel. Later, at the party, Robert began to act woozy and, only seconds before midnight, he collapsed down a flight of stairs! Everyone believed that Robert's fall was part of the game, but Sean confirmed that the terrifying tumble was for real. Seeing Robert immobile, Kate screamed in horror! Was Tangeneva's prediction about Robert dying by the hand of a blond before the end of the year actually coming true?

Meanwhile, word reached Julian Jerome that Duke was still alive. Now bitter and vengeful, Julian pledged to track Duke down and kill him! Taking a job in Port Charles, he waited for Duke to return. Duke was at an airport en route to a new safehouse when he learned of Victor's death. Thinking it was now safe for him to live in the outside world, he slipped away from the witness protection program agents.

Simultaneously, Anna, in the same airport, stopped dead in her tracks when she spotted— Duke? Shaking it off, Anna was convinced that her sighting was merely a vision. Eventually, Julian tracked Duke to a clinic in Rio where he was about to undergo cosmetic surgery to change his face. Commandoes sent by Julian arrived on the scene and riddled Duke's bed with bullets. But, once again, Duke Lavery had eluded death, this time by stuffing his bed with pillows to fool his killers! Back in Port Charles, Julian Jerome began to ingratiate himself to Anna and Robin, who were unaware he had accepted mob money to hunt down Duke in exchange for his promise to head the family in Victor's place. One day, a lonely Duke placed a call to his wife, only to have Julian Jerome answer the phone. Crazed with anger, Duke quickly left for home....

1990

Dr. Monica Quartermaine faced the Port Charles press and issued a grim statement. "Police Commissioner Robert Scorpio suffered a massive heart attack this evening. We did everything we could, but were unable to revive him. He was a very dear friend to all of us in Port Charles. This is a tragic loss."

The news stunned everyone. Robert's daughter Robin cried. Her mother Anna held her close. Robert's fiancée Katherine felt faint and Sean quickly lent her an arm. But their tears weren't real.

Sean brought Katherine to the secret room in his penthouse. As soon as she walked in, she saw Robert's dazzling smile! He'd faked his death. He was on to the murderous Jimmy O'Herlihy. Sean had persuaded Monica to publicly pronounce Robert dead to help them trap Jimmy.

Everyone turned out for Robert's funeral... except Robert, who was searching Jimmy's room at Katherine's house. He found David's taped confession about killing Tucker, but no proof Jimmy killed David. And until he did, Robert would let Jimmy think He'd gotten away with his own murder as well! He told Anna what to do.

With Robert "dead" and Anna named "acting" police chief, Anna arrested Tracy Quartermaine for David's murder. Tracy was scared. She was counting on her lawyer, Scotty Baldwin, to come through for her. She knew he'd work hard. He needed her support to be named chief legal counsel for ELQ. Or so Tracy liked to think.

Scott did want the job. His father Lee once had it, and Scott wanted to make him proud by following in his footsteps. But Tracy wasn't the only Quartermaine in town, and Scott always played more than one angle. He also approached Tracy's brother and ELQ rival, Alan, and offered to help him undermine Tracy and her son Ned.

Alan gave Scott a chance to prove himself, if not the job. Scott wanted to celebrate his small victory with his favorite woman, Lucy Coe. But Lucy'd set her sights on Alan, whom she was determined to marry. The way her eyes flashed with devious anticipation, Scott knew Alan didn't stand a chance! But Scott wouldn't let Lucy forget his hold over both her and Alan!

Out of spite, Scott put the pendant that crime boss Victor Jerome had choked on into an envelope addressed to Police Chief Devane and dropped it in the mail. Frantic, Lucy snuck into police headquarters to retrieve it before Anna found it and reopened the investigation into Victor's death.

Back from her successful letter-filching mission, she waved the envelope in Scotty's face.

"Okay, pal, you gave me a scare. But now I've got the pendant. And you have nothing!"

"Guess again, peabrain." Scott smirked. "Open the envelope."

She did, only to find an Oreo cookie! Scotty had made a switch! She wanted to belt him. But his grin turned her anger into laughter. They shared a mad night of love!

But Lucy still wanted Alan. She'd seduced him into bed, but not into marriage. He wouldn't divorce Monica. The ELQ rivalry war and Tracy's arrest had hurt ELQ and the family business couldn't afford another scandal. Alan needed to preserve his marriage.

Monica wasn't making it easy for him. She was completely preoccupied with her newfound daughter, Dawn. As was Alan's nephew Ned. Dawn knew Ned loved her but she kept seeing him huddled with her mother.

A suspicious Dawn finally asked, "Did you and Ned have an affair?"

"No, don't be silly! What an absurd idea!" Monica lied, but her cheeks burned at the memory of her romp with Ned at Green Meadows Spa.

The more Alan tried to show Monica he loved her, the more she gave him the cold shoulder. He bought her a diamond watch. She rejected it...and him! So Alan gave it to Lucy, who never saw a diamond she didn't want. Even after her horrible experiences with Olivia over the Jerome diamonds!

The Jerome crime family, weakened by Victor's death, regrouped under his son Julian, who had two objectives: to neutralize his dangerous sister Olivia and to see Duke Lavery truly dead. Julian knew that

Duke had been reborn in Brazil with a new face and a new name...Daniel Lund. But his men lost track of "Lund." Julian didn't know what Duke looked like, but he knew that Duke would resurface in Port Charles. Then Julian would kill Duke...and frame Olivia for the crime!

Olivia was already facing trial for her crimes against Anna in her attempt to steal Anna's husband, Duke. Anna Devane Lavery despised Olivia Jerome. That witch caused Anna to miscarry Duke's baby! She couldn't wait to see Olivia put away forever, which upset Anna's friend Colton Shore, who was certain Olivia had changed. She could have escaped and left Colton to die in that mountain cabin. But she didn't. Anna was annoyed when Colton posted Olivia's bail.

The more Colton defended Olivia to all his friends, the more in love with her he became. Olivia enjoyed his attention...and his kisses. With Colton on her side, she knew she'd be acquitted. In the meantime, she wanted her rightful place in her father's organization. Julian let her talk, biding his time.

Robert took action. He disguised himself as Katherine's old Russian piano teacher, Maestro Vladimir Diaganoff, and moved into Katherine's house to protect her from Jimmy. He used a doctored version of David's taped confession to gaslight Jimmy. "You killed me. You'll pay." David's voice accused Jimmy of murder! When Jimmy's Aunt Mary, Katherine's housekeeper, found proof of her nephew's villainy, Jimmy snapped and took her hostage. Robert strode in as the old Maestro, enraging Jimmy further. But Jimmy crumpled when Robert revealed himself.

Having captured his killer, Robert "returned to life!" His friend Bobbie Jones felt a little hurt that she wasn't part of the inner circle who knew he hadn't died.

Robert and Katherine set their wedding date, celebrating their engagement with a big party. Everyone showed up and romance was in the air. Frisco and Felicia made plans to remarry. Dawn danced with a very smitten Ned, but couldn't stop staring at Colton's brother, Decker Moss, who stared back intensely!

Dawn's mother Monica was staring at Lucy Coe, who was dancing with Scotty Baldwin, and wondering why Lucy was wearing the very same diamond watch that Monica had refused to accept from Alan! Monica felt Alan had some answering to do, but doubted it was even worth asking the questions!

Lucy loved driving Alan crazy by dancing with Scotty. He'd set her up in their own little love nest. But if she was going to be his mistress, she intended to be mistress of his mansion...as his wife! Still the family man, Alan wouldn't consider divorce. However, when he found the chance, he gleefully forced his sister Tracy to resign from ELQ!

Alan's mother Lila stared at Edward's portrait. "Oh, Edward, look how you've set your children against each other! You should be ashamed!"

The portrait stared back! "Oh, Lila. Watching Alan and Tracy go at it...I never had this much fun when I was alive. Now, where is Jennings with our martinis?"

Lila sat back in her new wheelchair. After a bad fall, she'd opted to live her life in a wheelchair rather than risk an uncertain future by undergoing dangerous back surgery. Her friend and doctor, Steve Hardy, gave her good counsel and comfort based on his own wheelchair experience.

To please Monica, Alan invited Dawn to move into the mansion. But Ned was even more pleased than Monica. His mother Tracy, free of the murder charge, only pretended to accept Dawn. Tracy was hellbent on breaking up her son and Monica's bastard daughter. She asked Decker, her mother Lila's part-time mechanic, to help because she could tell Decker liked

In 1990, Duke Lavery returned to Port Charles with a new face and new name, Jonathan Paget. Sadly, his plan to take Anna and Robin to Scotland went awry and Duke was shot and killed.

After learning from Olivia Jerome that Jonathan Paget was really Duke, Anna rushed to his prison cell where she was joyously reunited with her husband.

Dawn. Decker listened to Tracy and wondered what kind of a family Dawn was getting herself into.

Decker learned about Monica and Ned's affair from his loose-lipped cousin Lucy and went to Green Meadows Spa. Posing as Ned Ashton, he found a security tape which had recorded Monica and "Ward's" assignation. And he met a young attendant, Wendy Masters, who was quite taken by the rich young man Decker claimed to be.

Thoughts of becoming a very rich Quartermaine obsessed Lucy. She knew what she had to do.

"If Alan won't divorce Monica, I'll just have to get Monica to divorce Alan!" Lucy hugged herself with glee as she schemed!

Pretending to be Monica, Lucy hired Curry, a sleazy private eye, to investigate her husband Alan.

"He's having an affair with a rather beautiful young woman," Lucy said, picturing herself, "and I want pictures, lots of pictures...if you get my drift, Mr. Curry."

He got her drift and the address of her little love nest. The rest was up to Lucy—and that night she left Alan breathless.

"How did I manage to spend so many years in such a narrow life with Monica?"

"Oh, Alan!" she cooed, nibbling on his ear.

"Lucy, I knew you were good. But tonight you've outdone yourself!"

And she had!

While Lucy plotted divorce, Monica's daughter Dawn had agreed to marriage...with Ned. Dawn's friend, student nurse Meg Lawson, was thrilled for her. Meg was interested in Dr. Harrison Davis, but he had a thing for Simone Hardy. Simone's husband Tom had moved out after Simone confessed that she wasn't sure if Tom or Harrison was Tom Jr.'s father!

Tom's mother Audrey worried about her son's marriage. Both Tom and her husband Steve still blamed her for not telling Tom about Simone's affair. Audrey told herself they'd come around eventually as she got ready for Dawn's engagement party.

The gala at the Quartermaine's was a disaster. The *Port Charles Gazette* arrived with headlines screaming sex, lust, and scandal...and steamy pictures of Alan and Lucy to back them up! Monica stormed over to Alan and Lucy, who'd come with Scotty, and dumped a tray of canapes on them.

"What the hell is the matter with you Monica?!" asked a stunned Alan.

"Read all about it!" she shouted back, thrusting the newspaper in his face.

Monica also had a few choices words for Lucy. "If you want him, you can have him!"

Alan was speechless. But Lucy, never at a loss for words, told the world how much in love she and Alan were and that he'd only stayed married because of Monica's precarious mental state.

As soon as Monica flew off for a quickie divorce in Mexico, Lucy announced that she and Alan were getting married—a decision that calmed the roiled waters of the once-again-scandalized ELQ. When Monica returned, Lucy was engaged to Alan.

"Alan, how could you!" Monica was livid!

Alan mumbled, "Well, it seemed like the best thing to do for the family business."

"Congratulations, Alan, you finally are your father's son!" Monica's words hurt.

When Lucy married a thoroughly miserable Alan, the bride wore red, fire engine red...thanks to a dress shop mix-up! She looked more showgirl than bride, but Lucy finally was Mrs. Alan Quartermaine.

Felicia was once again Mrs. Frisco Jones. At their second wedding, Frisco wrote his own vows.

"Felicia, the two years I was away from you I realized some things. One is that I love you with all my heart and secondly, you're my life. I want to marry you and I want to be with you the rest of my life. So I'm vowing that from this day forward, I will love you and I'll protect you for the rest of your life."

The newly remarried Joneses honeymooned in Europe. While there, Frisco told her he'd be touring as a rock singer, but he was really on a mission for the WSB. Ross, the WSB head, told him his friends' lives were in danger.

Duke Lavery finally returned to Port Charles... with a new face, a new name, and no Scottish accent. As art dealer Jonathan Paget, he handled Sean Donely's purchase of some rare Chinese porcelain, the Wellington Collection. Duke wanted to go right to his beloved wife Anna, but he knew Julian Jerome was on his tail.

At Jonathan's request, Sean had Anna act as security for the porcelain's arrival. At the warehouse, Jonathan came face to face with Anna. But she was with Julian, who'd decided the fastest way to find Duke was to stay close to Anna. Upon seeing Julian, Jonathan reached for his gun, a reflex which surprised and annoyed Anna. She disliked Jonathan from the start. Julian was suspicious of him.

Anna's daughter, Robin, however, met Jonathan and instantly liked him.

"He reminds me of Duke," she told an irritated Anna.

"That man is nothing like Duke! Enough of all this nonsense."

But Robin persisted. "His eyes twinkle like Duke's."

Talking about Duke unnerved Anna. She pressured an agent at the Witness Protection Program to confess that Duke was really alive with a face altered by plastic surgery. But all traces of him as Daniel Lund had vanished. Anna wondered if he might be the mysterious Jonathan Paget...'til she overheard Jonathan talking with Julian.

"You're Duke Lavery," Julian challenged Jonathan with clear menace in his voice.

Anna held her breath! She couldn't believe what she was hearing.

"No, I am not Duke Lavery," Jonathan lied, sweating bullets. "I killed Duke Lavery in Brazil!"

With those words, Anna's hopes crumbled. Duke died all over again.

Anna arrested Jonathan for her husband's murder. Julian laughed at how Jonathan was charged with killing himself. He never believed Jonathan's lie, and as Julian plotted Duke's demise, he wondered how he could keep Robert Scorpio off his back.

Mark Broxton, the mob lawyer for Julian's late father Victor, assured Julian that they could neu-

Olivia Jerome's reign of terror came to an end in a Port Charles courtroom where she was gunned down by her own brother, Julian.

tralize Robert Scorpio. But Broxton didn't tell Julian about his "Billion Dollar Baby" file, given to him by Victor, who said it contained records of a baby boy born to Scorpio's ex-girlfriend Cheryl Stansbury. Cheryl was told her baby had been stillborn though it had been adopted by Bobbie Meyer who later married Tony Jones. Broxton guarded this information dearly.

After Jonathan was arrested, Robert and Anna refused to believe his story that he was Duke. Julian kidnaped his sister Olivia to frame her for the murder-to-come once he broke Duke out of jail. While being held, Olivia overheard Julian's plan. She had to warn Anna!

Olivia's trial was underway, but the defendant was missing. An angry Anna told Colton she always knew Olivia would bolt. Colton addressed the court with an impassioned plea on Olivia's behalf. Then Olivia burst in, waving a gun!

She'd escaped from her captors, grabbed a gun and rushed to the courthouse. Olivia shouted. "Anna, there's something you have to know!"

A shot rang out. Olivia collapsed. In the pandemonium her appearance caused, Julian had shot his sister and slipped away. Anna rushed to the wounded Olivia, who spoke haltingly, trying to atone for her crimes against Anna and Duke.

"Anna. It's Duke. You must be with him. Go to him. Prison." Olivia passed out. Colton rushed her to General Hospital. His love had changed her. With her dying breath, she told him, "I didn't run. I love you." She died in his arms.

Anna rushed into Duke's arms. After a tearful reunion, they consulted Robert. He felt Duke was safer in jail as Jonathan 'til Robert could safely arrange his escape. Then Duke would meet Anna at the cabin and leave for Scotland with Robin.

Anna and Duke's new beginning was scheduled for Robert and Katherine's wedding day. Katherine couldn't help wishing that Robert had less time for Anna and more time for her. Still, this was her wedding day.

With the prison warden on Julian's payroll, Julian's men were able to break Duke out before Robert's men could. Duke went to the cabin. Julian was waiting for him with a gun. They struggled. Two shots! Julian died. Duke left the cabin.

Anna was leaving to meet Duke when he arrived at her door. She was surprised to see him there. Then, she saw the blood. Duke had been shot, too. But he wouldn't let himself die without seeing her one more time. She cradled him.

"I love you as much today as the first moment I saw you. Promise me, when I'm gone, you'll get on with your life." Anna promised through her tears. Duke died as she rocked him.

News of Duke's unexpected death arrived moments before Robert and Katherine's ceremony.

"If you'd like to postpone the wedding, I'd understand," Katherine offered to a shaken Robert, secretly hoping he'd say "no." Robert dashed her hopes. He kissed Katherine and ran off to Anna.

A few days later, Robert flew to Scotland with Anna, where she scattered the ashes of the man she had loved so passionately. Together, they reminisced about their own marriage and how it had gone so wrong. Shortly after double agent Anna married WSB agent Robert, her DVX partner forced her into a disastrous final mission by threatening to kill Robert. Anna betrayed the WSB and Robert, destroying their marriage, all because of Cesar Faison! How she hated him! Robert reminded her that Faison was long dead and promised that their daughter Robin would never learn of Anna's treason.

Home in Port Charles, Robin found a unique crystal on Spoon Island. She showed it to Tiffany Hill on her television show. In an Alpine hideaway, the noted writer PK Sinclair watched a tape of that program.

Sinclair was fascinated by Robin. "She reminds me of someone," he thought while puffing on his cigarillo. Sinclair was the notorious Cesar Faison, and he wanted Robin's crystal. His assistant, Desiree, entered to report on their "guest" in France.

Their guest was Felicia, who'd been abducted while on tour with Frisco. Sean quickly joined Frisco's search for her. The sinister Faison deliberately led them on a chase right to Felicia, who was being treated like royalty! She hardly felt kidnaped. The food and wine were too good! Then they returned to Port Charles, which was what Faison wanted them to do. He was heading there himself!

Frisco told Sean that Felicia didn't know he'd been working again for the WSB and that he'd tracked down a dying scientist. His last words were: "Lumina. Port Charles. Annihilation." Sean had a bad feeling. Strange things were happening.

One night, Robin's crystal filled her room with a cool, blue light which spread to the workshed across the yard. Inside, in a blazing show of lights and lasers, a visitor arrived. He looked like a man but seemed surprised by his own human appearance. Seeing that he was naked, he put on some work clothes left in the shed and went to sleep.

Robin met the extraordinary Casey Rogers the next day. His arrival made the security alarm go haywire. Neither Robin nor Olin, Anna's housekeeper, could fix it. Casey simply passed his hand over it and it was fine!

"How did you do that?" Robin kept asking, until Casey told her he'd come from another planet, Lumina, to retrieve Robin's crystal and others like it which were from his world. Twelve-year-old Robin instantly believed him. Casey sensed more crystals on Spoon Island. Robin promised to help him and keep his origin secret!

PK Sinclair moved to Spoon Island, renting Windemere from Ned. The Quartermaines welcomed the noted writer with a party.

Lila gushed, "You're my favorite author. I found the exploits of your heroine Davnee in ALPINE EXPRESS quite thrilling!" Sinclair smiled. Davnee, an anagram for Devane, was his favorite creation, and Anna was his inspiration.

Wendy Masters came to town looking for Ned, whom she soon learned wasn't Decker but the man she once knew as "Ward." Realizing that Ned and his fiancée's mother, Monica, had had a fling, Wendy smelled money to be made. She sent Monica an

GREAT MOMENTS

One stormy night, an extraterrestrial was "born" in Anna Lavery's garage. Taking human form, the alien from the planet Lumina befriended little Robin Scorpio.

anonymous note threatening to reveal the affair. Afraid of losing her daughter all over again, Monica returned to Green Meadows Spa to find the blackmailer. Discovering that Lucy had been there, Monica jumped to the wrong conclusion.

Lucy was appalled when Alan told her that Monica owned the Quartermaine mansion. Meekly, Lucy asked Monica if she and Alan could live there with Lila, whom she called "Mother Quartermaine" in a way that set Monica's teeth on edge. (Lila's, too!) Monica, assuming Lucy was the blackmailer, agreed as long as Lucy didn't reveal what she knew.

Since a very confused Lucy didn't know anything, she instantly agreed to Monica's demand and happily ensconced herself in the mansion. Monica and Dawn moved to the Port Charles Hotel. Lucy

generously offered them the use of the mansion for Dawn's wedding, which Lucy was sure would be the social event of the season.

Returning from Scotland, Anna was annoyed by Robin's constant chatter about Casey and the crystal. Robin went to Spoon Island without Anna's permission. Anna went to fetch her, paying a call at Windemere. As Desiree told her she hadn't seen Robin, Anna noticed a cigarillo burning in an ashtray. She reflexively shuddered. Spying from above, Faison was thrilled to learn Robin was Anna's daughter. It was destiny.

Anna grounded Robin for her disobedience and threw Robin's crystal into the trash on the docks. Without the crystal, Casey grew weak. Robin ministered to him in the catacombs. But he was near death when Anna found them there. She rushed Casey to General Hospital.

Casey's illness confounded his doctors, Alan and Harrison. Test results indicated he was dying of old age, yet he looked young! Robin was desperate to find the crystal!

Somehow, the crystal wound up in a lab at the hospital. It caused all the lab equipment to go berserk, delaying all hospital test results, including the paternity test on Tom Hardy Jr.

Tom Jr. gnashed his teeth. He and Simone had gotten back together despite Harrison's intense interest in her. Tom's mother Audrey told them she'd seen Harrison whispering with Simone's mother Pauline. The Hardys didn't trust Harrison, who wanted Tom's wife and child…and Tom's father Steve's job as Chief of Staff! Harrison saw the Casey Rogers case as his big break.

Robin located her crystal and brought it to Casey. Anna and Tom walked in to witness Casey's amazing rejuvenation with both him and Robin bathed in a blue light! They learned the truth about Casey, which Tom recorded in a file. Harrison stole Tom's file and leaked the news about the alien to the press, creating a public scare!

Confiding in Frisco and Sean about Casey, Anna traced the story of Lumina back to an old Air Force file labeled "Extra-terrestrial." They decided to help send Casey back home…though Frisco still had a hard time believing Casey was from another planet!

Helping Casey, Anna returned to Windemere where she came face to face with Faison! Alive! And still despicably charming! Anna reeled. This man could destroy her! Robert, searching for the "alien" who'd escaped from the hospital, found Anna with Faison. He, too, was shocked!

Faison captured Anna, Robin and Casey. He took Robin's crystal and another they'd found and joined them to a third crystal of his own, causing a catastrophic blackout throughout Port Charles! Casey explained that the explosive reaction occurred because a small, stabilizing crystal was still missing. Using his otherworldly skill, he restored the city's power.

Under Faison's orders, Desiree stole the porcelain dog from Sean's Wellington Collection. With Frisco in pursuit, she brought it to Spoon Island. During a struggle, the dog shattered. Robin found the missing piece of crystal inside. Anna handed it to Casey.

"Now you can go home," she smiled. She would miss him. They'd grown close during their adventure. Casey realized how painful human love could be as he said good-bye. He left for Lumina with a parting message: "Be good to one another."

Robert, Sean and Anna feared Faison and his knowledge of Anna's treason. Faison told them he also knew how Sean had deceived Robert and Anna in the aftermath of Anna's final DVX mission. As head of the WSB, Sean lied to them that their friend Swede had been executed for Anna's treason, shattering Robert's image of Anna...and their marriage. Robert became furious with Sean! But Sean wasn't the enemy. Faison was.

To remove Faison from their lives, Anna became engaged to him. She was his Achilles' heel. He commissioned a family portrait of himself, Anna and Robin. She pilfered a gold coin from his pocket watch. It was a piece of the Roman Gold, four coins held by the heads of the DVX. When all the Roman Gold came together, thanks to Robert and Sean's brilliant scheming, the powerful Remondo, Faison's most deadly enemy, was instructed to hunt Faison down!

Robert gave Faison fair warning about Remondo's imminent pursuit.

"Personally, I hope Remondo finds you and kills you. But I'm giving you a chance to save your skin. I'd advise you to take it and leave Port Charles."

Feeling Anna's betrayal, Faison looked at her. He still loved her. But he took Robert's advice and left. Robert and Anna resumed their everyday lives.

Robert's fiancée Katherine transformed Duke's Club into her own nightclub, Delafield's, where she and Frisco regularly performed. Felicia, unhappy to learn about Frisco's renewed WSB activities, left

him briefly, but returned to tell him they were going to have a baby.

Bobbie and Tony's son Lucas became ill and went into a coma. When Dr. Simone Hardy diagnosed juvenile diabetes, Lucas recovered. But Bobbie worried that she knew so little about Lucas's medical history.

But Wendy Masters knew plenty. The little blackmailer went to work for Decker's brother Colton at his new health club, Body Heat, while she put the screws to both Ned and Monica. Ned even began an affair with Wendy to shut her up! When Monica learned about it, Ned assured her it was necessary or Wendy would hurt Dawn—and them—with the truth!

Wendy also began a secret vendetta against Decker. In the end, she was killed...knifed on a carousel! On the day Dawn married Ned! News of Wendy's death reached their reception. Afraid that Ned killed her, Monica confronted him. Dawn heard them talking and learned all about their brief encounter. Her mother and her new husband! She left the reception and ran away with Decker...who became Robert's prime suspect in Wendy's murder. As a juvenile, Decker was convicted of killing a fellow carnival worker in a knife-throwing incident.

While Ned tried to find Dawn, the new mothers-in-law, Tracy and Monica, worried about their children. Lucy felt left out. Nobody, especially Alan, paid any attention to her. She also saw Alan and Monica getting closer when their son, Alan Jr., got in trouble at school. Lucy feared losing Alan...and her newfound social standing.

And so...Lucy told Monica and Tracy she was pregnant! She wasn't. But she was determined to get pregnant! Which wasn't easy. Alan was so annoyed with his greedy wife he avoided her...even in bed!

Lucy tried to vamp her ex, Tony, into bed. But he'd been there, done that and wasn't going to do it again! She nixed a sperm bank as too yucky. Finally, she arranged an assignation with Gunther, a friend of Larry Ashton's.

She entered the dark hotel room. Gunther motioned Lucy to join him in bed.

They made love. Gunther turned on the lights! Lucy gasped!

She hadn't been between the sheets with Gunther. Scotty Baldwin had pulled another switch!

"Gotcha!" He grinned. He really did love this gal! But she wanted no part of him! She was furious...and finally pregnant!

Alan didn't believe Lucy was pregnant…but the tests proved him wrong. Alan groaned.

Harrison also had the proof he needed. The paternity test showed that he was Tom Hardy Jr.'s father. Harrison sued for custody! He didn't want his child raised by an interracial couple like Tom and Simone. To improve his chances, he manipulated innocent Meg Lawson into marriage. They moved into his posh new condo at Willow Shores.

Tom found evidence that Harrison and Simone's mother Pauline falsified the test results. Tom was Tommy's father after all! Simone banished her mother from her life. Steve, Tom's father, instantly fired Harrison, promising that his unethical behavior would cost him his medical license. Harrison turned to Meg for comfort, but her eyes were open. She threw him out!

Meg's friend Dawn, on the run with Decker, wound up in Midvale, where Decker confronted ghosts from his past. Tiffany Hill and her new reporter, Shep Casey—who bore a startling resemblance to the visitor from Lumina—tracked them to Midvale, and so did Ned. Decker fought his old friend Drago who had killed Wendy and framed Decker, as he'd done years before. When Drago pushed Decker over a scaffold, Ned actually saved his rival's life by pulling Decker to safety.

Charlene was happy. Her son Decker was cleared of the murder charge and her other son Colton finally found true love…with Carla Greco, an illegal alien from Santo Moro. Colton helped Commissioner Scorpio safeguard democracy in Carla's country by preventing the assassination of El Presidente in General Hospital. After Carla killed Rico, a man who had raped her, when he was about to kill Colton out of jealousy, Carla proposed to Colton. He lovingly said yes.

Dawn also said yes—to Decker's proposal!—after her marriage to Ned was annulled. Ned still wanted Dawn. When Decker left town to deal with his gambling problem, he left a note for Dawn—which Ned found and forged into a "Dear Dawn" kiss off! After she read it, Ned hoped she'd return to him. She slapped him instead.

Dawn moved in with Meg at the Willow Shore condo which Monica purchased for them from the departing Harrison. When a mystery developed at Willow Shore, Dawn fell ill and was hospitalized.

Alan was sick, too…of Lucy.

"You're the greediest person I know, incapable of any genuine feeling. I'll provide for you and our child, but don't think we have a marriage!" he railed.

Lucy wasn't listening. Lucy had diamonds on her mind. Robert Scorpio told her that in a few short months the Jerome diamonds "tossed into her car" would be hers!—if no Jerome heir was found!

Scott asked Lucy to dump Alan and forget the diamonds. Scott wanted Lucy and their baby. She laughed in his face.

Scott, hurt and angry, confronted Alan with Victor's incriminating locket and demanded that Alan appoint him ELQ's Chief Legal Counsel. In exchange for the evidence, Alan gave Scott the job. Then, to end Lucy's endless nagging about ELQ, Alan withdrew from the company, turning the reigns over to Tracy.

Intent on proving herself the kind of child her father Edward never had in Alan, Tracy brought Edward's favorite stockbroker, Cheryl Stansbury, back to Port Charles.

Cheryl met Shep Casey at the Port Charles Bar and instantly went to bed with him. They became an item, but Cheryl kept fantasizing about her ex-lover Robert. Tiffany welcomed her sister back, helping Cheryl move into a garden apartment in Bobbie and Tony's brownstone.

On Halloween night, while dressed like a clown, Felicia found herself both locked out of the brownstone…and in labor! She tried to climb through a window, but an approaching Frisco stopped her. He thought she was a burglar 'til she said, "Frisco, it's me!" They rushed to the hospital where his brother Tony helped deliver their new baby daughter, Maria Maximilliana. Named for Felicia's grandmother and uncle, they called her Maxie.

Cheryl bonded with the brownstone children, Maxie, Tommy, BJ and Lucas. Lucas was her favorite. Bobbie felt jumpy whenever she saw Cheryl hold Lucas.

"He looks like the baby Robert and I might have had," Cheryl told Tiffany and Bobbie.

Hearing that Cheryl had given birth around the time Lucas was born, Bobbie did a little investigating and was rocked to discover that Lucas was Cheryl and Robert's son! Bobbie decided not to tell anyone, especially Tony! Her straight-laced husband would insist they return Lucas. Bobbie refused to lose her son!

Cheryl had a secret, too. A secret room at the Port Charles Hotel where she brought gifts she'd purchased for Robert. Katherine noticed the way Cheryl looked at Robert, but she knew her fiancé hadn't forgiven Cheryl for her past lies. Katherine thought Robert still loved Anna! Robert and Anna laughed over the notion there could ever be anything between them again. But Robert and Katherine both knew their romance was over. They parted as friends and Katherine left on a long concert tour.

Lucy's breakup with Scotty was hardly friendly. He joined forces with Tracy to break up Alan and Lucy. Tracy had barely tolerated Monica as Alan's wife, but Lucy was impossible! While scheming to find a Jerome heir to keep Lucy from getting the diamonds, Scott and Tracy fell into bed together, surprising themselves— and Scotty's parents Lee and Gail!

A Jerome grandson turned up…in Germany. A music videomaker who called himself Edge. Scott went to Berlin and, baiting Edge with diamonds, lured him to Port Charles. Anna met Edge, didn't trust him and proved him a fraud!

With no Jerome heirs, Robert placed the diamonds in Lucy's hand, and her fist locked tight!

"Oh, I love you, I love you, I love you!" Lucy cooed to each dazzling stone. Then, the IRS agents walked in.

"We'll take those, Mrs. Quartermaine. They should just about cover Victor Jerome's back taxes."

"No, they're mine. Mine, mine, MINE! DO YOU KNOW HOW LONG I'VE WAITED FOR THEM!!!"

Finally, they pried the diamonds out of her grip. Lucy was in shock. Robert smiled at her misfortune and turned to his investigation of the mystery illness at Willow Shore. Robert told Frisco, who was back on the police force, that it bothered him that Victor Jerome's crooked lawyer, Mark Broxton, owned Willow Shore.

Bobbie also investigated Broxton. She discovered he knew about Cheryl's baby…and had Lucas's medical file in his office. Bobbie had to get that file! When Broxton caught her in his office, she pretended to be a condo buyer, not knowing that Broxton knew who she was!

At the hospital, Bobbie's husband Tony was working overtime with a nurse, his ex-stepmother Rita, to find the cause of the Willow Shore "flu." They'd had a fling long ago. Rita was still interested in him.

Tony and Rita found that the water at Willow Shore was contaminated and confronted Broxton! Bobbie dropped an earring rushing out of Broxton's office before they saw her. Rita found it while

At Halloween, Felicia Jones barely made it to the hospital to give birth to her daughter, Maxie. In a madcap adventure, Frisco mistook his wife for a burglar when she climbed through his window dressed as a circus clown!

Broxton stonewalled Tony.

When Bobbie tried to steal his "Billion Dollar Baby" file again, Broxton caught her.

He was through playing games.

"Call your husband off the Willow Shore investigation, Mrs. Jones."

"Even I can't stop Tony when he's determined to…"

"You'll find a way, Bobbie," Broxton leered. "Because if you don't, you and Tony can kiss your little boy good-bye!"

Bobbie was terrified! Then, her missing earring arrived with an ominous note. Frisco found Rita's fingerprints on the earring, but Robert stopped Frisco from mucking up the situation by asking Rita questions. Robert was convinced that Bobbie was mixed up with Broxton!

When Cheryl's kidney condition flared up, she collapsed in Robert's arms. He brought her semi-conscious to General Hospital, where Bobbie overheard her moan, "Dr. Perry, please save my baby!" Bobbie wondered if Cheryl might somehow know that her baby didn't die! Bobbie felt scared…and guilty.

Thanks to Tony's hard work, Dawn recovered from her Willow Shore "flu." Decker returned when he heard she was sick and they reaffirmed their love. But Edge, the phony Jerome heir, had his own plans for the young heiress.

1991

As Dr. Alan Quartermaine approached, Tiffany reached for her husband Sean's hand. She expected grim news about her sister Cheryl's condition. Alan smiled.

"She's passed the crisis."

Tiffany sobbed her relief on Sean's shoulder and went in to see for herself. She was shocked when Cheryl told her about her baby.

"Dr. Perry told me he was born dead. But Tiffany, I heard him cry. My baby is alive! My baby and Robert's!"

But Tiffany, concerned about Cheryl's obsession with Robert, thought that Julian Jerome could have been the baby's father. Which is what Cheryl let Robert believe when she begged him to help her find her baby.

Bobbie reluctantly accompanied Tony to a medical conference in Florida. Tony had insisted that they have this time together because she'd been acting so weird lately. He turned over to Robert his findings about the contaminated water at Willow Shore.

Robert confronted Rita about the earring she sent Bobbie. Rita felt that Bobbie was having an affair with Broxton. But Robert was sure Rita was up to no good. He knew enough about her shady past to persuade her to leave town.

Bobbie panicked and left Tony in Florida. She rushed back to snatch the baby file from Broxton's office just as Robert and Frisco arrived. Frisco saw her leaving and later asked what she was doing there.

Bobbie broke down, telling him the entire story right through her burning of the file. To her astonishment, Frisco promised to cover for his sister-in-law.

Scotty had been covering for Lucy. Having convinced Alan to set up a huge trust fund for their baby, Lucy promised Scotty that he could liberally raid it with her—as long as he didn't tell Alan he was really her baby's father.

Alan's sister Tracy didn't like Lucy manipulating Scotty. Tracy showed Scotty that Lucy was double-crossing him. When Scotty told Alan that he, and not Alan, had fathered Lucy's baby, Alan went ballistic! He started to throw Lucy out of the mansion when she went into premature labor. The baby didn't survive. Lucy lost everything all at once. Her baby, her husband, her mansion. She was depressed. So was Scotty. They planned to sue Alan for assault—'til Alan's mother Lila sent Lucy on a six-week cruise to cool down.

Monica was sorry Lucy lost the baby, but she was delighted Alan had come to his senses about his conniving second wife. Monica shared her daughter Dawn's excitement about Dawn's impending marriage to Decker.

When Ned couldn't win Dawn back, he spitefully foreclosed the mortgage on Decker's brother Colton's health club, Body Heat. Colton moved, with his mother Charlene and fiancée Carla, to the ranch in Santo Moro which El Presidente had given him for saving his life. Decker's new partner, Edge, convinced Decker to buy

A devastating earthquake rocked Port Charles, wrecking Bobbie's brownstone. Frisco Jones valiantly combed the rubble to rescue his wife Felicia and their baby girl, Maxie. Felicia was temporarily paralyzed in the disaster, but rapidly recovered.

Body Heat as home base for a video bootlegging operation. Edge told Decker to tell Dawn it was an advertising agency, happily anticipating the eventual outcome of Decker's lies to Dawn. Edge was alarmed to hear that his old nemesis, Helmut, was in Port Charles and looking for him. Edge had stolen money from Helmut's bootlegging operation in Berlin—and he was out for revenge.

The crooked Broxton worked feverishly to repair the pipes in the catacombs that supplied the tainted water to Willow Shore. When Robert caught up to him, Broxton threw Cheryl's baby in Robert's face. But Robert had already learned the truth. He dispatched Broxton to the justice system and confronted Bobbie.

"I know Lucas belongs to Cheryl, not you!"

"Did Frisco tell you?" a frightened Bobbie cried. Robert was stunned. He felt like he'd lost two friends, Bobbie and Frisco. Robert told Bobbie to turn Lucas over to Cheryl or he'd get a court order to force her.

Bobbie had no choice. She told Tony, who was furious—especially when Bobbie tried to run away with Lucas. Robert stopped her in time and pulled the little boy out of her arms. Tony packed up his and BJ's things. He'd had it with Bobbie's deceit and lies.

"Tony, I won't let you and BJ leave. I won't let you!" Bobbie wailed.

"Don't you dare make a scene," Tony fumed at his wife. "You've done enough already!" Leaving Bobbie shattered and in tears, Tony and BJ moved back to his old house.

Robert handed Lucas to Cheryl. "He's yours."

"No, Robert, he's yours." Cheryl's heart soared. She would have her baby—and Robert! But he wouldn't believe her 'til a paternity test proved it.

Shep Casey ended his one-sided relationship with Cheryl and left town. Bobbie tried apologizing to her, but Bobbie's words only provoked a bitter fight. Tiffany took Cheryl's side against her former friend.

Robert, disappointed in Frisco, fired him from the police force. Frisco told Felicia that he'd quit. He became a Mr. Mom while Felicia worked for Anna and Sean at their detective agency.

Anna was annoyed that Robert greeted Cheryl's news so coldly.

"You know, Robert, you play with women's hearts like it's a hobby. Cheryl. Katherine. You build up their hopes—and dash them."

"Who the hell are you to tell me I'm cold and unfeeling after the way you kept me from being a father to Robin for seven years!" Robert glared at Anna. "You're turning into a prune-faced nag. It isn't very attractive!"

The paternity test proved that Robert was *not* Lucas's father. Cheryl continued dreaming of a life with Robert. But he was so busy fighting with Anna that he never noticed her. Finally, Cheryl took Lucas and moved away.

On Valentine's Day, Robert and Anna's daughter Robin played Cupid by sending them valentines signed with each other's names. They went to Robin's dance recital together, where Anna began playing footsy with Robert. She rubbed her foot seductively up and down his ankle and Robert was turned on. They shared a romantic dinner and went back to his place. She worked him into a heat, sensually removing her long black stockings. Then she tied him up and gagged him with them!

"Do you think I look like a frump now?" taunted Anna. "Do you think I look like an old hag? I'm sexy. I know how to turn someone on. I know how to get dressed up. I know how to tie someone up, obviously! Robert, did you write the book about being sexy? Tell me that. Because if you did, I think you need to look in the mirror. You look quite ridiculous right now." She triumphantly walked out.

Robert was embarrassed when Frisco found him the next day. Yet Robert had enjoyed Anna's little game in spite of himself.

The Quartermaines were waiting for their ship to come in—literally. The fortunes of ELQ, the family business, were sinking. CEO Ned assured the family that the machinery arriving on the *SS Tracy* would revitalize their cannery.

At Kelly's Diner on the docks, Robin Scorpio helped Jenny Eckert and other members of the Greenbelts, an environmental safety organization, prepare to protest the arrival of the *SS Tracy* for carrying unsafe chemicals. When the ship appeared, Jenny launched the protest in a speedboat.

Suddenly, the *SS Tracy* exploded—and sunk! Police Commissioner Scorpio led the rescue effort as crewmen struggled in the Port Charles Harbor. Robert pulled one bedraggled survivor onto the safety of the dock. But as soon as he saw the man's face, he scowled, "You!" and pitched him back into the water!

The man was Mac (Malcolm) Scorpio, the brother Robert never told anybody he had! Not even his ex-wife Anna or their daughter Robin.

As soon as Mac was on dry land, the brothers were fighting. Chief Guy Lewis tried breaking up the brawl. But Mac landed a haymaker on Guy and was instantly arrested. Jenny, who was also under arrest as a suspect

GREAT MOMENTS

On Valentine's Day, 1991, Anna proved she still had what it took to seduce her ex-husband Robert. Then she bound and gagged him!

ANNA

"Do you think I look like an old hag? I am sexy. I know how to turn someone on. I know how to get dressed up. I know how to tie someone up, obviously! Robert, did you write the book about being sexy? Tell me that. Because if you did, I think you need to look in the mirror. You look quite ridiculous right now."

in sabotaging the ship, liked Mac from the moment she first saw him.

Jenny's brother, Bill Eckert, was a crewman on the boat along with their cousin Joey Moscini. When the boat exploded, Joey saved Bill's life. Bill had a head injury and was taken to General Hospital. Nurse Bobbie Jones couldn't believe her eyes when she saw him.

"Luke? Is that you?"

Bill looked like Bobbie's brother Luke. Bill was Bobbie's cousin. Years of bad blood between the Eckerts and the Spencers had kept each side of the family a stranger to the other.

Bill left the hospital and went home to his father Fred, mother Angela and his ten-year-old son Sly, who had arrived in Port Charles ahead of him. The Eckerts ran a successful bakery and coffee shop. Fred hoped

Bill was finally ready to settle down in Port Charles with Sly. Bill had recently divorced Sly's mother Nancy. He got custody because Nancy had no interest in children, unlike Angela and Fred, who lived for their children and were worried sick about the trouble their headstrong daughter Jenny had just gotten herself into.

Monica's daughter Dawn was in grave danger. Helmut and his henchmen tied up Edge, Decker and Dawn and left them to die in Body Heat, which they set ablaze. Dawn was upset to learn Decker had lied. Edge freed himself and bludgeoned Decker and Dawn with a lead pipe, which he placed in Decker's hand. Dawn didn't survive.

Robert rehired Frisco, who cleared Decker of Dawn's murder when he found a videotape of Edge killing her. Decker left town. The police later found Edge's body. Helmut's men had finished him.

As Alan helped Monica grieve for her lost daughter, he and his ex-wife grew closer. Monica moved back into the mansion and ordered her ex-sister-in-law Tracy and Tracy's ex-husband Larry Ashton out of the mansion and into the gatehouse where they could live with their son Ned. The cramped quarters prompted the free-loading Larry to take his leave of Port Charles.

Ned was furious with Jenny Eckert for her part in ELQ's troubles. He fired her from the ELQ cannery where she worked. As her father Fred posted her bail, Jenny said she didn't sabotage the ship.

When Jenny heard the Quartermaines were planning a big party, she decided to show up so she could tell Ned off in front of everybody. She borrowed a "to-die-for" red dress from Wyndham's Department Store, where her friend Patrick worked, and crashed the party. But it wasn't a party. It was a wake for Dawn, Ned's ex-wife. Ned disliked Jenny even more.

Ned told the Quartermaines that the sinking of the *Tracy* was a disaster for ELQ. He hadn't kept up the ship's insurance payments. He didn't notify the Environmental Protection Agency that dangerous PCBs were on board. They lost the machinery needed for the cannery. ELQ was in serious trouble.

Lila turned to Edward's portrait for solace.

Edward's ghost was grim. "Lila, if I wasn't already dead, this would have killed me!"

Alan and Monica could no longer trust Ned or Tracy to run the company. They began searching for someone who could help pull ELQ back from the brink. They found Paul Hornsby, a brilliant businessman and lawyer. He examined ELQ's financial situation and recommended the company sell off some of its assets.

Jenny was cleared of the sabotage charge. Robert suspected Mac was the saboteur. Mac hadn't blown up the ship, but he was working for the man who had ordered the sabotage. Mac called his mystery boss and asked who did it. He got no response.

For assaulting Chief Lewis, Mac was ordered to perform community service in the morgue. There, he met the sprightly Finian O'Toole, a civil servant who managed to do as little as possible at every city agency he worked at—and he'd worked them all. Mac and Finian forged an instant friendship.

Jenny asked Mac to dive down to the *SS Tracy* and get some water samples to check for toxic chemicals. He retrieved the samples for her, and also the tools that would have incriminated him in the sabotage. Robert learned about Mac's dive and arrested him as the saboteur. When Mac jumped bail, Robert handcuffed him and hauled him back to Port Charles on a bus.

Harlan Barrett of Barrett Enterprises came to Port Charles to salvage the *SS Tracy*. He was impressed with Bill Eckert, who invented a unique machine that raised the ship. Harlan hired Bill as chief engineer and promised him a bright future with his company. Tracy Quartermaine was very taken with the boisterous Harlan, and he liked her. He liked all the ladies, but he seemed to be after Tracy.

Lucy returned to Port Charles from her cruise and barricaded herself in Monica's mansion until her lawyer Scotty hammered out a divorce settlement for her. Lucy got 25% of Alan's ELQ stock, and Scott took a third of that as his fee.

As ELQ's financial situation worsened, Bill suggested Harlan buy the cannery. Paul pressed the Quartermaines to sell, but they refused—until arson destroyed part of it. Under suspicion of setting the blaze themselves to collect the insurance, the Quartermaines sold the cannery to Harlan.

As a newcomer to Port Charles, Paul Hornsby kept running into a lively young woman who never failed to make him smile. He saw her at the bakery. He saw her at the Port Charles Grill. Paul decided he'd like to get close to Jenny Eckert. Ned felt that given Jenny's history with ELQ, Paul's interest in her might be perceived as a conflict of interest. But Ned was falling for her himself!

Robin Scorpio liked her new uncle Mac from the start, even if her father ordered her to steer clear of him. But someone didn't like Robert: He was shot at in Wyndham's and trapped in a smoke-filled elevator. Robert and Anna suspected Mac of trying to kill him.

Upon arriving in Port Charles, Mac Scorpio was thrown in jail—twice! First, the sexy Aussie was arrested for punching Police Chief Guy Lewis. Then he was tossed in the slammer and charged with sabotaging the sunken ship, *SS Tracy*.

As Frisco became Robert's bodyguard, Anna began to realize just how much Robert meant to her!

An exploding hockey puck was hurled into Robert's office, gravely wounding him. Anna kept a constant vigil at the hospital. A worried Mac sneaked in to see his brother—and Anna blew up when she saw him!

Robert told Anna that he hated his brother because Mac had deserted him and their parents in the Australian desert after he crashed a plane with all of them aboard. Robert blamed Mac for their parents' death.

Mac was arrested for the attempted murder of his brother. Scott Baldwin was Mac's lawyer, but Jenny asked her new lawyer friend Paul to help Mac, too. Paul went to the jailhouse, but Mac cursed him out. Paul was the mystery man who had hired Mac to sabotage the Quartermaine ship!

Robert made a slow recovery at General Hospital, where Bobbie threw a party for the graduating student nurses. Jenny's cousin Joey, a big flirt, toasted the graduates, Meg and Sheila. But it was Sheila who got his biggest smile!

Audrey was pleased to see another class graduating. But she was exhausted. She'd become a full-time surrogate mother to her grandson Tommy after her daughter-in-law Simone took a leave of absence to work with orphans in Romania. Audrey and her husband, Steve, were happy and relieved that their son Tom stayed behind. Steve still hoped Tom would one day become his assistant chief of staff.

Lucy saw Tom dining with his cousin Scotty at dinner one night and invited herself to join them. Scotty wasn't in a Lucy mood and quickly left, but a lonely Tom enjoyed talking to her. After several meetings with Lucy, Tom woke up one morning in her bed. He felt guilty. He never thought he was the kind of man who could cheat on his wife.

Lucy pooh-poohed Tom's self-induced misery and focused on Harlan Barrett, trying to flirt her way into a job with him. Tracy walked in to see Harlan kissing Lucy and was not amused. She wanted Harlan for herself—until she discovered he was secretly buying huge blocks of ELQ stock, which had gone public at Paul's urging.

Tracy marched up to Harlan. "You rat!" She slapped him!

Tracy, Monica and Lucy, in a rare show of unity prompted by mutual ELQ greed, taught Harlan a lesson by seducing him into great expectations with each of them—and then plastering him into a full body cast!

Robert was released from General Hospital into Anna's care, and they grew closer. Finally the old sparks between them ignited into a night of passion. They made love and the earth moved! Literally.

A major earthquake hit Port Charles. Bobbie's brownstone was a wreck. Frisco had to dig Felicia and Maxie out from the rubble to save them. Felicia was temporarily paralyzed. Tony invited Bobbie to stay with him and BJ. "For BJ's sake," he said. Bobbie accepted. And their reconciliation began.

The quake rattled open the door of Mac's jail cell, and he walked out. Jenny and her nephew Sly hid him in the Eckert basement for a while. Stealing the habit of Jenny and Bill's visiting aunt, Sister Mary Dorothy, Mac left dressed as a nun.

Robert put out an all points bulletin on Mac as Finian helped Mac hide on the docks. Robert heard voices in the catacombs. He thought he'd found Mac, but it was only Joey making out with Sheila! Finally Robert caught up with Mac on a ship. They fought! Tumbling overboard, Mac was presumed dead when no one could find his body. Robert was indicted for manslaughter. Guilty and grieving, he resigned from the police force.

But Mac hadn't died. He escaped to the Finger Lakes with Finian's help. Unfortunately, Finian let Paul Hornsby know Mac's whereabouts, and Paul dispatched Rory, the *SS Tracy* saboteur, to kill Mac. Paul

tried seducing Jenny, but she was thinking about Mac, who had phoned to say he was alive!

Robert became suspicious about Mac's "death" and traced him to the Finger Lakes. Robert came face to face with Mac and a shot rang out. Rory's bullet tore through Robert's arm. Mac fired back, instantly killing Rory! At the local clinic, Mac donated blood to Robert. Lying side-by-side during the transfusion, Robert accused him of deserting the family after the plane crash.

Mac blinked back the tears. "Robert, I didn't abandon you. I went for help." Robert listened as Mac poured out his grief at having killed his parents, and how Robert was gone by the time he could get back. Robert's heart ached as he realized what Mac had gone through. He'd felt it himself when he thought he'd killed Mac. The brothers Scorpio were reunited at last. But they were in trouble—under arrest for Rory's death!

In adjoining cells, Mac confided to Robert that ELQ's savior, Paul Hornsby, had hired him to sabotage their boat, but not blow it up! While Mac and Robert bonded, Anna left Robin with Sean and Tiffany, and went in search of them.

Escaping from jail, Mac and Robert met Anna. They took refuge at a luxurious estate named Serenity, where their beautiful and wealthy hostess Dominique Taub charmed Mac thoroughly. Robert and Anna enjoyed a reunion of their own while Mac tried getting to know Dominique. He could tell she was attracted, but she kept sending out mixed signals. He discovered she was deaf—and very unhappily married.

Mac, Robert and Anna returned to Port Charles. The charges against both brothers were cleared up. Dominique arrived. She'd left her husband and wanted Mac's help because she knew Taub would do anything to force her back.

Finian helped Mac find Dominique an apartment above a closed nightclub. Mac bought the club. Hiring another newcomer in town, a singer named Connor, Mac planned for the opening of The Outback.

Robert and Anna's daughter Robin was ecstatic when Robert and Anna told her they decided to remarry. Meanwhile, Alan Quartermaine Jr., who had started calling himself AJ, began guilt-tripping his parents because they had divorced.

From boarding school, AJ had been calling for—and getting—money from his father, mother and grandmother. Together, Alan, Monica and Lila began wondering why AJ needed so much.

Alan and Monica were informed that he had been caught cheating on his final exams. He ran away from school and was arrested for drunk driving. AJ looked to his unhappy parents for help and put the screws to them. All his trouble, he said, began when they got their divorce. Alan and Monica felt guilty even though they suspected it was a snow job!

When Bill and Jenny's father Fred died of a heart attack, their mother Angela moved to Portland. Jenny returned to Port Charles University and moved in with nurses Amy, Sheila and Meg. Bill moved into an abandoned lighthouse with his son Sly and Finian O'Toole, whom Bill had hired as a housekeeper.

Bill Eckert had become a wealthy man when he inherited land in Alaska worth three million dollars from a man named Willoughby. Bill's ex-wife Nancy, having heard about his inheritance, suddenly wanted custody of their son, Sly. But Bill knew what she really wanted and wouldn't give in to her blackmail.

Lucy made a play for Port Charles's newest millionaire. But as much as Bill enjoyed flirting with her, he wasn't about to give her anything more than a job as his secretary. The worst secretary in Port Charles, as it turned out, but "Miss Lucy" amused Bill.

Harlan Barrett brought his daughter Julia to Port Charles and set her up as co-owner with Bill of the cannery he'd purchased from ELQ. Julia was a hot-shot marketing genius but she didn't know anything about fish oil, Bill observed, as she fell into a vat of the gunky stuff on her first tour of the factory. Bill and Julia fought—a lot! Then they stopped fighting and made love—even though the competitive Julia resented the way Harlan was grooming Bill—and not her—for bigger and better things.

Julia was on Bill's side when Nancy sued for custody of Sly. Scott Baldwin represented Bill—but he also advised Nancy. Scott's pal Lucy had met Nancy on her post-marriage cruise. Using whatever information Lucy might overhear in Bill's office, Scott and Lucy were helping Nancy, who promised them a cut of whatever she could squeeze out of Bill.

On Robert and Anna's wedding day, Dominique freaked out. She flashed back to her own wedding to Leopold Taub, which was when her father had been shot to death. In a confused state, Dominique grabbed a gun and pointed it at Mac, but he was able to calm her down.

With the wedding about to begin, Anna was a no-show. She'd been detained by the unwelcome reappearance of Cesar Faison! He begged Anna to forget Robert and go off with him. Robert found them togeth-

Dominique Taub frightened the guests at Robert and Anna's wedding when she freaked out and pointed a loaded gun at Mac Scorpio!

er, sent Faison packing and married Anna.

Frisco rejoined the WSB and left Port Charles, and his wife Felicia went to work for Mac at the Outback. When Frisco asked Felicia to join him at her grandmother Maria's ranch in Texas, she went and decided to stay there so she and Maxie could be closer to Frisco.

Bobbie's brownstone was restored and she moved back with Tony and BJ. Tom Hardy moved back with Tommy and Simone, who had returned from months of aiding orphan children in Romania.

Tom confessed his one-night affair with Lucy. Simone was angry, yet she forgave Tom. But she got into a real catfight with Lucy the first chance she got.

AJ Quartermaine entered Port Charles University, where he set up a junior league loan-sharking operation, and the kids who couldn't pay him back got roughed up. When AJ became interested in Sheila, he framed her boyfriend Joey for theft, forcing him to leave town.

AJ had a drinking problem and did poorly in school. Quarreling bitterly and constantly with his father, AJ knew he was a disappointment to Alan.

Alan and Monica realized they never stopped loving each other. That, plus guilt over AJ, prompted them to remarry in a quick ceremony at City Hall.

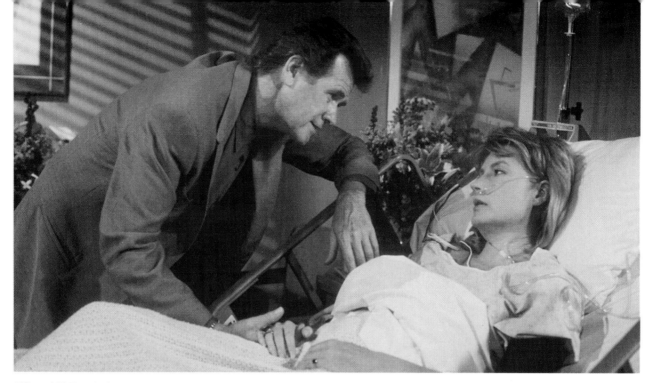

Tiffany Hill Donely fell deathly ill when the evil Faison poisoned her milk with a deadly virus. Faison used the virus to control Tiffany's husband Sean by providing him with a pill that would keep Tiffany alive for thirty days at a time.

Lila promised to give her grandsons AJ and Ned their inheritance immediately—if they could avoid scandal for six months.

Piece of cake, thought AJ, who went bar-hopping one night and fell into the company and bed of Nancy Eckert. She turned out to be the older woman from hell. As their affair went on, she began asking, then demanding, money from her rich young lover, or she'd tell his parents they were lovers. AJ couldn't afford the scandal.

Nancy continued her suit against Bill for custody of Sly. Through Lucy's snooping at Bill and Julia's cannery, Nancy heard about—and later filched—a vial of carbon disulfide which makes people appear drunk in small doses and kills them in large ones!

The carbon disulfide was manufactured in a secret room at the cannery. Harlan Barrett bought the cannery as a front for an evil cartel of global movers and shakers. The cartel, headed by Harlan, Leopold Taub and Cesar Faison, intended to force the world to do their bidding. They'd forced Paul Hornsby to involve himself with the Quartermaines so they could gain control of ELQ and its assets.

The villains had concocted a fatal virus which they administered to Paul's six-year-old daughter, Susan, who lived with Paul's mother. To get the pill which temporarily controlled the disease, Paul had to work for them. Faison also used the virus to control Sean Donely, Faison's old nemesis and Robert Scorpio's good friend.

After Faison poisoned Tiffany's milk with the virus, she became deathly ill. Paul promised to supply Sean with the temporary antidote one pill at a time as long as Sean fed the cartel information about Robert's investigation. After thirty days, the pill would wear off and Tiffany would be facing death all over again!

Sean took the pills from Paul and fed the cartel false information supplied by Robert. Dr. Tony Jones and his new assistant, Dr. Eric Simpson, worked feverishly to find a permanent cure for Tiffany's mystery disease.

Leopold Taub arrived in Port Charles with more than cartel business on his mind. He wanted his wife Dominique back. Taub battled Mac endlessly for control over her. In a struggle with Taub's men, a gunshot restored Dominique's hearing. But when Taub was named her guardian, he had her declared mentally incompetent and committed her to Shadowbrook Sanitarium. Mac, however, was determined to save Dominique.

Faison tried to control Robert and his wife Anna through mind control. He made Anna, under hypnosis, spy on her new husband Robert by whispering the phrase, "Can you hear the waters weeping?"

Faison also hypnotized Robert into seeing images of Faison and Anna making love! Robert began to doubt Anna.

The cartel ordered Paul Hornsby to marry Tracy Quartermaine and take control of her ELQ stock. Tracy was flattered by Paul's unexpected attention and fell deeply in love with him. But Paul really wanted Jenny, who wouldn't give him the time of day—especially after he became engaged to Tracy. Tracy's son Ned began courting Jenny, who loved the way Ned got along with her nephew, Sly.

The cartel's video camera caught Sly's mother Nancy snooping in their secret room at the cannery. Nancy exposed Bill to the carbon disulfide just before he testified in the custody suit. Bill was so disoriented that he lost the case.

In defeat, Bill went out and got really drunk. Robert, reeling from images of Anna and Faison, was on a bender, too. He and Bill bonded over booze at Jake's Bar and drunkenly crashed Tracy and Paul's engagement party, where Robert accused Anna of adultery and Bill punched out Paul, who was looking funny at Bill's sister Jenny, Ned's date.

Scott Baldwin felt awful. He had stabbed his own client, Bill, in the back. Nancy gloated. She decided she'd use Sly to remarry Bill and get all his money. And she wouldn't give Scott or Lucy a red cent. Scott couldn't stop her because Nancy could destroy his career as a lawyer. She had a tape of their unethical deal. Hating himself for helping consign the boy to his monster of a mother, Scott became a good friend of Sly's.

Barrett and Taub told Faison that Nancy Eckert had to be eliminated. She was not only snooping, she was distracting Bill, Harlan's pick as a new major player in their cartel. Faison tried to hypnotize Anna to kill Nancy. But Anna and Robert had become wise to Faison's mind control. With Tom Hardy's psychiatric help, they became immune to it.

It was a dark and stormy night—and Bill's lighthouse was a busy place. When Nancy showed up for a meeting with Bill, AJ was lurking nearby. Scotty came and went. So did Lucy. And Bill's girlfriend Julia. And Faison. When the night ended, so did Nancy's life.

AJ was sweating bullets. He hoped Sheila would lie and provide an alibi for him. When she didn't, he had a friend rough her up. Sheila's friend, Eric Simpson, urged her to tell the truth, and AJ was hauled in for questioning. Scott and Lucy also sweated out the investigation.

When Bill was charged with the murder, Sly was devastated. Bill looked at his son and said, "I'm so sorry, Jellybean. I swear I didn't do this to your mother."

Robert didn't really think Bill did it, so when he arrested Bill he asked him to go undercover with the cartel. Bill agreed. Robert gathered all the murder suspects at the lighthouse and forced Nancy's killer to come forward. It was Finian O'Toole! He'd argued with Nancy about her taking Sly from Bill and had accidentally killed her.

Alan and Monica found out about AJ's involvement with Nancy and insisted that he get his life together. They forced him to work at the hospital as an orderly and Lila cut off AJ's inheritance.

"Tough luck, cuz!" Ned laughed in his cousin AJ's face.

Learning of Lucy and Scott's involvement with Nancy, Bill fired Lucy and had Scotty's license to practice law suspended for six months.

Harlan introduced Bill into the cartel. Taub, Barrett and Faison told Bill he had to prove himself. His assignment: Kill Robert Scorpio!

Robert and Bill staged the scene for Harlan's benefit. Bill "shot" Robert on the docks. Harlan sauntered over to them.

"Nice work," said Harlan. "But you know, I'm funny about these things. Let's give him another bullet just to make sure."

Bill was horrified when Harlan aimed his gun at Robert's head. To save his friend, Bill shot Harlan dead!

Bill's romance with Harlan's daughter Julia had become intense. But it was over the instant he told her he'd killed her father to save Scorpio's life. She couldn't believe her dad was a bad guy.

Paul begged the cartel to let him out but they wouldn't. As ordered, Paul married Tracy, but on their honeymoon, Tracy felt Paul pull away from her. She wondered if he found her repulsive because she was older than him. The more Tracy tried to seduce Paul, the guiltier he felt about deceiving her and the more he wanted to be with Jenny. Paul reluctantly slept with his wife and settled into married life. Tracy

Why the grim looks on the faces of the guests during Paul Hornsby and Tracy Quartermaine's wedding? Perhaps they suspected that the groom didn't want to marry his cold, rich bride. In truth, Paul had been ordered by a secret cartel to marry Tracy and take control of her ELQ stock.

Robert Scorpio held his brother Mac back from attacking Leopold Taub who, after being named his wife Dominique's guardian, had her committed to a sanitarium. Mac vowed to set Dominique free!

didn't like seeing her son Ned pant after Jenny Eckert. She despised that girl.

After Tracy noticed Lila talking with Edward's portrait, she examined the painting and found a letter taped behind it. A letter from Edward. In it, he described how he'd refused to do business with the cartel. He feared they might try to kill him.

Anna learned that Edward's plane accident two years earlier had been no accident. Upon investigating, she discovered that Edward was alive, living in the Bahamas as a beach bum named Hank! Until recently he'd had amnesia. When his memory returned he had stayed away to protect the family. But Anna returned Edward to his loved ones.

Lila's eyes sparkled to see her husband. "I never believed you were dead! You were always alive in my heart!" Edward kissed her.

"And now, my boy," Edward turned to his grandson Ned, "let's see about saving ELQ!"

When Paul failed to get control of Tracy's ELQ stock, Faison ordered him to kill her so he'd inherit it. Paul refused, grabbing the virus vial which had put both Sean and him into the cartel's power. Faison stabbed Paul, who got away.

As Dr. Monica Quartermaine operated on Paul, she heard him mumble, "I love you, Jenny." Tracy was annoyed when Jenny joined her vigil for Paul at the hospital. Jenny told Paul she loved him, too, but his marriage to Tracy made their love impossible.

Using both the virus and the pills he got from Sean, Tony found a permanent cure for Sean's wife Tiffany and Paul's daughter Susan.

The Founder's Day event in Port Charles was hosted by Steve and Audrey Hardy, and everybody was there. Faison and Taub planned to test their carbon disulfide by killing them all. Faison unleashed the dead-

ly gas through the balloons. One by one everyone passed out. A deathly stillness filled the room.

As Faison and Taub toasted their success, Robert and the WSB arrested them. Scorpio had figured out their plan and asked the gala guests to play dead!

Faison looked at Anna. "We will meet again." he assured her. In a daring escape attempt, Faison got away, but Taub was killed.

Released from Shadowbrook, Dominique returned to Port Charles as a very wealthy widow. She hoped to pick up her relationship with Mac. He was impressed with her new independence.

Mac's friend, Connor Olivera, was an illegal alien from Mexico. Connor was searching for El Patron, an American whom he suspected was his father. Sean, who was once called by that name in Mexico, confided in Robert that he might be Connor's father.

The truth about Paul's marriage to Tracy was revealed. Sean helped clear Paul of criminal charges by explaining that he had been coerced. Paul asked for a divorce, but Tracy refused. With Edward's backing, Ned retained control of ELQ over Paul. Ned kept an eye on his new stepfather. When Ned saw Paul kiss Jenny, he warned him about hurting Tracy. Then Ned proposed to Jenny—and Tracy had a fit!

AJ tried to make up with Sheila, but when she began dating Dr. Eric Simpson, he planted drugs in Simpson's locker.

Alan and Monica's other son, Jason, came home from boarding school for good. AJ took pleasure in reminding his brother that he was Alan's illegitimate offspring. But Jason was as generous in spirit as AJ was mean-minded, and forgave him.

Anna, Robert and all their friends received mysterious packages containing initials in the mail. They were alarmed to realize the ominous message the initials spelled: FAISON KILLS.

In her dinky room above Kelly's Diner, Lucy was growing flowers. Her landlady Ruby thought she was growing pot. But Lucy had begun to market her own perfume line.

"After all, who knows more about perfume than I do!" she told Scotty.

With his help, she developed a scent which attracted many investors, from Steve Hardy to Ruby herself. At Christmas, Scotty surprised her with a prototype bottle for her new product. She told him she was naming her perfume "Deception."

"Well, who knows more about 'deception' than you," Scotty smiled. And they kissed.

1992

Alan and Monica Quartermaine hoped their son AJ would straighten out his life after confessing how he'd planted drugs in Dr. Eric Simpson's locker. They were grateful their friend Steve Hardy had decided that dismissing AJ as an orderly at the hospital was punishment enough.

Drinking heavily, AJ went for a joy ride in Alan's car.

At the same time, AJ's younger brother Jason was helping a rescue team drag scores of injured people from a plane crash. Doctors Alan and Monica were treating the survivors at the hospital when the police called Alan. AJ had driven into a ditch and was arrested for drunken driving. At the police station, Alan was relieved to see that AJ was okay, and AJ was relieved to see Alan.

"Can you believe they arrested me! Dad, you've got to bail me out!"

"No. Maybe a night in jail is what you need." Alan walked out on his son.

Monica was already operating on crash victim "John Doe" when she got her first look at his face. She gasped. Her hand slipped. Surgical nurse Bobbie Jones quickly steadied her. But the patient's aorta ruptured. Monica wasn't sure if her scalpel had caused it. Finishing the operation, she asked her assistant, Eric Simpson, to close for her.

Monica had recognized "John Doe" as David Langton, a world-famous humanitarian. In her college

years, he had been her first love. When he left for Vietnam, she remained in school and never told him they'd had a daughter, Dawn. Flashing back, Monica recalled how he called her "Nikki." No one had ever called her that before—or since.

Robert Scorpio was also shocked by the return of a lost love. He'd gone to Dominique Taub's New York City apartment where she was throwing a birthday bash for his brother Mac. While there, during a blackout, he saw Dominique's mysterious new neighbor, Sabrina, by candlelight and couldn't believe his eyes! Robert gazed at the strikingly beautiful visage of a woman he knew all too well.

"Holly?"

Sabrina bolted before Robert could say anymore. Sabrina was Robert's late wife, Holly! When he finally caught up with her, Holly informed her stunned former mate that she hadn't died in a plane crash in Australia after all. She had actually gone to England to see her family and had been in a car accident that left her in a lingering coma. When she finally recovered years later, Holly was horrified to hear that Robert had remarried his first love, Anna. Choosing not to unsettle his life, Holly made the painful decision to stay away from Robert.

Having returned to her deliciously wicked Sutton family, Holly was running a scam with her cousin Barry. They were after the Sphinx stamp in Dominique's collection for a mysterious client who hadn't told them why he wanted it.

When Robert returned to Port Charles, Anna was missing. She had gone to confront the parents of a bully who'd been pestering Robin at school. It was a trap. Once again, Anna faced Cesar Faison!

"I told you we were meant to be together, Anna!"

She tried to escape but Faison knocked her out and carried her off.

Robert knew Faison was behind Anna's disappearance. He refused to believe the note from Anna telling him that she loved Faison.

Faison knew that Anna would never be happy without her daughter. He became as determined to kidnap Robin as Robert was to find his wife.

Scorpio learned from Sean Donely that the WSB

Good guy Jason Quartermaine always provided a helping hand to his alcoholic brother, AJ. AJ especially needed his brother's love when he was left at the altar by his bride-to-be, Nikki. This abandonment nearly destroyed AJ, sending him to the brink of suicide, then to an alcohol rehab clinic.

On their wedding night, Jenny Ashton got a lesson in love-making from her groom, Ned. Little did Ned know that years earlier, his "virgin" bride had miscarried a baby fathered by prominent Senator Jack Kensington.

was also after Anna for her past activities as a double agent. If they found her, they'd kill her.

Sean found proof that he was Connor Olivera's father. As Connor was about to be deported as an illegal alien, Sean stepped forward. The son of an American, Connor was allowed to stay in the U.S. Sean's wife Tiffany welcomed Connor warmly into the family, though Sean and Connor's relationship remained chilly.

Tiffany yearned to have a child of her own—especially after visiting her sister Cheryl and nephew Lucas in Phoenix. She reported news of Lucas to a grateful Bobbie, who still missed the little boy who had been her son.

Bobbie was impressed with a book, *Violence Tamed,* by convicted cop killer Joseph Atkins. In it he described how he'd turned his life around in prison. Bobbie, who'd turned her own life around since her days as a hooker, wrote to him. He wrote back, asking her support in his attempt to win parole. Bobbie's husband Tony hit the roof when Atkins began calling their home. Finally, Bobbie decided that she couldn't support Atkins and told him so.

"You'll be sorry, Bobbie!" When Atkins slammed the receiver down, Bobbie knew she'd made the right decision.

But she wasn't sure about Monica's decision to continue treating her ex-lover, David Langton. Monica confided in Bobbie—and in psychiatrist Tom Hardy, who advised her to keep a journal in which she could sort through her private feelings. Monica took Tom's advice as her husband Alan grew increasingly annoyed with her attention to this patient.

As David slowly recovered, he and Monica remembered their past. Monica met David's grown daughter Nikki, whom Monica felt resembled Dawn. David had named Nikki after Monica, although Nikki didn't know that. And Monica didn't know that David didn't like or trust his daughter very much, or that Nikki only pretended to want her father's recovery.

Monica's sister-in-law Tracy was desperate to save her marriage to Paul Hornsby.

"Divorce me and I'll send you to jail for all your crimes!" she threatened.

"Marriage to you is like being in prison!" Paul responded. He wanted to marry Jenny Eckert. But she'd agreed to marry Tracy's son Ned Ashton.

Tracy despised Jenny, but decided that Jenny marrying Ned would be good for her own marriage. Tracy threw an engagement party for them just as Paul finally convinced Jenny to break up with Ned.

At the party, Tracy grabbed the spotlight from Ned and Jenny to make a big announcement.

"I'm pregnant!" Tracy stared triumphantly at Jenny, who was in shock. So was Paul. Tracy had played her trump card and won back her husband. Jenny told Paul she'd marry Ned after all. And Paul resigned himself to his hell of a marriage to Tracy.

After the party, Ned wanted to make love to Jenny, but she confessed that she was still a virgin. He promised to wait until their wedding night when he would make her first time very special.

The law punished Ned's cousin AJ for driving under the influence by suspending his license, by ordering him into community service at the high school cafeteria and ordering treatment for his drinking problem. Dr. Tom Hardy had a very resistant patient in AJ, who clearly felt deprived of his father's love and approval.

Nikki Langton felt similarly deprived. She felt that her father cared more about Monica, his doctor, than her, his own daughter. Her suspicions were confirmed when she overheard David call Monica his first love, "Nikki!"

In New York, Holly learned that Faison was the mysterious buyer of Dominique's Sphinx stamp. She returned to Port Charles to tell Robert, and to inform him that Faison was also the son of Nanny McTavish, the kindly woman who'd been nanny to both Holly and Anna in their youth. In fact, that was how Faison first met Anna.

Holly and Robert brought Nanny to Port Charles, where she went on TV to beg her son to return Anna. When Faison saw his mother in the park, he roughed her up. Then he made several attempts to grab Robin, but Holly saved her.

Nanny was torn. She wanted her son to be happy. Finally she decided to help Faison get Robin. Robert had planted a tracking device in Nanny's earring, and Nanny led him to Faison. Robert saved Robin but Faison, feeling betrayed by Nanny, shot his mother and got away. Before she died, Nanny told Holly that the Sphinx stamp box contained a microchip with information about the "Nanny Network."

Faison left Port Charles with a flourish of mayhem. To settle his old grudge against Paul Hornsby and the Quartermaines, he planted a bomb in Jenny's bridal bouquet. But Paul, sensing danger, grabbed it out of Jenny's hand and tossed it outside, where it exploded safely. For being a hero, Paul's reward was dubious: he got to see his beloved Jenny marry his stepson Ned.

On their wedding night, Ned made passionate love with his virgin bride. Jenny felt loved and convinced herself that she loved Ned.

Leaving Port Charles to search for Faison and Anna, Robert asked his brother Mac to take care of Robin until he returned, although he doubted he and Anna could ever return because of the WSB threat.

Mac was flattered but concerned. He knew nothing about raising a teenage girl. Robert asked Holly to move in with Mac and Robin, and she agreed.

Upon leaving, Robert told Holly, "You're still my wife, but I love Anna." A few weeks later, Holly received divorce papers from Robert's lawyer. She decided to wait 'til he returned to sign them.

Holly settled into her new life in Port Charles. She and Mac became Robin's surrogate parents. She also worked for Mac part-time at the Outback. Dominique became jealous of Mac's time with Holly. Mac ignored her while he and Holly worked to crack the nursery rhyme code of the "Nanny Network" microchip. When they did, they found a file detailing Anna's life as a double agent. Mac was rocked by the news, which Holly had long known. They agreed that Robin must never know. Together, they used Robert's old WSB computer to break into WSB files. They discovered a "Black Box" around Robert's and Anna's names—meaning that Robert and Anna were as good as dead!

Mac and Holly rushed to Sean Donely, who had been made police commissioner. He reported devastating news from the WSB: Robert, Anna and Faison had all been terminated! Robert had caught up with Faison and Anna on a boat. But rather than lose Anna to Robert, Faison blew up the boat with all of them on it. According to all reports, no one survived!

Tears welled up in Holly's eyes as she tore up her unsigned divorce papers. She still loved Robert.

Mac broke the news to Robin, who took the news bravely. Her parents would have been proud. The entire town turned out to mourn its two fallen heroes.

David Langton's death turned Monica's life upside down. Though she felt close to David, Monica loved her husband, Alan. She gave David a comforting kiss to put their past behind them. David's daughter Nikki saw the kiss and later accused David of loving Monica more than her. Nikki's harangue caused David to have a massive heart attack.

Eric Simpson and Monica rushed to his side, shooing Nikki away. As David died in Monica's arms, he looked at her and whispered, "Nikki, my love."

Eric told Nikki that her father's final words were about her. But Nikki knew better. After her father's funeral, Monica invited Nikki to move into the Quartermaine mansion. Pretending to be grateful, she moved in and began snooping in Monica's bedroom for proof of her past with David. Though attracted to Eric Simpson, Nikki began dating Monica's son AJ to see if he knew anything. When Monica found Nikki snooping, she threw the girl out. Too late. Nikki already filched a page of Monica's journal declaring that she could never love Alan as much as David, her first love.

David died in debt, leaving Nikki penniless, so she decided to charge malpractice in her father's death. She asked Scott Baldwin to represent her without saying why but, since Scott was still under suspension, he recommended another lawyer, Jessica Holmes.

Unable to practice law, Scott helped Lucy Coe launch her perfume line. Lucy sold a major order of Deception to Wyndham's Department Store, promising the manager in-store endorsements from Ann-Margret, Barbra Streisand and Bette Midler. When the manager actually demanded that the celebrities show up Lucy became desperate!

"What am I going to do?" Lucy begged for Scott's help.

"I ought to let you stew in your own mess," he taunted. "But I love you, so I'll get you out of this."

Scott found some ordinary Port Charles citizens who happened to have celebrity names. He convinced Lucy to present "Streisand" and company to Wyndham's. The manager was angry until Scott explained, "Don't you see! That's what we're selling—Deception!" The manager broke into a smile.

Deception became a big success. Lucy hired her one-time boss, Julia Barrett, to manage its advertising. Julia sold her ELQ shares to Bill Eckert in exchange for

Bill Eckert and Holly Sutton sailed to San Sebastian where they fended off bullets, soldiers, sharks and jaguars. But Bill and Holly couldn't escape this trap. The net result? They fell in love!

his half of the cannery. Then she sold the cannery. As a 36% owner of ELQ, Bill became a major mover in Port Charles. He became Mac's partner in the Outback, where he was quite taken with Holly Scorpio. Holly couldn't get over how much Bill looked like her first love, Luke Spencer. Bill also went into partnership with Paul Hornsby to turn the decaying Pier 52 into Pier 5 Promenade, a lavish new shopping mall.

Lucy grew restless quickly. Julia disappointed her by hiring Dominique as signature model because Lucy felt that she herself was the obvious face of Deception. When a big New York City advertising mogul, Gregory Bennett, offered Lucy a fat executive salary to work for him, Lucy jumped! She told Scott she was leaving.

"I love you. You're my best pal, but you know me. I'll always want more. Forgive me."

Scott forgave her—after he tossed her into a fountain! She'd hurt him deeply. He took over all her shares of Deception as she walked out on their contract with a bittersweet farewell.

Scott, Julia and Dominique became partners in the perfume—and close friends despite constant squabbling. Scott began an affair with attorney Jessica Holmes, who was on the State Bar Ethics committee. He hoped she could help shorten his suspension. But he regretted having sent Nikki to Jessica for legal advice. If he had only known what Nikki was up to!

The Quartermaines were celebrating Monica's birthday with a big party at the mansion when the papers were served. Nikki was suing Monica, Bobbie and General Hospital itself for malpractice resulting in her father's death. She excluded Dr. Eric Simpson in

her suit. Nikki had a "fatal attraction" for him. But when Eric continued to choose nurse Sheila Cantillon over her, Nikki sued him as well.

Jessica promised Nikki that if she won the malpractice suit, she could even sue Monica for the mansion! Scott hated what Nikki and Jessica were doing. After he looked into Nikki's past in Washington, D.C., he advised Monica's lawyer to speak with Nikki's old psychiatrist.

Nikki, the tearfully wronged daughter, testified to her love for her father on the witness stand. But she was lying. Her psychiatrist said that Nikki was a disturbed girl who argued constantly with her parents and may have even set the fire in which her mother died! Finally, proof was offered that David had a prior heart condition. Monica, Bobbie, Eric and the hospital were cleared.

Alan felt hurt and betrayed and was furious with Monica when he heard Jessica read Monica's words about loving David more than Alan. But he stood by his wife lovingly throughout the ordeal. Tony supported Bobbie as well, though he criticized his wife for poor judgment in allowing Monica to continue treating David.

AJ never stopped seeing Nikki, despite Alan's orders. In fact, when Nikki began to realize she might lose, she even tried seducing AJ, but he'd passed out from too much booze. After she lost, Nikki left town. AJ went after her.

He found her in Washington. Nikki was playing a tape of her parents telling her psychiatrist that they didn't love her. AJ felt sorry for her and persuaded her to return to Port Charles with him.

When Alan heard AJ brought Nikki back, he blew his top! "How could you—after what this girl has put us through! I'm disgusted, AJ. Where's your sense? Just once, why can't you be more like your brother Jason?"

AJ stormed over to Nikki. Drinking himself into a stupor, he took her out for a drive and crashed her car into a tree. AJ was unconscious when Nikki pulled him from the car moments before it exploded! He had a concussion. She wound up in surgery, losing her spleen. Afterward she lied to the police that she'd been driving to protect AJ. AJ's family, however, sensed the truth.

AJ's brother Jason had started working on Dr. Tom Hardy's new hospital Teen Hot Line. Along with freshman Robin Scorpio and fellow junior Karen Wexler, Jason manned the telephone to help teenagers in trouble. Jason and Karen discovered that they both wanted to become doctors one day. Karen was sympathetic as Jason talked about his brother's drinking. Her mother Rhonda drank too much, but Karen didn't want anyone to know.

Every time Jason offered to drive Karen home she

turned him down. Jason was concerned about Karen's taking the bus so late. He knew the streets could be dangerous at night.

Late one night, after Ruby Anderson closed Kelly's Diner, three young toughs broke in. One of them tried to shoot her, but another pushed Ruby out of the way. The bullet hit him in the neck as his friends ran out. He was rushed to General Hospital, where Dr. Tony Jones saved his life. Personally, Tony hoped the kid would be put away for a long time for trying to rob Tony's wife's Aunt Ruby.

The kid was John Cates. He called himself Jagger. He was a street kid, a drop-out, somewhat wild, but he had a decent streak. As he recovered in General Hospital, his lowlife friends visited him: "Rat on us and you're dead meat!" Jagger kept silent. Police Commissioner Sean Donely wanted to help him but the wayward boy wouldn't help himself. When he was about to be released to jail, he tried escaping. Hospital volunteer Karen saw him take the stairwell to the roof. He tried lowering himself over the side. But he froze. Karen pulled him to safety. He admitted to a lifelong case of acrophobia, a dizzying fear of heights. Karen helped Jagger back to his room without giving him away.

Ruby refused to testify against the boy who saved her life and Jagger was set free. Ruby helped send his friends to prison when the police arrested them without Jagger's help.

Homeless, Jagger was sleeping under the pier when Bill Eckert first noticed him. Bill persuaded Ruby to give him a job at Kelly's and a room. Bill also gave him some work on his waterfront renovation project.

When Jagger accidentally cost Karen her job at a burger joint, he persuaded Ruby to hire Karen at Kelly's as well. Ruby enjoyed mothering the two kids. There was a chemistry between Jagger and Karen. But she'd begun dating Jason Quartermaine and fought her attraction to Jagger, who nobly kept his distance.

Jason didn't like the way Karen looked at Jagger anymore than Robin liked the way Jason looked at Karen. Robin confessed her crush on the older Jason to Holly, who warned her that love is no less complicated when you're older.

Dominique and Mac ended their relationship because of her jealousy for Holly. Connor Olivera hoped to win Dominique's heart. But Mac wasn't as interested in Holly as Bill Eckert was.

Bill and Holly fell in love during an improbable adventure on the high seas and in San Sebastian that had them fending off bullets, soldiers, sharks and jaguars! After they helped Holly's look-alike half sister Paloma

restore freedom to her small country, they returned to Port Charles, and consummated their romance with a night of passion at the Port Charles Hotel.

The hotel had changed ownership in the weeks they'd been away. When Ned Ashton and Julia Barrett purchased it as partners, their business meetings drew them close. But they fought the impulses they felt. After all, Julia was Ned's wife Jenny's best friend. Julia even hired Jenny to design the hotel's new spa.

Ned wasn't happy about Jenny's pursuit of a career. He didn't want his wife working but the more they quarreled over her job, the more Jenny's thoughts turned to Ned's stepfather Paul. Paul and his wife Tracy had bonded somewhat during Tracy's pregnancy. When Tracy went into premature labor, Jenny rushed her to the hospital to give birth to Dillon. Jenny and Ned became Dillon's godparents.

A troubled Felicia Jones returned to Port Charles from Texas with her daughter Maxie. They'd just arrived at Bobbie's brownstone when someone shoved a cloth in Felicia's face. Bobbie and Tony found Maxie unharmed and Felicia unconscious. When she came to, Felicia had amnesia. All she knew was that Maxie was her baby!

Mac Scorpio hired the perky amnesiac as a bartender at the Outback. His customers really flipped for the "Felicia Flip," her own delectable concoction. But Felicia herself was flipping out with nightmares of running from a man across a rocky terrain and of a man stabbing a woman with an ice pick. Felicia was also being stalked!

Dr. Ryan Chamberlain had come to Port Charles from Texas where, under the name of Todd Wilson, he'd fallen for Felicia. Ryan had caused Felicia's amne-

While working together at the Outback, Mac Scorpio grew close to Felicia Jones, who was suffering from amnesia. For months, Mac and Felicia flirted, sparred and gazed longingly at each other, before finally consummating their romance.

sia because she'd seen him kill a woman! As long as Felicia had amnesia, he was safe. And so was she. Ryan wanted to keep Felicia safe. He loved her.

Ryan, a pediatrician, charmed everyone in Port Charles. He took care of Maxie. He saved Robin's life when she began to choke. Robin's Uncle Mac was grateful but he didn't like Ryan who was dating Felicia. Mac was jealous.

Mac got his detective's license and began investigating what had happened to Felicia, who was being treated by psychiatrist Tom Hardy. Ryan resented Mac. When he heard Mac planned to fly to Texas, Ryan tampered with Mac's plane. Ryan didn't know that Felicia had decided to leave town with Mac.

Their plane almost crashed but Mac landed in a field. He and Felicia spent the night together in a barn. They were so close they could feel each other's heat. Something was happening between them, but neither was sure just what. They held back.

When Mac and Felicia finally arrived in Texas, Felicia had a memory breakthrough. She recognized her grandmother Maria, who told Felicia how she had divorced Frisco after he had taken another dangerous WSB assignment. Upon their return to Port Charles, Ryan tried spiking Felicia's drink with a memory-loss concoction. He was jealous of her new closeness with Mac, who finally admitted his feelings for Felicia to himself—and her. They decided to take their relationship slowly as Ryan fantasized about marrying Felicia.

Jason dreamed of getting to know Karen better. He invited her to his cousin Dillon's christening. Finding Karen's invitation, her mother Rhonda invited herself as well and embarrassed Karen when she showed up at the Quartermaine mansion. But Alan and Monica welcomed Rhonda. They liked Karen and her mother.

But they could never approve of AJ's interest in Nikki. AJ and Nikki began living together and he helped pay her medical bills, although Nikki enjoyed some free medical attention from Eric Simpson, who was attracted to her in spite of himself.

While visiting Karen at General Hospital's Teen Hot Line, Rhonda ran into Scotty Baldwin. They reminisced about having dated in high school. Rhonda was glad that Scotty had become a lawyer. She'd only become a beauty parlor shampoo girl.

While selling Deception on the road, Scott grew close to Dominique. But Scott kept coming back to Jessica's bed—even though she never did help shorten his suspension. Scott kept up his friendship with Sly Eckert, who was woefully neglected by his father Bill.

As coach for Sly's Little League team, Scott had the entire team cut their hair in his own famous Baldwin buzzcut style.

Jason Quartermaine invited Karen for a summer afternoon on the Quartermaine cabin cruiser. Her friend Jagger Cates had been hired to tune up the boat's engine for their outing. Below deck, when he heard Jason and Karen come on board, Jagger got up to leave, but hit his head and knocked himself out.

On the open water, Jason was less than thrilled to see Jagger suddenly appear on the boat with him and Karen. Then suddenly a storm hit, the boat sank and the three teens washed up on a deserted island!

Stranded on the island, Jagger laughed when "boy scout" Jason couldn't make a fire by rubbing two sticks. Then Jagger whipped out his cigarette lighter. He still carried it even though Karen had convinced him to stop smoking. The three of them became close friends during their island adventure.

Jason's father Alan prayed they would find Jason. He dreaded calling Monica (who was at a medical conference in China) with unspeakable news about their son. Alan and Karen's mother Rhonda worried together about their children's safety while Ruby feared for Jagger. The kids were missing for days!

Jagger's convicted ex-friend Cal had broken out of jail with his convict brother, Joseph Atkins. They'd also landed on the island. Cal saw Karen and tried to rape her, then he dragged her to the top of a cliff. Jagger, forgetting his fear of heights, rushed to save her. Jason got there in time to see Cal plummet to the shore below. Convinced that he was dead, the teens made a pact to keep what had happened a secret.

The search party had finally been called off. But AJ insisted that he and Alan go out again to search for Jason. Alan was glad he listened to AJ, because they found Jason, Jagger and Karen. Alan's prayers had been answered—and he was proud of AJ!

Rhonda was overjoyed to see her daughter. But she suspected Jagger had caused the bruises Cal had left on Karen's arms. One of Rhonda's loutish boyfriends beat Jagger up for hurting Karen. Jagger didn't tell Karen at first but, when she finally found out, she was angry with her mother.

Nikki pressed AJ to make peace with his father. She had decided to marry AJ for his money. Joseph Atkins also wanted some of the Quartermaine money.

He blackmailed Jason, Karen and Jagger with ominous notes. "I know what you did. You won't get away with it!" Jason stole his grandfather Edward's coin collection to help pay Atkins the $25,000 he demanded for his silence about Cal's death. With Jagger and Karen, Jason also stole a car. Suspicious of the teenagers, Sean had them tailed.

They went to pay Atkins and were shocked to find Cal alive and well with his brother. A shoot-out occurred when the police arrived, with Jagger suffering a minor wound. Cal was arrested, but Atkins escaped.

He hid in Bobbie's brownstone, where he took her hostage and tried to rape her. When her husband Tony tried to save her, Atkins tied him up. Finally, Atkins arranged to escape in a police helicopter flown by Mac Scorpio but he was caught after Mac's stunt flying caused Atkins to drop the gun. Tony and Bobbie felt lucky to be alive after their brush with a killer.

Scott Baldwin also felt lucky. He'd broken the bank in Vegas! He asked Dominique to join him in Atlantic City to win some more. A few days later they woke up together in Las Vegas—hungover and married! They didn't believe the wedding license until they saw the Vegas chapel videotape of their ceremony! Simple loving vows of friendship and support that both touched and surprised them. Still, Scott, whose suspension was over, filed the papers for a divorce. They decided if they enjoyed being married, they'd call the divorce off during the waiting period.

Jessica Holmes was livid when her lover Scott returned married to Dominique. A disappointed Connor congratulated Dominique and left town.

Nikki manipulated AJ into proposing and moving back home—with her! Monica, realizing how Nikki saved AJ's life, tried to be gracious. But Alan resisted the situation at every turn. He was angry.

So was Brenda Barrett! The teenage spitfire turned up on her big sister Julia's doorstep demanding to know why Julia had frozen her trust fund. Julia said she'd heard Brenda had dropped out of her European jet set school. "No school, no money," she said, persuading Brenda to move in with her and enroll in Port Charles High.

When Jagger Cates also enrolled at PC High, Brenda was instantly attracted to him. She could tell he liked Karen, whom Brenda instantly disliked. Jagger liked Brenda's style, and Karen teased him about her.

"Why are you so interested in my love life?" he teased back.

Despite the birth of their son, Tracy's marriage to Paul grew shakier. She met Marco Dane, a fast-talking, quick-thinking con artist from Llanview, Pennsylvania, when he was impersonating her own son Ned! Tracy hired Marco to dig up some dirt on her daughter-in-law/rival Jenny. Marco dug up a mountain. Jenny had a miscarriage by Senator Jack Kensington when she was 16! Tracy was delighted. To see Jenny squirm, Tracy invited the Senator and his family to dinner at the Quartermaines. Later, Tracy and Marco taped Jenny and the Senator talking about their affair.

Tracy blackmailed Jenny with the tape. "If you ever speak to Paul again, your marriage and the Senator's career are history!"

Jenny was shaken. She made it clear to Paul that anything between them had to end. He was bewildered.

Julia Barrett wondered why Tracy was paying Marco's expenses at the Port Charles Hotel. With her passkey, she entered Marco's room, found the tape—and took it! Julia realized how easily she could break up Jenny and Ned and have him for herself. But Jenny was her friend and Julia planned to give the tape to her.

Alan wanted to protect his son AJ from Nikki. On the morning of their wedding day, Alan drew Nikki aside. "I know you're only marrying my son for his money. But listen to me. If you marry AJ, there won't be any money. Not one thin dime. He will be disinherited. On the other hand, if you leave town now, you can be rich."

He showed her a check for one million dollars. Nikki took the check and jilted AJ at the altar. Totally crushed, AJ drowned his sorrow in booze.

Monica was horrified to hear how Alan betrayed their son. AJ hired a private eye to find Nikki with Alan's blessing. But Alan paid the detective even more money *not* to find her!

Ryan Chamberlain convinced Felicia to join him for a mountain cabin weekend. When her memory returned while she was there, she panicked. She'd seen Ryan as Todd kill a woman in Texas! Felicia felt trapped. Ryan showed her a wedding ring and wedding dress and proposed instant marriage! She bolted from the cabin and Ryan went ballistic. Tossing the dress in the fire, he lunged at her. Felicia picked up a knife.

Mac, meanwhile, knew she was in trouble when she missed Maxie's birthday. He headed for the cabin through a snowstorm and arrived to find Felicia standing over Ryan's body.

Monica operated on Ryan and he survived. Recuperating at General Hospital, he told police commissioner Donely and new Assistant District Attorney Holmes that Felicia had suddenly attacked him for no reason. She was charged with attempted murder!

"See you in court, counselor," Jessica sneered at Felicia's disbelieving attorney, Jessica's ex-lover Scott.

Scott and Dominique had grown to love each other

Stranded on an island off the coast of Port Charles, General Hospital's torrid teens, Jagger, Karen and Jason, fought the elements—and fugitive Cal Atkins.

but after a big fight over nothing, they decided to let their divorce go through. At the hearing, the judge asked why they were splitting up. When neither could offer a reason, the judge threw the divorce out of court. Scott and Dominique breathed a sigh of relief and kissed.

But two other marriages exploded. Brenda found the incriminating Jenny/Kensington tape in Julia's room. Thinking that she'd help Julia land the classy Ned Ashton, Brenda put the tape in Ned's car stereo. When he learned all about his wife's long-ago affair with the Senator, he threw Jenny and all her "virgin" lies out of his life!

Paul walked out on Tracy after hearing how she blackmailed Jenny. She, in turn, threatened him with the loss of his son, Dillon.

AJ began drinking in the Quartermaine garage, passing out with the motor running. Alan and Monica found him in the nick of time. They feared that their son might have deliberately tried to kill himself.

When Tiffany Hill's sister Cheryl died after a car accident in Phoenix, Tifffany and her husband Sean brought their nephew Lucas back to Port Charles. Bobbie and Tony offered sympathy and both were happy to see Lucas again. In a video will, Cheryl requested that Bobbie and Tony raise Lucas as their own. Ironically, Cheryl didn't think Tiffany wanted children. She had spent months persuading Sean they should have a child but she still hadn't become pregnant. When Tiffany vowed to fight Cheryl's will, Sean and Tony anticipated trouble.

Holly moved out of Mac and Robin's house, taking a residential room at the Port Charles Hotel so she and Bill could have private time together. Bill paid a fortune for a painting, "Summer at Provence," which

he lent to Holly. He also lent it to an art show benefit for the hospital. But when it was returned, he noticed it was a fake! In fact, all the paintings donated by Port Charles citizens had been replaced by fakes. The art show was an art heist and Bill was furious.

Lucy Coe slinked back to Port Charles. Her job with Greg Bennett had fizzled and a new partner-in-crime, Richard Halifax, had welched on paying her. She was dead broke. Seeing Scott kissing Dominique at Kelly's Diner, she kept her distance, crying to think what she'd given up.

Returning to Kelly's, Jagger saw a poor stranger, Lucy, huddled in tears beneath the pier. That was him not so long ago, he reflected as he gave her some money. His thoughts turned to his brother Mike and sister Gina and how he'd lost track of them. Their family was split up after their mother skipped out on them.

Lucy didn't give up on Scott, who came home to find Lucy waiting for him—in his shower. "I'm back," she cooed. But Scott pulled her off him and told her that he had married Dominique. Lucy was crushed as Scott made it clear: He loves his wife. Scott gave Lucy money to tide her over. She moved back to Kelly's.

To defend Felicia, Scott investigated Ryan's past in New York City. He stumbled upon news that incriminated Lucy in the Port Charles art heist. He told Bill and Holly, who deduced that Lucy had supplied information about the local paintings to the wealthy Richard Halifax.

When Halifax realized Bill and Holly were on to him he arranged the return of all the art—except Bill's painting, "Summer in Provence," the only painting Lucy couldn't have known about. Halifax swore he knew nothing about Bill's painting, but Bill didn't believe him.

Nobody believed Felicia when she announced that Ryan had broken into her apartment. Dr. Simone Hardy reported that he was asleep in his hospital bed when he was supposedly with Felicia. Ryan fooled all of them. But he wasn't fooled when Felicia confronted him at the hospital. She wore a wire that recorded Ryan endlessly forgiving her for having stabbed him for no good reason. Felicia felt defeated!

Brenda was triumphant when she boasted to her sister Julia about planting the tape in Ned's car. Brenda expected Julia to thank her. Instead, Julia slapped her! Brenda ran to Jagger for comfort. In his room at Kelly's, they made love.

Julia didn't tell Ned that she knew about the tape as he began dating her in earnest. On New Year's Eve at midnight, they, too, were making love.

Paul comforted Jenny. They were simply in love.

"No, you may not copy my homework!" Karen Wexler shot Jagger Cates a look of exasperation as she went to class. She knew he could do well in school if only he'd apply himself. But now that he was living with that wild Brenda Barrett, he was constantly distracted.

"What did you expect from that goody-two-shoes!" Brenda asked Jagger, "Now what'll we do?"

"Don't worry," Jagger said, grinning as he "accidentally" set off the fire alarm. As the school emptied out, Brenda and Jagger laughed. So much for that class. He received a warning for that little stunt!

All that Brenda enjoyed about her senior year at Port Charles High was her job as photographer on the school paper. Her only friend, besides Jagger and Karen's boyfriend Jason Quartermaine, was sophomore Robin Scorpio. Brenda was insecure about her relationship with Jagger, and with good reason.

While Jagger was motoring Karen to a college interview in Syracuse on his cycle, they became stranded in a snowstorm. They spent a night and a day talking and snuggling in a deserted cabin. After they admitted their feelings for each other, she told him she'd break up with Jason.

Upon returning, Jagger told Brenda to patch things up with her sister Julia and move back. Brenda was hurt—and ready to hurt back.

She took her camera into the girls' locker room, secretly photographed Karen while she was showering and slipped a naked snapshot of Karen in every boy's locker! Karen was mortified. Jagger heard the boys snickering and, defending Karen, lashed out with his fists. Jagger was expelled.

Jason comforted Karen with tender words. Seeing how he calmed her, Jagger decided Jason was better for her than he was, left her a farewell love note and left town.

Karen confessed her feelings for the now-absent Jagger to Jason. He didn't care. He asked her to go steady. She smiled and said, "Yes," through her tears.

Jason's cousin Ned Ashton was already going steady with his partner Julia Barrett. They'd developed a lusty relationship. Although he'd served divorce papers on Jenny, Ned grew increasingly jealous of his stepfather Paul Hornsby's relationship with her.

Ned threatened Paul that he'd make Jenny's underage affair with Senator Jack Kensington public if Paul didn't fork over his shares of ELQ. As soon as Paul gave in to Ned's demands, Ned leaked the story to the press anyway.

Ned's mother Tracy forbade Paul from seeing their son Dillon. She asked her cohort, Marco Dane, to help her frame Paul for embezzling from ELQ. She'd see her wayward husband in jail yet!

Scott Baldwin believed he and his wife Dominique were the happiest couple in Port Charles. He didn't know she'd been having severe headaches and that Dr. Tony Jones had diagnosed a terminal brain tumor! She swore Tony to secrecy.

Felicia's murder trial went badly. Dr. Tom Hardy testified that Felicia's amnesia and nightmares indicated instability. Mac Scorpio testified to seeing her with the knife over Ryan's bloody body. There was no proof to support Felicia's tale of having seen the respectable Ryan kill a woman in Texas. And in the witness box, Ryan himself was only full of love and concern for Felicia. He just knew she didn't mean to hurt him when she went nuts. The verdict: Guilty! The sentence: 5 to 15 years in the State Mental Hospital.

"Tell Maxie I love her!" Felicia screamed as she was taken from the courtroom. She was terrified her young daughter would forget her. Mac, Scott and Police Commissioner Sean Donely swore they would find proof to help her.

Prosecutor Jessica Holmes was triumphant as she glared at her ex-lover Scott. Scott's other ex-lover Lucy Coe still wanted him back but felt it was hopeless. After seeing Dominique get dizzy, Lucy guessed she was pregnant. But Dominique collapsed and begged Lucy to rush her to Tony Jones, a neurosurgeon. Lucy was aghast to learn the truth. Dominique tearfully thanked her for promising to keep it a secret from Scott just as he walked in.

Scott thought Lucy had provoked Dominique's tears and ordered Lucy to leave his wife alone. Lucy accepted Scott's anger. Finally, Dominique told Scott her sad news. He was devastated. Scott and

Dominique had a poignant second wedding ceremony with all their friends present. Lucy kissed and steadied Dominique just before she walked down the aisle.

To give Scott a child before she died was Dominique's one desire. She had so little time, but there was a medical solution. Her fertilized egg could be implanted into a gestation mother who could carry the baby to term.

Dominique wanted Lucy, someone she knew both she and Scott loved, to carry their baby. So Scott asked Lucy, who was very touched. And so Lucy became pregnant with Scott and Dominique's baby.

Tiffany Hill Donely, obsessed with getting custody of her nephew Lucas from Tony and Bobbie Jones, angered her husband Sean by informing the social worker of Bobbie's past as a prostitute. Sean warned Tiffany that if Bobbie's past came up at the hearing, he wouldn't testify. When Tiffany's attorney tore into Bobbie, Sean walked out. Without him, Tiffany lost Lucas to the Joneses.

"Sean, our marriage is over!" she told him. Tiffany meant business and he moved to the Port Charles Hotel. When Jessica Holmes heard they split up, she set her cap for Sean, and lured him into bed.

Tiffany began to drink and she asked Alan to prescribe pills to help her sleep. But he canceled her prescription when he discovered she was pregnant. Tiffany was thrilled!

Alan's son AJ had come home from the rehab center, where he finally learned to control his alcoholism. He still wanted to know why Nikki Langton left him at the altar. Monica fumed that she had to keep her husband's million-dollar check to Nikki a secret from their son. Monica and Alan's arguing about it didn't end when AJ discovered the truth.

After another nasty fight with Alan, AJ finally found Nikki—in Malibu—and he begged her to pick up with him again. She felt sorry for him, but she said, "That's impossible, AJ."

"Why?"

"I'm married."

Nikki's husband came home, and on his flight back to Port Charles, a shaken AJ downed a double vodka.

Alan started dining on macaroni-and-cheese, playing pool and dancing the Texas two-step with Rhonda Wexler. She couldn't believe that a man like Alan enjoyed her company. Alan's wife Monica suspected they were having an affair.

Rhonda's daughter Karen and Alan's son Jason were Queen and King of the Valentine's dance at school. Jagger, who'd realized he couldn't live without Karen, showed up at the dance.

"Karen, I love you," he said. She left with him, leaving Jason humiliated in front of all their friends. Jagger had hurt Brenda, Karen had hurt Jason, and both regretted it—but Jagger and Karen knew they were meant to be together.

AJ consoled Jason. Together, they agreed, "Women, who needs them!" AJ was furious with Jagger for hurting his little brother. To put his own life together, AJ got his cousin Ned to give him back his old job as desk clerk at the Port Charles Hotel.

Dr. Tom Hardy resigned as Chief of Psychiatry to work in the Emergency Room. But Tom remained restless. Finally he announced he was leaving for a while to work with the relief effort in Somalia. His wife Simone and son Tommy kissed him good-bye. Tom's parents, Steve and Audrey, hoped he'd return soon. Steve still dreamed of Tom succeeding him as chief of staff some day.

At the mental hospital, Felicia was bedeviled by visits from Ryan and by a guard who threatened rape. Mac helped her escape through some air ducts. On the run, they delved more into Ryan's past and realized he was a serial killer. They found the name of the woman he'd killed in Texas and tracked down a friend of "Gloria" named Michelle Bales. When Michelle guessed what Ryan had done and tried to blackmail him, she was never seen alive again.

Mac and Felicia discovered Ryan's fiancée Linda had also died at his hands! They decided to gaslight their psychotic nemesis into confessing. Sean Donely helped them, along with their former adversary Jessica Holmes, Sean's new lover.

Jessica told Ryan that while on the run, Mac and Felicia went to Texas, where they were in a car accident. Ryan reeled when he learned that Felicia had been killed. He went to General Hospital, where a "wounded" Mac had been flown, then to the funeral parlor, where he saw Felicia in her casket. Meanwhile Felicia, made up to look dead, prayed that she soon wouldn't be!

Ryan was distraught, believing that his beloved Felicia was dead. Then he started getting phone calls from her!

"I'm with your mother, Ryan." Felicia's voice spooked him.

"My mother's dead," said Ryan, rattled. He remembered setting the fire that killed her.

He really started to crack when his computer screen began flashing messages from his mother, accompanied by her picture, which Bobbie Jones had stolen from Ryan's desk. "You've been a bad boy, Ryan. But then, you always were."

Sly Eckert was a good boy, but he had trouble getting any attention from his father Bill. Bill traveled to Lisbon and then to Paris searching for his missing painting. Bill's lover, Holly Scorpio, finally learned that he was sentimentally attached to "Summer in Provence" because it reminded him of his first love, Victoria Parker, whose affection Bill had stolen from her fiancé, Richard Halifax. Stealing the painting was Richard's revenge.

Bill reclaimed his painting in Paris. Holly stood by him until Victoria, whom Bill believed was dead, proved to be alive. Richard had been supporting Victoria, who'd been blinded in a not-so-fatal accident, for years.

When Bill realized Victoria was alive he brought her to General Hospital, where eye surgery restored her sight. Richard warned Holly not to trust Bill, but Holly continued to believe that Bill loved her, not Victoria.

Bill, however, had rekindled his affair with Victoria, while continuing his relationship with Holly. After Holly saw Bill and Victoria in bed together at his lighthouse, she left unseen, determined to make two-timing Bill pay for deceiving her.

Holly invited Victoria to tea in her hotel suite. She also invited Bill over for a tryst a half hour earlier. When he showed up, he undressed and jumped into Holly's bed. And that's where he was when Victoria arrived.

But Holly was with Richard at Bill's lighthouse. While Bill tried explaining to Victoria, Holly and Richard smashed all the rare wines in his wine cellar. Richard also stole back the painting. On a cruise ship leaving Port Charles, Holly felt hurt but satisfied. "Here's to revenge. Funny, it tastes bitter to me," she sighed, settling into her deck chair.

Bill almost won Victoria back. But when she saw him slap his son Sly—who merely wanted Bill to spend time with him—Victoria realized Bill wasn't the man she thought he was. She walked out on him, too. Sly ran away to his Aunt Jenny, but Bill forced Sly to come back. He wanted Sly to grow up, be more of a man in dealing with disappointment. Bill wouldn't accept that Sly was only a boy.

When Paul was arrested for embezzling from ELQ, Jenny tore into a gloating Tracy. Their bitter quarrel in a parking garage left Tracy in a blind rage. Storming to her car, she drove out and accidentally ran into Jenny!

Fearing Jenny was dead, Tracy panicked. She anonymously car-phoned the police with news of the "hit-and-run" she'd "witnessed," then sped off.

Ned and Julia found Jenny's crumpled body and rushed her to General Hospital. Julia saw that Ned still cared for his ex-wife.

At the hospital, Jenny thanked Ned for saving her life, wondering if they could be friends again. Ned smiled his dimpled grin. "Sure." Ned decided to win her back.

She told the police she didn't know who hit her. But she did.

"Okay, Tracy," said Jenny to her former mother-in-law. "Here's the deal. Drop your phony charges against Paul and divorce him! Or go to jail!" Jenny'd learned how to play nasty from a master.

Tracy begged her father Edward for help: "How do I get out of this, Daddy?"

Edward was furious to hear what Tracy had done. He told her to give in to Jenny and get out of his house. He banished her from Port Charles as he had once done years before. Even Monica felt sorry for her sister-in-law when she found Tracy crying over her packed bags.

But Tracy had one final hurrah. She took her son Dillon with her. Paul could be free, but he'd never have his son! Paul had no idea where Tracy went.

Late one night in the hospital lecture hall, Ryan saw Felicia's ghost! She was wearing a hidden microphone.

Shrinking at the sight of her, he cried, "Go away. Go away. Why are you torturing me like this. I didn't kill you!"

"No, but you killed all the others, didn't you? Linda, Gloria, Michelle, Helen, Magi. You can tell me. I can't hurt you anymore.

"Ryan," Felicia said soothingly, "did you kill all those people?"

Ryan was sobbing. "I didn't want to. But they kept criticizing me—nagging me. I begged them to stop. But they wouldn't. So I stopped them. Just like I stopped my mother!" He fell to his knees.

Startled by his confession, Felicia stumbled and cut her elbow. Ryan saw the blood.

"Ghosts don't bleed!" Ryan went ballistic, charging after her! Mac saved Felicia—but Ryan got away.

The next morning, Audrey Hardy opened her front door to a frantic Ryan.

"Mother, I need to talk with you."

Alarmed, she went along with Ryan's delusion that she was his mother, and Ryan began to calm down. Audrey's husband Steve walked in, saw Ryan and ordered him out. Steve moved to call the police. Ryan ripped the phone out of the wall. Steve tried to fight him off but Ryan knocked him out.

Ryan turned to Audrey. "Now it's your turn, Mother."

When Steve came to, he found Audrey beaten to a pulp! But Monica operated on her and saved her life.

The telephone rang. "Hello, Felicia. It's Ryan. I have your daughter. Say hello to Mommy, Maxie."

Felicia turned white. Was there no stopping him? After a desperate showdown in Texas, Mac finally captured him. Felicia had her daughter and her freedom. And Mac, if she wanted him. They agreed to take their relationship slowly.

Audrey recovered physically and, after much therapy, she testified against Ryan. Ryan was convicted and sentenced to the same mental hospital Felicia had been in.

Ryan swore he'd get all of them, including Jessica Holmes, for betraying him. Then he slit his wrists. His wretched life was saved in General Hospital.

Jessica felt betrayed by Sean. He ended their affair when he learned his wife Tiffany was pregnant. Jessica had even told Sean that she thought she was pregnant, but he still wanted to be with Tiffany.

When Sean confided in Mac that he might have gotten Jessica pregnant, Tiffany overheard them. She doubled over in pain and was rushed to the hospital, where she prematurely gave birth to a boy. He didn't survive. Tiffany was so despondent that she attempted suicide by swallowing a fistful of pills, but Tony and Bobbie Jones saved her.

After she recovered, a contrite Jessica told Sean she wasn't pregnant.

Sean begged Tiffany's forgiveness. By the time she was ready to forgive him, Jessica learned that she really was pregnant. Jessica demanded that Sean do right by her or she'd tell Tiffany.

"I'll kill you if you do!" said Sean, thinking of Tiffany's fragile state.

As Robin Scorpio entered her uncle Sean's hotel room, she saw him holding a bloody statue over Jessica's body. Secretly fearing that Tiffany had killed her, Sean said he killed Jessica! But when Mac and Felicia proved that Ryan had escaped custody briefly to kill yet again, Sean was cleared. He and Tiffany slowly reconciled.

Dominique lived long enough to hear her baby's heartbeat as it grew inside Lucy. Scott filled her final

With snowflakes falling gently on an early spring day, Scotty Baldwin cradled his beloved wife Dominique in his arms as she took her last breath of life. Moments later, she died from an inoperable brain tumor, leaving Scotty devastated—and vulnerable to the charms of Dom's "friend," Katherine.

weeks with love and tenderness and she died in his arms. Lucy cried for them both. But her eyes brightened just a tiny bit when she heard that Dominique had left Scott $100,000,000.

As Jagger and Karen fell deeper in love, she wanted to make love with him. But she froze whenever he got too intimate. Jagger told her he'd wait 'til she was ready. She began having disturbing flashbacks.

Karen encouraged Jagger to search for his missing brother and sister. He located Gina, who told him that their brother Mike had lived with her and her new family briefly. But he stole from them and ran away. Jagger hired Felicia (who was helping Mac in his detective business) to find his 16-year old brother.

A letter arrived for Dominique from an old friend, Katherine Crawford. Scott realized Katherine couldn't know Dominique had died. He wanted to meet her, because she could tell him about Dominique as a child. When Katherine came to Port Charles, Scott hung on her every word. Drawn together by their love of Dominique and their shared loss, they found instant comfort in each other. Lucy hated her. She also didn't trust the crafty Katherine.

It *was* a con. Katherine told Scott her late husband's debts were causing gangsters to harass her at every turn. All lies! But Scott gave Katherine $250,000 to buy off the thugs. She was very pleased with herself. Every time Lucy uncovered a lie, Katherine sweet-talked Scott into forgiving her, even when she had to confess that she was really Katherine Bell, the cook's daughter at Serenity, the estate where Dominique grew up. Scott forgave Katherine time and again. Lucy fumed when Scott and Julia named her as public relations director for Deception perfume.

Ray Conway, an old boyfriend of Scott's receptionist, Rhonda, had come back to town and Rhonda invited him to stay with her and Karen. Soon after seeing Ray, long repressed memories flooded back to Karen: He had abused her when she was a child! Whenever her mother passed out from drinking, Ray entered her room, drew the shades and forced himself on his little "Carrie," as he called her.

He still called her "Carrie" as he attempted to reprise the past. Karen cursed him and threatened to tell. He dared her to, reminding her how much "she liked it."

Bad student Brenda couldn't believe that she actually made it to graduation day. Jason and Karen made top honors. But Karen didn't feel good about herself. She felt so dirty.

At Jake's Bar, AJ, Jason and Brenda noticed how much Alan liked being with Rhonda. They even saw him kiss her!

Running into Karen and Jagger, AJ taunted them, but Jason really exploded: "You're a slut, just like your trampy mother!"

Jagger's hands turned into fists, but Karen told him it wasn't worth fighting.

At home, AJ nailed Alan for his infidelity as Monica walked in.

"Save your breath, AJ," Monica told him. "I know all about it."

Alan said he and Rhonda weren't having an affair. He just found her easy to talk to.

"You know, Alan, that hurts me even more than if you were having an affair."

Monica asked her friend Bobbie how she could win her husband back.

"Make him jealous," Bobbie suggested.

Remembering just how dangerous a jealous Alan could be, Monica shuddered but decided to do it. She bought herself flowers and jewelry and made sure Alan learned her gifts came from "Rod." When Alan finally fell for Monica's ruse, she confessed and they fell into each other's arms.

Alan told a disappointed Rhonda they had to stop seeing each other.

Karen began wearing trashy-flashy clothes and wandering into teen "raves." At a wild party, someone slipped the drug "ecstasy" into her drink. A kid named Stone saw how zoned out Karen was. When the police raided the rave, Stone got her away safely.

Karen felt unworthy of Jagger, who had started to box with Marco Dane as his manager. She broke up with him.

"I'm going to college, Jagger. I'm going places. You're going nowhere." She hated hurting him, but she couldn't reveal her dirty secret.

GREAT MOMENTS

Snowbound in a cabin with Lucy in labor, Scotty Baldwin rolled up his sleeves and assisted in the delivery of baby Serena.

ISSUES

In 1993, General Hospital *documented the stirring tale of a model-teen-gone-wrong, Karen Wexler. Raised in a single parent home by her alcoholic mother, Rhonda (pictured here), Karen slowly came to realize that she had been sexually abused by her mother's boyfriend, Ray Conway, when she was a child. Filled with shame and self-loathing, Karen became an exotic dancer in the Paradise Lounge, a strip club managed by Sonny Corinthos. She nearly trashed her goal of a pre-med education with a downward spiral into drugs, lies and isolation from her friends and family.*

"This was one girl's story," explains executive producer Wendy Riche. "It was a very dark journey for Karen, as it is for countless young women in our country. It was our hope that, through Karen, others might find the strength to seek help." To that end, actress Cari Shayne, who portrayed Karen, appeared in a public service announcement urging victims of sexual abuse to call a toll free number (1-800-422-4453) for help.

Brenda was eager to comfort an angry and confused Jagger. Brenda was working as a personal assistant to Jason's grandmother Lila when Lucy Coe—who had rejoined the Deception team—offered Brenda the opportunity to be the perfume's new sig-

nature model. Brenda's sister Julia okayed the job as long as Brenda went to college.

Julia's affair with her Port Charles Hotel partner, Ned Ashton, was still hot, but cooling. Ned's grandfather Edward pressured Ned to show his cousin AJ the ropes in the hotel business. So Ned "invited" AJ to attend a business meeting with him and Julia in the Bahamas. The Bahamas were very steamy—for AJ and Julia. To her utter surprise, Julia gave in to AJ's advances—and loved the way AJ made love!

Despite his involvement with Julia, Ned decided to pursue his ex-wife Jenny. He sent her lover Paul on a wild goose chase to Italy with a false clue that Tracy and Paul's son Dillon were there. With Paul away, Ned saw more of Jenny.

Still, Ned blew up when he discovered his cousin AJ having an affair with his partner/lover Julia. When Ned took it out on Julia via their partnership, Julia had finally had enough and moved to London. In a parting jab against Ned, she sold her half of the hotel to AJ, who borrowed the money from his grandfather, Edward, who found the competition between his two grandsons amusing. Edward's wife Lila invited Julia's sister Brenda to live in their mansion.

"I'm going to win my wife Jenny back," Ned told his old prep school buddy, Damian, who'd come to town. But Jenny learned how Ned maneuvered Paul out of the country and stormed over to Ned and Damian's table at the Port Charles Grill. Jenny dumped a bowl of soup on Ned's head, which Damian found amusing.

Damian had a lover. Katherine Bell! They'd been together in New York City. But they pretended to meet in Port Charles. Damian approved of her plan to marry Scott for his money—so long as she didn't sleep with him. Furthermore, he'd help Katherine by keeping Lucy Coe from getting in her way.

A scheme of his own was also on Damian's mind. After causing ELQ trouble with the Environmental Protection Agency by tainting water samples, Damian told Ned that he could solve the problem. For Damian's help, Ned sold him 2% of ELQ, one quarter of which Damian secretly gave to Katherine. Ned championed Damian's plan for ELQ to build a toxic waste incinerator. The rest of Ned's family was opposed.

Karen developed a friendship with Stone, who introduced her to the Paradise Lounge, a strip joint. His boss and benefactor, Sonny Corinthos, owned it. Stone lived in Sonny's apartment above the club. Karen was appalled that women could so degrade themselves. Then she met Sonny. He told her how women, by stripping, controlled men, got them drooling. Cleverly and seductively, Sonny dared her to try it. Soon Karen became "Carrie, the Schoolgirl," Sonny's star attraction.

Karen told Sonny how she'd been abused by Ray when she saw him in the club. Sonny had Ray thrown out and led Karen to his own bed. Soon she was addicted to stripping, Sonny—and pills! Karen kept her new life a secret while she worked at Kelly's and the hospital and went to class at Port Charles University.

While searching for Jagger's brother Mike, Felicia met a drugged-out street kid named Crystal. After Crystal fatally overdosed, Felicia learned that a young teenager had paid for her burial. She was certain it was Mike.

Jagger showed up for Crystal's funeral, and so did Mike. They had a shaky but warm reunion over her grave.

Jagger brought Mike back to Kelly's. Karen was there. She was shocked. Jagger's brother Mike was Stone—from her secret life! When Karen pretended they'd never met, Stone played along. With Sonny's permission, Stone moved in with Jagger.

Jagger boxed his final amateur bout against AJ, who'd waited a long time for a crack at Jagger. In a hard-fought fight, Jagger K.O.d AJ. Marco couldn't wait for his prizefighter to turn pro.

After Jagger and Stone argued over Stone's going back to school, Jagger followed him to the Paradise Lounge, where he saw Karen stripping.

"Is this what you meant by going places!" Jagger was disgusted with Karen. He threw a crumpled bill at her feet and left.

In tears, Karen fell into Sonny's arms.

When Jagger calmed down, he felt concerned about Karen and went back. Jagger found Karen in bed with Sonny—and beat him up.

Sonny put a hit out on Jagger. His thugs locked Jagger in Sonny's basement, but Stone saw him there. Jagger begged Mike to help him, but Stone wouldn't cross Sonny. He owed Sonny more than he owed Jagger.

Karen knew Sonny's men would kill Jagger, so she ran to Marco for help. Marco promised Sonny a piece of Jagger's boxing action in exchange for Jagger's life. Sonny liked the idea of "owning" Jagger and agreed.

When Karen's pill-popping increased, Sonny cut off her supply. Karen asked Stone to get her more. He refused, remembering how his friend Crystal had

Coached by Marco Dane, Jagger Cates took up boxing. In his final amateur bout, Jagger skillfully squared off against AJ Quartermaine, and promptly knocked him out.

died. Even Alan grew concerned upon seeing Karen so strung out. He warned her about drugs—but that didn't stop her from stealing pills from the hospital.

Curious over how mysterious Karen had become, Brenda followed her to the Paradise Lounge one night. Karen told Sonny she wanted to quit stripping, but he wouldn't hear of it.

"This is what you wanted, what you asked for. You know you like it. Now get on stage." Sonny's smile was hard.

Slipping into the strip joint, Brenda's eyes popped to see Karen's gyrations! Karen felt dizzy. The room was spinning and she collapsed. Brenda saw it all and told everyone.

Everyone rallied around Karen, who was clearly in trouble. Jason apologized to Karen for being so mean. Alan gave Rhonda a check to underwrite Karen's college education to ease the pressure on the girl. Even Brenda befriended Karen. But Karen's greatest support came from Jagger.

Vowing revenge on both Karen and Jagger for having crossed him, Sonny Corinthos gave orders to Marco Dane: "Tell your boy Jagger he's taking a dive

Luke and Laura Spencer knew what the explosion of their truck outside the Triple L Diner meant—Frank Smith had found them! Once again, they were on the run—and headed home to Port Charles.

in his next fight, or his girlfriend's gonna get hurt!"

Jagger refused to take the dive. He knocked out his opponent, grabbed Karen and ran. They hid in the cabin they'd once stayed at. She told him about how Ray had abused her as a child and finally let herself make glorious love to Jagger.

Police Commissioner Sean Donely closed Sonny's Paradise Lounge for hiring underage kids like Karen and Stone.

When Karen told her mother Rhonda about Ray's abuse, Rhonda scoured Port Charles looking for him. At Kelly's Diner, she let Jason and Brenda know exactly why she was looking for the bum. When Rhonda found Ray at home and lit into him, he attacked her.

Jason told Alan what Rhonda said about Ray. Concerned, Alan called Rhonda, who grabbed the phone while Ray was hitting her. Arriving at Rhonda's apartment, Alan found Ray kicking her unconscious body. He threw Ray against the wall, killing him!

Alan panicked. He didn't want Monica to know he'd been to Rhonda's. He anonymously called an ambulance for Rhonda and dragged Ray's body away.

Life was peaceful at Luke and Laura Spencer's Triple L Diner in Canada. Laura couldn't believe that after years of running, she and her husband Luke had finally established a normal life for their 11-year old son Lucky. Life with Luke had turned into a waltz.

But their peaceful life was about to explode. Without warning, a bomb killed a friend of theirs who had turned the ignition key in the Spencer's truck. Luke and Laura knew the bomb was meant for them. Their old enemy, Frank Smith, had found them. Once again, they'd be on the run. Only this time, they decided to run home—to Port Charles.

Luke was determined to settle the score once and for all with Frank, who ran his mob from behind bars. Luke and Laura sent Lucky to his Aunt Ruby Anderson on his own. They felt he'd be safer away from them.

Laura grabbed the carpetbag of mementos and incredibly useful odds-and-ends which had sustained her through countless adventures and closed the door on her life in Canada. Luke stole a plane, but it sputtered out of gas. Wearing parachutes, they knew they'd have to jump.

Laura landed in a river, but Luke managed to save her before she plummeted over a waterfall. Somehow, they and the carpetbag made it to Port Charles. They acquired a pink Cadillac along the way.

They hid out in a large abandoned house that Laura fell in love with. Lucky reached Ruby at Kelly's. The Spencers were reunited and welcomed back tearfully by all their friends.

Lucky made a new friend in his distant cousin Sly

Eckert, whose father Bill looked like Luke. When gangsters chased Lucky, he and Sly ran to the catacombs for safety. Bill went after them. The gangsters shot him, thinking they got Luke.

"Who'd have thought the last face I'd see is my own!" Bill died staring at Luke, who had just arrived.

When Damian heard that the Frank Smith mob was responsible for Bill's death, he went to the State Penitentiary.

"Dad, I'm setting myself up as a businessman in Port Charles. I don't need fallout from your activities right now." Damian was Frank Smith's son! He proposed a plan to Frank, who agreed.

Arranging to meet with Luke through Luke's sister Bobbie, Damian informed Luke that his father, Frank Smith, would guarantee the Spencer family's safety if Luke would help smuggle certain people into the country for Frank. Luke's liaison with Frank would be Sonny Corinthos, who became Frank's front man in Port Charles after his strip joint had closed. Luke agreed.

Luke told Laura he'd work for Frank only until they found a way to get him out of their lives for good.

The Spencers replanted their roots in Port Charles and Laura bought the house they had hidden in. She sensed a lot of family love and warmth in its walls.

As Damian's girlfriend Katherine Bell seduced Scott into proposing, she actually fell in love with him. Katherine loved making love with Scott almost as much as she loved telling Lucy Coe about it. Lucy sputtered as she told her new confidante Damian what that witch Katherine had done. Damian frowned to realize Katherine betrayed him.

Scott's first wife Laura wished him well. She was glad they'd been able to get past the old hurts. He invited her to his wedding.

With Katherine about to marry Scott, Damian suggested to Lucy that Scott might wonder why Katherine came to town using a fake name if she really didn't know Dominique was dead.

With that question, Lucy stopped Katherine's wedding before the "I do's." Scott blasted Katherine, who swore she was really Dominique's half-sister. He left her at the altar.

In a cabin during a snowstorm, Scott helped Lucy give birth to his and Dominique's baby. They named her Serena in honor of Dominique's home. After Scotty saved Serena from being kidnaped, he knew he had to take her away from Port Charles. He gave Lucy

his 4% share in ELQ and, tearfully, they parted. Only Scott's receptionist Rhonda, who survived Ray's beating, knew his whereabouts.

Lucy felt her heart break. She thought of Serena as her own.

Sly went to live with his Aunt Jenny. She inherited Bill's 36% share of ELQ. Ned tried buying it, but Jenny wouldn't sell it to her ex-husband. She sold it to Damian Smith for $250,000,000—dirty money Damian borrowed from his father. But that was his secret. Mob money would have made the sale illegal.

Damian and Ned needed Lucy's 4% of ELQ to

In the catacombs, young Sly Eckert raced to the aid of his dad, Bill, who took a bullet meant for Lucky Spencer. Moments later Bill died a hero, in the arms of his look-alike, Luke Spencer.

vote in approval of their toxic waste incinerator plan. When Damian couldn't convince Lucy to vote her shares their way, he bet that he could charm any woman she could name into bed.

"What do I get when I win?" she asked.

"What do you want?"

"How about one of *your* shares of ELQ?"

Damian smiled. "Done! And when *I* win, I have the option of buying your 4% of ELQ at fair market value, plus a night in bed with your beautiful body! A night you won't forget, I might add."

Soon after arriving back in Port Charles for the first time in a decade, Laura Spencer honored the memory of her mother, Lesley Webber, by paying a tearful visit to her grave.

With the wager set, Lucy wondered which woman in Port Charles was the most seduce-proof!

Ned went to Buffalo on business. At the hotel bar, he heard the Idle Rich, a rock band he knocked as "so-so."

"Oh, yeah. And what do you know about it?" The band's manager, Lois Cerullo, a feisty go-getter from Brooklyn with indescribably long, decorated fingernails, challenged Ned. Having sung in college, Ned hopped on stage and wailed with Lois's band. He tore the place down.

Lois turned to Ned, "I'm gonna make you a star! What's your name?"

"Eddie Maine," Ned lied as she led him to her bed for an incredible night of passion.

After Mac and Felicia at long last became engaged, they met a newcomer to Port Charles. Dr. Kevin Collins found the town incredibly inhospitable. Everywhere he went, people either screamed when they saw him, or punched him out. Kevin was the demonic Ryan's identical twin brother. They'd been separated since they were four. Kevin had an international reputation as a psychiatrist. He'd heard about Ryan's case and wanted to see if he could bring his brother to some degree of sanity.

Mac didn't trust Kevin at all. "Something about his looks," he told Felicia, who saw no reason to blame Kevin for Ryan's crimes.

Kevin visited Ryan in the mental hospital. Ryan gave Kevin a hard time, but he needed his brother and looked forward to Kevin's return. Soon Ryan began practicing how to *be* Kevin!

Ray Conway's body was found outside the ELQ Petrochemical Plant. AJ found Alan's cuff link and confronted him: "You killed him!"

Alan confessed. They both agreed Conway deserved to die. Monica, guessing the truth, forgave Alan. They found keeping the secret a constant strain. AJ decided to help his father by framing Jagger for the crime. Learning that their son caused Jagger's arrest, Alan and Monica pressured AJ to clear him. He did. The police continued investigating.

Lucky trailed his father Luke when he met with a hit man named Ivan, who worked for Frank. Sonny warned Luke that Ivan might really be working for Frank's enemy. As Luke left Ivan, the killer took aim at him. The bullet hit Lucky, and Luke shot Ivan dead.

Luke and Laura spent New Year's Eve at General Hospital praying for their son's recovery.

*P*ure exhilaration! After singing with the Idle Rich, Ned experienced the kind of rush that he usually felt only after he'd made a corporate killing. And all Lois Marie Cerullo, the band's manager, had to do was look at him and Ned felt ten feet tall.

Ned enjoyed his new singing alter ego, Eddie Maine. It allowed him to perform without compromising his mogul status as CEO of ELQ. The gig was fun. But Lois was serious about turning "Eddie Maine and the Idle Rich" into a major rock group. As she supervised his first CD recording session, Lois dreamed of the day Eddie would finally give up his day job as a traveling pharmaceutical salesman.

"Where in tarnation is Ned?" grumbled Ned's grandfather, Edward Quartermaine. Ned's new double life kept him shuffling off to Buffalo, to Lois and the band.

Luke and Laura Spencer got good news from Dr. Tony Jones about their son Lucky. He would recover from the shooting. Their initial fears about permanent paralysis soon disappeared. Lucky would eventually walk again.

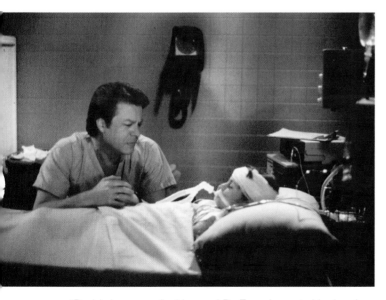

"Daddy loves you," whispered Dr. Tony Jones to his daughter BJ after she was severely injured in a school bus crash in May 1993. Knowing his daughter was brain dead, Tony made the painful decision to turn off her life-support systems. BJ's death was not in vain, however, because Tony and his wife Bobbie elected to donate their little girl's heart to save the life of her critically ill cousin, Maxie.

Luke and Laura were terrified when rival gangsters to Frank Smith, retaliating for the death of their hitman, Ivan, attacked them in the hospital. Laura grabbed Lucky, carrying him down the stairwell, and her sister, nurse Amy Vining, let Laura commandeer an ambulance to drive him away.

At the Bradley Ward House for Children, Laura felt she and her son would be safe. The grandmotherly Mary Mae Ward (Mae Mae to her friends) started the home in honor of her son Bradley, a community leader who had disappeared twenty years earlier.

Pediatrician Simone Hardy, a volunteer at Ward House, introduced Laura to Mae Mae. Mary Mae, an energetic African-American woman, had raised her own family in the house that Laura and her family now lived in. Laura had sensed Mary Mae's love from the first moment she'd entered her new home, and she and Mae Mae became friends instantly.

Furious that his family had been threatened, Luke complained to Sonny Corinthos, Frank Smith's lieutenant in Port Charles. But Laura went to see Frank in prison herself and exacted a promise from him that no harm would befall her or her son. Frank wouldn't guarantee Luke's safety, but he directed Sonny to smash the Garfield gang's threat.

Frank's son Damian smiled when Lucy Coe finally pointed to the woman she was betting he'd never be able to seduce: Bobbie Jones, the most happily married, most devoted wife and mother Lucy knew in Port Charles. Damian wasted no time getting to know Bobbie better. And she didn't mind. As she told her husband Tony, she'd cultivate Damian to get information about his father to help her brother Luke.

Damian knew Bobbie was using him, but Lucy didn't, and she began to get nervous that Bobbie might actually fall for the charming scoundrel. Lucy didn't want her ex-husband Tony, who was now Bobbie's husband, to get hurt. Lucy agreed to vote her ELQ stock in favor of Damian's incinerator proposal. But he refused to call off the bet. Damian enjoyed flirting with Lucy while he flirted with Bobbie.

The incinerator vote would have passed if not for Katherine Bell, Damian's secret ex-lover. When she learned how Damian helped Lucy break up her

"You have to listen to me, Mac—he's Ryan!" shouted Dr. Kevin Collins in the midst of a melee at Mac Scorpio's wedding to Felicia Jones. A vengeful Ryan had tied up his twin brother and showed up at Mac and Felicia's nuptials with a bomb strapped to his chest. When Kevin suddenly appeared, rotten Ryan threatened to blow everyone up, but Mac managed to save the day and Ryan was apprehended.

wedding to Scott, Katherine instantly voted her .5% share in ELQ with Damian's opposition. Ned told Damian he'd romance Katherine to get her to vote her meager, though now crucial, share for their project.

As Ned, he seduced Katherine, who enjoyed his wealthy attention. As Eddie, he began falling for Lois, who was head over heels for him.

Running errands for Frank Smith kept Luke busy. To buy a helicopter for Frank from an amorous Russian, Luke and Laura slipped into their undercover alter egos, Roger and Lulu, and nailed the deal. In spite of herself, Laura loved helping Luke run scams. This was the man she'd fallen in love with!

After a check-up, their son Lucky found a pug-ugly pooch who had been injured in the hospital parking lot. Lucky fell for the dog and adopted him. Lucky named him Foster. Luke called him Skillethead.

Realizing that Frank was plotting his own prison break out, Luke told Laura he'd help spring Frank and have a final show down with him. Laura didn't like what Luke was proposing, but she trusted him to make things right. She found a "safe house" for Luke to bring Frank to after his escape.

When Luke told Sonny they were going to break Frank out of jail, Sonny was impressed with Luke's daring. "Count me in," he told Luke, secretly fearing reprisals from Frank if anything went wrong. Sonny told Stone Cates that he had a job for him, driving the getaway van. Stone was excited.

He and his brother Jagger still had their differences about Stone's working for Sonny, Jagger's worst

enemy. But even so, Stone and Jagger had finally rekindled the warm relationship they'd had as kids.

Jagger stopped boxing. He decided to become a cop and Commissioner Sean Donely promised to help him enroll in a police academy in Chicago once Jagger earned his graduate equivalency diploma. Karen Wexler was very proud of her fiancé. And Jagger was proud of her. She'd received a scholarship to study medicine at Northwestern University. After setting their wedding date, Jagger asked Stone to be his best man.

Karen and Jagger's friend Robin Scorpio was pleased Stone and Jagger had made up. She'd developed a crush on Stone, although her uncle Mac had no use for him whatsoever. Mac felt Stone was bad news—a streetkid, a dropout and, worst of all, a friend of that hood, Sonny Corinthos. The more Mac ordered Robin to keep away from Stone, the more Robin wanted to see him. And did!

Mac's fiancée Felicia Jones advised Mac to go easy on Robin and Stone. Felicia, who had helped to raise Robin after the untimely passing of her parents, talked to her about the ramifications of falling in love. Taking a straightforward approach, Felicia gently advised Robin not to sleep with her boyfriend until she was truly ready, and told her how to protect herself when she was. When Mac found a condom that Felicia had given Robin, he hit the roof. But Robin told Felicia that sex was the furthest thing from her mind.

Feeling very sexy while luxuriating in a warm bath, Robin's friend Brenda Barrett fantasized turning on the hottest men in Port Charles. But the one who turned her on the most was a gangster: Brenda couldn't get Sonny Corinthos out of her mind.

Sensing Brenda's interest in him turned Sonny on to Brenda even more.

"Is danger what you're looking for?" Sonny flashed his dimpled smile at Brenda.

Brenda denied it. "Why do you say that?"

"Because ever since we met, every move you made has been flirting with danger."

Brenda continued flirting. She was completely over her obsession with Jagger Cates.

Before Jagger and Karen's wedding day, a suicidal patient at the hospital almost plunged out a window—with Karen—but a new orderly, Miguel Morez, saved them both. The heroic and hard-working Miguel, who needed money for his family in Puerto Rico, took on a second job when Mac hired him as bartender at the Outback. Miguel saw how Jagger felt about Karen and had a pang. He had once been in love like that.

Jagger couldn't hold back the smiles as he joyously prepared to marry his love, Karen. On the very same day, Jagger's brother Stone tried desperately to quell his fears as he prepared to assist in a prison break. Jagger followed his brother Stone when he realized Stone was about to drive the getaway van carrying Frank Smith out of jail. When Jagger couldn't convince Stone to go back to the wedding with him, he slugged his wayward brother and put him on his cycle and sped off. Tragedy struck when the bike spun out into a snowdrift. Hitting his head on the icy pavement, Jagger was knocked out.

Stone got help for Jagger as he directed the police away from where he knew Luke would be taking Frank. Luke and Sonny had broken Frank Smith out of jail, but it had gone wrong. The cops were everywhere. There'd been a shoot-out and Sonny took two bullets, but he got to his car and drove off. He passed out, crashing his car just as Brenda was passing by in the brand new car she bought herself with earnings from her work as the face of Deception Perfume.

Brenda drove Sonny to his apartment and called for help, as he directed, and a mob doctor patched him up. In the midst of this life-threatening crisis, Brenda realized that she had truly fallen for this sexy and dangerous man. Brenda's blood was needed for a transfusion.

When Luke got Frank to the safe house, he took out his gun and pointed it at the mobster, intending to shoot Frank. But just then Laura arrived. Frank grabbed her as a shield and got away, later letting her go.

Dr. Ryan Chamberlain also escaped from his prison cell. Knocking out his visiting twin brother Kevin Collins, Ryan traded places with him. Ryan would never let Felicia marry Mac. He showed up at the church on their wedding day wearing a bomb! No one suspected he was Ryan and not Kevin—until Kevin burst in. He'd finally convinced the guards who he was. Ryan threatened to blow everyone up, but Mac got the bomb away from him, tossing it to Paul Hornsby, who detonated it safely outside the church. Mac and Ryan struggled and crashed through a second floor railing to the floor below. Ryan was captured.

But Mac was injured and couldn't marry Felicia. Paul and Jenny, who had longed to be together, seized the moment and took their place at the altar. Following this impromptu and heartfelt ceremony, Paul and Jenny Hornsby left on an instant honeymoon in the South Pacific. Upon their return, Jenny's nephew Sly moved in with them.

After Mac recovered, he and Felicia postponed their wedding again when Felicia's daughter Maxie became terribly ill.

Jagger recuperated from his motorcycle spill and married Karen in a touching wedding ceremony. It was a day filled with love—and surprises. Karen's mother Rhonda dropped a bombshell when she tearfully revealed to her daughter that Scott Baldwin was Karen's father. Karen, overjoyed by the news, happily hopped on the back of her new husband's motorcycle and sped off to a new life in Chicago. Karen and Jagger—together at last!

Stone stayed behind with Sonny, who'd been nursed back to health by Brenda. The Quartermaines weren't happy with Brenda's new man but, still, Lila encouraged Brenda to trust her heart.

Neutralizing Frank Smith consumed Luke Spencer, who finally realized how he could do it without shedding blood. He could control Frank if he had some dirt on Frank's beloved daughter Jennifer, whom Luke almost married. Jennifer was Frank's Achilles' heel.

Luke's brother-in-law Tony grew jealous of his wife Bobbie's spying on Frank's son Damian for Luke. Tony put his foot down when Damian invited Bobbie for a weekend at his sister Jennifer's Atlantic City casino. Luke decided he and Laura ought to check out Jennifer's place.

Jennifer, who was no longer the thin and willowy woman Luke remembered, couldn't keep her hands off Luke. Her husband Billy Boggs developed instant hots for Laura! Fending off the oversexed couple, Luke and Laura escaped—with proof of larceny that could put Jennifer behind bars for years. Gotcha, Frank, Luke thought.

After hearing from Sonny that Frank was in San Joaquin, Luke and Laura flew to see him. Police Commissioner Sean Donely, who suspected Luke helped Frank escape prison, followed them—and *he* was followed by his reporter wife Tiffany.

Laura whispered to Luke, "With Tiffany following Sean following you following me following Frank Smith, it's beginning to look like a conga line!" It did, but Luke won Frank's promise to lay off the Spencers with the information Luke had on Jennifer. Luke even saved Sean's life from an alligator attack arranged by Frank's men!

Life became sweet for Luke and Laura, who discovered she was pregnant. Their son Lucky was thriving in his first perfectly normal home. He and his friend Sly went into business, selling worm farms which they called Mother Nature's Own Garbage Disposal Unit.

When they sold one to Lila Quartermaine at her mansion, Lucky's dog Foster accompanied them. Foster met Annabelle, the pedigree dog Edward bought for his wife, and the two dogs fell deeply in love. But Edward Quartermaine despised Foster from day one. He was a mutt from the wrong side of the tracks.

After Lucky and Sly found a gun and a blood-stained dressing gown while playing in the attic, Luke and Laura found a body in their yard. It was Bradley Ward, Mae Mae's long-missing son. He'd been murdered!

Bradley's son Justus came to Port Charles for the funeral. He was a lawyer—and community-minded, like his late father. Mary Mae greeted him with tears. It was good to have him home. And Keesha, Mary Mae's granddaughter, had come home, too.

Mary Mae thanked Edward Quartermaine for coming to her son's funeral. Luke Spencer was surprised to see him there. Mary Mae had told him that Edward and his partners from 20 years ago, who included Jack Boland and Frank Smith, before his mob activities were known, had fought Bradley bitterly over his opposition to their projects.

With Justus, Luke investigated Bradley's death. Keesha began dating Jason Quartermaine. Neither Mary Mae nor Edward seemed pleased that their grandchildren were going out together.

After eavesdropping on Alan and Monica talking about Alan's guilt in Ray Conway's killing, Damian stole the incriminating evidence from police headquarters. He blackmailed Alan and Monica with it for their ELQ votes backing his incinerator project. Alan

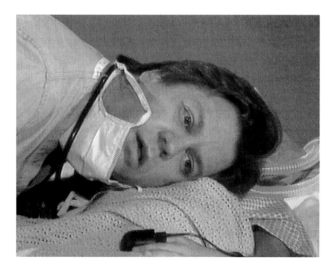

When the transplant of BJ's heart into Maxie's body was completed, Tony Jones put his head on Maxie's chest and listened in wonderment to the sound of his precious daughter's heart beating. BJ had given Maxie life!

refused to submit to Damian's blackmail.

"Go to hell! I'd rather go to jail!" Alan was fit to spit.

Damian discovered he couldn't turn Alan in. Alan's son AJ paid Luke Spencer to steal the evidence from Damian's safe—but AJ kept the evidence himself.

Edward feared that his other grandson Ned and his no-good friend Damian might get the votes they needed for their damned toxic waste incinerator. AJ proposed that he and Edward could make money from Damian's plan by buying up the land where the incinerator should be built with a dummy corporation and selling it back to ELQ at a huge profit. Edward liked the idea and invited his friend Jack Boland to join them.

The designated site, Charles Street, housed the Bradley Ward home. The street was home to a vibrant African-American community in Port Charles. Also to Luke and Laura. And Miguel Morez.

Miguel saved the day for Lois Cerullo when her hot band, the Idle Rich, was booked into the Outback. Ned didn't dare perform as Eddie Maine in Port Charles, so he faked laryngitis and was a no-show. When Miguel sang with the band to help Lois out, she knew she'd found another star. But Miguel said he didn't want to sing professionally.

Ned loved his double life—mogul by day, rock singer by night—too much to give it up. And he'd begun caring about Lois, who was increasingly in Port Charles. Ned took Brenda into his confidence and introduced her to Lois as sort of a "little sister" when Lois demanded that she meet someone he knew. Eddie had already met all of Lois's family in Brooklyn. And she found an old friend from her Bensonhurst neighborhood when she met Brenda's boyfriend.

"Sonny Corinthos! How are you! You know, my brother Louie still wants that $300 you owe him!"

Sonny and Lois had a warm reunion. Since Frank's escape and his involvement with Brenda, he decided to go legit. When Lois and Brenda decided to open their own record company, L&B Records, Sonny backed them as a partner. While keeping his identity as Eddie Maine a secret from Sonny, Brenda begged Ned to tell Lois the truth.

Ned was still trying to win Katherine's ELQ vote, and Katherine was trying to win *him*. She saw Ned kissing Brenda's friend Lois and decided that she had to act fast. When Katherine proposed to Ned, he turned her down, but she wasn't taking no for an answer.

Having overheard a conversation between Alan and AJ about the stolen evidence incriminating Alan in the death of Ray Conway, Katherine stole it

Dr. Monica Quartermaine felt discomfort in her breast but chose to ignore the symptoms. When she finally went for a mammogram, it was too late. In 1994, she underwent a mastectomy and chemotherapy treatments, only to have another lump appear on the incision. In excruciating detail and with unrelenting realism, viewers followed Monica's battle to survive as well as the effect her illness had on the entire Quartermaine family.

from AJ's office. Katherine then went to Edward Quartermaine and told him to order his grandson Ned to marry her or his son Alan would go to jail.

The Quartermaines forced Ned to marry Katherine. But first Ned eloped with Lois and honeymooned with her at Coney Island. Ned made sure she never learned his real name—and that their wedding was not legal.

"I don't deserve you. But I sure do love you."

"Oh, Eddie!" They kissed and kissed again.

Then Ned exacted a share of ELQ from each member of his family, forced AJ to resign from the Port Charles Hotel, secured the family's ELQ voting rights for 5 years and finally married Katherine. She moved into the Quartermaine mansion with him and turned over the evidence—which Alan burned.

Then, at Lila's invitation, Lois moved into the Quartermaine gatehouse. It became home both to her and to L&B Records.

Like walking a tightrope, Ned hopped from bed to bed! Brenda couldn't believe his stamina. Feeling very disloyal to her friend, Lois, she begged Ned to end the charade.

Eager to sign up Miguel, Lois learned that he'd been a singer in Puerto Rico, but his contract was owned by a mobster. With Miguel's permission, Lois told Sonny. He used his clout as a Frank Smith lieutenant to buy back Miguel's contract from Rivera, the Puerto Rican gangster who owned it. Sonny forced Rivera to lay off Miguel and his family in the future. Back in Port Charles, Sonny persuaded Miguel to sign with L&B.

When Ned and Damian announced plans to build a toxic waste incinerator on Charles Street, Laura Spencer led the community protest of the controversial project. Jack Boland, Edward's partner in the dummy corporation, wasn't about to lose a fortune because Laura opposed the plan. He hired some thugs to frighten her into silence.

Foster tried to protect Laura, but she fell in the basement while hiding from her tormentors. Finding her, Luke got Laura to the hospital where she gave birth to their daughter, Leslie Lu, named for Laura's mother Lesley and for Laura's alter-ego, Lulu.

Lucky loved rocking Lesley Lu. "I'm your big brother. It's my job to take care of you," he told his baby sister lovingly. But when Laura and the baby were threatened in the hospital, Luke sent mother and daughter to Beechers Corners, where their favorite couple, the Whitakers, could keep them safe.

Accusing his family of environmental racism, Jason joined the protest against the incinerator. Alan and Monica were proud of their son, though they feared for their other son AJ's soul because of his fervor for the project.

Damian's seduction of Bobbie was working. She couldn't stop thinking about him. When she made love to her husband Tony, she thought about Damian Smith.

After she and Damian kissed, Bobbie tried to end it. To maintain their connection, he underwrote the General Hospital Nurses' Ball to benefit AIDS research and patient services. When he arranged for Bobbie to be named Chairwoman of the Event, Lucy wangled her way in as Bobbie's co-chairperson and decided she had to break them up.

Trying to understand why she still found Damian attractive, while she hated the way he toyed with Tony and Bobbie's marriage, Lucy sought advice from Dr. Kevin Collins. He found the self-centered Lucy amusing. Her attempts to do the right thing only made the mess she'd wagered herself into even messier. But Kevin was annoyed when he dated her and saw Lucy using him to make Damian jealous!

Felicia barely held herself together when the doctors told her that her daughter Maxie was dying from Kawasaki Syndrome, congenital heart failure, pneumonia and an extremely rare genetic P-factor. The frail youngster desperately needed a heart transplant, and it was highly unlikely a match would be found. Mac and Felicia stood vigil at Maxie's bedside. Finally he left to find and bring Maxie's father Frisco to her side.

Thanks to Mac, Maxie smiled. "I love you, Daddy."

Mac saw that even Felicia smiled to see Frisco. He also saw that Felicia had never looked at him the way she was now looking at Frisco.

Bobbie Jones was impatient. Her daughter BJ was dawdling as Bobbie, distracted by thoughts about Damian, sent her off to school. Bobbie went to the hospital where Damian motioned her into the stairwell. Bobbie followed him like a moth to a flame. Tony opened the door and saw them embracing. Tony punched out Damian and stormed off.

"Tony!" Bobbie screamed and followed him. How could she make him understand when she barely understood herself? Bobbie caught up with Tony. He was yelling at her when nurse Amy Vining found them.

"Tony, Bobbie. There's been an accident. It's BJ!"

BJ's schoolbus had been hit by a drunk driver. BJ was badly hurt. As soon as Tony saw her, he knew she was brain dead. He made a decision. He told Bobbie they had to donate BJ's heart to her little cousin Maxie. Bobbie shook her head no.

"Bobbie, nothing's going to bring her back."

Bobbie couldn't comprehend that her little girl was gone. She choked on her tears as she said goodbye.

Tony took his daughter's hand. "When you give your heart to Maxie, I will give my heart to you. And we will both be safe." Tony sobbed. "Bless you, BJ. I love you."

When the transplant was completed, Tony put his head on Maxie's chest and heard BJ's heart beating. A miracle! Tony and Bobbie's tears were tempered by the knowledge that their beloved daughter's heart would beat on in the body of her cousin.

Lucy Coe was also in tears. BJ had once been her stepdaughter. Lucy ran into Damian, who was sympathetic, but he still planned to bed Bobbie to win their bet. Lucy realized Damian was evil.

After BJ's funeral, Tony threw Bobbie out of the brownstone. She showed up at Damian's door and wound up in Damian's bed. Lucy barged in to find them between the sheets!

"You bastard!" Lucy yelled at Damian. Bobbie was unfazed. She was where she wanted to be. When Damian suggested she return to Tony, Bobbie wasn't sure she wanted to.

"It was a bet, Bobbie! Damian doesn't love you!" Lucy wanted to shake her to get Bobbie to see Damian for the louse he was.

Lucy gave Bobbie the key to her apartment and dared her to watch Damian collect his winnings. The next night, when Bobbie used the key and found Lucy

in bed with Damian, she was devastated. She dumped a bucket of ice water on Damian and left. Then Lucy kicked Damian out of her bed before he collected his winnings. She wouldn't pay him anything. Damian was furious.

Watching Frisco and Felicia together during Maxie's crisis, Mac realized that in their hearts, Felicia and Frisco belonged together. And so he set her free. "It's over, Felicia."

Felicia and Frisco shared a night of pure passion. As much as they cared for each other—and they cared deeply—Felicia understood that her beloved Frisco would not be happy living a life of domestic tranquility. She could never tame his wanderlust—danger was Frisco Jones' life blood. With a tender kiss, Felicia sent Frisco back to his adventures with the WSB.

The death scene from *Romeo and Juliet* is supposed to be tragic, but everyone laughed when Robin and Stone performed it at the Nurses' Ball. "Juliet" kissed her dead "Romeo," and "Romeo" kissed back.

"You're supposed to be dead," Robin muttered.

"I'm not that dead," Stone replied.

Mac fumed to see his niece kissing the boy he'd forbidden her to see.

As the talent show continued, Lucy tried to reunite Tony and Bobbie by secretly pairing them in a tango number. Tony saw Bobbie on stage and walked off. She was humiliated. Damian chivalrously took to the stage and danced a hot tango with her. He exited to applause—and a punch in the jaw from Tony. Damian had Tony arrested.

Monica Quartermaine woke up and her left breast felt sore. She knew she needed a mammogram, but kept putting it off. When she was finally tested she learned that she faced surgery and a possible mastectomy. Her husband Alan held her tenderly. On the night before her surgery they made love.

When Monica awakened after her surgery, she felt she'd lost herself and not merely a breast when Bobbie told her the tumor had been malignant.

Alan was strong. "I won't lose you, do you hear me. I will not let you go. We will fight this cancer."

"I can't fight."

"Oh, yes you can. And you will!" If he had to, Alan would force Monica to take care of herself. She began an exhausting regimen of chemotherapy.

Tiffany Hill broadcast the fight to stop ELQ's toxic waste incinerator at a city council meeting. Edward insisted all the Quartermaines attend to defend the plan, which he still hated. Lois glanced at the TV set.

She saw the camera pan across all the Q's, as she called them. She saw Katherine, the witch that Ned, the only Q she hadn't met, had married. And by Katherine's side, she saw....

"Eddie?"

Nobody in the Quartermaine family could stand Katherine. After she hit Lila's dog Annabelle with a shoe, Lila turned to Reginald, her butler, and sighed.

"Will no one rid us of that accursed creature!"

Katherine threw herself a birthday party at the Outback and demanded that her new family celebrate with her. A giant cake was rolled out and Lois popped out of it!

"Happy birthday to Mrs. Ned Ashton from the other Mrs. Ned Ashton!"

Ned's double life was over! So were his two marriages!

Ned had hired Mac to dig up some dirt on Katherine so he could divorce her safely. He learned that she was an embezzler—and that she'd been Damian's lover for years. Now he could control her. But it was too late.

Bobbie still wanted Damian. Whenever Damian turned around, Bobbie was there. He found her a nuisance. When Damian was kissing Lucy, Bobbie saw them and threw a fit—in public!

"Get out of my life!" Damian ordered.

Bobbie realized she'd thrown her life away on a man who wasn't worth it. She sought revenge. Pretending to be a mysterious admirer, she lured Damian to the catacombs before revealing herself.

"Bobbie! You?"

"Listen closely, Damian, because the next sound you hear will be your introduction to my version of hell!"

Bobbie severed the power line in the tunnel and left, slamming the door. Damian was lost in the dark. He couldn't get out. A storm hit. Water in the catacombs began rising. Damian tried to climb out. Falling, he broke his back! He couldn't move, trapped in rising water with rats crawling across his chest. That's when Lucky Spencer and his dog Foster found him.

Ironically, Tony operated on Damian and saved his worthless life.

While recovering, Damian's only visitor was Katherine. He encouraged her to tough it out with the Quartermaines. After calling them all together to demand Ned divorce Lois and remarry her, she collapsed and fell down a flight of stairs.

Someone tried to poison Katherine and she was

"Happy Birthday, Mrs. Ned Ashton. —from the other Mrs. Ned Ashton!"

Lois Cerullo picked the perfect moment to shock her two-timing, multi-married husband, Ned "Eddie Maine" Ashton, when she popped out of a giant birthday cake at his other wife Katherine's birthday party. Ned's double life was over. So were his two marriages!

comatose for weeks. Damian visited her bedside constantly. When she came to, they swore revenge on all their enemies in Port Charles—especially Lucy Coe. Damian learned that Lucy helped Luke Spencer discover he'd used mob money to buy his major share of ELQ. Ned forced Damian to sell it back—at a loss.

Police Commissioner Sean Donely questioned the Quartermaines about Katherine's poisoning. He still suspected their involvement with the Conway killing—but he simply couldn't prove it. Monica suggested to her old friend (and lover) that without a shred of evidence the case should just be forgotten. They flirted with each other for old times sake, and Monica felt better about herself than she had since she'd first heard about her breast cancer.

Sean knew he'd be coming back to the Quartermaines. Evidence in the Bradley Ward murder pointed to Edward as the killer, who swore to Mary

In a Puerto Rican graveyard, mobster Frank Smith engaged in a final showdown with his longtime nemesis, Luke Spencer. When Luke shot and killed Smith, his long vendetta was finally over.

was taken over by ELQ. Ned, however, let Lucy run her former company. She began dating Kevin Collins, who became less interested in Felicia the more he saw of Lucy. Besides, Felicia discovered she was pregnant by Frisco.

"Good heavens, the butler did it!" Edward's eyes popped when Reginald confessed to poisoning Katherine. The Quartermaines rallied around Reginald. AJ successfully framed Katherine for attempting to kill herself. When Katherine realized that the police considered her the prime suspect in her own near-murder, her blood boiled. But that was how the investigation ended.

Edward was tried for Bradley Ward's murder. He was furious when his so-called friend Jack Boland slandered him on the witness stand.

Laura and Leslie Lu returned to Port Charles in time for Luke and Laura's 13th wedding anniversary.

Mae that he didn't kill her son. She told him that she knew that.

Edward was indicted anyway. His friend Jack Boland had lied to the police to incriminate Edward. Luke suspected Frank Smith was a more likely suspect and pressed on in his investigation with Justus.

Ned told Lois the entire truth about his deception and marriage to Katherine. She didn't want to have anything to do with him. Eddie was gone forever and she had no use for this Ashton, this "Nedley," as she began calling him. She wasn't going to forgive him. It even took her a while to get over her anger at her business partner Brenda.

Sonny was annoyed with Brenda for keeping Ned's secret and jeopardizing their business. But he forgave Brenda. L&B Records launched Miguel Morez's career with a mega-concert in his native Puerto Rico. Sonny located Lily Rivera, Miguel's lost-love and song-writing inspiration. She was the daughter of the Puerto Rican crime boss.

Lily's love for Miguel hadn't died after Lily's father forced them apart. He'd forced Lily to give up her child by Miguel. Their boy was now six, Lily told him. In Puerto Rico, they searched for and found their son Juan. That he'd been adopted into a happy home eased their heartache a little.

Lucy dropped Damian totally after learning he had destroyed her chance to buy Deception, which

"Rainbow of Hope"—the theme of the 2nd Annual G.H. Nurses Ball, was ably represented in a fun-loving rendition of *The Wizard of Oz* featuring Alan (The Cowardly Lion), Tony (The Scarecrow), Kevin (The Tin Man) and Emily (Dorothy) as part of the ball's amateur talent show. The glittering gala is held yearly in the Versailles Room to raise funds for the Combined AIDS-related Programs at General Hospital.

As they kissed, Luke and Laura vowed they'd never be separated again. They belonged together.

Frank Smith was angry that Luke was sniffing into his affairs again because of the Ward murder case. Frank had a plan.

Police Commissioner Sean Donely got a tip that Jack Boland had been murdered. Sean arrived to find Luke standing over Jack's body. Luke and Sean both knew that Luke had been set up. Luke knew it must have been Frank.

Lucy couldn't convince Kevin to take her to Puerto Rico to hear Miguel sing, so she went alone.

Frank Smith was now hiding out in Puerto Rico. He summoned Sonny Corinthos to a meeting. Sonny called Luke to fill in for him. Luke told Sonny that he would meet Frank in Sonny's place.

Sean tailed Luke to the meeting. Sean slipped. Frank whirled and shot! Sean was hit. Luke stepped out as Frank aimed at Sean again.

"Appropriate place to meet, Frank!" They were in a cemetery.

"Spencer!" Frank fired at Luke.

Luke shot back. Frank fell. Luke shot him again—to be sure. The long vendetta was over.

Damian was making love to Katherine when the call came. "Your father's dead."

Together, they went to Puerto Rico to retrieve his body.

News of Frank Smith's death spread quickly. Rivera, Lily's gangster father, heard and was delighted. No more Frank Smith. No more having to give in to Sonny Corinthos.

Sonny feared trouble from Rivera and met with him. Brenda followed him and was caught. With Luke's help, Sonny and Brenda escaped from Rivera's men. They leaped into a speedboat but a bullet hit Luke. He fell overboard, shouting at Sonny and Brenda to keep going.

At the concert site, Lois wondered where her partners were. Ned had shown up and, for the first time, Lois's icy attitude began to thaw. Ned felt hopeful.

Breathless, Sonny and Brenda arrived in time to hear Miguel sing to thundering applause. After the concert, Brenda, Sonny, Miguel and Lily were all kidnaped by Lily's father.

Sonny told Rivera that he was taking over, filling the power vacuum left in the mob by Frank's death. Sonny liked the sound of it even as he was trying to tough his way out of the bad situation. Rivera wasn't buying any of it. His daughter Lily convinced him to

In one of General Hospital's *most powerful and realistic storylines, Monica Quartermaine furthered her bout with breast cancer by entering the La Mesa Wellness Community. Away from the turbulent confines of the Quartermaine mansion, Monica was finally able to let down her guard and share her painful feelings of loneliness, despair, fear and anger with her fellow patients.*

To make the story of Monica's ongoing recovery process as true to life as possible, actress Leslie Charleson, Executive Producer Wendy Riche and head writer Claire Labine visited Wellness Communities to research what Monica would go through during her fictional stay at La Mesa.

In addition, some of the women in her support group were actual cancer survivors. "The Home Show's" Cathy Masamitsu, a leader in the battle against breast cancer, played the part of an oncologist and Riley Steiner, who portrayed Monica's dear friend, Page Bowen, is a survivor of cervical cancer.

release them all by daring him to kill her when he killed the rest of them. He couldn't do it. They flew back to Port Charles—with sad news.

"Luke is not dead. I would know. I would feel it," Laura declared when she heard he was missing. While others mourned, Laura assured her son Lucky that his father would be back.

Laura was right. Luke, though wounded, had found his way to Lucy Coe's room. She helped nurse him back to health and smuggled him home. Luke and Laura held each other dearly. Their years of running from Frank Smith were truly over.

Luke's sister Bobbie got her estranged husband Tony to agree to marriage counseling. Hopefully, Kevin Collins could help salvage their marriage. As soon as Tony agreed, he disappointed Bobbie by accompanying his ex-sister-in-law Felicia to Cairo so she could tell Frisco they were going to have another baby.

Monica held her breath. After all the exhaustion and hair loss, she'd finally completed chemotherapy. The report on Monica's condition was disappointing. A new lump was found on her incision and she faced another round of chemo. Alan hesitated before reassuring her. He'd come to feel that his words of support sometimes irritated Monica. Thank God he had Monica's best friend Bobbie to help him support Monica through this ordeal. Bobbie was grateful for Alan's support since she separated from Tony.

Edward's trial went poorly. Proof that Jack Boland had actually killed Bradley was inconclusive. Then Bradley's mother Mary Mae announced why Edward couldn't have killed Bradley. He was Bradley's father! Mary Mae described how she was a lonely war widow singing blues in a saloon in 1942 when she and a navy lieutenant, Edward, connected. Bradley was the result of their brief encounter.

Edward was acquitted. His concern was for his wife Lila, who forgave him his indiscretion despite her hurt.

Justus Ward couldn't believe Edward was his grandfather. Being a Quartermaine—and being related to white folks—would take Justus some time to get used to. Justus ran for a city council seat. His staunchest campaign supporter was Dr. Simone Hardy. Though he was interested in Simone, Justus held back. She was committed to her long-absent husband Tom, who was doing relief medicine in Africa.

When Simone went out to dinner with Justus, he was surprised when her son Tommy ran to Steve and Audrey Hardy.

"Grandpa. Grandma!" Justus realized Simone's husband was white. Seeing Justus with Simone, Audrey feared for her son Tom's marriage. Audrey's husband Steve told her they shouldn't interfere.

Lucy's relationship with Kevin Collins progressed. He'd been having nightmares that he'd killed his lover Grace by drowning her in a car, but Lucy helped him discover he was innocent. Kevin's fears

Dr. Tom Hardy's return from Africa was met with anything but enthusiasm from his son, Tommy, who barely recognized him, and his estranged wife, Simone, who questioned Tom's motives for insinuating himself back into their lives.

that he might be a killer like his twin Ryan disappeared and he fell deeply in love with Lucy. Their feelings were mutual.

Miguel and Lily had never fallen out of love. At Christmas they became engaged.

Brenda suggested that she and Sonny live together. "Bad timing," thought Sonny, who, unbeknownst to Brenda, was taking over Frank Smith's gang. Still, he helped her move into his place.

Ned promised Lois he'd take a leave from ELQ to concentrate on his music. He hoped she'd learn to love Ned as much as she'd once loved Eddie.

For Bobbie and Tony, the holidays brought a tentative truce in their marital rift. For months they had separately mourned their heart-breaking loss. Now, as the new year loomed, the Joneses tried to focus on happy memories of the past as they came together in a mutual need to heal their family.

"Will BJ get presents in heaven?" little Lucas asked his parents.

Of course she would. Tony would see to that. He returned with a multi-colored assortment of helium balloons. On the brownstone stoop, tears filled Bobbie and Tony's eyes as they watched their son let go of the balloons, sending them up to heaven.

1 9 9 5

*L*ucy Coe never had so much trouble getting a man into her bed! It seemed like forever before interruptions and misfortunes like patients, hives, a flaming sofa and a slippery bathtub subsided enough for Lucy and Kevin to finally make love. They liked it so much, they did it again!

Kevin paid a final visit to his twin, Ryan. Ryan asked about life in Port Charles and was genuinely sorry to hear of BJ's death. Kevin told him he'd rid himself of all his demons—including Ryan, and that he'd never see him again.

"You see, Ryan, the big difference between us is that I can love and you can't."

"Oh yeah?" challenged Ryan. "How's Felicia?"

"Pregnant—with Frisco's child." Kevin left Ryan seething.

When Ryan's naive new occupational therapist, Connie Cooper, taught him how to crochet, Ryan's mood improved. He'd crochet and talk. She'd watch him crochet and listen. Before long, he'd crocheted his way into her heart.

"This is too easy!" Ryan giggled to himself. He'd come up with a plan.

So had Edward Quartermaine. To improve his relationship with his new African-American grandson Justus Ward and to turn all his recent bad publicity around, Edward proposed setting up a foundation to fund new businesses on Charles Street, an area his company had once targeted for its aborted toxic waste incinerator. Even Justus, who'd been voted in as city councilman, liked the idea. Justus was wary about working with his new cousin, AJ. But AJ's brother Jason, whom Justus liked, also joined the Charles St. Foundation Board.

Dr. Simone Hardy was excited about how quickly Justus had become a leader in Port Charles. Her mother-in-law Audrey Hardy smiled grimly every time Simone began praising Justus. She wished her son Tom would come home. He'd been away two years.

Audrey's wish came true. Dr. Tom Hardy came home—to find Justus feeling very at home with Tom's wife and son Tommy. Justus left, knowing that Tom and Simone had a lot to talk about.

Tom confessed that he'd had an affair with a col-league in Rwanda, but that he didn't love her. Tom loved his wife Simone. He asked her and Tommy to move to Africa with him, but she refused to uproot their son. She suggested that she and Tom end their marriage and they decided to divorce as Tom went back to Africa.

Tom's father Steve Hardy was particularly disappointed that Tom had cheated on Simone. Audrey couldn't change Steve's mind.

"Robin, I'm so proud of you!" Mac Scorpio was ecstatic. His niece Robin had been accepted to Yale. But his smile dropped when she told him she didn't want to move so far from Stone Cates. Mac and Robin had been fighting for almost a year about her seeing him.

Stone had come down with the flu. As Robin nursed him with chicken soup, he persuaded her to go to Yale. After all, he'd be out of town a lot himself, on band tours with L&B Records' hottest groups. Meanwhile, they still had the rest of her senior year and all summer to be together.

Lois Cerullo (Ashton) drove her husband Ned mercilessly on his whirlwind tour as Eddie Maine, the rock singer. Finally she collapsed on the bed in their Schenectady hotel room and Ned whispered, "You want a commitment from me? I'll run you into the ground, my love."

Luke Spencer formed a partnership with Sonny Corinthos in a blues club with a little back-room gambling action. Sonny provided the space—his old strip joint, the Paradise Lounge. Sonny, Brenda and Stone were living in the apartment above.

While Luke readied the club for its big opening, a drifter named Mike Corbin asked him for a job. A likable conman, Mike got Luke a good deal on the club's dinnerware, which Mike had stolen. An unsuspecting Luke hired Mike as his maître d'.

Mike swiped a great pair of speakers from a van parked at the Outback and presented them to Luke. When Luke showed Sonny their club's new speakers, his partner was fit to be tied. Pointing to the "Idle Rich" logo on them, Sonny told Luke that they belonged to his company's band.

Confronting Mike, Luke informed him he had stolen the speakers from the "baddest dude" in Port Charles. "Mike Corbin, meet Sonny Corinthos."

Dr. Ryan Chamberlain cleverly coaxed his occupational therapist, Connie Cooper, into helping him escape from prison. Connie's pipe dreams—and life—came to an abrupt end when Ryan snapped her neck, ironically with the very scarf she taught him to crochet.

The two men stared at each other. "Hi, kid," Mike offered.

Luke was totally confused. "The two of you know each other?"

"Oh, yeah," Mike muttered.

"He's my father," said Sonny turning his back—but he let Mike stay on. Mike tried to reach his estranged son, but Sonny ignored him.

Sonny's decision to take over Frank Smith's gang brought him into another partnership—with Luke's enemy, Damian Smith. From his inheritance, Damian provided Sonny with money to run Frank's crime empire, chuckling to think how his old dad would love the fact that his son was finally getting his hands dirty.

"Just as long as nobody knows," Damian whispered in Katherine's ear, his only confidante.

Ned Ashton didn't trust Sonny Corinthos from the start. He knew his wife Lois loved the guy like a broth-er, and Sonny was her partner in L&B, not to mention their friend Brenda Barrett's lover. But Ned wanted Sonny out of all their lives, so he hired Mac Scorpio to investigate Sonny.

While Mac was in Brooklyn learning about Sonny and Scully, Mac's niece Robin invited Stone to their home. Robin had lost so many of the people she had loved in her young life she just wanted to hold on to Stone. In the year they'd been seeing each other she had fallen more deeply in love than she could ever have imagined, and she wanted to show Stone how much she cared. She was ready to make love with him, but Stone pulled back.

"What's wrong?" Robin asked.

"I don't have any protection." Stone and Robin cooled down and decided to wait. As he left the house, he ran into the returning Mac, who flipped out and grounded Robin.

Edward Quartermaine was apoplectic when his prize dog, Annabelle, ran off with that Spencer mongrel, Foster, and the two dogs behaved like animals! But Edward really lost his temper when Annabelle disgraced the family by becoming pregnant!

"I'll drown the damn puppies if they look like Foster!" he declared.

"Drain the jacuzzi, Reggie," Edward's wife Lila instructed. She wasn't going to take any chances. She promised Lucky Spencer, Foster's owner, the pick of the litter.

Newly engaged, Miguel and Lily decided to wait until their wedding night to make love. Lily fantasized about all the children they'd have. Miguel laughed. He wanted kids, too—but not until his career had taken off.

Brenda never waited. She was deliriously happy with Sonny. Her lover, her partner, her life. She never suspected he was keeping so many secrets from her.

They yelled. They screamed. They cried. They maintained stony silence. Bobbie and Tony Jones were finally exploring what had gone wrong with their marriage in sessions with Dr. Kevin Collins. It was painful, but it was working. Though Bobbie wasn't too thrilled with her therapist's choice of lover when she realized he and Lucy Coe were an item.

On Valentine's Day, Lucy gave her psychiatrist boyfriend a rare first edition of Freud. Kevin, in turn, gave Lucy some jewelry—and a duck! She named her

After slipping on the ice and breaking his leg, Edward Quartermaine was comforted...and kept alive...by his dog Annabelle. Edward's bad break occurred while searching for the family's pregnant pooch during a winter storm.

new pet Sigmund, and it became the love of her life. After Kevin, of course.

Katherine Bell hated Lucy. She and her lover Damian Smith weren't finished getting their revenge on her.

Monica Quartermaine decided to go through her second round of chemotherapy at La Mesa Wellness Group in Arizona. Her husband Alan wanted to take her to the airport, but Monica didn't want him to. Alan had begun to wonder just what she wanted from him. But he knew he would always be there for her. More and more, he appreciated being able to confide his hurts and frustrations to Bobbie Jones.

At the Wellness Group, Monica slowly bonded with other women who were fighting cancer. She became particularly close to Page Bowen, a widow with an eleven-year-old daughter named Emily. After Monica and Page had a good cry listening to "La Boheme" together, they became friends forever.

After a particularly rough chemo session, Monica waved Page away. Page asked Monica a disturbing question. "Why don't you want anybody to help you?"

Monica thought about what Page said and phoned Alan. She needed her husband and wanted to share her experiences at the Wellness Group with him. Alan flew out immediately.

When he arrived, Monica felt that she looked like a mess, gaunt and bald from the chemo, and lopsided from the surgery.

Alan smiled at her. "You've never looked more beautiful to me in your life."

"Liar," Monica laughed.

Alan wanted to be alone with her. But Monica constantly included Page and Emily in their time together. Alan liked them both, but he grew frustrated.

Alan wanted to hold Monica. He wanted to make love to her. But she kept her distance as Alan tried to remind her how good sex between them had always been. She wondered how he could expect her to be "in the mood" at a time like this.

Monica whirled around to face Alan and angrily peeled off her robe.

"Do you honestly think *this* is sexy? Try making love to this!" she dared, revealing the scar that had replaced her breast.

"I miss you, Monica. Not your breast."

They embraced and made love. But it was unsatisfying.

"I was so aware of needing you, or needing to be near you, Monica—and you weren't there at all." They

ISSUES

As part of its commitment to compelling, informative storytelling, General Hospital *presented a saga of classic romantic resonance and contemporary social urgency in 1995. The story involved young lovers Robin Scorpio and Stone Cates who were in the heady throes of first love when Stone was diagnosed with the AIDS virus.*

This dramatic love story took place in real time, and was not rushed for the sake of accommodation. General Hospital *viewers saw the affects AIDS had on the lives of these young characters on a daily basis. And viewers would learn life-enhancing information as the story—and the disease—progressed.*

"This is a story of choices," explained executive producer Wendy Riche when the story was announced to the public. "Knowledge is power, and we hope with this story to empower our audience with practical information about the choices individuals have regarding sex in the '90s. Protection, contraception, HIV blood tests, monogamy and abstinence are all factors that must be considered by any person in this age who considers sexual expression. We're offering this information dramatically through the most intimate experiences of these two young lovers."

Here, a stunned Robin learns the devastating news from the young man she loves.

were two people—alone in the same bed.

Luke gave Laura, Lucky and Foster the grand tour of his new club.

"Luke, I love it," said Laura. "Really cool, Dad!" Lucky liked it, too. Foster seemed indifferent.

"Thanks, Skillethead." Luke's opening was to be the next night. But as they were leaving, Luke's Club was firebombed! No one was hurt but Laura was terrified. Was it starting all over again for them?

"Luke, were you the target?" she asked.

Luke didn't know. But Sonny soon found out that Frank Smith's lawyer, Phil Cusack, had tried to muscle in on Sonny's action. Sonny dealt nonviolently with the thugs who bombed Luke's for Cusack.

Soon after, Cusack was found dead. Sonny's friend and confidante, Harry Silver, told him Joe Scully had ordered the hit on Cusack. Scully had been like a father to Sonny. "More of a father than Mike Corbin," Sonny sneered to his girlfriend, Brenda.

Brenda liked Mike, but she couldn't get Sonny to forgive Mike for having walked out on Sonny's mother when Sonny was a boy. Sonny's stepfather Deke had beaten Sonny's mother mercilessly—and Sonny, too. Until Sonny left home and met Scully. Scully had Deke rubbed out—for Sonny. Sonny owed him ever since!

But Sonny never believed he owed him as much as Scully wanted: control of Frank's gang and a piece of Luke's Club. After Sonny and Luke stalled Scully, Luke sent Laura and their baby, Leslie Lu, back to Beechers Corners for their own protection.

"It's only 'til we settle this Scully thing," he promised. Laura left, confused. She'd hoped her days of running were over.

Mac learned of Sonny's connection to Scully and told Police Commissioner Sean Donely, who made it clear to Scully that he'd be keeping a close eye on him.

Damian Smith asked Scully to help him in his latest effort to exact a little revenge on Lucy Coe. Damian wanted him to steal incoming supplies and outgoing products from Lucy's successful business, Deception.

Luke's Club opened. The star attraction, B.B. King! A triumph! But Luke missed Laura. He wanted to celebrate his success with her.

Stone Cates, who worked at Luke's Club for Sonny and Luke, invited Robin to watch B.B. King on the monitors in Sonny's apartment when her uncle Mac forbade her to attend the opening with Stone. Mac attended.

He's so unfair, Robin thought. But Uncle Mac was downstairs in the club and she was alone with the young man she loved. This was the night Robin and Stone had been waiting for. But before they could give themselves to each other, Mac unexpectedly came through the door. Seeing Robin undressed with Stone in Sonny's apartment, Mac went ballistic! Luke restrained him while Stone and Robin ran off. Nothing Mac could say or do could keep them apart when their hearts told them that they were meant to be together.

Stone checked them into a motel room. In each other's arms, Stone and Robin felt at home. Stone was prepared with a condom. He assured Robin he'd been tested and was HIV negative. They made love for the first time.

"Are you really okay?" Stone tenderly asked.

"How could being that close to you be anything but wonderful!" Robin sighed. Their night was perfect.

The next morning, Robin confronted Uncle Mac. He hadn't slept all night and was about to ground her for life when Robin stopped him.

"Save your breath, Uncle Mac. We did it."

Mac stormed over to Felicia, who calmed him down and went back to make sure that Robin was okay. Robin wished that Mac could see that Stone was a wonderful person.

She and Stone developed an ongoing sexual relationship. As soon as Robin got herself on the pill, they stopped using condoms. She and Mac eventually reached an understanding that they could both live with about her dating Stone. He didn't like it but he had to let her grow up. If Stone could just shake the flu he'd had all winter, things would be perfect.

Luke's Club was a major success. He invited Mary Mae to sing one night. It was the night Felicia decided to give birth. She delivered her baby under a table at Luke's. She and her healthy little girl were taken to General Hospital and Luke took the microphone and introduced Mary Mae Ward.

"Felicia's going to be a tough act to follow," Mary Mae told the crowd. She knocked them out with her singing. Lois Cerullo Ashton just knew she had to sign Mary Mae to a contract at L&B Records.

Ryan Chamberlain convinced his only friend, Connie Cooper, that he'd be murdered in his cell if she didn't help him. She bought the medication and made all the arrangements.

Kevin got the phone call and turned pale. He turned to Lucy and said, "Ryan is dead."

Kevin and Lucy went to the prison hospital's morgue and saw Ryan's body. They saw him in his casket. They saw him buried.

Connie Cooper, who watched them leave, started digging for dear life—Ryan's life. He looked so dead. She hoped the medication that slowed down his heart didn't kill him after all. When she reached his coffin, she let herself hope. When Ryan sprung out of it, her heart leaped.

She hugged him. "Oh, Ryan, I'm so happy I could die!" As she went on about their life together, he took out the scarf he'd crocheted. He tied it tightly around her and snapped her neck, burying Connie in his grave.

Stealing into Kevin's home, Ryan stole clothes, money and, once again, his twin's identity.

"Georgie? What kind of a name is Georgie?" Felicia asked her daughter. But Maxie said she had a boy's name, so why couldn't her new baby sister be called Georgie? Felicia named the baby Georgie.

Ryan renamed her Celeste when, posing as Kevin, he kidnaped the newborn baby from the hospital. Ryan dreamed of raising her as his own but, on the run, the baby wouldn't stop crying. Ryan felt the rage building inside himself. But Ryan the pediatrician *loved* children. He didn't want to hurt her. He made a desperate call to Kevin that was traced by the authorities, who were hot on Ryan's trail.

Realizing his mistake, Ryan grabbed the baby. In the car, his mother's ghost appeared and criticized his behavior mercilessly. To get away from her, he leaped out of the car with the baby and headed to a deserted amusement park.

Kevin, Lucy, Mac and a frantic Felicia tracked him there. They rescued Georgie from the carousel. Inside the house of mirrors, Ryan caught Lucy and Felicia and tied them up. Kevin freed them, fighting with Ryan as they ran out. A gas pipe broke and Ryan set the place ablaze. Kevin was horrified to see his twin brother fall back into the flames—into the arms of their mother! He blinked the image away. Ryan was finally gone.

When Lily Rivera decided she wanted to have a child right away, she told her fiancé Miguel Morez that they needn't wait for their wedding. Miguel felt Lily wanted to replace their son, Juan. After they'd confided their identities as Juan's biological parents to his adoptive parents, Lily became even more obsessed with children. She began pressuring Miguel just as he most wanted to concentrate on the steamy music video he was going to make with both her and Brenda Barrett.

But as their arguments continued, Lily dropped out of the video. She ended her engagement to Miguel, who was hurt and angry. She confided more and more in Sonny Corinthos. Sonny felt comfortable around Lily. But Brenda grew more jealous each time she saw Lily with Sonny. They, in turn, were jealous every time they saw Miguel and Brenda rehearsing that hot video.

Brenda's best friend Lois was concerned. Lois wanted the whole world to be in love ever since she found it in her heart to trust in her "Nedley." She'd promised herself she'd get used to calling him, "Ned." He'd moved in with her at the gatehouse. They were planning a church wedding.

Robin discovered that Stone couldn't read. She suspected he was dyslexic and directed him to Dr. Kevin Collins, who confirmed it. Kevin began working with Stone to help him read. But he was concerned about Stone's unshakable flu. Kevin ran tests and discovered the worst possible news. Stone was HIV positive.

He asked Stone to come to his office, wondering how you tell a nineteen-year-old kid this kind of news.

Stone left Kevin's office in tears.

Robin saw him. He ran past her. Why was he so upset, she wondered? Kevin couldn't tell her. When his girlfriend Lucy came to his office, her problems didn't seem too important to him. Later, Stone went to see Robin at her house, but couldn't bring himself to reveal the deeply tragic news.

For weeks, Lucy's essences for Deception perfume and her store deliveries kept getting stolen. Someone was destroying her company! Frantic, she turned to Luke Spencer, who owed her for saving his life in Puerto Rico. Now she was depending on him to save her company.

Luke asked his partner Sonny to find out what was going on, and Sonny got the word from his friend, Harry Silver. Joe Scully's mob was sabotaging Lucy's company. Luke asked Lucy if she wanted to help him and Sonny get Scully.

"What do I have to do?" Lucy asked. Kevin feared for Lucy's involvement with Luke. Danger seemed to follow him everywhere. But Kevin couldn't stop her.

Luke couldn't wait to stop Scully. The more he and Sonny had been stonewalling Scully, the more impatient Scully grew. Perturbed at Luke and Sean's threats to his plans, Scully plotted to take care of both of them simultaneously. He called Luke, inviting him to gangland's infamous No Name Club to "clear the air." Luke accepted, but packed a "piece" for protection.

Scully arranged for Sean Donely to tail Luke to the No Name. Luke turned Scully's apology down and even put him down. "You're no Frank Smith!" he declared, walking out.

As Luke reached his car, one of Scully's men fired a shot from behind. Startled, Luke turned around as Sean stood to investigate. In the frenzy, Luke accidentally shot Sean!

"Donely, what are you doing here?!" Luke screamed.

"Dying, I think," Sean muttered as he fell limp into Luke's arms. An ambulance rushed Sean to General Hospital.

Sean survived, but his recuperation wouldn't be as simple as his recovery from Frank Smith's bullet in Puerto Rico. Tony Jones sent Sean and his wife Tiffany, who ironically had finally become pregnant again, to Boston where Sean could begin his lengthy rehabilitation at Mass General. Sean and Tiffany left Port Charles amid a sea of tearful goodbyes.

Luke and Sonny began their sting operation against Scully with Lucy as the bait. She vamped Scully, dropping hints about her Deception shipments so Scully could steal them. It was a setup. With Mike Corbin's help, Luke planted drugs stolen from Scully himself on Lucy's truck and tipped off the police. They showed up to bust Scully with the drugs.

Out on bail, Scully wanted some answers about the setup from Lucy Coe.

Kevin was frantic when Mac Scorpio told him she'd been kidnaped. It was Damian who supplied Luke and Sonny with Scully and Lucy's whereabouts. Damian wanted to hurt Lucy, not kill her.

Sonny went to face off with his old mentor, Scully, while Luke secretly freed Lucy. But Scully didn't trust Sonny anymore. Scully shot at him, but Sonny's father Mike dashed out of his hiding place and took the bullet instead! Sonny shot Scully dead. Mike survived, his life saved by Dr. Monica Quartermaine.

It was Monica's return as a surgeon to General Hospital after her own surgery. She'd come back from the Wellness Group in Arizona with guests in tow. Her own prognosis indicated a complete recovery. But her friend Page had a recurrence of cancer.

Page had very little time left. Monica, with Alan's blessing, told Page that Emily could live with them after Page was gone. When Monica returned to Port Charles, she introduced Page and Emily to their new home, the Quartermaine mansion.

Laura Spencer had also returned to Port Charles when Leslie Lu spiked a fever. She was tired of hiding out in Beechers Corners. Lucky welcomed her home, delighted his family was together again.

Laura was singing a lullaby to Leslie Lu when a mob faction attacked Luke's Club.

Robin finally found Stone outside of the club. He refused to tell her why he'd run away from her. Suddenly, a spray of machine guns!

Brenda was luxuriating in a shower when the bullets riddled her privacy!

Luke, Lucky and Sonny were in Luke's living room when the bullets blasted through the windows and door.

And Laura stopped singing.

Stone had shielded Robin, but took a bullet in the leg. He screamed when he saw his blood on Robin and ran away!

Brenda had ducked in the nick of time. A few cuts, but she'd be okay.

Sonny took Lucky to the basement. Laura came downstairs. She saw a hitman about to shoot Luke in the back. She had their shotgun and used it, killing the man instantly.

"It's over, Luke. I won't live with the violence anymore. I want our children to grow up safely. You have to leave."

Robin found the wounded Stone in the motel where they'd first made love.

"I'll take you to the hospital and they'll treat your wound and you'll be fine."

Stone was crying. "I'm telling you, they can't help me. Why can't you get it?"

"I don't understand. Why do you keep saying that?"

"Because," Stone was uncontrollably sobbing, "I'm HIV positive!"

They cried together. Robin took Stone back to Kevin for answers. He'd tested negative, but hadn't taken a necessary retest six months later. Apparently, his addict girlfriend Crystal had infected him, though Stone had also had unprotected sex with other runaways.

Dr. Alan Quartermaine discovered that Stone had already developed full-blown AIDS. His was a particularly virulent case. He and Kevin set up a treatment regimen for Stone, but their most constant thought was, "What about Robin?"

Robin tested negative, but she'd have to retest for a year and a half before they could be certain that she

Ryan or Kevin? Real or Reflection? Such was the dilemma during the pursuit of Ryan after he kidnaped Felicia's newborn daughter, Georgie. Ryan led Kevin and Lucy into a dangerous game of cat-and-mouse inside a house of mirrors at an abandoned amusement park.

hadn't been infected. Robin respected Stone's wish to keep his disease a secret until he was ready to tell people.

Sonny was devastated when Stone told him. Brenda could tell Sonny was upset, but he refused to tell her why, respecting Stone's request. Brenda annoyed Sonny by guessing that it had something to do with Lily. He was growing tired of her jealousy.

The Quartermaine dog, Annabelle, had her puppy. Only one. Old Edward had almost killed himself chasing the pregnant pooch and her ardent Foster into a cave just before Annabelle delivered. Lucky Spencer felt that the puppy belonged to him because Edward's wife Lila had promised him the pick of the litter. But Edward refused to give Lucky the puppy. Secretly, he wanted the cuddly creature for himself!

Jason Quartermaine continued to see Keesha Ward. Before they made love in Paris during their spring break, Keesha confessed to Jason that she was a virgin. He smiled and told her that he was, too. And then, they weren't.

Jason and his brother AJ tried to cheer up Page's daughter Emily as best they could. Generally, the Quartermaine brothers got along, but Jason wasn't too thrilled when AJ hired Keesha to assist him at the Charles Street Foundation. Jason could tell that AJ had a thing for her.

Ned waged a campaign to win approval from Lois' mother and father. Gloria gave Lois her blessing. But Carmine still considered Ned a weasel for having hurt his daughter, Lois.

"Yeah, Pops, but he's *my* weasel!" Ned smiled at Lois. Somehow it sounded better when she said it.

Lois's partner and best girlfriend Brenda turned 21. Brenda's boyfriend Sonny threw her a big party at Luke's Club. Brenda confided in Lois that she was certain Sonny would give her an engagement ring. But he didn't and, while struggling to hide her disappointment, Brenda concentrated on a wedding. Not hers. Her best friend's.

It was "All aboard the Quartermaine Express!" as nearly all of Port Charles chugged to Brooklyn for the pleasure of seeing Ned and Lois become man and wife. The Quartermaines and the Cerullos celebrated on the Quartermaine yacht with a pre-wedding cruise near Coney Island. The yacht almost sank, but still Emily Bowen had fun. She was with Alan. Monica had stayed behind to be with Page, who had taken a turn for the worse. Lois invited Emily to be a bridesmaid.

An old boyfriend begged Lois to dump the bum, but Lois told Danny Zacharowitz that she was already married to him and to feel happy for her—and to get out!

In a glorious church wedding, Lois and Ned were married in front of their tearfully happy families.

Emily returned from the wedding for a final day with her mother. After Page died, Monica found that the girl seemed closer to Alan than to her. Monica felt hurt, but Alan assured her that it was natural. Emily wasn't ready to replace her mother just yet. To comfort Emily, Edward and Lucky agreed to end their feud about ownership of Foster and

Annabelle's puppy and gave him to Emily. With Lucky's help, she named him Raoul, which rhymed with "howl"—sort of.

When Lucky's father Luke told him to guard Laura and the baby, Lucky took his responsibility seriously. He fired the shotgun, narrowly missing the prowler who turned out to be Luke. That near-tragic accident convinced Laura even more that Luke had to leave them. She loved him but could no longer live with the danger. And she knew Luke couldn't live without it. They were both miserable. Luke began to realize that maybe his life with Laura was truly over.

Robin said nothing to Mac about Stone's illness. As she graduated from high school, he knew something was terribly wrong, and her silence was killing him. At the Outback, Katherine Bell tried to cheer Mac up. She liked flirting with him. Mac liked flirting back. But Katherine's lover Damian didn't like seeing her with Mac any more than Katherine liked seeing Damian with Lucy Coe.

Damian underwrote the AIDS fund-raising Nurses' Ball for General Hospital to get Chairperson Lucy's goat. For his support, he made her promise to sing with him in the talent show.

Damian couldn't interest Katherine in his latest plot to ruin Lucy's life. Katherine decided she'd had enough of Lucy Coe to last a lifetime, and she didn't quite trust Damian's interest in Lucy.

Damian arranged for Madame Maia Montebello, a self-proclaimed psychic, to peddle her new book, *Life: What Was, What Is, What Will Be*, in Port Charles. He paid her to bamboozle Lucy with her auras and convince Lucy to dump her boyfriend Kevin and take up with Damian himself. There was something Damian wanted even more than revenge on Lucy. He wanted Lucy!

Lucy and her friend Jon Hanley, who was living with AIDS, staged the 1995 Nurses' Ball around a "Rainbow Of Hope" theme. When AJ Quartermaine cracked that these days only an idiot gets AIDS, an angry Stone announced that *he* had AIDS. AJ felt awful. Stone felt relieved. Robin felt so proud. She told Mac, who exploded when he realized that Robin had been exposed.

Mac shared his anger and his fear that he hadn't worked hard enough to protect the little girl he loved. Felicia, too, feared for Robin.

Felicia's ex-husband Frisco came home briefly in the spring of 1995. He told her he was home for good, but Felicia knew he hadn't gotten the WSB out of his system. She told him to go as soon as his partner, Rakeem, announced their next assignment. Rakeem himself would have liked to stay a little longer to get to know Mary Mae Ward. He'd taken a liking to her.

Mary Mae's grandson Justus and Dr. Simone Hardy became an item. She'd sent her husband Tom the divorce papers. But Tom returned to Port Charles without having signed them. He made sure Justus knew that Tom intended to get his family back. Simone's anger at Tom softened when she saw that the atrocities Tom had witnessed in Africa had taken a toll. She was afraid he was having some kind of a nervous breakdown.

Steve Hardy lost confidence in his son. When the Board vote was tied between Tom and Kevin for the position of chief of psychiatry, Steve's vote gave the job to Kevin. Tom joined the staff under Kevin.

Felicia was glad to see Tom back in town. She remembered how he'd tried to support her during those awful times with Ryan. And she could see he was grateful for her support as he grappled with the realization that he had truly lost Simone to another man, Justus Ward.

Madame Maia charmed Lucy Coe completely. Kevin couldn't believe that Lucy was falling for her psychic mumbo-jumbo. Even Katherine was surprised, but Damian wasn't. "She talks to a duck, for heaven's sake," he told Katherine.

Damian and Lucy's duet at the Nurses' Ball made Katherine see red. She's had it for Damian, but she was falling for Mac Scorpio, a man who could see past her games into her vulnerabilities. She began to see even more of Mac.

Mac Scorpio refused to deal with Stone and tried to avoid him. But once Stone tried to speak to Mac, and Mac let him have it. "You may have signed Robin's death warrant!" He blasted Stone and he wasn't sorry.

With a renewed zest for life, Monica launched herself into setting up a Wellness Group at General Hospital. She kept Alan at arm's length. He spent more and more time with Bobbie, who was surprised to find herself strongly attracted to him. Why, Bobbie wondered, was she flooded with thoughts about Alan, just as she and Tony were getting back together?

Sadly, another couple was coming apart. Brenda realized Sonny might be a mobster. She told Lois, who told Ned, who told Mac. They persuaded her to wear a wire to get the goods on Sonny. Brenda felt disloyal, but she knew Sonny'd never trusted her enough to tell her the truth.

Lily discovered what Brenda was up to and warned Sonny. He frisked Brenda, found the wire and blew up at her. They were finished. Miguel was disgusted with Lily for what she'd done. They, too, were finished. Out of the ashes, two new couples arose. Brenda and Miguel, who had consoled each other in friendship, became lovers. And Sonny turned to Lily in pain, after witnessing Brenda, the woman he truly loved, in Miguel's arms.

When AIDS threatened to blind Stone, even Mac found it hard not to feel for the kid.

Then Robin came down with a flu. Was it AIDS? Robin was instantly retested. At the hospital, a panicked Stone saw an equally frantic Mac.

"If there were anything I could do to make Robin safe, I would." Stone was crying and didn't notice that his poignant words were reaching Mac's heart. Stone turned to leave.

"Stone. Wait." Mac opened his arms and embraced him.

As much as Mac feared what the future might hold, he finally understood the depth of this dying young man's love for his niece. Why hadn't he seen it before? In an instant, Mac realized he could never have kept Robin and Stone apart. The little girl he'd raised had found true love. Stone was Robin's destiny.

Family and friends, both near and far, showered Stone and Robin with love and compassion—even as they struggled on with their own complicated lives and loves. That's the kind of town Port Charles is, where adventure can begin in your very own backyard. Where your worst enemy can become your best friend. And where the unexpected is around every corner. A community of people who care about each other, people who rally in times of need, people we've come to cherish through years of heartache and humor. People who have become our friends.

We want Bobbie to realize she belongs with Tony!

We yearn for Monica to let Alan sweep her off her feet!

We can't wait to see Brenda in Sonny's arms once again!

We thrill to hear Ned serenading Lois, Edward cackling over his latest dirty deal and Lucy driving all her men crazy.

And we long for Luke and Laura to show us that theirs is still the greatest love of all!

GENERAL HOSPITAL ON LOCATION

It is a long-standing tradition for *General Hospital* to treat viewers to stimulating doses of provocative drama, intriguing romances and stirring adventures set against a backdrop of exotic locales. This legacy began back in 1974, when the soap first took a small crew and several actors on location to the nearby Hollywood Palace Theater. Elaborate and extensive remote sequences carried out by a battalion of cast and crew are practically routine events these days. From the sandy beaches of Puerto Rico to the treacherous jungles of Mexico, the people of Port Charles are forever on the go.

According to Executive Producer Wendy Riche, "Puerto Rico has a magic of its own that we wanted to capture in the stories we were telling on *General Hospital*." The adventurous love story of Sonny and Brenda was among the stories featured in GH's most elaborate and extensive location shoot, taped in the historical streets of old San Juan and the romantic, seductive sites around the glamorous El Conquistador Resort and Country Club in San Juan.

It was a dream come true for Brooklyn native Lois Cerullo when she honeymooned with her new husband "Eddie Maine" at Coney Island, the historic amusement park, which had always been dear to her heart. In the summer of 1994, *General Hospital* spent a spectacularly romantic day following the couple as they enjoyed the boardwalk, munched on cotton candy and even rode the classic Cyclone roller coaster.

Newlyweds Scotty and Laura enjoyed an idyllic summer honeymoon in Southern California, where they visited the famous Chinese Theater on Hollywood Boulevard.

South Dakota's historic Mt. Rushmore served as the breathtaking backdrop for 1987's action-packed espionage story featuring young lovers Terry O'Connor and her beau Dusty Walker.

Singer Terry O'Connor fulfilled her lifelong dream when she traveled to Nashville to audition for the Grand Ol' Opry. While singing her heart out on the historic stage, she was blissfully unaware that a stalker waited in the wings with a gun aimed right at her!

On Location

"For the return of our popular characters, Luke and Laura Spencer, we wanted to bring an even richer and more textured feel to our story by going on location," explains Executive Producer Wendy Riche. "Thirty years ago, the creators of *General Hospital* conceived that the city of Port Charles was in upstate New York, perhaps near Buffalo. We scouted several locations and felt that the Rochester area was perfect for our vision of the city." A local diner was re-dressed to become the Spencers' own "Triple L Diner."

The 1993 remote scenes around Rochester involved exciting and intricate action, including aerial shots, boats, parachuting and explosions. In this harrowing scene, a helicopter swooped down to rescue Luke and Laura just seconds before their raft would have plummeted over the falls (above).

Newlyweds Duke and Anna enjoyed an idyllic honeymoon at a Scottish manor where Anna was unable to master Duke's favorite sport—fishing. The lush Scotland highland scenes were actually shot on location at the Disney Ranch in California (left).

In 1991, *General Hospital* taped location scenes at Southern California's picturesque San Pedro Bay, home of Los Angeles Harbor. For two days, this Southland hub of commerce and tourism was transformed into the Port Charles waterfront. In the drama, Jenny Eckert led a huge group of environmental protesters who wanted the ELQ ship out of the harbor because they believed it was leaking toxic chemicals.

During 1983's DVX/WSB power struggle over the dangerous "Prometheus Disc," the campus of the University of Southern California provided the perfect setting for Expo 83, a huge festival of nations held in Port Charles. In this scene, Grant Putnam tends to his wife Celia, who had been held hostage by the enemy.

General Hospital ventured north to Canada for the first time when Luke, Holly and Robert went to British Columbia. In this dramatic sequence—which played out on the streets of Vancouver—Luke Spencer commandeered an ambulance to rescue his love, Holly Sutton, who had been kidnapped by her corrupt relatives, the Durbans.

Jagger Cates, Jason Quartermaine and Karen Wexler never suspected that their afternoon would turn to disaster when a sudden storm shipwrecked their boat on an island off the coast of Port Charles. California's Big Bear Lake and its rustic surroundings in the San Bernardino Mountains stood in for the eastern environs in this adventurous 1992 escapade.

Frisco and Felicia joined forces to search for an Aztec treasure in 1984. The hunt took them into the treacherous jungles of Mexico.

"We have technical masters who perform miracles on our show every day," says *General Hospital* Executive Producer Wendy Riche, explaining why the soap chose to visit the Shining Star of the Caribbean. "But there's nothing in the studio that can re-create the spellbinding ambience of a golden sunset on the shimmering shore of Puerto Rico." In the story, reunited lovers Miguel Morez and Lily Rivera returned to their homeland to explore the mystery and heartache of their long-ago relationship.

In a thrilling chase scene that took them atop a tram and racing through the Caribbean in a speedboat, Sonny and Brenda narrowly escaped death. Here, in the aftermath of their heart-stopping Puerto Rican escapade, the water-soaked lovers celebrate the fact that they survived the ordeal.

YOUNG LOVE

What could be more exciting than to be young and in love? For nearly three-and-a-half decades, *General Hospital* has gifted viewers with many of daytime TV's most sensitive and heartwarming love stories. The more labyrinthine their struggle to find happiness, the harder we pull for these kids to get together. Sadly, the harsh reality of adult life often breaks the magic spell of youthful passion. But for one moment in time—that one moment—life was oh-so-sweet.

Scotty and Laura

Laura Webber's tragic affair with an older man left her feeling she could never trust a man again. But through support and compassion, young Scotty Baldwin showed her she could love again. When they married, Laura believed she would be with Scotty until the day she died, but it was a promise the troubled teenager couldn't keep because by then another man had stirred feelings deep inside her. His name was Luke Spencer.

Angie and Eddie

General Hospital's first pair of young lovers—Angie Costello and Eddie Weeks—actually lived happily ever after. In 1963, a drunken Eddie crashed his car and nearly killed Angie. Together the teenagers had a baby out of wedlock who was given up for adoption. After marrying two years later, the kids decided they wanted their baby back, so they snatched the child and went on the run. Through these turbulent times, one thing remained certain for Angie and Eddie—their love for each other.

Lou and Blackie

Rock-and-roller Blackie Parrish showed his sensitive side when he discovered teenage runaway Louise (Lou) Swenson hiding out in a construction trailer. Blackie put his own life on the line to rescue Lou from a dangerous pimp. Their youthful attraction led briefly to a love affair. But Blackie, more attracted to the lure of stardom, brazenly gave Lou the brush-off and had an affair with his sexy blonde manager. Blackie blamed himself for Lou's untimely death and, though he didn't kill her, he refused to defend himself against manslaughter charges and went to jail.

Jade and Yank *(above)*

General Hospital's version of *West Side Story* brought together Jade Soong and intern Dr. "Yank" Se Chung, innocent victims from opposite sides in a violent war between two factions in Port Charles' Asian Quarter. Their love was put to the test when Yank killed Jade's corrupt brother Kim, who planned to blow up a cannery run by the opposition. Jade, devastated by the trauma of learning that her lover had killed her brother, suddenly went blind and shunned the man she loved. Eventually, however, they found their way back together.

Jeff and Anne

Romance blossomed in the halls of *General Hospital* when Dr. Jeff Webber fell for nurse Anne Logan. Their love was tender and innocent—because virginal Anne refused to sleep with Jeff until they could be married. But he couldn't commit to her because he was already married to Heather, who was committed to a sanitarium. Sadly, Heather's horrible machinations succeeded in keeping these star-crossed lovers apart forever.

Jagger and Karen

After months of simmering attraction, Jagger Cates swept Karen Wexler off her feet on Valentine's Day, 1993. Their love remained strong until Karen became haunted by memories of a past in which she was molested by her mother's old boyfriend, Ray. The secret chewed away at Karen, causing her to scorn Jagger. Feeling worthless, Karen entered the underground world of rave parties and began to work as a stripper. After stumbling upon her shocking new life, Jagger did not turn his back. Instead, he helped Karen come to grips with the dark memories that plagued her. With Karen's delicate psyche on the mend, she married Jagger and they began a new and happy life in Chicago.

Robin and Stone

Robin and Stone shared the tender passion of the very young until the harsh reality of the modern world broke their magic spell. The untimely news that Stone suffered from an advanced case of AIDS came as a shock to the young lovers, who bravely showed the world that love can endure even under the most painful circumstances.

Miguel and Lily *(opposite)*

Miguel Morez and Lily Rivera's tender love affair was plagued by heartache and separation. The lovers were sweethearts in their native Puerto Rico until Lily's overbearing father forbade her to see Miguel. Soon after, Lily discovered she was pregnant with her young lover's child, which she gave up for adoption. Years later, they reunited in Port Charles and returned to their homeland to find their son, Juan.

Decker and Dawn

Decker Moss, a rebellious conman with a heart of gold, couldn't believe that a girl like sweet and naive Dawn Winthrop could be interested in a guy like him. So a heartsick Decker stood on the sidelines and watched as Dawn walked down the aisle with blue-blooded Ned Ashton. But moments after they married, she made the startling discovery that her new husband had slept with her mother. Hurt and humiliated, Dawn ran away in Ned's Ferrari, which was all decorated for the wedding.

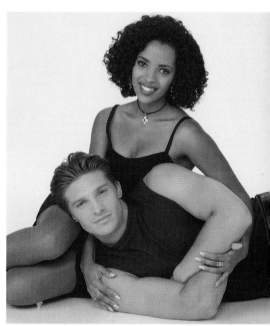

Keesha and Jason

Jason Quartermaine, a pre-med student with a warm personality and kind heart, found his perfect match in Keesha Ward. They were happy, but their families weren't. Much in love, the kids shoved reality aside and took a fairy tale trip to Paris where they made love for the first time.

Young Love

CLASSIC COUPLES

And they lived happily ever after....

That's the way fairy tale romances are supposed to end, but *General Hospital*'s love stories don't always conclude in storybook fashion. Happiness is elusive in Port Charles, and rarely do couples find eternal bliss. For GH's dynamic duos, tragedy and pain may litter the path to true love, but their reward for the search is worth the effort. These timeless twosomes gave us many unforgettable memories on the road to romance.

Rick and Lesley
No two people deserved happiness more than Drs. Rick and Lesley Webber—and none had less of it. After two stormy marriages marked by infidelity, scandal and murder, this troubled union came to a tragic end when Lesley's car skidded out of control on an icy road and she was killed.

Steve and Audrey
Is love better the second time around? For Steve and Audrey Hardy, three times were the charm. Fate threw up an endless series of obstacles before they were finally able to find marital tranquillity.

Sean and Tiffany (above)
Talk about strange couplings: Tiffany Hill was a flamboyant B-movie star turned TV reporter. Sean Donely was a spy and con artist turned detective. Together, they turned each other on.

Lee and Gail Baldwin (left)
Lee Baldwin and Gail Adamson had a terrible time making it to the altar because Gail couldn't get over the death of her late husband, Greg. After discovering that he had once had an affair with Monica, she became so depressed that she broke up with Lee. Devastated by his loss, he broke his Alcoholics Anonymous pledge and began to drink again. But eventually they found their way back together.

Classic Couples

Bobbie and Tony

Bobbie Spencer hadn't had the best luck with men—until the day she fell in love with Tony Jones. In 1989, Tony's heart was aching from his ill-fated liaison with Lucy Coe, while Bobbie's busted romances with Jake Meyer and Scotty Baldwin left her looking for a mate she could trust. Together, Tony and Bobbie found love among the ruins and married—twice!

Duke and Anna

They were a storybook couple in so many ways: Anna Devane with her lilting English accent, long auburn hair and graceful demeanor, and Duke Lavery with his Scottish brogue, chiseled features and elegant sense of style. Sadly, Duke was gunned down, bringing this foreign and fascinating fairy tale to an untimely end.

Alan and Monica
Just when you think they've had enough of each other, theirs proves to be one of the most enduring romances in Port Charles.

Lucy and Tony
So the way to a man's heart is through his stomach? Not for Lucy Coe. When she set her sights on wealthy widower Tony Jones, Lucy did her gourmet cooking in the bedroom! Lonely Tony was powerless to resist Lucy's seductive appeal, but good sex only lasts for so long. In rapid time, Tony unceremoniously gave his scheming wife the heave-ho.

Lois and Ned
Straight-laced, buttoned-down Ned Ashton took a walk on the wild side when he strolled into a Buffalo bar and grabbed the mike. Calling himself "Eddie Maine," naughty Ned sang his heart out, and this impetuous star-turn caught the eye of rock promoter Lois Cerullo. Lois and "Eddie" quickly became a team—and an item!

209

Classic Couples

Star-Crossed Lovers:
FRISCO AND FELICIA

Fate has a strange way of bringing star-crossed lovers together. Frisco Jones might never have met Aztec princess Felicia Cummings if it hadn't been for a simple gold ring that he purchased at an art fair. Little did he know that the ring was part of an Aztec treasure that rightfully belonged to Felicia. She desperately wanted it back, so one night in the summer of '84, Felicia disguised herself as a boy and crept into Frisco's bedroom. He caught his intruder, but she captured his heart. Together, they became *General Hospital*'s most popular pair of young lovers in the 1980s. Long after Frisco's incurable appetite for danger and intrigue caused him to join the WSB and leave the "lady of his heart" behind, their love remains pure, strong—and unconditional.

Colton or Frisco? Frisco or Colton? After a nasty bout with amnesia, Felicia decided to return to Frisco rather than start a new life with the man she had recently married, Colton Shore. After years of heartache, Frisco and Felicia's second wedding in 1989 was even more heartfelt and poignant than the first.

Portrait—1984

Through long and painful separations and personal crises, Frisco has always cared deeply for Felicia. Here he sings a tender love song to "the lady of my heart."

Long before he met Felicia, Frisco was the lead singer for Blackie Parrish's rock band, The Riff Raff.

After returning from a middle eastern prison, Frisco tried to revive Felicia after she fainted from the shock of seeing the husband she had given up for dead. When she came to, Felicia was faced with a dilemma because she was now married to two men—Frisco and Colton. She chose Frisco.

A pair of senior citizens out for a Sunday stroll on the boardwalk in Atlantic City? Not exactly. This elderly pair of tourists was actually Frisco and Felicia in disguise and on the run in the seaside gambling town.

In the fall of 1986, the newlyweds put their super-sleuthing skills to good use when they went undercover at the circus to crack a money laundering ring operated by the notorious Mr. Big. Frisco and Felicia didn't find Mr. Big under the big top—but they did find a big elephant.

Frisco and Felicia

THE ROMANTIC ADVENTURES OF LUKE AND LAURA

Never before in the history of daytime soaps has one couple so captivated an entire nation. Luke and Laura! The incredible chemistry of actors Genie Francis and Anthony Geary, combined with a powerful story chock full of intriguing danger and powerful passion, propelled *General Hospital*'s popular lovers onto the cover of *Newsweek* and forever into the hearts of millions of adoring soap opera fans. Luke and Laura's fabled love story was capped with a storybook wedding watched by millions and attended by the one and only Elizabeth Taylor. After a decade away, Luke and Laura brought their legendary magic back to Port Charles in 1993 for a new series of exciting adventures. Here's a look back at some of their amorous escapades.

At the Whitaker farm in cozy Beechers Corners, Luke and Laura posed as Lloyd and Lucy Johnson and befriended the affable, guitar-strumming Hutch, who was actually a hitman sent by Frank Smith to do away with them.

During the summer on the run, a blanket, strategically draped over a rope, kept Luke and Laura a safe distance apart in their cheap motel.

LAURA
"Being on the run kind of gets lonely."

LUKE
"It wouldn't be nearly as lonely if we slept in the same bed."

LAURA
"I want to be able to love you without any hangups at all."

LUKE
"When a woman says that to a man, he can wait — but not too long!"

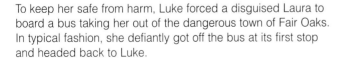

To keep her safe from harm, Luke forced a disguised Laura to board a bus taking her out of the dangerous town of Fair Oaks. In typical fashion, she defiantly got off the bus at its first stop and headed back to Luke.

While hiding from the Port Charles mob, Luke and Laura defied danger and danced the night away in Wyndham's department store. As the strains of "Fascination" filled the air, they shared an unforgettably romantic evening and pledged their undying love to each other (opposite).

213

Portrait – 1981

After solving the mystery of the Left-Handed Boy and finding Frank Smith's stash of gold, Luke and Laura triumphantly hopped onto a nearby motorcycle and roared back to Beechers Corners, where the "Walls of Jericho" came tumbling down in a night of pure passion.

With the seconds ticking away, Luke frantically searched for the correct password to disarm the Cassadine weather machine. Moments later, Luke triumphantly hit the mark when he typed the phrase to thwart the deep freeze. The code? "I-C-E P-R-I-N-C-E-S-S"!

The Luke and Laura phenomenon brought national attention to Anthony Geary and Genie Francis.

**The Spencer Family 1995
—Laura, Lucky, Lesley Lu, Luke**

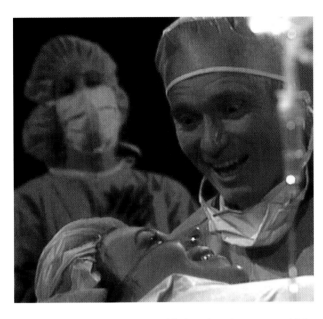

"It's a girl!" shouted an amazed Luke when Laura gave birth to their daughter Lesley Lu in the fall of 1994.

Luke and Laura made a conspicuous return to *General Hospital* in a pink Cadillac. When they were stopped by a policeman, Laura feigned that she was in labor, prompting the officer to offer the clever pair a high-speed escort to the hospital (below).

DANGEROUS LIAISONS

Passion—with a price! *General Hospital* wouldn't be half as much fun without these charismatic couples engaging in seductive sexual encounters and risky affairs of the heart. Despite their differences, they make sparks fly. Add a third party to the mix and you've got a sizzling triangle. Dangerous liaisons—they're the stuff that soaps are made of!

Robert, Anna, Duke
In the winter of 1988, Robert Scorpio realized that he still loved Anna Lavery, the mother of his child. But now Anna was married to the attractively off-center Duke Lavery. The two men squared off in an eternal triangle when Anna was kidnapped by the villainous Grant Putnam. In a heartstopping climax in the snow-filled Adirondack mountains, Duke became odd man out when Robert saved Anna's life.

Alan, Monica, Rick
The tangled trio of Rick, Monica and Alan became even more entwined in 1980 when Monica gave birth to a son, Alan, Jr. Was the child a product of her marriage to Alan or her affair with Rick? Delirious during labor, Monica muttered that Rick Webber was the father of her baby. But the presence of a family birthmark, followed by more blood tests, revealed that the child was fathered by Alan, not by Rick.

Alan and Susan

Dr. Alan Quartermaine began his back-room affair with sexy Susan Moore in 1981. Led by his libido, Alan secretly installed his mistress in a waterside gatehouse down the road from his family's elegant mansion. Monica caught on to their affair when she spied on her mate and his lover through a telescope. Too late, though. In rapid time, Susan was carrying Alan's love child.

Scotty and Bobbie

In 1978, hooker-turned-nurse Bobbie had the hots for respectable law student Scotty Baldwin. Scotty loved Laura Webber, so Bobbie tried everything in her power to bust them up. When nothing worked, her last resort was to trap Scotty into marriage by claiming that she was pregnant with his baby. To give the phantom baby a name, Scotty nearly married Bobbie, but her desperate charade was uncovered just in time.

Heather and Jeff

Dr. Jeff Webber's love life was chock full of turmoil thanks to the conniving Heather Grant. Jeff married Heather only after she had given birth to their son, then fled to New York to become a star. Scared and broke, she sold her child on the black market, and told Jeff that he had died of pneumonia. It took years for Jeff to discover his wife's deceitful lies.

Robert, Holly, Luke

After nearly dying in an avalanche, a paralyzed Luke was too proud to let his lady love, Holly, know he was alive until he could walk again. After months of grueling therapy, he returned "from the dead" in 1983 to find Holly married to his best friend, Robert Scorpio.

Dangerous Liaisons

Noah and Tiffany

Noah Drake sizzled with sexy Tiffany Hill in 1982. Seeking a steady commitment from the playboy doc, Tiffany made Noah jealous when her old boyfriend, Tom Clark, came to town for a short visit. But the tables turned on Tiff when Noah's former flame, Bobbie Spencer, returned to town and headed straight for Noah's bed.

Justus, Simone, Tom (with Tom, Jr.)

Two years after leaving his wife Simone and son Tom, Jr. behind to go on a medical mission to Africa, Dr. Tom Hardy paid a house call on his family and found another man, attorney Justus Ward, making himself quite at home. Could Tom make up for lost time and win back his wife's affections? Or was the rift in their marriage too deep to mend? Justus held the key to both questions.

Terry and Mark

With his catatonic wife Mari Ellen confined to a mental institution, Dr. Mark Dante fell deeply in love with torch singer Terri Webber Arnett. To their shock, Mari Ellen recovered enough to come home, where an obedient Mark was forced to resume their sham of a marriage.

Lucy, Damian, Bobbie
The ever-scheming Lucy Coe presented Damian Smith with the ultimate challenge when she bet him that he couldn't seduce the seemingly happily married Bobbie Jones. Bobbie tried desperately to fend off Damian's advances, but soon she found herself fantasizing about her sly and sexy suitor. Unable to resist any longer, she made Lucy a loser when she gave in to her desires and slept with Damian.

Scotty and Heather
Scotty Baldwin was a changed man when he came back to Port Charles after being dumped by Laura. Bitter and vindictive, this "new" Scotty was just ripe for a relationship with the scheming Heather Webber. In 1982, these two hard-hearted scoundrels hooked up, then cooked up several nasty schemes to separate Heather's cousin Susan Moore from her money.

Katherine, Ned, Lois
Double-dealing Ned Ashton found himself wedged in a messy marital triangle when his family forced him to tie the knot with black-mailing businesswoman Katherine Bell. The Quartermaines didn't know that Ned (calling himself "Eddie Maine") was already married—to rock manager Lois Cerullo. Throughout 1994, naughty Ned tap-danced his way between these two very different women, trying to keep his two wives and lives from crossing paths.

Dangerous Liaisons

Ned and Monica

At the exclusive Green Meadows Spa, Monica encountered a young tennis pro named Ward who offered to help her with a lot more than serves and volleys. After a carefree roll in the hay with her sexy pro, Monica headed home. Imagine her surprise when Ward turned out to be none other than Ned Ashton—Tracy Quartermaine's son.

Sonny and Brenda

Brenda Barrett is a risk-taker, enticed by danger. And hot-tempered mobster Sonny Corinthos is a dangerous man. For months, these two hot-blooded kids toyed flirtatiously with each other's libido. Finally lust exploded into passion and they made love.

Brenda, Jagger, Karen

With his dark, brooding looks and sculpted torso, Jagger Cates was a sexual magnet. In 1993, this dangerous rebel had one woman too many. His heart belonged to wholesome pre-med student Karen Wexler, but his bed belonged to sexy Brenda Barrett. Brenda stopped at nothing to keep Jagger and Karen apart, even going as far as to plant nude photos of Karen in the lockers of her schoolmates to humiliate her innocent competitor.

Lucy and Alan
"How did I manage to spend so many years in such a narrow life with Monica?" asked a sexed-up Alan in 1989 of his latest mistress, Lucy Coe. In the midst of another midlife crisis, Alan set his lover up in a penthouse love nest, but soon discovered that life with Lucy was no party.

Sam, Frisco, Felicia
Felicia wasn't thrilled when Frisco decided to pursue a dangerous career in law enforcement. And she was less than enthused that her future husband's new partner in the Port Charles P.D. was the beautiful Samantha Welles.

Jason, Karen, Jagger
A college student with med school aspirations, Karen Wexler dreamed of living the wealthy life with the decent Jason Quartermaine, but she couldn't deny her attraction to the brooding Jagger. Over the summer of '92, the tension in this hot young triangle escalated as the kids survived a shipwreck. Returning to shore, Karen left Jason in the dust when she allowed herself to be swept off her feet and onto the back of Jagger's motorcycle.

THE HOSPITAL

For over 8,000 episodes, life and death dramas have filled the corridors of *General Hospital*, a busy metropolitan institution located in the heart of Port Charles. When the story began in 1963, it revolved almost entirely around Chief of Internal Medicine Dr. Steve Hardy, Nurse Jessie Brewer and the professional and personal lives of their fellow staff and patients. Over the years the prescription changed quite a bit, with action and intrigue supplanting the medical dramas that gained GH its initial success. Today, high-powered drama once again flourishes within the four walls of the hospital, and after 30+ years, the prognosis for healthy drama is excellent!

For nearly thirty years, dedicated Nurse Jessie Brewer assisted Dr. Hardy with the patients on *General Hospital*'s seventh floor. Though never romantically involved, Jessie and Steve were the closest of friends and confidantes.

Dr. Steve Hardy, Nurse Jessie Brewer and her philandering husband, intern Phil Brewer, formed GH's initial triumvirate of skilled medical professionals.

Originally a flight attendant trained in nursing, Audrey March Hardy landed on the staff of *General Hospital* in 1964. Now Administrator of Nursing, Audrey is a sensitive, dedicated and strong-willed woman who is always there to comfort a troubled co-worker or friend.

Originally *General Hospital*'s head of Internal Medicine, Dr. Steven Hardy became Chief of Staff in the late 1970's. Dr. Hardy is a fair and caring doctor, but a stickler for playing by the rules. As well as being the pillar of the hospital staff, Steve is a civic leader, and important part of Port Charles society. Perhaps the one thing he loves more than *General Hospital* is his wife Audrey.

No-nonsense nurse Lucille March ruled the seventh floor's student nurses with an iron hand (and a heart of putty) during *General Hospital*'s first decade. Among her "subjects" was eager-to-please Sharon McGillis Pinkham.

GENERAL HOSPITAL
FLOOR BY FLOOR

BASEMENT
X-ray
Emergency Room
Radiology
Storage
Lecture Hall
Morgue

MEZZANINE
Therapy Room

ONE
Main Entrance
Library
Boardroom
Book Storage
Cafeteria
Admissions
Lounge for Medical Staff
Chapel
Records Room

CARDIAC WING
Cardiac Intensive Care Unit

TWO
Chief of Staff's Office
Doctor's Offices
Administration
Boardroom
Clinics
Examining Rooms
Labs

THREE
Orthopedics

FOUR
Pediatrics
Obstetrics
Nursery
Newborn Intensive Care Unit
Tania Jones Day Care Center
Pediatrics ICU

FIVE
Gynecology
Urology
Infectious Diseases

SIX
Eye, Ear, Nose and Throat

SEVEN
Internal Medicine
Pharmacy
Co-ed Lounge

EIGHT
Psychiatric Ward
Burn Ward
Staff Psychiatrist Offices
Neurosurgery

NINE
Geriatrics
Physical Therapy

TEN
Surgery
Intensive Care (ICU)
Recovery Rooms

ROOF
Heliport

Barbara Jean Spencer began as a flighty student nurse in 1977. By 1981, "Bobbie" had become a well-respected member of the staff which included her boyfriend, surgeon Noah Drake and aunt, Ruby Anderson, who was a custodian.

Presently a general practitioner, Dr. Alan Quartermaine was introduced as a promising young surgeon. Alan's ambitions came to a halt when he injured his hand in an attempt to kill Monica and Rick Webber (who were having an affair), and the injury has prevented Alan from returning to the operating room.

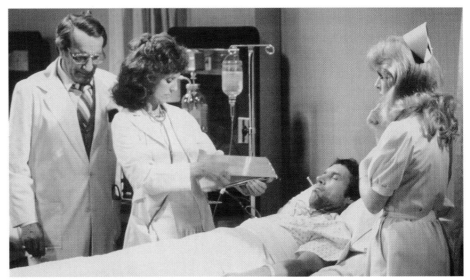

Lesley and Steve treat a patient. Beautiful Dr. Lesley Williams joined the staff in 1973 and immediately distinguished herself with her winning bedside manner. She remained to treat hundreds of patients (like the one pictured above) over the next 11 years. Dr. Hardy and busybody nurse Amy Vining appreciated and respected Lesley's skills.

For over ten years, Dr. Peter Taylor served as *General Hospital*'s top psychiatrist. His wife, Diana, was a staff nurse. Both died tragically—Peter of a heart attack and Diana was murdered!

In 1988, the entire Hardy family worked under the roof of *General Hospital*. Pictured here are Steve (recovering from back surgery), Audrey, their son Tom, a staff psychiatrist, and his wife Simone, a pediatrician.

Surgeons Rick Webber and Monica Quartermaine rarely had time to share a laugh in the corridors of *General Hospital*. The doctors often teamed up in the operating room—and the bedroom!

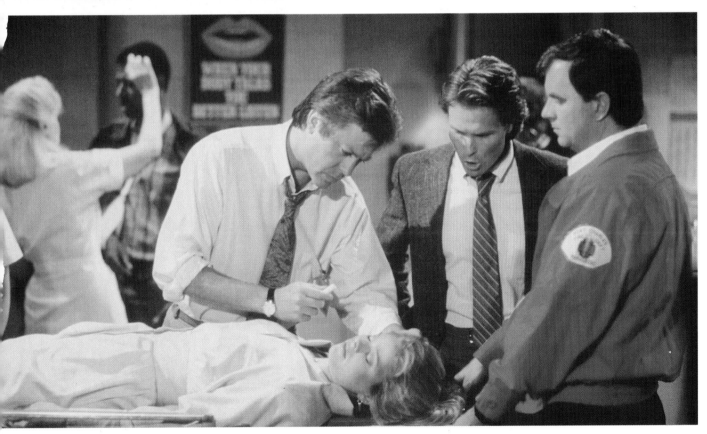

As the hospital's respected Head of Neurology, Dr. Tony Jones treated his sister-in-law Felicia when she was injured in a fire at the Brownstone in 1988.

After giving Stone Cates the diagnosis that he was suffering from AIDS, Dr. Kevin Collins and Dr. Alan Quartermaine provided their patient with life-enhancing information and the latest information on the treatment available to deal with the deadly virus. Stone's girlfriend Robin stood by her man throughout the entire ordeal (opposite).

The Hospital

HEROES AND HEARTTHROBS

The Macho Men of Port Charles

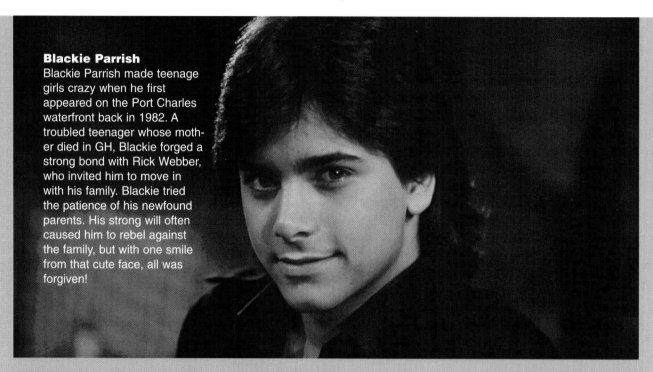

Blackie Parrish
Blackie Parrish made teenage girls crazy when he first appeared on the Port Charles waterfront back in 1982. A troubled teenager whose mother died in GH, Blackie forged a strong bond with Rick Webber, who invited him to move in with his family. Blackie tried the patience of his newfound parents. His strong will often caused him to rebel against the family, but with one smile from that cute face, all was forgiven!

Frisco Jones
When singer Frisco Jones discovered that he thrived on danger more than rock and roll, he smoothly moved from pop music to police work. Though he loves Felicia and his two darling children dearly, this world-class adventurer can't seem to tame his wanderlust. A good soul, Frisco's desire to make the world a better place keeps him on the move, but not on the make.

Scotty Baldwin
Over the course of his long and rollicking run in Port Charles, Scotty Baldwin progressed from a sweet, lovesick kid to a struggling law student and finally a sexy scoundrel with a heart of gold. Scotty is a very smart and able attorney who could have done well except he was always trying to take shortcuts in search of riches, power and respect. He is equally clever in matters of the heart, where he uses any means to get the woman he wants—just ask Laura, Heather, Lucy and Bobbie!

Joe Kelly
The twinkle in Joe Kelly's Irish eyes made lots of lassies smile, but this handsome fellow never seemed to get the girl! Joe had been deeply in love with Anne Logan. However, his attention was not returned because Anne had fallen in love with Joe's best pal, Jeff Webber. On the rebound, the lawyer turned his attention to his client, Heather Webber, but she was more interested in scheming (and sleeping) with Scotty Baldwin. Do nice guys really finish last? Say it ain't so, Joe!

Decker Moss

Growing up in the carnival taught Decker Moss to survive by his wits. This sexy grifter became a very skilled con man and he crisscrossed the country breaking countless hearts along the way. Decker was not the type to stay in one place for too long. He traveled light both with his possessions and his emotional entanglements.

Duke Lavery

Duke Lavery did a lot of bad things, but always with good intentions. This handsome gentleman with chiseled features and a deep Scottish brogue knew just how to court a woman: whispered poetry on bended knee… a sprig of heather… Duke made plenty of women swoon, but only one captured his fancy—and her name was Anna Devane.

This chorus line of heartthrobs lined up at Duke and Anna's wedding. Check out the specs and pecs on Duke Lavery, Jake Meyer, Sean Donely, Tom Hardy, Tony Jones and Patrick O'Connor.

Jagger Cates

Soap Opera Digest called Jagger Cates "the sexiest character on the soaps." If a picture is indeed worth a thousand words, look closely at that chiseled torso and those bedroom eyes and judge for yourself! When he motored into town, Jagger was a wanted man. Wanted by beautiful Brenda Barrett! But this heartthrob only had eyes for Brenda's rival, Karen Wexler.

Miguel Morez

General Hospital viewers first met heroic hunk Miguel Morez when, as a hospital orderly, he talked a suicidal woman off a ledge, then risked his life to save a bunch of school kids whose bus had crashed and was about to explode. After keeping his singing talents under wraps for months, Miguel took center stage.

Mac Scorpio (opposite)

Mac Scorpio is an Australian adventurer who has mastered the All-American art of romance. Mac was a romantic rogue with a dangerous edge when he sailed into Port Charles in 1991. Over the next four years, this dimpled darling underwent a dramatic transformation that elevated him to virtual "white knight" status. Still, nobody flirts like good-guy Mac. He's a heartthrob with heart!

Kevin Collins

Urbane and sophisticated Dr. Kevin Collins is a hot number for women who prefer brains over beefcake. Kevin's a respected psychiatrist, a skilled marriage counselor and (as Lucy finally found out) quite a Lothario!

Sonny Corinthos

Dark and brooding mobster Sonny Corinthos is one tough customer. But the chosen few who really know him are aware that this hot-blooded heartthrob has a soft center buried deep beneath his hard-as-nails exterior. A restless soul, Sonny doesn't explode—he smolders!

Jason Quartermaine

Is Jason Quartermaine too good to be true? This level-headed young man is the kind of guy you want to show up at the front door for your daughter's first date. Jason's moral, muscular and he's even studying to be a doctor, just like his parents. Irresistibly charming and intelligent, Jason is every mom's dream!

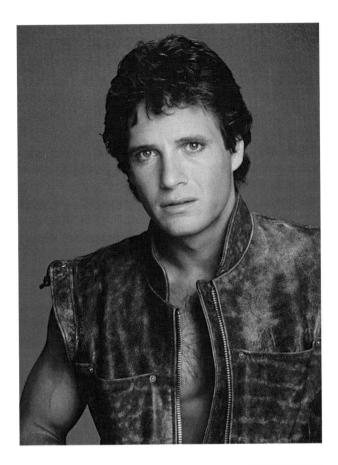

Jimmy Lee Holt

In 1983, a handsome young man with piercing blue eyes roared into town on his motorcycle. His name was Jimmy Lee Holt, and he'd come straight from Indiana to deliver the shocking news that he was Edward Quartermaine's illegitimate son! The blue-jean clad hunk boldly staked his claim to both the Quartermaine fortune and their distant relative Celia who was engaged to another man, Grant Putnam. But when Celia gazed into Jimmy Lee's baby blues, she was instantly smitten!

Ned Ashton

Tall, dark and dimpled, Ned Ashton is as ruthless in business as he is lovable in bed! As treasurer of ELQ, he nearly ran the company into the ground, but had much better success in his second career as a rock and roll heartthrob. Squeezing into a pair of tight leather jeans, "Eddie Maine's" gyrating hips made female patrons swoon.

AJ Quartermaine

The black sheep of his flock, AJ Quartermaine is an intense competitor who wants what his relatives have—their money, their respect and their women.

ROBERT SCORPIO

Whether chasing dangerous criminals or beautiful women, super-spy Robert Scorpio displayed a style and polish seldom seen in provincial Port Charles. A handsome Australian export with piercing blue eyes and a disarming grin, Scorpio brought an air of international intrigue to a series of action-packed adventures and sexy escapades that kept viewers enthralled for over a decade.

The 1991 "reunion" of Robert Scorpio and his kid brother, Mac, was charged with animosity. Robert blamed Mac for the long-ago deaths of their parents and Robert's fiancée. When Mac arrived in Port Charles, he was framed for the attempted murder of his brother, who eventually saved him, restored their fraternal bond and helped to capture the real villains.

Robert Scorpio's first marriage to beautiful WSB agent Anna Devane took place in the piazza of a tiny Italian village. The newlyweds were deeply in love, but the demands of the spy game drove them apart when the evil DVX blackmailed Anna into acting as a double agent. Upon discovering his wife's dastardly deception, a heartbroken Robert divorced Anna.

In 1985, Robert arrived home to find a little girl on his doorstep. The pint-sized princess turned out to be Robin, the daughter he never knew he had! They became instant chums.

Over the years, Robert Scorpio and Sean Donely were alternately comrades and adversaries in a series of explosive storylines. In Europe, Sean had been Robert's boss at the World Security Bureau, and was one of the few people who knew of his marriage to fellow agent Anna Devane. In 1984, Scorpio solicited the help of his old friend Sean to help locate the missing Aztec Treasure. Unbeknownst to Robert, self-serving Sean planned to steal the treasure for himself!

Instantly and indisputably, there was a certain chemistry between Robert Scorpio and charming and sophisticated Katherine Delafield—though neither would admit it. Their tempestuous courtship began when Robert leased a quaint cottage in the woods, only to discover that the owner, Katherine, was still in residence. Landlord and tenant agreed to share the tiny house, sparking a series of arguments spiced with a strong sexual undercurrent.

First came marriage and then came love for Robert and Holly. Believing that his best friend Luke had died in an avalanche, the ever-loyal Scorpio married Holly, who was pregnant and about to be deported. After Holly miscarried Luke's baby, her platonic marriage to Robert turned passionate!

 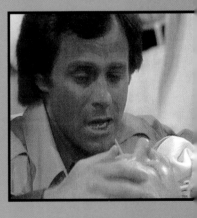

Cheryl Stansbury's brains and beauty were the two qualities that captivated Robert Scorpio in 1988. However, Cheryl's unbreakable ties to an old lover, Julian Jerome, and a passion for deception, drove the lovers apart.

"No!," screamed Robert Scorpio in horror upon the death of his mentor and surrogate mother, WSB Agent O'Reilly, who was gunned down on the docks during the early stages of the Ice Princess caper. In a tearful farewell, Scorpio held his dying friend, and vowed revenge on the evil Cassadine clan!

WEDDINGS

The march down the aisle is rarely an easy trek for the romantic couples of Port Charles. Over the years, viewers have followed every unpredictable twist and turn in anticipation of the joyous day when man and wife are joined together in holy matrimony. *General Hospital* wedding ceremonies are seldom mundane because guests often see red, brides wear red and not-so-late spouses have been known to return from the dead at the most inopportune moment. Whether they tie the knot in an ornate church or an austere hospital room, GH couples seldom find everlasting happiness. Nevertheless, they have provided us with enough wonderful memories to last a lifetime. Share the joy and the sorrow of *General Hospital*'s greatest weddings!

Audrey March and Steve Hardy (1965)
In 1965, Lyndon Johnson was president, the Beatles were the rage and Audrey March became Mrs. Steven Hardy for the first time. A lifelong bachelor, Dr. Hardy dragged his feet before agreeing to marry Audrey, a former swinging airline stewardess. After a painful divorce, they married again eleven years later.

Al Weeks and Lucille March (1974)

Hospital handyman Al Weeks, a widower, found love in the golden years with crusty nurse (and perennial old maid) Lucille March. Dr. Henry Pinkham served as Al's best man in the much-anticipated 1974 wedding which was held in the hospital chapel. Tears flowed freely when Lucille's dear friend, Steve Hardy, sang "Oh Promise Me" to mark the occasion.

Cameron Faulkner and Dr. Lesley Williams (1975)

Dr. Lesley Williams and wealthy financier Cameron Faulkner married soon after the groom was shot while saving Lesley from an obsessed patient who had kidnaped her. The Faulkner's marriage disintegrated when Cameron became fiercely jealous of Lesley's relationship with her long-lost daughter, Laura.

Dr. Peter Taylor and Jessie Brewer (1969)

Believing that her husband Phil Brewer died in a plane crash, Jessie turned to her dear friend, Dr. Peter Taylor, for comfort. Their simmering affection blossomed into love and marriage but, when Phil turned up alive, the union was rendered invalid. Jessie returned to Phil, and Peter subsequently married pregnant waitress Diana Taylor—who was carrying Phil's child!

Lee Baldwin and Caroline Chandler (1975)

After years of mourning his late wife Meg, Attorney Lee Baldwin found love again with adoption counselor Caroline Chandler. After a Port Charles wedding, Lee and Caroline started a new life in Florida. Less than a year later, Caroline and her son, Bobby, were killed in a boating accident. Heartbroken, Lee moved back to Port Charles.

Weddings

Scotty Baldwin and Laura Webber (1979)
Young lovers Scotty Baldwin and Laura Webber overcame many obstacles to marry in a casual June wedding held in Port Charles Park. Moments before the long-awaited wedding, Laura nearly panicked when Scotty was nowhere to be found! Due to a mix up, he arrived just in time to take Laura as his teenage bride.

Dr. Steve Hardy and Audrey March (1976)
A wheelchair-bound Steve Hardy refused to marry his true love, Audrey, until he could walk down the aisle. After intensive therapy, Dr. Hardy proudly took the walk, but happiness for Steve and Audrey was short-lived. On their Hawaiian honeymoon, Steve and Audrey discovered that Audrey's "late" husband, Tom, was alive!

Luke Spencer and Jennifer Smith (1980)
Though he loved Laura, Luke was pressured into marrying mob "princess" Jennifer Smith. But the wedding never happened—thanks to Laura's husband, Scotty, who burst on the scene and punched out Luke. Luke fell overboard, then went on the run with his true love, Laura.

Robert Scorpio and Holly Sutton (1983)
Holly Sutton was about to be deported to her native England after her fiancé Luke was presumed dead in an avalanche. Problem—Holly was pregnant with Luke's baby. Solution—Luke's pal, Robert Scorpio, agreed to marry Holly to keep her in the country and give her baby a name. In February 1983 they tied the knot with a quickie city hall wedding, but soon their marriage of convenience became one filled with love.

Dr. Rick Webber and Dr. Lesley Faulkner (1981)
Rick and Lesley Webber proved that love can be better the second time around. After Rick's affair with Monica, the couple divorced, but found their way back and married in an intimate ceremony held in their living room in 1981.

Brian Phillips and Claudia Johnston (1983)
Brian Phillips suffered a case of last minute nerves and nearly backed out of his marriage to wealthy Claudia Johnston. Fortunately, Dr. Rick Webber talked some sense into the bashful bridegroom in time to bring their four-year courtship to an end—in marriage.

Dr. Kevin O'Connor and Terry Brock (1985)
Prior to her marriage to Dr. Kevin O'Connor, Terry Brock was plagued by a series of horribly grotesque flashbacks. If only she had known that her intended hubby was secretly a psychotic mad-man responsible for a series of murders in their hometown of Laurelton!

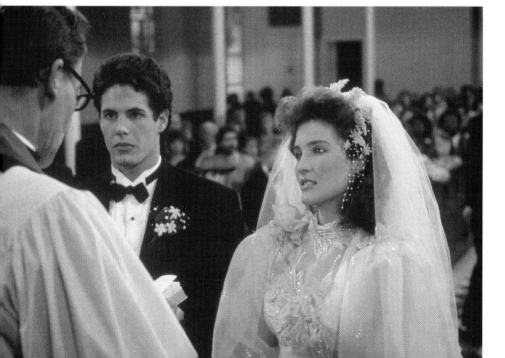

Weddings

Grant Putnam and Celia Quartermaine (1983)
While planning her society-page wedding to all-American Dr. Grant Putnam, Celia Quartermaine carried on a passionate affair with rugged Jimmy Lee Holt, who was not about to let go of his lady love. Jimmy Lee kidnaped Celia on her wedding day, but she refused to break Grant's heart. Escaping from her captor, the bride hitched her way back to Port Charles on the back of a truck filled with chickens, arriving just in time for the ceremony.

D.L. Brock and Bobbie Spencer (1983)
In a ceremony presided over by Port Charles Mayor, Lee Baldwin, Bobbie Spencer fell in love and married strong-minded financier D.L. Brock, unaware she would soon become a target of his raging temper and unending mental and physical abuse. Bobbie's torment came to an end when her husband was shot and killed by Ginny Blake—though at first Bobbie was charged with the crime.

Jake Meyer and Bobbie Brock (1986)
After her rocky, ill-fated marriage to D.L. Brock, Bobbie settled down with her friend, lawyer and business partner, Jake Meyer. Their marriage suffered when Jake slept with Lucy Coe, who became pregnant with his child. Though Bobbie forgave Jake's indiscretion, she never let Lucy off the hook!

Frisco Jones and Felicia Cummings (1986)
Nearly two years after they met, young lovers Frisco Jones and Felicia Cummings hitched up in June 1986—but not without last minute complications. Felicia almost called off the nuptials when her fiancé refused to leave his dangerous career with the Port Charles Police Department. At the last minute she relented and, after a mad dash to locate a minister, Frisco and Felicia were married.

Duke Lavery and Anna Devane (1987)
It took two tries, but a kilt-wearing Duke Lavery finally made it to the altar with Anna Devane in October 1987. Five months previous, their nuptials were interrupted mid-ceremony by tabloid reporter Mark Carlin and a herd of reporters who accused Duke of being an accomplice to a long-ago murder.

Colton Shore and Felicia Jones (1989)
"Widow" Felicia Jones found love again with handsome Colton Shore. In June 1989, they married in Port Charles Park. Unbeknownst to the newlyweds, Felicia's not-so-late husband, Frisco, had escaped from a middle eastern prison and arrived home just in time to witness his wife's shocking ceremony.

Dr. Tony Jones and Bobbie Meyer (1989)
At first, Bobbie Meyer and Dr. Tony Jones just wanted to be friends. Burned by their ill-fated marriages to Jake and Lucy, neither wanted to admit the obvious—they had fallen in love! In a radiant October 1989 wedding held in Puerto Rico, Bobbie happily became the third "Mrs. Tony Jones."

Sean Donely and Tiffany Hill (1988)
Port Charles' most unlikely couple got together in December 1988 when straight-laced former secret agent Sean Donely (who swore he would never marry) took the leap with outrageous former B-movie star Tiffany Hill. Furious with her groom, Tiffany had to be dragged kicking and screaming to the altar!

Dr. Tom Hardy and Dr. Simone Ravelle (1988)
Drs. Tom Hardy and Simone Ravelle overcame the outside pressures of their interracial romance and became man and wife in the hospital chapel in 1988. After their wedding, Tom and Simone's problems did not go away. Tom was suspended after losing his temper and slugging a prejudiced patient and Simone left on a world cruise after miscarrying their unborn child.

Robert Scorpio and Anna Lavery (1991)

What could be more romantic than a wedding in June? Possibly a wedding in which the bride and groom, forced apart in the past by betrayal, felt that this time fate had brought them back together. Robert Scorpio and Anna Devane reunited in 1991 with their old WSB comrade, Sean Donely, serving as best man in the English country garden wedding held on the grounds of the Quartermaine estate.

Ned Ashton and Jenny Eckert (1992)

The courtship of virginal Jenny Eckert and blue-blooded jet-setter Ned Ashton culminated in a traditional church wedding in 1992. The couple weathered a stormy courtship marked by murder, blackmail and family turmoil, but their union could not survive Tracy Quartermaine's shocking revelation that Jenny had been involved in an affair with Senator Kensington when she was sixteen years old.

"Eddie Maine" and Lois Cerullo (1994)

Rock and roll promoter Lois Cerullo thought she was marrying singer Eddie Maine when she tied the knot at the Justice of the Peace in 1994. Little did she know that her new husband was an imposter.

Weddings

Jagger Cates and Karen Wexler (1994)
The long-awaited marriage of heartthrob Jagger Cates and troubled Karen Wexler nearly failed to take place when Jagger was seriously injured just before the wedding (right). Upon his recovery, close relatives and friends were on hand to wish the happy couple well before they triumphantly hopped on Jagger's Harley and roared out of Port Charles.

Dr. Alan Quartermaine and Lucy Coe (1990)
In March 1990, wealthy Dr. Alan Quartermaine became the latest in Lucy Coe's long line of "victims." The very embodiment of a Jezebel for the '90s, Lucy snared Alan for one of the most bizarre daytime TV weddings ever. It's true that Jezebel wore red—but Lucy didn't intend to, not for this event. It seemed the wedding gown she ordered didn't arrive—another dress did—and she had no choice but to wear the garish, jungle red outfit to the nuptials.

Ned Ashton and Lois Cerullo (1995)
Brooklyn, NY, was the setting for the second wedding (in June 1995) of hometown girl Lois Cerullo and her beau, Ned (opposite). Friends and family journeyed from Port Charles to attend the long-awaited nuptials which survived a last ditch effort by Lois' former boyfriend, Danny, to reclaim his girl!

LUKE AND LAURA'S WEDDING

What's left to do after you've tossed the world's most diabolical villain into an icebox and saved mankind from a deep freeze? How about a wedding! Not just a wedding—the wedding. The biggest party that Port Charles had ever seen. On a beautiful Indian summer afternoon in the fall of 1981, Luke and Laura put their turbulent past behind them and married on the grounds of the Port Charles mayor's mansion. Two thorny, uninvited guests—Scotty Baldwin and Helena Cassadine—crashed the wedding to bring an extra-added air of excitement to an otherwise elegant affair. Relive the romance of that very special day!

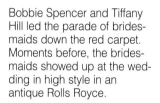

Bobbie Spencer and Tiffany Hill led the parade of brides-maids down the red carpet. Moments before, the brides-maids showed up at the wedding in high style in an antique Rolls Royce.

ABC-TV invited the world to tune in to the daytime wedding of the decade!

The bride wore a gorgeous hand-beaded gown to complement her groom's dashing grey tuxedo. Luke and Laura's long-awaited nuptials, plus the presence of Elizabeth Taylor, served up the highest ratings in Soap Opera history.

The groom and his best man, Robert Scorpio, chugged to the ceremony in an antique jalopy driven by their pal, cabby Slick Jones.

A pensive and emotional Laura listened as the mayor asked her to recite the vows of marriage to her husband-to-be.

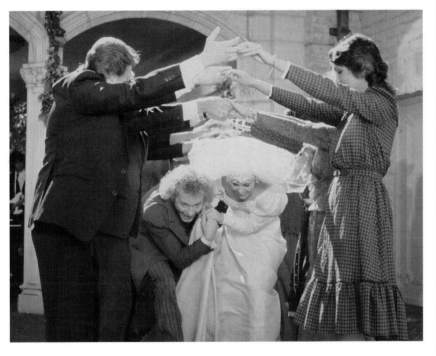

At the wedding reception Luke and Laura were the main attraction in a square dance led by the friendly country folks from Beechers Corners.

Lurking in the background during the wedding ceremony, a vengeful Helena Cassadine offered some parting words to the bride and groom.

HELENA
"A curse on you, Laura and Luke. A curse on you both!"

Flanked by the mayor (who presided over the ceremony) and his best man, Robert, Luke anxiously awaits the arrival of his bride.

The beaming bride and handsome groom danced the first dance to the melodic strains of their special love song, "Fascination."

With a bevy of eligible women poised below, Laura prepared to toss her bouquet from the balcony of the mayor's mansion.

Laura's ex-husband, Scotty Baldwin, provided the fireworks when he appeared out of the blue to catch Laura's wedding bouquet! Luke jumped from the balcony of the mayor's mansion and pummeled his long-time rival.

QUARTERMANIA

They are as delightful as they are dysfunctional! The upper-crust Quartermaines are one of the wealthiest and most prominent families in Port Charles. The family patriarch, Edward, is a crafty and cranky business tycoon who craves power and money. His effervescent and wonderfully wacky wife, Lila, has made a fortune of her own peddling pickle relish. Their battling brood of children and grandchildren—both legal and illegitimate—has kept Port Charles alive for years with the sound of their bickering. But as ferociously as they fight, the Quartermaines will fiercely protect any member of their mansion who encounters troubles with outside forces. Here's an intimate look at that quibbling clan—the Quartermaines.

Edward and Lila: Their love has endured for decades. Perhaps the greatest strain on their half-century of marriage occurred when Edward's plane crashed in the Bermuda Triangle. Assuming that her husband had perished, Lila began conversing and sharing martinis with his portrait! After two years suffering from amnesia, Edward regained his memory on a Caribbean island and eventually came home to the surprise and delight of his waiting wife.

Edward Quartermaine didn't get to the top by being a softie. At home, the family patriarch could be cold and aloof or tender or caring, depending on his mood. Every Quartermaine learned to steer clear of Edward's bad side—or they'd better watch out!

In 1980, Edward and Lila welcomed the newest member of the Quartermaine family dynasty when they attended the christening of Alan Quartermaine Jr.

Lila Quartermaine knows better than anyone that the Quartermaine clan can be a very difficult group to control. Unlike her domineering husband, the family matriarch has learned that you can get more out of people with honey than with vinegar. Though, on occasion, Lila is forced to lay down the law—especially when it comes to keeping her hubby, Edward, in line.

Edward Quartermaine's illegitimate offspring, Jimmy Lee, married distant cousin Celia in 1985, but their marriage fell apart when Jimmy Lee's bad business deals caused him to go broke. Unable to handle Jimmy Lee's poverty and infidelity, Celia left her mate and departed Port Charles.

With lots of idle time on their hands, the Quartermaines often fill their days by making mischief!

Happy moments were rare for Alan Quartermaine and his sinister sister, Tracy. The Quartermaine siblings engaged in an endless series of heated arguments—usually over money. Years ago, Tracy felt that the money to be inherited by Alan's newborn son should actually go to her boy, Ned. This cold-blooded cobra tried every trick in the book to get her way, and when she failed to get her hands on daddy's dough, Tracy left town—penniless.

In 1990, the guests were aghast when the newest Quartermaine—Lucy—came to her wedding dressed in an outrageous red gown. Although he was forced into the short-term marriage, Alan looked mildly amused.

The Quartermaine clan—circa 1994. Clockwise from top: Alan, Monica, Edward, Ned, Jason, Lila and AJ.

Tracy Quartermaine is arguably the most despicable woman ever to bedevil the people of Port Charles. Just when the Quartermaines thought that their unscrupulous offspring was gone for good, the bitch came back! After gadding about Europe for nearly a decade, Tracy Quartermaine slithered back to town in 1989 to resume her tempestuous relationship with her "beloved" family.

Still together after all these years... Edward and Lila's long-lasting love affair is stronger in the '90s than it was in the '40s. That's when he had an affair with torch singer Mary Mae Ward!

Through volcanic fights and all-out war, those Quartermaine doctors, Alan and Monica, always seem to find their way back to each other. Their unlikely union can best be described as one hell of an emotional rollercoaster ride—one they keep taking again and again! Alan and Monica's incessant sparring conceals the couple's underlying love for each other.

The Quartermaines—circa 1993. Clockwise: Monica, AJ, Alan, Jason, Tracy, Lila and Edward.

In a gracious act of friendship, Monica offered to let the dying Page Bowen and her daughter Emily live in the Quartermaine mansion. The family welcomed Page and Emily with open arms, though Alan became jealous of Monica's close relationship with her fatally ill friend. Stricken with inoperable cancer, Page died with Emily by her side in June 1995.

He squandered her fortune and cheated on her. Still, years after they parted, the divorced duo of Lord Larry Ashton and Tracy Quartermaine continued to harass each other.

Alan and Monica—1995

Two families—one blue-collar, one blue-blooded—came together in holy matrimony when Bensonhurst's Lois Cerullo tied the knot with Port Charles' Ned Ashton in a neighborhood church in Brooklyn. Afterward, the newlyweds celebrated with a kiss!

"I'll stay with you until you go into the operating room,"

whispered Alan to his wife, Monica, on the night before she underwent surgery for breast cancer in 1994. Monica's courageous bout with the disease brought out a compassion in Alan that she had never witnessed in all their years of marriage.

Patriarchs Carmine Cerullo and Edward Quartermaine smoked a peace pipe, uh, make that cigar to mark the special occasion of Ned and Lois' 1995 wedding.

In 1982, Monica returned from France with a studly Frenchman, Phillipe, on her arm! As part of a vicious game to make Alan jealous, Monica invited her suave new friend to stay in the Quartermaine mansion. His visit did not last long—because Phillipe realized that Alan might kill him if he found him in Monica's bed!

Edward proved to be more irascible than ever in the winter of 1995 after breaking a leg while pursuing his pregnant pooch, Annabelle, and her lover dog, Foster. Slipping on a slick patch of ice, Edward fell and—crack!—he busted a gam. Back home, Annabelle tried and failed to console her irritable master.

STARS!

No doubt about it—Port Charles has star power! Over the years, memorable appearances by a long line of luminaries have been incorporated into the fabric of the *General Hospital* storyline. Legendary celebrities, among them Elizabeth Taylor and Sammy Davis Jr., checked into *General Hospital* because they were huge fans of the soap. Several of today's mega-stars—including Demi Moore—began their rise to the top in roles on *General Hospital*. And top recording artists have filled our afternoons with beautiful music. Check out this illustrious group of luminaries who have called Port Charles home…

Two of today's top stars, Janine Turner and Demi Moore, played sisters on *General Hospital* back in 1982. At the tender age of 19, film superstar Demi Moore beat out one thousand actresses to win the role of investigative journalist Jackie Templeton on GH. Long before she rose to fame as *Northern Exposure*'s spunky Maggie O'Connell, Janine portrayed the equally spunky Laura Templeton.

From Monica to Heather to Anne to Diana… For five years (1976-81) viewers followed the tumultuous love life of *General Hospital*'s Dr. Jeff Webber, played by Richard Dean Anderson. The handsome actor went from battling disease to fighting crime as the star of ABC-TV's hit action/adventure series *MacGyver*.

The late Sammy Davis Jr. rarely missed an episode of *General Hospital*. The talented performer had the chance to appear on the show when he played Eddie Phillips, a recovering alcoholic who sought to reunite with his estranged son, Brian Phillips, and his new wife, Claudia. Sammy brought tears to the eyes of the *General Hospital* cast when he sang "It Had to Be You."

Mae Clarke, the actress who had a grapefruit smashed in her face by James Cagney in the 1931 film classic, *The Public Enemy,* was an original GH cast member. Mae portrayed Marge, a tough seventh floor nurse.

Long before he donned pointed ears to play *Star Trek*'s Mr. Spock, Leonard Nimoy appeared on *General Hospital* as a pill pusher named Bernie. In this 1963 scene, Bernie showed up at Peggy Mercer's door with a home delivery for her beau, Roy Lansing.

Stars!

Long before he journeyed through the heavens as Luke Skywalker in *Star Wars,* a fresh-faced Mark Hamill was a regular on *General Hospital* as Jessie Brewer's teenage nephew-with-a-chip-on-his-shoulder, Kent Murray.

In 1968, *Cagney and Lacey*'s Tyne Daly gave a riveting performance as Caroline Beale, a young mother dying from kidney failure. In this scene, Caroline is about to be told the heartbreaking news that she is not a candidate for renal dialysis.

Luke and Laura Spencer were in for quite a surprise when they traveled to Atlantic City and met up with Luke's former fiancée, Jennifer, and her husband Billy "Baggs" Boggs, played by Roseanne and her then-husband, Tom Arnold. "When Roseanne told me that she is a devoted fan of *General Hospital,* I invited her to be on the show," explains Executive Producer Wendy Riche. The madcap tale that followed was both intriguing and amusingly amorous as Jennifer and Billy tried to seduce the surprised Spencers!

As dapper Dr. Noah Drake, rock star Rick Springfield wooed Tiffany Hill (and Bobbie Spencer) during the week on *General Hospital,* then jetted off to arenas throughout the U.S. to perform rock and roll before thousands of screaming teens! While on GH, Rick's song "Jessie's Girl" rose to the top of the *Billboard* charts.

When Luke Spencer opened his new blues nightclub in Port Charles, he invited the legendary B.B. King to be the opening act. The appearance marked Mr. King's daytime drama debut, who added that, "Tony Geary (Luke) gave me some great advice about acting, though he doesn't know he did. He taught me to just relax, be myself and be honest. It's a lot like playing the blues."

Just one year before he became Captain Frank Furillo on *Hill Street Blues,* Daniel J. Travanti played *General Hospital'*s Spence Andrews, a former football player who entered group therapy after his wife left him. Also in the group was Rick Webber's estranged wife, Lesley, who found comfort in her deepening friendship with the handsome Mr. Andrews.

"I had a ball—I'm wild about that show!" Elizabeth Taylor told *People* magazine after her unforgettable five-show guest stint in 1981, which brought unequaled status to *General Hospital.* Dripping with diamonds, Liz portrayed Helena Cassadine, the vengeful and rich widow of mad scientist, Mikkos. The legendary screen star graciously donated her $2,000 paycheck to two Virginia hospitals.

Stars!

Scotty Baldwin surprised his wife Dominique with an impromptu concert by Broadway and country western singer Gary Morris. Looking back, Morris remembers, "Dominique was on the verge of dying from her brain tumor and Tiffany, who knew me from her days back in Nashville, got me to sing for Dominique and Scott in the gazebo. The cast was wonderful. My fans gave me excellent feedback from the appearance. And I was surprised how many of them were faithful viewers of *General Hospital*."

Grammy Award-winning recording star Melissa Manchester played herself in 1994. In the story, Melissa called her old friend Mac Scorpio to tell him she was in town on tour. Later, Melissa thrilled the patrons at the Outback with a song. "It was pure nepotism that I sang on *General Hospital*. The show introduced me as being a friend of Mac's but, in reality, my manager is a cousin of one of the producers. The cast was so generous to me as fellow actors, and my day on the set was lots of fun!"

International superstar Julio Iglesias made a 1994 cameo appearance when music manager Lois Cerullo took her budding singer Miguel Morez through a high-tech recording studio on a visit to New York City. To their surprise, they discovered Julio Iglesias recording in the same building. Ricky Martin (Miguel) remembers that Julio was impressed with the recording studio set that *General Hospital* constructed especially for the scenes. "Can I record here?" he asked Ricky with a laugh.

Ten years after he made his debut as teen hero Blackie Parrish, John Stamos (*Full House*) returned to his roots at *General Hospital*. This time, John played himself in a calamity-filled restaurant scene with Scotty Baldwin and Julia Barrett. "If I'm anywhere, it's because of *General Hospital*. I'll never stop appreciating what GH meant to me," explains John today. "My major break as an actor came with my role on *General Hospital*. It taught me a lot. Training on a soap really prepares you and it was a great learning experience for me…I've always been very grateful to the show for what it did for me and my career."

"Mr. Television," Milton Berle, suavely kissed Laura Spencer's hand when he guest-starred as Tiffany Hill's wisecracking theatrical agent, Mickey Miller, in 1981. "Uncle Miltie's" character played a pivotal role—it was Mickey Miller who launched Laura's modeling career as "Miss Star Eyes."

Weight loss guru Richard Simmons climbed the pyramid to success by playing himself in 1979. Soon after joining the cast, Simmons did his first solo mall appearance in South Bend, Indiana. "We couldn't get into the mall it was so crowded. I said to the driver, 'My God, who's here?' He said, YOU'RE HERE. They see you on *General Hospital* helping all the overweight women. They are here to see YOU!' Appearing on *General Hospital* changed my life."

Stars!

BEHIND THE SCENES:

Through the years...

Constructed in 1977, the nurses station, known as "the hub," is the only permanent set on the *General Hospital* studio floor.

The cast—circa 1969

1976 cast

After seven years on the air, *General Hospital*'s vital signs were excellent! John Beradino (Steve) led 1970's anniversary celebration (left).

The 1977 cast

The 1980 cast

Genie Francis (Laura), John Beradino (Steve), Rachel Ames (Audrey), Denise Alexander (Lesley), Georganne LaPiere (Heather) and Peter Hansen participated in a cake cutting to mark *General Hospital*'s 15th anniversary in April 1978 (below).

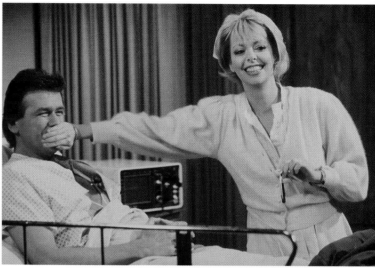

Shell Kepler (Amy) quiets quipster John Reilly (Sean Donely) during a funny moment between takes in 1985.

Emma Samms (Holly) and Anthony Geary (Luke) study their lines while on location in 1982. The scenes, taped at the Franklin Canyon Reservoir in the Hollywood Hills, marked Emma's *General Hospital* debut.

The Cassadine island—complete with lagoon and a real waterfall—was constructed on the *General Hospital* sound stage at Sunset-Gower Studios in Hollywood in 1981. Executive Producer Gloria Monty (back to camera), Anthony Geary (Luke), Genie Francis (Laura) and a member of the crew tend to final adjustments before taping a scene.

GENERAL HOSPITAL HAPPY 20th

Emily McLaughlin (Jessie) and John Beradino (Steve) sweetly celebrated *General Hospital*'s 20th anniversary on April 1, 1983.

April 1, 1983: Chris Robinson (Rick), John Beradino (Steve) and Anthony Geary (Luke) raise their glasses in celebration of *General Hospital*'s anniversary.

The cast celebrated a quarter-century on the air in April 1988.

Behind The Scenes

Director Marlena Laird instructs Antonio Sabato, Jr. (Jagger) and Cari Shayne (Karen) where to move on the Hollywood set of *General Hospital* which had been transformed into an island off the coast of Port Charles for this summer 1992 scene.

During the taping of the 1995 Nurses' Ball, ABC's Daytime Senior Vice President Maxine Levinson posed with her very own Cowardly Lion (adorably portrayed by Stuart Damon).

General Hospital marked yet another monumental milestone when it aired its 7,000th episode on Thursday, August 9th, 1990. The soap is the longest-running daytime drama on the ABC Television Network.

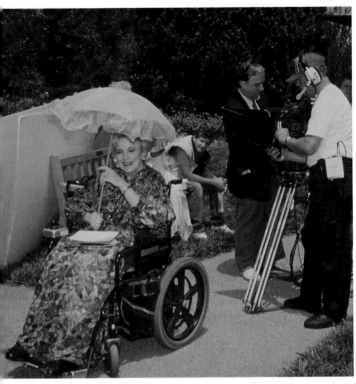

Anna Lee (Lila) brought along her own parasol to ward off the midday sun's rays during a 1991 location shoot at the historic Greystone Mansion in Beverly Hills, which is used for exterior shots of the Quartermaine mansion (left).

April 1, 1993: Thirty years of *General Hospital*.

July 5, 1994: The cast gathers on the set to mark the occasion of the taping of *General Hospital*'s 8,000th episode.

Behind The Scenes

BACKSTAGE PASS

A peek behind the scenes at some of the people who make *General Hospital* happen five days a week, fifty-two weeks a year.

Supervising Producer Francesca James, Consulting Producer Shelley Curtis and Producer Julie Carruthers are integral parts of the dream team that has shaped *General Hospital* into one of daytime television's most sophisticated and popular dramas.

With notable success in many areas of television production, Executive Producer Wendy Riche brings an acute understanding of the importance of rich character development and involving storylines to *General Hospital*. The soap has enjoyed a remarkable resurgence since Ms. Riche arrived to captain the ship in 1992.

"What are we doing next Tuesday?" asks coordinating Producer Jerry Balme of Associate Producer Marty Vagts as they review the "breakdown board." The board shows, at a glance, the hundreds of scenes to be taped over the coming week.

Director Shelley Curtis discusses the finer points of the script with Kimberly McCullough (Robin Scorpio), John J. York (Mac Scorpio) and special guest Maty Monfort from ABC-TV's "Mike and Maty."

"Sit here!" barks director Joe Behar to Kristina Wagner (Felicia Jones), who is busy working out the kinks in John J. York's (Mac Scorpio) aching back!

Production Designer Matthew C. Jacobs (foreground) reviews plans for a new set with Art Director Mercer B. Barrows and Assistant Art Director Jim Jones. The production team has constructed everything from lighthouses to tropical islands in *General Hospital*'s spacious studio 54.

Whenever you hear a telephone ring or a doorbell chime, it's sound effects engineer Sandy Masone pressing the buttons!

It's not unusual for Casting Director Mark Teschner to receive over 100 photos and resumes a day from aspiring actors seeking a plum role on *General Hospital*.

In his ground floor dressing room, Wally Kurth (Ned Ashton) brushes up on his lines while relaxing between scenes.

"Should Mac fall for Katherine?" *General Hospital*'s team of writer's assistants confer daily via telephone with GH Writers and consult their trusty 8-ball to forecast upcoming plotlines. From left, Writer's Assistants George Doty IV, Davis Goldschmid and Marc Alan Dabrusin are joined by Elizabeth Korte, who handles script continuity in this playful "behind-the-scenes" moment in their fifth floor office.

Make-up artist Donna Messina Armogida applies the finishing touches to Rena Sofer (Lois Cerullo Ashton).

Hairstylists Robin Rollins and Sue Darling team up to give Vanessa Marcil (Brenda Barrett) a glamorous hairdo.

Rosalind Cash (Mary Mae Ward) is on the cutting edge of chic thanks to this crimson gown, which was submitted for her approval by Costume Designer Bob Miller.

BACKSTAGE TALES

Did you ever wonder what *General Hospital*'s stars say and do backstage? Here are some tasty tidbits about life behind the scenes in Port Charles.

Vanessa Marcil

Steve Burton

Leslie Charleson (Dr. Monica Quartermaine): Monica's brief reunion with her long-lost lover David was sweet. Right after poor David died of a terminal storyline, Jeffrey Pomerantz, who played him, really got me with a practical joke. I was taping a bedroom scene with Stuart Damon when Jeffrey popped up swathed in bandages like a mummy! He scared the "bejeebers" out of me!

Jon Lindström (Dr. Kevin Collins): The *General Hospital* crew once gave me a door as a present. It stems from the time that I was supposed to throw a picture frame at a door and watch it shatter. Well, I threw the frame just like I was supposed to and it stuck right in the middle of the door. Bulls eye! The next day, I arrived at the studio only to find the very same prop door (complete with picture frame) in my dressing room—wrapped up in that yellow police department tape you find at crime scenes. Some gift, guys!

Vanessa Marcil (Brenda Barrett): I spent my first year on *General Hospital* trying to break up Karen and Jagger so I could have him for myself. But the first time I got Jagger into bed with me, Cari Shayne, who played Karen, burst into the room and bounded onto the bed with us, as a goof. And my love scenes with Antonio often cracked me up. We were such good friends, it was like making love to your brother!

Wally Kurth (Ned Ashton): Ned's been involved with Monica, Dawn, Jenny, Julia and Katherine, but never anyone like Lois before! From the Brooklyn accent to the outrageously long and decaled fingernails, she's one of a kind, and Rena Sofer as Lois is hilarious! Those fingernails are trouble though. Once during a love scene, she lost two nails and we had to stop tape to look for them!

Lynn Herring (Lucy Coe): Playing Lucy's sexy, steamy love scenes can be tricky. Once when Brad Maule as Tony picked me up, my teddy unsnapped, and I was just sort of hanging there with not much on in front of the crew. All I could do was look up and smile!

Steve Burton (Jason Quartermaine): You have no idea how much action I see backstage at *General Hospital*. During those long waits between scenes, John York, who plays Mac, whips out his squirt guns and nerf ball guns, and before you know it, it's a madhouse! If you just want to sit back and learn lines, forget it.

Rena Sofer (Lois Cerullo): Fans are always reminding me of the day I popped out of that cake. If they only knew! On the first try, the prop department attached the lid on so tight that I couldn't break through. I had to crouch down inside that giant prop until someone rescued me. On the second try, I burst through with such force that the strap on my dress broke! It took three tries to get the scene you saw on TV.

Mary Beth Evans (Katherine Bell): Playing unconscious isn't as easy as it looks. When Katherine was in a coma, I got pretty squirmy just lying there in bed. And once, I even grunted a word in a scene. I thought no one heard me. But afterward, Wally Kurth who plays Ned said he heard something, so we had to tape the whole scene over!

David Lewis (Edward Quartermaine): I played lots of comedy, but often the funniest stuff happened off-camera. Once, I was supposed to grab my coat from the closet and exit in a huff. Well, I couldn't get that coat! It got tangled on the hanger. It fell on the floor. Five takes later, I opened the closet door and a hand shot out and gave me that blasted coat! Everyone broke up and we went for take number six.

Senait Ashenafi (Keesha Ward): When I heard that Jason and Keesha were flying off to Paris on their spring break, I got excited. I thought we were really going to France! 'Till I found out that Paris was upstairs in the studio... right between the Outback and the Nurses' Station! C'est la vie!

Leslie Charleson (Dr. Monica Quartermaine): Despite 17 years of battling with Alan, I have no scars. Though our make-up artist once almost gave me some for real when she accidentally sponged glue on me instead of moisturizer! I was up untill 1:00 a.m. scrubbing my face until it looked like I had leprosy. She thought it was funny, but I could have killed her!

Anna Lee (Lila Quartermaine): As Lila, I'm often described as "gracious," but my backstage reputation changed after I accidentally rolled my motorized wheelchair over the toes of Stuart Damon who plays my son Alan. Now when the cast and crew see me barreling down the corridors, they shout, "Look out, here comes Anna!" And Leslie Charleson even gave me a crash helmet naming me "The British Bullet!"

John Reilly (Sean Donely): Over the years, Sean was shot no fewer than five times! But scripted wounds are easy. It's the off-camera injuries that really hurt! While taping scenes, I slipped and cracked ribs, cut my finger with a hunting knife and was splashed with caustic acid! But I was in real agony when Sharon Wyatt (Tiffany) stomped on my foot during our tumultuous wedding ceremony. Her heel went right through my shoe and drew blood!

John Beradino (Dr. Steve Hardy): I've mellowed over the years. Steve used to have quite a temper! I'd often slam my fist on my office door. But the day my soft plywood door was replaced with solid oak, no one told me. I punched it and (crack!) broke my hand. I was in agony, but the show must go on! Somehow I made it through *General Hospital*, then I made a beeline for a real hospital!

Bradley Lockerman (Casey Rogers): When I arrived as Casey Rogers, space alien, the special effects people were working full tilt. I arrived in a blaze of lasers and dry ice smoke. My crystal glowed, and so did I, thanks to fiber optics! They were threaded through my clothes and attached to my fingernails for that glowing fingers effect!

Cari Shayne (Karen Wexler): When my character Karen suffered a brutal attack, I carried the scars for days! Those awful-looking bruises the make-up wizards painted all over me wouldn't come off at the end of the day,

Mary Beth Evans

Carol Lawrence

Jacklyn Zeman

Jennifer Guthrie

no matter how hard I scrubbed. One guy in a store saw me and said, "Oh my God, what happened to you?" But the make-up folks were happy—they knew exactly where to reapply my bruises every day!

Carol Lawrence (Angela Eckert): Like Angela, I'm an Italian mother in real life, too, which means I love to cook. In fact, the *General Hospital* prop department would whip up my recipes to feed my hungry TV brood. Sometimes I'd even bring in the food myself. So, now you know, when you saw us enjoying Angela's lasagna, we were really feasting on Lasagna a la Lawrence!

Jacklyn Zeman (Bobbie Jones): I loved dancing the tango at the 1994 Nurses Ball Talent Show. I thought I'd be dancing with Brad Maule (Tony) but the writers revved up the passion by pairing me with Leigh McCloskey, my lover Damian. During dress rehearsal, for a goof, Leigh and Brad ran into each other's arms instead!

Jennifer Guthrie (Dawn Winthrop): I couldn't trust anybody backstage, because any one of my fellow actors could get me with the dreaded… clothespin! It was our favorite backstage game, "Gotcha," which left an unsuspecting actor walking around with a clothespin dangling around his back.

Jon Lindström (Dr. Kevin Collins): It took months, but I finally made love to Lucy. Wouldn't you know it, when we finished taping our big love scene, everyone was standing around with lit cigarettes, moaning and groaning as if they'd just done it themselves. They'd planned their little joke for weeks! It was so sweet, and I was laughing so hard that I nearly wet my pants!

Peter Hansen (Lee Baldwin): Peggy McKay, who played my secretary Iris, was a prankster. Pat Breslin, who played my wife Meg, was in a room somewhere. Iris was to knock on Meg's door to enter the scene. Off stage, Peggy put on a rubber witch mask complete with warts and hair sticking out of the nose and false hands that looked like claws. Peggy, in her grotesque mask, knocked on the door to do the scene with Pat. Pat answered the door, shrieked and almost fainted.

Peter Hansen (Lee Baldwin): I have my pilot's license, and often gave people on the show rides. For an auction that was given by Leslie Charleson and her fan club, a lady bid a few thousand dollars to go up in the air with me in my private plane. Leslie hadn't flown with me yet. To razzle her, I paced up and down the hall, in front of her open dressing room, with a thick manual of how to fly an airplane. She asked me what I was doing, and I told her that I had to get up off the ground somehow. We had a big chuckle about that.

Roy Thinnes (Dr. Phil Brewer): I would warm up John Beradino's pitching arm during our breaks. I would be his catcher while he was getting ready for charity baseball games. And coffee and tea with Emily McLaughlin, that was always special for me.

Rachel Ames (Audrey Hardy): In the old days, memorizing the lines was the most difficult part of being on the show. I would sometimes write little crib sheets with cue words on a piece of paper and tack it up on the refrigerator door in Audrey's apartment. I would lean against the door, always with a cup of coffee in hand, and say my lines. We would carry the script behind the hospital charts as well. Lights would pop, cameras would fall, but we would still continue with the taping. We had to!

Joseph Phillips (Justus Ward): Tony Geary makes really funny observations that crack me up. One day, right before taping, he said something that dropped me to my knees. The dog, Foster, was also in the scene, and during the break, the dog was, to put it delicately, cleaning himself. Tony said to me, "Can you imagine if we could do that? We would never leave the house." I could not stop laughing. That was one of the funniest things I ever heard.

Norma Connolly (Ruby Anderson): My favorite scene on the show was when I came out of a cake the night before Luke's wedding, bumping and grinding to the song "Anything Goes." I said to the costume director, "I am not putting this old bod into a bikini for anybody, so you just think of something else for me to wear, thank you." So, they gave me a bright red leotard, with five-inch heel shoes and a red feather boa. It was very funny!

Ricky Martin (Miguel Morez): The hardest part of doing the show for me is memorizing my lines. It is doubly hard for me because English is not my first language. There are times when I read the script in English and have no idea what Miguel is even saying. I run over to Lilly Melgar and she helps me. She is like a teacher to me.

Richard Simmons (Richard Simmons): Gloria Monty was stricter than any Catholic nun who taught me in school. She made me sweat like I just went to the best Mexican restaurant. But three days a week I would turn the tables on her. I would go into her office, make her take the phones off the hook and I would exercise her for an hour.

Doug Sheehan (Joe Kelly): The hardest scene that I ever had to do was when I had to punch out Scotty, played by Kin Shriner, when he discovered me in bed, wearing very little clothing, with Heather. My character was not a fighter, and Gloria Monty wanted me to act nauseous from the physical confrontation. Kin and I just kept cracking up. It was hard going from rehearsal, where we would comment and joke about how foolish these character's behavior was, to being completely serious about the work during taping.

Joseph Phillips

STORYLINE STUFF

Although the actors on *General Hospital* are further ahead in the story than the fans are (they typically tape the show two weeks before it airs), they still wonder, "What will happen next?" Here are some anecdotes relating to those scintillating storylines!

Brad Maule

Steve Burton (Jason Quartermaine): I didn't mind when Karen dumped Jason, because I think it made him a little tougher. I really appreciated it, because you have no idea how annoying it can be to play "just plain nice" all the time! I'd never have ignored all those looks between Karen and Jagger the way Jason did. My instinct would have been to pull out of a bad situation. Of course, if the writers had followed my instinct, I'd have had no story!

Rena Sofer (Lois Cerullo): The thought of riding the Cyclone, that world-famous giant roller-coaster, terrified me. I begged the producers, "Get a stand-in!" But Wally (Kurth) convinced me to try it, and it was great! Though when we taped, I think he screamed even more than I did.

Brad Maule (Tony Jones): Amnesia is the one malady I haven't had in my years as Tony Jones. As a doctor, I'm *General Hospital*'s best patient! I've taken bullets in the head and heart, been paralyzed, blind and impotent, and had so many brain surgeries, I think they ought to install a zipper!

Stuart Damon (Dr. Alan Quartermaine): In my eighteen years as Dr. Alan Quartermaine, Monica's breast cancer is the best story I've ever had, because the cancer is happening to him as well as to her...and the husband's suffering is rarely explored on TV. One *General Hospital* fan who also suffers with breast cancer wrote to me, "I only hope any woman unfortunate enough to have breast cancer will be lucky enough to have a husband like Alan!" I was floored.

Lynn Herring (Lucy Coe): Remember when Nancy Eckert was murdered? Everybody was trying to figure out who did it—including me! None of us in the cast knew who the killer was, because the producers like to keep us guessing as much as the audience!

Anna Lee (Lila Quartermaine): My favorite storyline was when I concocted my million-dollar recipe for relish, Pickle-Lila. What tickled me about it is that I've never been much of a cook, though I do like to make Yorkshire pudding and trifle!

Sharon Wyatt (Tiffany Hill): When my storyline took me near death, I really felt like I was dying. Those tubes they stuck up my nose were no picnic. And when I went into cardiac arrest, I squeezed my hands so tightly, I drew blood!

Shell Danielson (Dominique Taub): I was shocked that Dominique ended up married to Scotty. Neither Kin Shriner nor I had any inkling that our constant comic bickering on the show was really a prelude to romance and marriage... we were as surprised as the audience! In fact, the only person

I know who wasn't surprised was my real-life boyfriend. He said he saw it coming. I don't know… I was there, and I sure didn't see it!

Stuart Damon (Alan Quartermaine): I loved being caught between my wife Monica and my mistress Lucy—in my book, that was storyline heaven! I went to bed more times with Lucy in three weeks than I did in twelve years with Monica. You wouldn't believe how often I got to take off my clothes in those days!

Jacklyn Zeman (Bobbie Jones): No medical storyline has touched me more than the one in which my TV daughter BJ's death led to a desperately needed heart transplant for her cousin Maxie. As a mom in real life, it was horrific to play. This story really struck a chord with many of our viewers, though, and the show got tons of mail from organ donors and recipients alike, so I'm proud I was a part of it.

Tristan Rogers (Robert Scorpio): I must have done something right because the role of Robert Scorpio was only supposed to last for two days. I began during all that craziness with the Ice Princess storyline, which was an adventure the likes of which daytime TV had never seen before! It's probably always going to be my favorite storyline.

Tristan Rogers

Martin West (Dr. Phil Brewer): When Phil Brewer was murdered in 1975, the show filmed each of the five suspects doing him in. None of the actors knew which character was the real killer. For six months, I kept getting residual checks because each character would dream that they killed Phil, and the same scenes would play over and over. It was the easiest money I ever made in show business.

Kimberly McCullough (Robin Scorpio): The SNOWMAN story with Grant Putnam was my favorite. It was originally going to be Robin who was trapped in the cage, but at the last minute, the censors said there were rules against keeping kids in cages and showing them as victims of violence. The story had to be changed to Anna getting kidnaped and Robin being comatose due to the tragedy. Anyway, I had a great time being traumatized and staring into space and throwing trays of food at people. It was really fun.

Kristina Wagner (Felicia Jones): Playing Felicia has been a Cinderella story for me. Sometimes it takes people a lifetime to have their fantasies come true. We all know what it is like to be with your fantasy guy, but what about being on the back of a motorcycle, wearing a fur coat, all dolled up and with forty thousand dollars in cash floating behind you. And, with an audience of millions watching. That was one of my favorite stories, being on the run with Frisco.

Kristina Wagner

Leslie Charleson (Dr. Monica Quartermaine): I don't know what my favorite storyline is per se. To have ANY storyline is a good thing. Certainly the most profound and important storyline I have ever had has been the recent one we did on breast cancer. It was a great deal of work, but certainly the most rewarding. The storyline that was the most FUN to do was long ago when Monica had the affair with Rick, and Alan tried to murder her. That was exciting.

IN THE BEGINNING

Time marches on, even in Port Charles! Read on for some special memories from the *General Hospital* cast's first days on the set...

Rachel Ames

Jonathan Jackson

Rachel Ames (Audrey Hardy): When Audrey married Steve back in 1965, the folks at *General Hospital* really surprised me. They didn't tell me until the wedding day that they'd hired my real-life father, actor Byron Foulger, to play the minister! You can't believe how emotional the ceremony was for me.

Jonathan Jackson (Lucky Spencer): When I first began on *General Hospital*, Genie Francis, who plays Laura, clued me in on what to expect as a child actor on a soap. She wasn't much older than I am now when she first joined the show. Genie warned me that studying with a teacher on the set is a lot more lonely than in a normal school. And maybe the studying part is, but I've made too many friends at the studio to be lonely!

Leslie Charleson (Dr. Monica Quartermaine): Until I began as *General Hospital*'s Monica, I'd always played the good girl next door, but Monica back then was a real witch! I had to become very good at being very bad very quickly because the show was about to be canceled! But we survived. In fact, we're still going strong, though I'm not quite as bad as I used to be!

Norma Connolly (Ruby Anderson): As hard-working Ruby, I'm always at my restaurant, Kelly's, because the set that I used to go home to years ago is history! Oh, how I loved padding around that little apartment in my red fluffy slippers and bathrobe, which was a man's robe that must have been hanging in wardrobe for about 40 years. One look at it, and I knew it was Ruby, and I miss it!

Anna Lee (Lila Quartermaine): The renovation of our stately home was a thrill, but I confess to missing the old Quartermaine setting which was a part of my life and Lila's for a long time. Seventeen years! Goodness, I never dreamed I'd stay on *General Hospital* this long. That old Quartermaine living room sure has many stories to tell.

John Beradino (Dr. Steve Hardy): Money was so tight back in 1963. Every expense was spared. In fact, at one point, in order to build some sets, the producers actually asked me to take a pay cut, which I did!

Kevin Best (Dr. Harrison Davis): When I first appeared on the show, I just wandered through a few episodes as an extra. It was enough to get me watching *General Hospital* though...and get hooked!

Shell Kepler (Amy Vining): One of my first scenes was with Stuart Damon, who I'd had a crush on since I was a kid and saw him on TV as Prince Charming in Rodgers and Hammerstein's *Cinderella!* He was still charming when I met him as Amy. In our first scene together, my line was, "I feel like Cinderella." It just cracked me up!

Camille Cooper (Nikki Langton): My first day at *General Hospital*, we were shooting two shows, which would make anyone nervous! I wasn't as tense as I might have been though, thanks to Stuart Damon. He cracked so many jokes I actually felt relaxed in spite of myself.

Sharon Wyatt (Tiffany Hill): The first summer I joined *General Hospital* was during the famous Ice Princess storyline. We were on location on the Cassadine Yacht, which was really this endlessly swaying flat bottom boat that made everyone in the cast and crew seasick. Including me, but I wasn't about to let it mess up my new job! I was queasy green, but I kept working.

Shell Kepler

John J. York (Mac Scorpio): I'm not afraid of anything...except maybe forgetting my lines! I used to cheat. On heavy dialogue days, I'd plant a page of key lines on the set as a security blanket. One day Kin Shriner (Scotty) fed me a cue, but I was speechless...because my "cheat sheet" was missing. When Kin waved it in my face, I learned my lesson, which is why I always learn my lines now!

Crystal Carson (Julia Barrett): I began my new job on *General Hospital* by falling into a vat of fish oil, which was actually gooey, slimy, warm vegetable oil. If you've never stepped into gallons of the stuff (and why would you?), you can't know what it's like, especially when you dunk your head! For three days, I'd wake up to find oil on my pillow.

Paul Savior (Dr. Tom Baldwin): Tom was a great looking and charismatic guy who could not get laid. For the first four years he was on the show, he never had a date. I asked the producers what was wrong with Tom. I thought every nurse would be running to go out with the eligible doctor. The producer said, "Paul, you gotta understand. Lots of women basically fantasize about being with your character...to pair you up on the show with a love interest would ruin the fantasy."

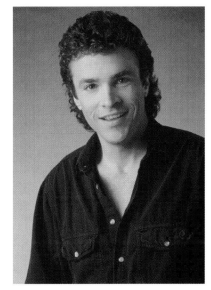

John J. York

AUDITION TALES

Would you have the courage to audition for a part, knowing that dozens of other talented actors are fighting tooth and nail for the same role? Some of the "chosen few" reminisce about how they won their *General Hospital* roles.

Rosalind Cash

Sean Kanan (AJ Quartermaine): I credit Stuart Damon, who plays Alan, for helping me every step of the way. He pulled a great performance out of me when he read with me at my audition. And the day before I began, he left a message on my answering machine that said, "We're excited you're coming on the show. You're gonna do great!" That made me a lot less nervous about my first day.

Vanessa Marcil (Brenda Barrett): After I auditioned for the part, it was days before I heard that I got it. And while I waited, I ate. That's what I do when I worry…I eat! I must have called my agent from every restaurant in Hollywood: "Have you heard yet? Have you heard yet?" Finally, I drove up to a pay phone and called and got the good news, and I started crying right there on the curb. People must have thought I was crazy until I screamed out, "I just got *General Hospital*! YES!"

Rena Sofer (Lois Cerullo): It still feels like yesterday that Mark Teschner, our casting director, asked me, "Can you do a Brooklyn accent?" And I said, "What, are you kiddin' me? I'm from New York for-godsakes. Wuddayou tawkin' about?" He said, "That's perfect!" Then I screen-tested with Wally Kurth, who plays Ned, and he must have liked me too because when we were done, Wally ran into the control room, found our producer and said, "She's it! Give her the part and let's go home!"

Rosalind Cash (Mary Mae Ward): When the producers of *General Hospital* were casting the role of Mary Mae Ward, my agent had to fight to get me an audition, because they felt I was too young! Well, thanks for the compliment, but I wanted that part! Thank goodness, he convinced them I didn't mind playing nearly 20 years older.

Jonathan Jackson (Lucky Spencer): When I auditioned, I didn't even know that Luke and Laura were daytime's most famous couple ever! When people heard who I was playing, they were like, "Wow! You're Luke and Laura's son!" I had to bone up on my soap history pretty fast!

Antonio Sabato, Jr. (Jagger Cates): My big break was winning the role of Jagger. When I first auditioned, I was up for the role of Frankie Greco. Now I'm kind of glad I didn't get it because poor Frankie wasn't around Port Charles for long!

Cheryl Richardson (Jenny Eckert): When I became Jenny Eckert, it was a dream come true. I grew up watching Tony Geary as Luke, and then he was my brother Bill! Before I was hired, the producers asked

Cari Shayne and Antonio Sabato, Jr.

me to dye my blonde hair red, which I never dreamed I'd do. But after two years of turn-downs at auditions, I'd have dyed my hair blue to get the job!

Brandon Hooper (Eric Simpson): To prepare for my residency as Dr. Eric Simpson, I went on rounds with a real-life emergency room doctor. It was one of the queasiest weekends of my life! Actually, I never expected to be a doctor on the show, because I first auditioned for the role of AJ Quartermaine.

Paul Satterfield, Jr. (Paul Hornsby): I originally auditioned for the role of Mac Scorpio. While I was testing, I started speaking with an Aussie accent all the time. Not getting the part was a relief, because playing Mac's accent all the time would have driven me (and everyone I know) nuts, if you know what I mean, mate!

Paul Satterfield, Jr.

Finola Hughes (Anna Devane): When I joined *General Hospital* as Anna, it was a part I never thought I'd get, because I'm as British as Emma Samms, and the producers wanted an American Anna. I was so surprised when they chose me, I jumped up and down for joy!

Jacklyn Zeman (Bobbie Jones): When I auditioned for the part, Bobbie was a little vixen. I got the role because the producer had liked my work as bad girl Lana McClain on *One Life to Live.* There was only one hitch—I had to lose ten pounds, but I was glad to do it. *One Life to Live* had asked me to gain fifteen pounds to play Lana!

Sharon DeBord (Nurse Sharon McGillis Pinkham): In 1965, I was working as a secretary at ABC in the typing pool and I got Kylie Masterson, who was the associate producer of *General Hospital*, to come and see me in a play. After she saw the show, she sent Jim Young, the director at the time, who then hired me as an under-5. I worked my way up to a contract role and stayed for ten years!

Robert Hogan (Burt Marshall & Phil Brewer): A year after Roy Thinnes left the show, another actor was hired to play Phil Brewer. A month after he started, this guy was doing a roofing job on his house and he fell off the roof. He was really injured and of course, he couldn't play Phil in a body cast. A show that I was appearing on called *Young Marrieds* was coming to an end and ABC just switched me over. I was delighted.

Jacklyn Zeman

Anna Lee (Lila Quartermaine): My agent wanted me to do the role of Lila Quartermaine. I had never seen a soap opera and wasn't sure if I would like it, so I told her that I would try it for three days and see what it was like. I instantly became hooked and stayed for another 17 years. Most people start in soaps and work their way up to films. I started in films and moved onto soaps. But I love it and plan to do it until I am a hundred-years-old.

Felecia Bell (Dr. Simone Ravelle Hardy): I first auditioned at GH for the part of a wealthy, poker-playing card shark who owned lots of companies. I thought she was great. I even learned to play poker for the audition. I got called back, and for the second call back, they gave me the sides for Simone. The card-shark character was a ruse. I guess nobody

Leslie Charleson

was supposed to know that the part was being recast, not even the actors auditioning.

Kristina Wagner (Felicia Jones): My photo somehow ended up on the desk of Mari-Lyn Henry, an ABC casting director in New York at the time. She said that I had a terrible resume but she liked my picture; it was this big pony-tail shot with dimples. I met Mari-Lyn and she sent me to audition for several soaps, but nothing happened. A month later, Mari-Lyn called to tell me G.H. was looking for a Felicia. I auditioned in Chicago for Gloria Monty. When I found out I got the part, I jumped up and down on my bed I was so happy.

Norma Connolly (Ruby Anderson): They read about 50 actresses and screen tested nine of us for the role of Ruby Anderson. One of the gals was Darlene Conley of *The Bold and the Beautiful*. The audition was 15 years ago. Whoever heard of an actor having a steady job for 15 years? It is unheard of.

Leslie Charleson (Dr. Monica Quartermaine): Tom Donovan, who was a producer at the time I started doing *General Hospital*, was also a producer of a soap called *Love Is a Many Splendored Thing* that I had done in New York. He called me up and asked if I wanted to play Monica. I really didn't want to do another soap, but Tom had been so special to me that I accepted. But soon after I started on *General Hospital*, he abandoned ship and left the show. That was pretty scary because he brought me in, and now I was on my own.

A FAMILY AFFAIR

With long hours on the set, sometimes the cast members of *General Hospital* see each other more than they see their own families. What do they really think of each other?

Robert Fontaine (Frankie Greco): Scott Thompson Baker, who played Colton, is a very generous man. One day, after hearing that I played the guitar, he gave me one that he said was just gathering dust at home. I couldn't believe it when it turned out to be a $1,200 instrument! You don't meet real-life good guys like Scott every day.

Vanessa Marcil (Brenda Barrett): Crystal Carson, who played my TV sister Julia, took me under her wing. She and my mother actually look alike! So maybe Crystal and I do look like sisters. We hung out together so much, we started to bond like real sisters. Sisters who got along a lot better than Julia and Brenda did!

Shell Danielson (Dominique Taub): Actually, my love scenes with John J. York (Mac) felt uncomfortable whenever his real-life wife Vicki was on the set. I mean, how would you like to do a love scene with a man while his wife was watching? Afterwards, I'd ask her, "Was it as awkward for you as it was for me?" and thank goodness, we both laughed.

Wally Kurth (Ned Ashton): When I joined *General Hospital*, I was reunited with Jane Elliot who played my demanding mother Tracy. When we last worked together, on *Days of Our Lives*, her character lusted after mine like crazy! Once I started playing her son, Jane said it was hard talking to me without wanting me to want her. Confused? Well, that's the soap life.

Lynn Herring (Lucy Coe): Oh, the men of *General Hospital*! Kin Shriner used to drive me crazy when I was in high school…I thought he was the cutest thing on TV! It was kind of weird to end up sleeping with him on TV! He's one of my favorite male co-stars because we did so much comedy together, but Brad Maule, who plays Tony, is the best kisser!

Tristan Rogers (Robert Scorpio): I watched Kimberly McCullough, who's played Robin since 1984, grow from this small little thing into a wonderful young lady. Finola Hughes, who played Anna, and I always made ourselves accessible to her because it's not easy to be in this business, no matter how old you are! For someone so young, Robin amazes me that she's remained as level-headed and well-adjusted as she is.

Jonathan Jackson (Lucky Spencer): I've got the coolest dog in Port Charles—Foster! But acting with a dog isn't easy. Once, in a pretty heavy scene with Tony Geary, who plays my dad Luke, I put a glass of milk down on the table. Before we knew it, Foster was lapping away at it! I don't know how we managed to finish the scene without cracking up, but we did. Though, believe me, I never would have finished that glass of milk!

Lynn Herring and Kin Shriner

Wally Kurth

Senait Ashenafi

Senait Ashenafi (Keesha Ward): Rosalind Cash, who plays my warm and wise Granny Mae, is my favorite pal on the set. We're always in each other's dressing rooms. We talk about everything! And I really listen to what she has to say. I grew up without a mother, and she's so loving, it's like I'm getting a taste of what I missed out on.

Sean Kanan (AJ Quartermaine): When I first began as AJ, I deliberately grew my sideburns long, but not because I wanted to look cool. I just wanted to be sure that the viewers didn't confuse me with Steve Burton, who plays my TV brother Jason, because we really do resemble each other. And the amazing thing is that after I was cast, Steve found out that we really are related...but only by marriage, second cousins twice removed or something like that!

John Reilly (Sean Donely): Sean Donely was not the jealous type, though we actors can be about our co-stars. Once, after I saw Sharon Wyatt, who plays my ever-loving Tiffany, in a scene with another actor, I asked why she called him, "Honey" six times! "John," she said, "I call everybody 'honey!'" And she does! She once called me a two-timer because Sean (not me!) had to romance another woman!

John Beradino (Dr. Steve Hardy): The lovely and gracious Rachel Ames, who played Audrey, was my leading lady almost since the very beginning. Originally, Audrey was supposed to die shortly after we got married. When I accidentally blabbed this fatal plot twist in an interview, the writers were so upset with me that they decided to let Audrey live! And the rest is history.

David Lewis (Edward Quartermaine): As Edward Quartermaine, the only thing I loved more than money was my dear sweet wife, Lila. I loved our more tender scenes together. Anna Lee, who plays Lila, always said there's no reason on earth why people our age shouldn't have a romantic relationship. And I agree.

Sam Behrens (Jake Meyer): The original best lawyer in town was Lee Baldwin, played for 20 years by Peter Hansen. Some years ago, Peter took me up in his private plane and rekindled my passion for flying, so I got a pilot's license and my own plane. I even managed to talk Jackie Zeman into going up, up, and away with me.

Denise Galik-Furey (Rhonda Wexler): Stuart Damon (Alan) and I used to do the Achy-Breaky Texas two-step together! I couldn't believe it, because I had the hugest crush on Stuart Damon when I was a kid in Cleveland. He was the young leading man in a whole string of musicals that I saw there. When I told Stuart, all he said was, "Please don't say you were a little girl. It makes me sound so old." So, don't tell him, but I was only eight!

Jacklyn Zeman (Bobbie Jones): My character Bobbie always had a soft spot in her heart for Scotty. In fact, when I first started on the show Bobbie did everything she could to win Scotty for herself. But when the writers tried to pair us up in 1988, it didn't work out again. Kin Shriner, who played Scotty, and I were such good pals in real life that whenever we looked at each other romantically, we'd crack up!

Paul Satterfield, Jr. (Paul Hornsby): I feel like I've been surrounded by talented and generous cast members from my very first day on the set. Stuart Damon really took me under his wing. "Listen, kid," he said, "You've got about 50 pages of dialogue here. Let's work on it." Which was great of him, especially when you consider how hard I worked to destroy his family fortune!

Stuart Damon (Dr. Alan Quartermaine): This job is sweet, and playing opposite Leslie Charleson as my wife Monica all those years made it even sweeter. We never stop laughing, and I can make her laugh any time I want to. Once I broke into a hospital scene to do my impression of Elmer Fudd going to the barber, you know, "just take a wittel off the top." Everyone cracked up, and we had to take the whole scene over again.

Anna Lee (Lila Quartermaine): I love all the young people on the show. Especially Lynn Herring and Brad Maule. They are so sweet to me. The acting on soaps is wonderful. I have made many films, and our actors on GH are the best I have ever worked with except for Spencer Tracy.

Stuart Damon and Leslie Charleson

Kimberly McCullough (Robin Scorpio): Jack Wagner would always make jokes on the set. I didn't know what he was talking about, but I pretended that I did. I would laugh along with everybody and they would look at me amazed that I understood the joke. Of course I didn't, but I didn't want them to know that.

Kristina Wagner (Felicia Jones): The very first love scene with Jack Wagner was really frightening for me. There was this bowl of fruit at the side of the bed, and when I wasn't looking, he pulled out this banana, made this whole presentation of it to the crew, and stuck it down his pants. When I got into bed, he started to push that banana up against my thigh. I didn't really know what was going on and I continued with the dialogue, but everybody started cracking up.

Doug Sheehan (Joe Kelly): Richard Dean Anderson and I were the bad boy pranksters on the set. He was more of a practical joker, but I was the guy who could sell the practical jokes. We got into trouble and misbehaved quite a bit, and of course Gloria Monty LOVED it.

Doug Sheehan

David Mendenhall (Mike Webber): We taped the show on the same stage as *Silver Spoons* and *Facts of Life*, so Kimberly McCullough and I would visit their sets during our breaks. We would try to challenge Ricky Schroder to little basketball games. He usually won, but we would play him anyway. It was a great time. Even though I had to give up things like playing sports with my friends at school, *General Hospital* was a great place to grow up and learn about the business.

FANTALES

It's possible that soap fans are the most passionate of all! Let's see what the GH actors think of the fans who can chase them down the street, or make their day.

Jon Lindström

John Ingle

Norma Connolly

Ian Buchanan (Duke Lavery): A couple of women came up to me and showed me tattoos of Anna and Duke that they had done on their arms. I was absolutely shocked! These women will have us branded on their bodies forever, but at least Finola (Anna) will always look twenty-five and I'll forever be twenty-nine.

Steve Burton (Jason Quartermaine): It's a little weird when the fans spot me while I'm driving my car. Once, while I was stopped at a red light, a couple of girls hopped out of the car in front of me just to ask for my autograph. Before I could give it to them, the light changed and they rushed back to their car. But at the next red light, they hopped out again to get it!

Jon Lindström (Kevin Collins): When I was just playing Ryan, I used to get some pretty strange mail. One woman who obviously doesn't get out enough wrote me a long list of how I could become a nicer person. "Be nice to Felicia," she advised me, and "do more volunteer work at the hospital." Well, that didn't work because Ryan went on a killing spree that landed him in prison for life.

John Ingle (Edward Quartermaine): Playing Edward isn't my first stint on *General Hospital.* Years ago in an Anna-Duke storyline, I played a state police commissioner on a recurring basis. I wouldn't expect anyone to remember me from that. But one of the fans did...and sent me a disapproving letter because of it. "How can I be Edward Quartermaine," it said, "because I had once played that other fellow!" Well, all I can say is I'm glad casting directors don't follow the shows nearly as closely as the fans do!

Norma Connolly (Ruby Anderson): I wouldn't have stayed with *General Hospital* for so long if I didn't love it! Especially the way the fans greet me like an old friend. Strangers come up and kiss me! I guess everyone wants an Aunt Ruby in their life. On a plane once, a fellow passenger saw me and cooed, "I know you, you're Aunt Ruby!" But I knew her, too...she was Julie Andrews!

David Lewis (Edward Quartermaine): When I became Edward Quartermaine on *General Hospital*, I was astounded at the reaction I got in public. A woman once plowed her car into another car in the parking lot because she was excited to see me. She ran up to me. I asked about her car. She didn't care. She was too busy meeting Edward!

Stuart Damon (Dr. Alan Quartermaine): I've never considered myself the type of man that women go screaming down the street to me. Yet, that's what happened to me in Denver a couple of years ago. I was making a TV movie with Sean Kanan, who plays my TV son AJ. I couldn't believe it when the young lovelies rushed over to me...and ignored Sean! I felt like such a stud muffin.

Rena Sofer (Lois Cerullo): I've gotten a lot of letters from fans who tell me they know someone just like Lois—same nails, same accent and same brains. I'm sure our headwriter, Claire Labine, knows a few Lois's too because she really lives in Brooklyn. In fact, Lois was given the last name Cerullo in honor of the Cerullos of Brooklyn, New York, who happen to be dear friends of Claire and her family.

Kevin Best (Dr. Harrison Davis): I got used to fans recognizing me as my character Dr. Davis, but I wasn't prepared the day two ladies spotted me doing my food shopping. They chased me all around the supermarket until they finally cut me off at the corn flakes. They only wanted to tell me how much they loved me on the show. I was flattered and embarrassed.

Kevin Best

Robert Hogan (Dr. Phil Brewer): This one woman regularly wrote me and told me everything that happened while Phil Brewer wasn't on camera. These letters continued most of my run on the show, and they would come almost daily.

Patricia Breslin (Meg Bentley Baldwin): A Harvard professor used to write me all the time. He started watching *General Hospital* after he had been ill and was in the hospital. He wrote that he fell in love with me. I could not believe a Harvard professor was watching *General Hospital*.

Paul Savior (Dr. Tom Baldwin): Little old ladies still come up to me in the supermarket and say, "Are you Tom Baldwin? What you did to Audrey was terrible." They still haven't forgiven me, 25 years later.

Kimberly McCullough (Robin Scorpio): I love the show *Blossom*, and I think Mayim Bialik is a great actress. I went to visit Finola on the set of her show, *Blossom*, and I wanted to meet Mayim. I was so nervous to meet her. It was Mayim's last show, everybody was around her, and Finola called, "Mayim, I have someone who wants to meet you." She came over, saw who it was, and screamed. She said," Oh my God, ROBIN, ROBIN, I'm your biggest fan." I said, "No. I am YOUR biggest fan." We just screamed and laughed. She was so cool.

Denise Alexander

Denise Alexander (Dr. Lesley Webber): I was in a very crowded restaurant, and a woman screams to me from across the room, "I can't stand it! I have to know. Are you going to have the baby or not?"

Leslie Charleson (Dr. Monica Quartermaine): I was in the airport, and a very well-dressed woman grabbed my arm and dragged me into a restaurant to meet her family. She knew me so well from watching the show, and she was convinced that I knew her too. Suddenly she looked at me and said, "My God, I am so sorry. You don't know me." She was very apologetic. She told me that because I was in her living room every day, she was convinced that we knew each other.

DOCTOR, LAWYER, INDIAN CHIEF?

The road to soap stardom can be a long and rocky one! Here are some examples of other occupations actors have tried on their way to their "big break."

Antonio Sabato, Jr.

Lilly Melgar (Lily Rivera): While I was on *General Hospital*, I hosted a Spanish language TV showed called *Moda*, which means "fashion," in which I wore designer gowns and went the glamour route in hair and make-up. I also hosted *Tu Musica*, a highly-rated video show, where I first met Ricky Martin, who played Miguel.

Rena Sofer (Lois Cerullo): Years ago on *Loving*, I was Rocky McKenzie, Trucker's sister, who was much more patient than Lois could ever be! As Rocky, I waited two years for my first love scene to come along. But as Lois, it took two episodes and bang!—I was in bed with Ned. Guess which role is more fun to play!

John Ingle (Edward Quartermaine): I took up acting as a profession only about 10 years ago...after 30 years of teaching high school! As drama director at Hollywood High, my students included Swoosie Kurtz, Barbara Hershey, Richard Dreyfuss and Louise Sorel.

Brad Maule (Tony Jones): In real-life when I was a band singer, I was a traveling man. In fact, for a whole year, I sang backup for Don Ho in Hawaii! What a life! Sun, surf and a nightly warbling of "okay hoo, oka mai hoo, hey oka mai, hey, hey!"

Wally Kurth (Ned Ashton): After a long day of lying and cheating and back-stabbing on *General Hospital*, I like to go home and unwind at my baby grand piano. Music's a big part of my life. I'm a singer and I like to write songs. I don't write them to burn up the charts though...I write them because they mean something to me, which is the best relaxation in the world.

David Lewis (Edward Quartermaine): I started at the Erie Playhouse where I worked for free for a whole year! Then they paid me six whole bucks a week. I got paid a whole lot more as Edward, but I liked playing him so much, I probably would have done it for free!

Antonio Sabato, Jr. (Jagger Cates): My real-life goal has always been acting. My father, who's a movie star in Italy where I was born, never wanted me to go into show business. But now he's very proud of my success in movies, TV videos and as a model in print ads and commercials.

Laura Herring (Carla Greco): Originally I never wanted to be an actress. But a producer who had seen me win the Miss USA pageant cast me in the TV movie, *The Alamo*. And then I danced the lambada as a Brazilian princess in *The Forbidden Dance*. *General Hospital* was my first really stable job in years!

Ricky Martin (Miguel Morez): When I was 12, I joined Menudo in Puerto Rico and traveled all over the world with them. While I was in the group, I began acting, and I've worked hard on both my singing and acting careers ever since. I'm no stranger to the soaps, either. I've appeared on them in Argentina and Mexico. But believe me, the soaps here are much harder. I mean, they're in English!

Sean Kanan (AJ Quartermaine): As AJ Quartermaine, I've been competing with my cousin Ned my whole life. And now that Ned's a rock star, I wish AJ could show him up by becoming a stand-up comic. That's been one of my dreams since I was a teenager. Back then, I quit my job at McDonald's so I could perform in comedy clubs. But I didn't tell my folks. They thought I was still serving burgers, which was my favorite joke!

Emma Samms (Holly Scorpio): Holly was a role I treasured, although I didn't plan to become an actress. I trained to be a prima ballerina until a hip injury ended that dream. I was a successful model, however, before I started acting, and in recent years I've become a professional photographer, too.

Sam Behrens

Camille Cooper (Nikki Langton): The hardest thing about playing Nikki was all that dialogue! I'd worked mostly in film and prime time TV, where you work on maybe two or three pages a day. But in daytime TV, it's not unusual to have to memorize 30 pages a day! Unless you have total recall, it isn't easy!

Sam Behrens (Jake Meyer): Before I ever walked into Kelly's Diner on *General Hospital*, I spent time at Ryan's Bar as Dr. Adam Cohen on *Ryan's Hope*. Before that, like any determined young actor, I worked nights waiting on tables, tending bar and driving a cab, while auditioning like crazy during the day. My first break was appearing on Broadway in *Grease*, but my best break was being cast as Jake on *General Hospital*.

Brandon Hooper (Eric Simpson): I'm not a doctor but I played one on TV! But seriously, I really am an athlete. I was on the U.S. Junior Olympic Ski Team, and some of my friends competed in the Olympic Games. There must be good genes in the family, because my brother Kendy is a rodeo champion!

Michael Lynch (Connor S. Olivera): My worst job was the summer I was a weed whacker in Colorado where I grew up. It was just me and my hatchet, chopping away under a blazing sun, nearly a hundred degrees every day, clearing out vacant lots of weeds that grew as tall as six feet. It was horrible!

Crystal Carson (Julia Barrett): Acting is the only career I've ever wanted, but in grade school I had to help my mother by taking calls on her home subscription service, a job I hated! I managed to make it fun by play-acting as a different character with each caller. When Mom saw what I was doing, she enrolled me in an acting program, and I've been acting ever since.

John Beradino (Dr. Steve Hardy): I'm very proud of the time I told the Christmas story to the kids in the hospital, because I wore the red ribbon that symbolizes love and support for people with AIDS. Our producers felt that Steve's wearing of the ribbon would send an important message about caring to our viewers. I was very honored.

Stuart Damon (Dr. Alan Quartermaine): My favorite scene was a doozy of a battle Alan and Monica had years ago. We really went at each other. I fell over a sofa. She knocked over a table. We were rolling around the floor ready to kill each other—but instead we made mad, passionate love! Ah, what a marriage.

John J. York (Mac Scorpio): It took over a year for Felicia and me to get to our first kiss. Before it happened, the script called for Felicia to shave off the beard I'd grown during our "love on the run" storyline. Well, she lathered me up, but during the commercial, I shaved myself, and then got creamed again so Felicia could shave me on camera...without using a real blade.

Peter Hansen (Lee Baldwin): The scene that won me the Emmy in 1979 was a long, protracted scene when Lee fell off the wagon. It was at a swank hotel bar, and Gail had not come around to marry Lee. She comes to the bar, having heard that he has fallen off the wagon from Scotty. They have a wonderful scene which lasted almost the entire show. I sent this clip in and it won me the Emmy.

Martin West

Martin West (Dr. Phil Brewer): We always had the lady from Broadcast Standards sitting and watching us film the show. She made sure that nothing racy ever got on the air. My character had been involved in an accident which rendered poor Phil impotent. I, at that time, had my eye on Jessie's stepdaughter, Polly, and we spent months giving each other the eye, but poor Phil could not perform. Well, months after the accident, I got the script when Phil, alone with Polly, realizes that he is finally cured. Today, if a scene were done on this subject, a character would be able to discuss his situation honestly. But no way back then. What we had to do was slip down behind the couch kissing, while Phil yells, "I'm a man. I'm a man." I was so embarrassed. I begged the writers to do it another way but there was just no way else to say it. In my whole acting career, this was my most memorable, and definitely my most embarrassing scene.

Maurice Benard (Sonny Corinthos): The hardest scene I ever had to do, and the one that I am most proud of, was a scene I had with Tony Geary that had three pages of a monologue, describing my relationship with Joe Scully and my abusive stepfather. I liked how that scene came out.

Anna Lee (Lila Quartermaine): I always loved the scene years ago when Edward wanted Lila to sign a document giving him power of attorney. I constantly refused to do it. I was in the spa, mud all over my face, and Edward asks again for Lila to sign it, thinking with mud all over her face that Lila would not know what she was signing. Lila signs the papers and Edward leaves very pleased with himself. Edward goes to his lawyer and shows him the papers. The lawyer says, "This is no good. It is signed 'MRS. PRESIDENT LINCOLN.'" I thought that was so funny.

GENERAL HOSPITAL'S EMMY AWARD WINNERS

It stands sixteen inches high, weighs four pounds and is covered with 24-carat gold plate. Given each year by The Academy of Television Arts and Sciences, the Emmy Award signifies excellence in daytime drama. Through 1995, *General Hospital* has been awarded nearly 20 of the prestigious golden statuettes, including Outstanding Actor honors to Anthony Geary (Luke Spencer) in 1982 and Outstanding Actress honors to Finola Hughes (Anna Devane Lavery) in 1991. On three occasions—1981, 1984, 1995—*General Hospital* has been chosen as the Outstanding Daytime Drama. *Here's to all of the distinguished nominees and winners!*

1979 OUTSTANDING SUPPORTING ACTOR PETER HANSEN
(Lee Baldwin)
General Hospital's first-ever Emmy went to Peter Hansen for his portrayal of recovering alcoholic Lee Baldwin, who fell off the wagon when the woman he loved, Dr. Gail Adamson, refused to marry him. Peter accepted his trophy saying, "When I was in the elevator the other day, I heard someone say, 'He's a late bloomer.' Well, better late than never!"

1981 OUTSTANDING DAYTIME DRAMA
General Hospital's Executive Producer Gloria Monty is credited by many for changing the face of daytime with her fast-paced storytelling and slick production values. In 1981, Ms. Monty accepted the Emmy with praise for the cast who "do their work with love and with joy. And to two members of our cast who have carried so much of the load this year—to Tony and Genie. For all of us, thank you."

Emmy Award Winners

1981 OUTSTANDING SUPPORTING ACTRESS JANE ELLIOT
(Tracy Quartermaine)
"I won a little portable television set in a raffle when I was thirteen years old and it really doesn't prepare you for anything like this!" spoke a delighted Jane Elliot, who had left the role of Tracy several months earlier. "I am very proud to have been a part of daytime drama. I think it's the hardest job there is in show business, television, to put out five hours of daytime and I think everyone deserves a piece of this… and I'm real glad to take it home!"

1982 OUTSTANDING ACTOR ANTHONY GEARY (Luke Spencer)
During the 1981–82 season, Anthony Geary held viewers spellbound as his character, Lucas Lorenzo Spencer, vanquished the villainous Cassadines, then married and lost the girl of his dreams. This riveting portrayal earned the talented Anthony Geary his first Daytime Emmy Award.

1982 OUTSTANDING SUPPORTING ACTOR DAVID LEWIS
(Edward Quartermaine)
During his prestigious career, David Lewis appeared in some 300 to 400 stage productions, and performed in an equal number of television roles. Forty-nine years after joining Pennsylvania's Erie Playhouse as an apprentice, David was recognized by his peers with a well-deserved Daytime Emmy Award.

1989 OUTSTANDING JUVENILE FEMALE KIMBERLY McCULLOUGH
(Robin Scorpio)
Eleven-year-old Kimberly was certainly thankful upon accepting her Emmy: "Wow, I am so surprised. My heart's beating so fast… Thank you to the academy and thank you to the fans for watching and thank you so much for this too. Thank you!"

1993 OUTSTANDING SUPPORTING ACTOR GERALD ANTHONY
(Marco Dane)
Eleven years earlier, in 1982, Gerald received his first nomination for playing the same role—Marco—on ABC's *One Life to Live*. In 1993, the talented actor brought madcap Marco to *General Hospital,* where his hilarious scenes with Jane Elliot (Tracy Quartermaine) earned him Supporting Actor honors.

1995 OUTSTANDING SUPPORTING ACTRESS RENA SOFER
(Lois Cerullo)
In 1995, Rena Sofer posed backstage with the Emmy she earned for her role as the feisty, tough-as-nails girl from Brooklyn, Lois Cerullo. Moments earlier, while accepting her Emmy, Rena was quick to praise the efforts of a cast mate who was nominated in the same category. "Jackie Zeman, I think you are the best and you should be up here!"

1995 OUTSTANDING DAYTIME DRAMA

What a team! Executive Producer Wendy Riche (center) was joined by headwriter Claire Labine and producers Julie Carruthers, Francesca James and Shelly Curtis. Earlier, Ms. Riche gave an emotional acceptance speech: "Thank you members of the academy for recognizing our hard work. I feel very privileged to accept this prestigious award on behalf of the cast, staff and crew of *General Hospital*. It's been a long time coming and every one here tonight and in Los Angeles is very proud to be honored by you. When so many people come together in collaboration without ego while maintaining their own personal integrity in pursuit of our excellence it's truly a cause for celebration. Teamwork is not just a word at *General Hospital*, it's a way of life and I'm very grateful for working with all these people."

1995 OUTSTANDING WRITING—DRAMA SERIES
GENERAL HOSPITAL WRITING TEAM

The TV Academy honored the *General Hospital* writing team in 1995. Flanked by associate Headwriters Matthew Labine and Eleanor Mancusi, the distinguished headwriter Claire Labine praised "Pat Fili-Krushel, Maxine Levinson, Barbara Bloom and our beloved Wendy Riche, who never says no to us about anything. Francesca James, Julie Carruthers, Shelly Curtis. All of our directors. Everyone in production. And most particularly, the acting company of *General Hospital*, who make us want to be working on this show."

1995 OUTSTANDING YOUNGER ACTOR
JONATHAN JACKSON (Lucky Spencer)

Anthony Geary and Genie Francis (Luke and Laura) proudly flank their *General Hospital* son, Jonathan Jackson, in the backstage press room at New York's Marriott Marquis Hotel. In his impromptu acceptance speech, the talented teenager expressed his gratitude to his TV parents by pointing at Tony and Genie saying, "I want to thank them—for everything you've done for me!"

Emmy Award Winners

GH DAYTIME EMMY NOMINEES

General Hospital Daytime Emmy Nominations & *Winners

1971-72
Outstanding Achievement — Jim Young, producer

1973-74
Outstanding Daytime Drama — Jim Young, producer
Best Actor — John Beradino
Best Actor — Peter Hansen
Best Writing — Frank & Doris Hursley Bridget Dobson, Deborah Hardy
Best Actress — Rachel Ames

1974-75
Outstanding Actor — John Beradino
Outstanding Actress — Rachel Ames

1975-76
Outstanding Actor — John Beradino
Outstanding Actress — Denise Alexander

1978-79
*Outstanding Supporting Actor — Peter Hansen
Outstanding Supporting Actress — Rachel Ames
Outstanding Supporting Actress — Susan Brown

1979-80
Outstanding Actress — Leslie Charleson
Outstanding Direction — Marlena Laird, Alan Pultz, Phil Sogard

1980-81
*Outstanding Daytime Drama — Gloria Monty, producer
Outstanding Actor — Anthony Geary
*Outstanding Supporting Actress — Jane Elliot
Outstanding Supporting Actress — Jacklyn Zeman
*Outstanding Direction — Marlena Laird Alan Pultz, Phil Sogard
Outstanding Writing — Pat Falken Smith, Margaret DePriest, Sheri Anderson, Frank Salisbury, Margaret Stewart

1981-82
Outstanding Daytime Drama — Gloria Monty, producer
*Outstanding Actor — Anthony Geary
Outstanding Actor — Stuart Damon
Outstanding Actress — Leslie Charleson
*Outstanding Supporting Actor — David Lewis
Outstanding Supporting Actor — Douglas Sheehan
*Outstanding Direction — Marlena Laird
   Alan Pultz
   Phil Sogard
*Outstanding Achievement in Design Excellence — Art Director: James Elling Wood; Set Director: Mercer Barrows; Lighting Director: Grant Velie, Thomas Markle, John Zak; Costume designer: Jim O'Daniel; Makeup: Pam P.K. Cole, Vikke McCarter, Diane Lewis; Hairstyling: Katharine Kotarakos, Debbie Holmes; Music: Dominic Messinger, Jill Farren Phelps; Music Composer: Charles Paul

1982-83
Outstanding Daytime Drama — Gloria Monty, producer
Outstanding Actor — Anthony Geary
Outstanding Actor — Stuart Damon
Outstanding Actress — Leslie Charleson
Outstanding Supporting Actor — David Lewis
Outstanding Supporting Actor — John Stamos
Outstanding Supporting Actress — Robin Mattson
Outstanding Direction — Marlena Laird, Alan Pultz, Phil Sogard
Outstanding Writing — Anne Howard Bailey, A.J. Russell, Leah Laiman, Thom Racina, Jack Turley, Jeanne Glynn, Robert Guza Jr., Charles Pratt Jr., Robert Shaw

1983-84
*Outstanding Daytime Drama — Gloria Monty, producer
Outstanding Actor — Stuart Damon
Outstanding Supporting Actor — David Lewis
Outstanding Supporting Actress — Loanne Bishop
Outstanding Writing — Anne Howard Bailey, A.J. Russell, Leah Laiman, Norma Monty, Thom Racina, Doris Silverton, Robert Guza Jr., Charles Pratt Jr., Peggy Schibi, Robert Shaw

1984-85
Outstanding Daytime Drama — Gloria Monty, producer
Outstanding Supporting Actor — David Lewis
Outstanding Supporting Actress — Norma Connolly
Outstanding Juvenile/Young Man — Jack Wagner
*Outstanding Achievement in Hairstyling — Debbie Holmes, Katherine Kotarakos, Mary Guerrero, Catherine Marcotte

1985-86
Outstanding Daytime Drama — Gloria Monty, producer
Outstanding Writing — Pat Falken Smith, Norma Monty, A.J. Russell, James Reilly, Patrick Smith, Robert Guza, Doris Silverton, Robert Soderberg, Maralyn Thoma
*Outstanding Makeup — Pam P.K. Cole—Head Makeup Artist; Donna Messina, Catherine McCann Davison, Sundi Martino, Becky Bowen

1987-88
Outstanding Daytime Drama — H. Wesley Kenney, exec. prod.
Oustanding Supporting Actor — David Lewis

1988-89
Outstanding Daytime Drama — H. Wesley Kenney, exec. prod.
*Outstanding Juvenile Female — Kimberly McCullough

1989-90
Outstanding Lead Actress — Finola Hughes
Outstanding Supporting Actor — Kin Shriner
Outstanding Supporting Actress — Lynn Herring
Outstanding Supporting Actress — Mary Jo Catlett

1990-91
*Outstanding Actress — Finola Hughes
Outstanding Supporting Actor — Stuart Damon
Outstanding Supporting Actor — Kin Shriner

1991-92
Outstanding Supporting Actress — Lynn Herring

1992-93
*Outstanding Supporting Actor — Gerald Anthony
Outstanding Supporting Actor — Kin Shriner
Outstanding Supporting Actress — Jane Elliot

1993-94
Outstanding Supporting Actress — Sharon Wyatt

1994-95
*Outstanding Costume Design — Bob Miller, costume designer
*Outstanding Younger Actor — Jonathan Jackson
Outstanding Younger Actress — Kimberly McCullough
*Outstanding Supporting Actress — Rena Sofer
Outstanding Supporting Actress — Jacklyn Zeman
*Outstanding Writing — Claire Labine, Matthew Labine, Eleanor Mancusi, Ralph Ellis, Meg Bennett, Michele Val Jean, Lewis Arlt, Stephanie Braxton, Karen Harris, Judith Pinsker
*Outstanding Drama Series — Wendy Riche, exec. prod.
Outstanding Lead Actor — Brad Maule
Outstanding Lead Actress — Leslie Charleson

* = Emmy winner

CHARACTER	ACTOR	DATE	CHARACTER	ACTOR	DATE
Abagail	Ivy Bethune	1987	Benny	George Brenlin	1981
Sarah Abbott	Eileen Dietz	1980	Dr. Walt Benson	Corey Young	1987
Dr. Tracy Adams	Kim Hamilton	1969	Bernie	Leonard Nimoy	1963
Dr. Addison	Richard Guthrie	1989	Dr. Yasmine Bernoudi	Lydia Denier	1989
Sister Agatha	Fran Ryan	1989	Zelda Bernstein	Sarah Simmons	1979
Al	Angus Duncan	1987	Bertha	Corinne Carroll	1984
Albert	William Beckley	1981	Aunt Bettina	Barbara McNair	1984
Alistair	Charles Shaughnessy	1983	Betty	Penelope Branning	1991
Cynthia Allison	Carolyn Craig	1963	Clyde Bingham	Walter Mathews	1981
Xanna Ames	Karen Dyer	1994	Councilman Blake	Rick Fitts	1994
Ruby Anderson	Norma Connolly	1979	George Blyth	Bruce Gray	1987
Dr. Grant Andrews	Brian Patrick Clarke	1983	Corey Blythe	George Lyter	1987
Jonelle Andrews	Mary Ann Mobley	1979	Doris Blythe	Mimi Cozzens	1987
Mrs. Andrews	Maida Severn	1972	Billy Boggs	Tom Arnold	1994
Spence Andrews	Daniel J. Travanti	1979	Jennifer Smith Boggs	Roseanne Arnold	1994
Angela	Deborah Ryan	1982	Jack Boland	Eddie Albert	1993
Anita	Leticia Vasquez	1990	Jack Boland	Tim O'Connor	1994
Armistead	Harry Basch	1983	Dr. Borden	Basil Langton	1984
Terri Webber Arnett	Bobbie Jordan	1976	Dr. Borez	Victor Mohica	1994
Dr. Dean Arnold	James Emery	1988	Emily Bowen	Amber Rose Tamblyn	1995
Arielle Ashton	Jane Higginson	1988	Page Bowen	Riley Steiner	1995
Lord Larry Ashton	Hugo Napier	1988	Dorothy Bradley	Susan Seaforth Hayes	1963
Ned Ashton	Kurt Robin McKinney	1988	Dr. Kyle Bradley	Daniel Black	1975
Ned Ashton	Wally Kurth	1991	Dr. Arthur Bradshaw	Martin E. Brooks	1981
Cal Atkins	Leif Riddell	1992	Steffi Brand	Elissa Leeds	1984
Joseph Atkins	Scott Lincoln	1992	Brenda	Sally Kirkland	1982
Bob Ayres	Yale Summers	1964	Brenner	Steve Matteucci	1990
Dr. Alex Baker	Phillip Abbott	1987	Dr. Phil Brewer	Roy Thinnes	1963
Larry Joe Baker	Hunter von Leer	1977	Dr. Phil Brewer	Robert Hogan	1966
Larry Joe Baker	Scott Mulhern	1977	Dr. Phil Brewer	Rick Falk	1966
Larry Joe Baker	Peter D. Greene	1977	Dr. Phil Brewer	Martin West	1967
Carolyn Chandler Baldwin	Augusta Dabney	1975	Dr. Phil Brewer	Craig Huebing	1967
Dr. Tom Baldwin	Paul Savior	1967	Jessie Brewer	Emily McLaughlin	1963
Dr. Tom Baldwin	Don Chastain	1976	Nurse Mary Briggs	Anne Helm	1971
Gail Adamson Baldwin	Susan Brown	1977	D.L. Brock	David Groh	1983
Lee Baldwin	Ross Elliott	1963	Sheriff Broder	Ron Hayes	1986
Lee Baldwin	Peter Hansen	1965	Broxton	Norman Snow	1990
Meg Bentley Baldwin	Patricia Breslin	1966	Felix Buchanan	Mark Travis	1975
Meg Bentley Baldwin	Elizabeth MacRae	1969	Nicholas "Domino" Van Buren	Joseph Mascolo	1989
Scotty Baldwin	Johnnie Whitaker	1965	Douglas Burke	Adolph Caesar	1969
Scotty Baldwin	Teddy Quinn	1966	Faith Burns	April Weeden Burns	1994
Scotty Baldwin	Tony Campo	1969	Butcher	Mike Muscat	1988
Scotty Baldwin	Don Clarke	1973	Dr. Ellen Cahill	Marilyn Rockafellow	1994
Scotty Baldwin	Johnny Jensen	1974	Callahan	John Milford	1989
Scotty Baldwin	Kin Shriner	1977	Dr. Campbell	Chris Cavy	1984
Tommy Baldwin	Christine Cahill	1971	Nurse Sheila Cantillon	Stacey Cortez	1991
Ballantine	William Wintersole	1980	Carl	Stan Kirsch	1992
Rory Banks	Bruce Young	1991	Carla	Fran Harrison	1994
Dr. Michael Baranski	Leigh McCloskey	1992	Mark Carlin	Gary McGurk	1986
Al Barker	Steve Whitmore	1982	Carmichael	Ryan Cutrona	1991
Nick Barnes	John Shepard	1991	Carruthers	Paul Petersen	1988
P.I. Nick Barnes	Richard Soto	1990	Barry Carter	Ron Perkins	1995
Brenda Barrett	Vanessa Marcil	1992	Carver	Tom Durkin	1990
Harlan Barrett	Michael Cole	1991	Shep Casey	Bradley Lockerman	1990
Julia Barrett	Crystal Carson	1991	Anthony Cassadine	Andre Landzaat	1981
Roger Barrett	Nathaniel Christian	1987	Helena Cassadine	Elizabeth Taylor	1981
Amanda Barrington	Anne Jeffreys	1984	Mikkos Cassadine	John Colicos	1981
Derek Barrington	Mark Goddard	1984	Stavros Cassadine	John Martinuzzi	1983
Hillary Bates	Kaye Kittrell	1988	Victor Cassadine	Thaao Penghlis	1981
Bea	Majel Barrett	1983	Petros Cassadine	John Colicos	1985
Caroline Beale	Tyne Daly	1968	John "Jagger" Cates	Antonio Sabato Jr.	1992
Katherine Bell	Mary Beth Evans	1993	Michael "Stone" Cates	Michael Sutton	1993
Bellows	Alan Ursillo	1986	Celeste	Jane Rogers	1987
Greg Bennett	John O'Hurley	1992	Baby Angie Cerullo	Morgan Rojas	1994

CHARACTER	ACTOR	DATE	CHARACTER	ACTOR	DATE
Carmine Cerullo	John Capodice	1994	Darius	John Boyle	1989
Chuck Cerullo	Louis Lorenzo	1994	Clarence Darrow	Danny Goldman	1991
Dee Dee Cerullo	Natalie Nucci	1994	David	Kale Brown	1983
Francine Cerullo	Zena Dell Stephens	1994	David	Stan Ivar	1986
Gerald Cerullo	Michael Santorico	1994	Davis	Jim Palmer	1995
Geraldine Cerullo	Lisa Fragner	1994	Dr. Harrison Davis	Kevin Best	1988
Gloria Cerullo	Ellen Travolta	1994	Howie Dawson	Ray Girardin	1968
Grandma Cerullo	Vanna Saviati	1994	Mrs. Dawson	Maxine Stuart	1968
Grandpa Cerullo	Mike Robello	1994	Mrs. Dawson	Phyllis Hill	1970
Lois Cerullo	Rena Sofer	1993	Nurse Jane Harland Dawson	Shelby Hiatt	1968
Louie Cerullo	Tony Mangano	1994	Phoebe Dawson	Lycia Naff	1989
Mark Cerullo	Richard Tanner	1994	Natalie "Natasha" Dearborn	Melinda Cordell	1983
Noreen Cerullo	Rae Dubow	1994	Debbie	Penny Johnson	1986
Patrick Cerullo	Jason Himber	1994	Beverly DeFreest	Louise Hoven	1979
Vincent Cerullo	Drew Himber	1994	Mrs. DeFreest	Vanessa Brown	1979
Rico Chacone	John Vargas	1990	Katherine Delafield	Edie Lehmann	1989
Mrs. Chamberlain	Joy Clausen	1995	Father DeLeon	Miguel Perez	1995
Ryan Chamberlain	Jon Lindström	1992	Delfina	Nita Talbot	1981
Bobby Chandler	Ted Eccles	1975	Denise	Beth Bowles	1991
Samantha Livingston Chandler	Kimberly Beck	1975	Dennis	Collin Bernsen	1989
Samantha Livingston Chandler	Marla Pennington	1976	Desiree	Chi-en Telemaque	1990
Chantal	Chantal	1994	Paul Devore	Joe Burke	1989
Constance Chapman	Patricia North	1992	Diem	George Takei	1985
Charlie	Whitney Kershaw	1991	Roy DiLucca	Asher Brauner	1978
Chet	Brett Baxter Clark	1988	Dimitra	Linda Cristal	1988
Civil Defense Chief	Tom Rosqui	1981	Dino	Chris DeRose	1988
Nurse Betsy Chilson	Kristin Davis	1991	Sean Donely	John Reilly	1984
Christie	Cathy Wellman	1988	Tiffany Hill Donely	Sharon Wyatt	1981
Won Chu	Nathan Jung	1974	Claude Donnet	Curt Lowens	1989
Dr. Yang "Yank" Se Chung	Patrick Francis Bishop	1985	Dorothy	Susan Seaforth	1964
Cindy	Denise Galik-Furey	1989	Sister Mary Dorothy	Kathleen Freeman	1991
Cindy	Christie Clark	1992	Dot	Jane Kean	1984
Nurse Judy Clampett	Robin Blake	1964	Drago	Pierrino Mascarino	1990
Mrs. Clancy	Nora Boland	1983	Dr. Noah Drake	Rick Springfield	1981
Autumn Clayton	Linda Sanders	1987	Martine Drake	Ward Costello	1981
Clayton	Alan Hunt	1989	Val Duncan	Jack James	1994
Josh Clayton	James McNichol	1984	Allistair Dunham	Randolph Kraft	1987
Beverly Cleveland	Sue Bernard	1968	Basil Durban	Warwick Sims	1982
Brooke Bentley Clinton	Adrienne Hayes	1965	Reginald Durban	George Lazenby	1982
Brooke Bentley Clinton	Indus Arthur	1970	Barry Durbin	Peter Kelleghan	1992
Noel Clinton	Dean Harens	1965	George Durnely	Paul Comi	1982
Noel Clinton	Ron Husmann	1965	James Duvall	Arthur Roberts	1981
Uncle Clive	Ian Abercrombie	1993	Dwight	Jack Orend	1990
Lucy Coe	Lynn Herring	1986	Angela Eckert	Carol Lawrence	1991
Dr. Collins	Chris Bart	1987	Bill Eckert	Anthony Geary	1991
Dr. Kevin Collins	Jon Lindström	1993	Fred Eckert	William Boyett	1991
DVX-backed Colonel	Henry Darrow	1987	Nancy Eckert	Linda Dona	1991
Commargo	Tony Perez	1990	Sly Eckert	Glenn Walker Harris Jr.	1991
Connie Cooper	Amy Benedict	1995	JoAnne Eden	Dawn Jeffory	1980
Nurse Linda Cooper	Linda Cooper	1971	Edge	Mark St. James	1990
Lamont Corbin	George E. Carey	1977	Electra	Terrah	1990
Lamont Corbin	William Bryant	1978	Cynthia Elliot	Wesley Pfenning	1982
Michael Corbin	Ron Hale	1995	Emil	Don Reid	1989
Corinne	Melanie Vincz	1981	Ron Engle	Eddie Zamit	1980
Adela Corinthos	Maria Rangel	1995	Lisa Erikson	Kirsten Devere	1994
Sonny Corinthos	Maurice Benard	1993	Dr. Diane Erskin	Brandyn Barbara Artis	1995
Corrigan	Frank Ashmore	1981	Carla Escobar	Nia Peeples	1983
Elena Cosgrove	Rebecca Holden	1987	Nurse Esther	Davey Davison	1990
Mike Costello	Ralph Manza	1963	Eugene	Willie Carpenter	1994
Craig	Donnie Jeffcoat	1990	Beverly Fairchild	Susan Bernard	1969
Jason Craig	Ivor Francis	1980	Iris Fairchild	Peggy McCay	1967
Crenshaw	John Mansfield	1991	Cesar Faison	Anders Hove	1990
Cruz	Cassandra Gavas	1984	Cameron Faulkner	Don Matheson	1975
Crystal	Karen Fredrik	1984	Kira Faulkner	Victoria Shaw	1974
Dr. Cunningham	Frank Whiteman	1983	Rosa Fernandez	Maria Rangel	1987
Phil Cusack	Rudolph Willrich	1994	Stella Fields	Jeff Donnell	1980
Marco Dane	Gerald Anthony	1992	Mary Finnegan	Mary Jo Catlett	1988
Connie Daniels	Jenny Gago	1987	Fred Fleming	Simon Scott	1963
Dr. Mark Dante	James York	1976	Janet Fleming	Ruth Phillips	1963
Dr. Mark Dante	Gerald Gordon	1976	Nurse Dorrie Fleming	Angela Cheyne	1977
Dr. Mark Dante	Michael Delano	1976	Ralph Fletcher	Edwin Owens	1983
Kathryn Corbin Dante	Maggie Sullivan	1977	Red Flynn	Thom McFadden	1986
Mary-Ellen Dante	Lee Warrick	1976	Dr. Irma Foster	Dwan Smith	1987

CHARACTER	ACTOR	DATE	CHARACTER	ACTOR	DATE
Francis	Michael Kostroff	1995	Teddy Holmes	James Westmoreland	1972
Colette Francoise	Amy Gibson	1988	Celia Quartermaine Putnam Holt	Sherilyn Wolter	1983
Freddy	Joseph R. Sicari	1995	Charity Gatlin Holt	Gloria Carlin	1986
Valerie Freeman	Keely Shaye Smith	1989	Jimmy Lee Holt	Steve Bond	1983
Frisco	Kevin Bernhardt	1984	Eddie Holton	James DePaiva	1985
Alex Garcia	George Alvarez	1992	Evelyn Hornsby	Patricia Allison	1991
Bill Garrett	Grant Wilson	1985	Jenny Eckert Ashton Hornsby	Cheryl Richardson	1991
Dr. Gary	Michael Ensign	1994	Paul Hornsby	Paul Satterfield Jr.	1991
Gary	Blake Bahner	1992	Susan Hornsby	Irina Cashen	1991
General Gastineau	Albert Paulsen	1988	Claire Howard	Diane McBain	1988
Mrs. Van Gelder	Alice Hirson	1982	Greg Howard	John Preston	1988
Phony Van Gelder	Boyd Hollister	1982	Gregory Howard	Alan Feinstein	1988
Real Van Gelder	George Ball	1982	Aunt Iona Huntington	Janis Paige	1989
George	George Pan Andreas	1983	Jefferson Smith Hutchins	Rick Moses	1980
Officer George	E.R. Davies	1989	Ida	Andrienne LaRussa	1983
Gravel Gertie	Jane Kean	1991	Julio Iglesias	Julio Iglesias	1994
Ray Gibbons	Spencer Milligan	1987	Dr. Greta Ingstrom	Kristina Wayborn	1987
Gloria	Margaret Mason	1990	Eric Ingstrom	John Ericson	1987
Gloria	Meg Wittner	1990	Irv	Milt Kogan	1995
Gloria	Janice Lynde	1990	Irving	Anthony DeLongis	1984
Dr. Goodman	Bill Bishop	1995	Elizabeth Jackson	Joan Pringle	1994
Vic Gower	Michael Heit	1980	Jacques	Ric Young	1990
Lois' Aunt Grace	Rhoda Gemignani	1994	Dr. James	Rosemary Forsyth	1992
Alexis Grant	Julie Sanford	1995	James	Roger Lodge	1992
Alice Grant	Camila Ashland	1976	Cal Jamison	Larry Block	1978
Alice Grant	Lieux Dressler	1978	Aunt Janet	Lynn Wood	1987
David Gray	Paul Rossilli	1982	Keith Jasper	Keith Washington	1991
Florence Gray	Anne Collings	1974	Ross Jeanelle	Tony Dow	1975
Gordon Bradford Gray	Howard Sherman	1973	Jed	Gene Dynarksi	1983
Gordon Bradford Gray	Eric Server	1974	Jennings	Frank Killmond	1984
Carla Greco	Laura Herring	1990	Reginald Jennings	Stephen T. Kay	1992
Frankie Greco	Robert Fontaine	1990	Julian Jerome	Jason Culp	1988
Nadia Greco	Anne Betancourt	1990	Olivia St. John Jerome	Tonja Walker	1988
Joe Green	Gordon Ross	1985	Victor Jerome	Jack Axelrod	1987
Damon Grenville	Will Jeffries	1986	Professor Hector Jerrold	Booth Colman	1983
Gretchen	Colleen Shelley	1986	Jody	Suzanne Ekerling	1992
Sally Grimes	Jenny Sherman	1975	Joey	Christian Svensson	1990
Mrs. Edna Hadley	Lesley Woods	1977	Buster Johnson	Peter Looney	1982
Ahmed Hakeem	Erick Avari	1991	Neil Johnson	David Strenstrom	1986
Richard Halifax	Randolph Mantooth	1992	Flora Johnston	Fran Bennett	1983
David Hamilton	Jerry Ayres	1977	Harve Johnston	Vince Howard	1993
Anthony Hand	John Warner Williams	1982	"Bobbie" Spencer Meyer Jones	Jacklyn Zeman	1977
Jon Hanley	Lee Mathis	1994	BJ Jones	Brighton Hertford	1989
Hannibal	Barry Williams	1984	Baby Maxie Jones	Ashley/Jessica Clark	1992
Swede, a.k.a. Lars Hanson	Allen Fawcett	1990	Dr. Anthony Jones	Brad Maule	1984
Audrey March Hardy	Rachel Ames	1964	Felicia Cummings Jones	Kristina Wagner	1984
Dr. Simone Ravelle Hardy	Laura Carrington	1987	Frisco Jones	Jack P. Wagner	1984
Dr. Simone Ravelle Hardy	Stephanie Williams	1990	Georgie Jones	Marina & Alana Norwood	1995
Dr. Simone Ravelle Hardy	Felecia Bell	1993	Georgie Jones	Ryan & Caitlin Cohen	1995
Dr. Steve Hardy	John Beradino	1963	"Maxie" Jones	Kahley & Chelsea Cufs	1990
Dr. Tom Hardy	Matthew Ashford	1995	Maxie Jones	Elaine & Melanie Silver	1993
Tom (Baldwin) Hardy	David Comfort	1977	Maxie Jones	Robyn Richards	1993
Tom Hardy	Bradley Green	1981	Slick Jones	Eddie Ryder	1981
Tom Hardy	David Walker	1982	Tania Roskov Jones	Hilary Edson	1984
Tom Hardy	David Wallace	1987	Juan	Rick Nahera	1987
Tom Hardy Jr.	Zachary Ellington	1994	Juan	Valentino Moreno	1994
Tom Hardy Jr.	Noelle Paige	1989	Alan Jr.	Eric Kroh	1980
Harper	Ryan MacDonald	1982	General Konrad Kaluga	Rod Loomis	1981
Peter Harrell	Judson Scott	1984	Young Karen	Jessie Anne Friend	1993
Prescott Harrell	Robert Newman	1985	Dr. Irene Kassorla	Dr. Irene Kassorla	1980
Sally Armitage/Max Hedges	Chris Morley	1980	Dr. Katz	Jordan Charney	1982
Helmut	Michael Keyes Hall	1991	Peter Kaufman	Eugene Glazer	1992
Dr. Gerald Henderson	Joseph DiSante	1975	Kay	Lisa Wilcox	1987
Henderson	Stuart Silbar	1986	Jim Kelly	Jim Kelly	1992
Hendrick	Kai Wulff	1983	Joe Kelly	Douglas Sheehan	1979
Lynx Henshaw	Elizabeth Savage	1989	Paddy Kelly	Frank Parker	1980
Hernandez	Rudolfo Hoyos	1976	Rose Kelly	Loanne Bishop	1980
Beatrice Hewitt	Anne Seymour	1984	Karen Kennedy	Kandace Kuehl	1988
Dr. James Hobart	James B. Sikking	1973	Betsy Kensington	Maeve Quinlin	1993
Lisa Holbrook	Janice Heiden	1978	Jack Jr. Kensington	Michael Stadvec	1992
Jessica Holmes	Starr Andreeff	1992	Mrs. Kensington	Marni Andrews	1993
Ted Holmes	David Doyle	1985	Sen. Jack Kensington	Stan Ivar	1992
Teddy Holmes	John Gabriel	1972	Kimo	Michael Yama	1981

CHARACTER	ACTOR	DATE	CHARACTER	ACTOR	DATE
Kincaid	Richard McGonagle	1990	Angus McKay	Guy Doleman	1986
B.B. King	B.B. King	1995	Sister Mary Camellia McKay	Liz Keifer	1986
King	Chris Babers	1990	Charles McKee	Dennis Robertson	1987
Rudy King	Joe E. Tata	1987	Martha McKee	Nancy Becker-Kennedy	1987
Kinley	George Shannon	1988	Melissa McKee	Ami Dolenz	1987
Louise Knotts	Kati Powell	1988	Rita McKee	Susan Watson	1987
Mr. Kosko	James Sweeney	1995	Skeeter McKee	Jamie McEnnan	1987
Dave Koz	Dave Koz	1993	Mac McLaughlin	Bert Douglas	1977
Dr. Kramer	Kathy Masamitsu	1995	Nurse Augusta McLeod	Judith McConnell	1973
Russ Krimpton	Ray Laska	1981	Nanny McTavish	Bibi Osterwald	1982
Kris	Ken Foree	1992	Nanny McTavish	Helena Carroll	1992
Pat Lambert	Laura Campbell	1976	Medina	Jose Rey	1994
Dr. Lane	Suzanne Cortney	1991	Peggy Mercer	K. T. Stevens	1963
David Langton	Jeff Pomerantz	1992	Philip Mercer	Neil Hamilton	1963
Nikki Langton	Camille Cooper	1992	Isaac Meyer	Cliff Norton	1983
Dr. Gary Lansing	Steve Carlson	1977	Jake Meyer	Sam Behrens	1983
Dr. Gina Dante Lansing	Anna Stuart	1977	Michael	Darryl Ferrera	1989
Dr. Gina Dante Lansing	Brenda Scott	1978	Michel	Jeremiah Sullivan	1986
Dr. Gina Dante Lansing	Donna Bacalla	1978	Coleen Middleton	Joyce Jameson	1979
Howard Lansing	Richard Sarradet	1978	Milar	Quentin Gutierrez	1994
Roy Lansing	Robert Clarke	1963	Dr. Miller	Ed Platt	1963
Roy Lansing	Roy Sullivan	1964	Mickey Miller	Milton Berle	1981
Anna Devane Lavery	Camilla More	1991	Minister	James Dale Ryan	1980
Duke Lavery	Ian Buchanan	1986	Assistant D.A. Abby Mitchell	Robin Christopher	1993
Jonathan Paget/Duke Lavery	Greg Beecroft	1990	Molly	Kathy Molter	1989
Meg Lawson	Alexia Robinson	1990	Det. Monahan	Tom Ormeny	1992
Meg Lawson	Lisa Canning	1993	Madame Maia Montebello	Anita Dangler	1995
LeBlanc	Philip Benichou	1988	Chiara Montgomery	Tracey Silver	1995
Sung Cho Lee	James Hong	1983	Packy Moore	Leonard Stone	1982
Orval Leeds	Gilbert Lewis	1995	Susan Moore	Gail Rae Carlson	1978
Beatrice LeSeur	Marcella Markham	1984	Angel Moran	Joseph diReda	1986
Dr. Todd Levine	Craig Littler	1978	Felipe Morez	Sam Vlahos	1994
Chief Guy Lewis	Don Dolan	1985	Jose Morez	Kevin Castro	1994
Ivy Lief	Chase Masterson	1994	Lydia Morez	Jacky Pinol	1994
Rita Lloyd	Kim Terry	1990	Marta Morez	Julia Vera	1994
Jeremy Hewitt Logan	Philip Tanzini	1978	Miguel Morez	Ricky Martin	1994
Nurse Anne Logan	Susan Pratt	1978	D.A./Mayor Morgan	Lloyd Haines	1984
D.A. Lombardi	Michael Canavan	1986	Dr. Kyle Morgan	Grainger Hines	1990
Priscilla Longworth	Allison Hayes	1963	Dr. Erna Morris	Angel Tompkins	1985
Lori	Diane Moser	1987	Gary Morris	Gary Morris	1993
Judge Lowell	George Petrie	1978	Morris	David Burr	1995
Peggy Lowell	Deanna Lund	1976	Chuck Morrison	John Medici	1986
Lucas	Nicholas Moody	1989	Dave Morrison	Sam Sablack	1968
Luis	Carlos Cantu	1992	Johnny Morrissey	Miles McNamara	1982
Charlie Lutz	Ken Smolka	1980	Maureen Morrissey	Carol Bagdasarian	1982
Emma Lutz	Merrie Lynn Ross	1981	Joey Moscini	James Morrison	1991
Mac	Sid Conrad	1989	Decker Moss	Michael Watson	1989
Brett Madison	James Horan	1985	Muriel	Carol Androsky	1993
Mai-Lin	Virginia Ann Lee	1974	Mouse	Melissa Hayden	1989
Claudio Maldonado	Sky Dumont	1989	Mouth	Garrett Morris	1991
Gregory Malko	Joe Lambie	1983	D.A. Chase Murdock	Ivan Bonar	1966
Melissa Manchester	Melissa Manchester	1994	Caroline Murray	Anne Wyndham	1972
Marge	Mae Clark	1963	Kent Murray	Mark Hamill	1972
Marino	Norma Maldonado	1995	Augie Nash	Rick Grassi	1983
Officer Marino	Robert Neary	1991	Eric Nash	Keith Amos	1990
Madolyn Markham	June Havoc	1990	Nathan	Shawn Donahue	1987
Burt Marshall	Robert Hogan	1973	Dr. Nelson	Pat Renella	1980
Kate Marshall	Monica Gayle	1976	Mrs. Nelson	Ann Morrison	1971
Dr. Ken Martin	Hunt a.k.a. Jack Powers Betts	1963	Nelson	Steve Stapenhorst	1995
Father Martin	Charles Boswell	1992	Nick	Ric Mancini	1989
Marty	Joseph Whipp	1991	Nina	Monica Hylande	1989
The Magus/Masters	Peter Breck	1982	Niven	George McDaniel	1982
Wendy Masters	Terri Hawkes	1990	Nora	Sandra McKnight	1989
Judge Matson	Jason Wingreen	1991	Noriko	Pat Li	1992
Andy Matthews	Ron Michael Hays	1987	Dr. Kevin O'Connor	Kevin Bernhardt	1985
Susan Matthews	Ebonie Smith	1987	O'Connor	Tom Epper	1995
Beth Maynard	Michele Conaway	1975	Patrick O'Connor	Guy Mack	1985
Elizabeth Maynard	Joan Tompkins	1977	Terry Brock O'Connor	Robyn Bernard	1984
Mayor	James Mendenhall	1983	Jimmy O'Herlihy	Nicholas Walker	1989
David McAllister	Patrick Strong	1989	Agent O'Reilly	Billie Hayes	1981
David McAllister	Geoffrey Scott	1989	Finian O'Toole	Arte Johnson	1991
Martina McBride	Martina McBride	1994	Olin	Beulah Quo	1985
Mountie McGraw	Christopher Murray	1995	Oliver	Neil Hunt	1982

CHARACTER	ACTOR	DATE	CHARACTER	ACTOR	DATE
Connor Olivera	Michael Lynch	1991	Ray	Cameron Bancroft	1991
Ancient One	Keye Luke	1985	Remondo	Darryl Roach	1990
Ric Ortega	Bernard White	1992	Jim Richardson	Jay Geber	1978?
brothel owner	Ron Reagan Jr.	1989	Madelyn Richmond	Sheila MacRae	1991
Victoria Parker	Terri Garber	1993	Mayor Richmond	Frank Aletter	1991
Blackie Parrish	John Stamos	1982	Officer Rick	Michael O'Connell	1994
Nigel Penny-Smith	Bernard Fox	1981	Ripley	Don Stark	1988
Percy	Edmund Gilbert	1982	Hernando Rivera	Ismael Carlo	1994
Dr. Tony Perelli	Antony Ponzini	1980	Lily Rivera	Lilly Melgar	1994
Dr. Tony Perelli	Michael Baseloni	1980	Nurse Doris Roach	Meg Wylie	1975
Paloma Perez	Emma Samms	1992	Roger	Jeremy Davies	1992
Perez	Raul Martinez	1994	Casey Rogers	Bradley Lockerman	1990
Dr. Perry	Gene Collins	1990	Roland	Roy Stuart	1984
Mrs. Perry	Anna Burger	1991	Rolf	David Newer	1995
Patti Peters	Andrea Walters	1995	Simon Romero	Frank Runyeon	1992
Police Commissioner	John Ingle	1986	Ron	Eddie Gammit	1980
Phillipe	Gilles Kohler	1982	Dan Rooney	Frank Maxwell	1978
Claudia Johnston Phillips	Bianca Ferguson	1978	Boris Roskov	William MacMillan	1984
Dr. Bryan Phillips	Todd Davis	1978	Ross	Marcus Smythe	1990
Eddie Phillips	Sammy Davis Jr.	1982	Yvonne Rousseau	Corinne Calvet	1987
Reverend Phillips	Charles Walker	1994	Rowdy	R.J. Williams	1989
Shirley Pickett	Roberta Leighton	1983	Rudolpho	Mike Henry	1988
Jonathan Pierce	Richard Venture	1991	Jonathan Russell	John Martin	1991
Pilgrim	Hurd Hatfield	1986	Leo Russell	John Callahan	1984
Dr. Henry Pinkham	Peter Kilman	1969	Jack Russo	Anthony Pennello	1994
Hank Pinkham	Maurice Marson	1969	Dr. Malcolm Rutledge	John Denos	1987
Nurse Sharon McGillis Pinkham	Sharon DeBord	1965	Ryan	David Goss	1989
Dr. Porchenko	Philip Bruns	1984	Sadie	Viola Kate Stimpson	1990
Mrs. Porchenko	Lidia Kristen	1984	Dottie Sandford	Patience Cleveland	1987
Dr. John Prentice	Barry Atwater	1964	Armando Santiago	Richard Miro	1994
Polly Prentice	Catherine Ferrar	1965	Dolores Santiago	Margarita Franco	1994
Polly Prentice	Jennifer Billingsley	1966	Saura	Monte Landis	1985
Nurse Georgia Price	Lisa Figus	1989	Nurse Schmidt	Barbara Schillaci	1990
Charlie Prince	Michael Tylo	1989	Wolfgang Von Schuler	William H. Bassett	1987
Priscilla	Sally Prager	1991	Maria Schuller	Maria Perschy	1977
Pritchett	Gene N. Wells	1987	Anna Devane Lavery Scorpio	Finola Hughes	1985
Carol Pulaski	Robin Curtis	1991	Holly Sutton Scorpio	Emma Samms	1982
Hank Pulaski	Larry Pennell	1991	Mac Scorpio	John J. York	1991
Marge Pulaski	Sue Anne Langdon	1991	Robert Scorpio	Tristan Rogers	1980
Patrick Pulaski	Noah Blake	1991	Robin Soltini Scorpio	Kimberly McCullough	1985
Dr. Grant Putnam	Brian Patrick Clarke	1984	Joe Scully	Robert Miano	1995
(maid) Quartermaine	Michelle Buffone	1995	Serge	Mark Chaet	1989
Alan Jr. Quartermaine	Abraham Geary	1983	Lorena Sharpe	Shelley Taylor Morgan	1984
Alan Jr. Quartermaine	Jason Marsden	1986	Ian Shelton	John Sanderford	1982
Alan Jr. Quartermaine	Christopher Ren Nelson	1988	Colton Shore	Scott Thompson Baker	1988
Alan Jr. Quartermaine	Justin Whalin	1989	D.A. Michael Shultz	Dennis Bailey	1991
Alan Jr. Quartermaine	Gerald Hopkins	1991	Dr. Silva	William Marquez	1989
Alan Jr. Quartermaine	Sean Kanan	1993	Harry Silver	Michael Fairman	1994
Alexandria Quartermaine	Renee Anderson	1980	Richard Simmons	Richard Simmons	1979
Annabelle (dog) Quartermaine	Treasure	1994	Warren Simon	Michael Muser	1992
Betsy Quartermaine	Peggy Walton Walker	1988	Charlene Simpson	Maree Cheatham	1987
Dr. Alan Quartermaine	Stuart Damon	1977	Dr. Eric Simpson	Brandon Hooper	1991
Dr. Monica Quartermaine	Leslie Charleson	1977	Mark Simpson	Gary Frank	1973
Edward Quartermaine	David Lewis	1978	Remi Sinclair	Suzanne Tara	1990
Edward Quartermaine	Les Tremayne	1988	Jack Slater	Randall England	1984
Edward Quartermaine	John Ingle	1993	Myrna Slaughter	Beverlee McKinsey	1994
Herbert Quartermaine	Will B. Hunt	1987	Damian Smith	Leigh McCloskey	1993
Jason Quartermaine	Quinn Carlson	1982	Frank Smith	George Gaynes	1980
Jason Quartermaine	Bryan Beck	1983	Frank Smith	Mitchell Ryan	1993
Jason Quartermaine	Steve Burton	1991	Jennifer Smith	Lisa Marie	1980
Lila Quartermaine	Anna Lee	1978	Pop Snyder	Milton Selzer	1979
Lila Quartermaine	Meg Wylie	1994	Filomena Soltini	Argentina Brunetti	1985
Quentin Quartermaine	Alan Miller	1983	young Sonny	Tyler Parker	1995
Tracy Quartermaine	Jane Elliot	1978	Nurse Jade Soong	Tia Carrere	1985
Tracy Quartermaine	Christine Jones	1989	Foster (dog) Spencer	Foster	1994
Kylie Quinlan	Brynn Thayer	1994	Laura Spencer	Genie Francis	1976
Rakeem	Ivory Ocean	1994	Lesley Lu Spencer	Kerrianne & Amanda Harrington	1994
Big Ralph	Chuck Mitchell	1981	Lesley Lu Spencer	Amanda Harrington	1994
Lord Rama	Kabir Bedi	1983	Lucky Spencer	Jonathan Jackson	1993
Maria Ramirez	June Lockhart	1984	Luke Spencer	Anthony Geary	1978
Capt. Burt Ramsey	Bob Hastings	1979	Nurse Stacy	Robin Eisenmann	1981
Vanessa Raphael	Tracy Brooks Swope	1983	Max Van Stadt	Jon Cypher	1981
Dr. Pauline Ravelle	Norma Donaldson	1987	Noel Van Stadt	Rosina Widdowson-Reynolds	1981

CHARACTER	ACTOR	DATE	CHARACTER	ACTOR	DATE
Stan	Saul Stein	1986	Dr. Wallace	Liam Sullivan	1988
Milton Stanis	Paul Carr	1994	Ling Wang	George Chiang	1974
Cheryl Stansbury	Jennifer Anglin	1988	Bradley Ward	Aaron Seville	1994
Lucas Stansbury	Kenny & Chuckie Gravino	1989	Bradley Ward	Aaron Seville	1995
Lucas Stansbury	Jay Sacane	1994	David Ward	Ron Canada	1994
Star	Karen Jablons-Alexander	1991	David Ward	Rif Hutton	1995
General Stark	John Hertzler	1990	Idios Ward	Joyce Douglas	1994
Professor Russell Stern	Beau Billingslea	1991	Isobel Ward	Michelle Davison	1994
Congressman Sterner	John Carter	1981	Justus Ward	Joseph C. Phillips	1994
Nurse Stevens	Maray Ayres	1989	Keesha Ward	Senait Ashenafi	1994
Stockton	Michael Ayr	1992	Margaret Ward	Karlotta Nelson	1994
Lt. Stoddard	Peter Miller	1980	Mary Mae Ward	Rosalind Cash	1994
Young Stone	Tex Weiner	1993	Roy Ward	Reggie Harper	1994
Dr. Joel Stratton	Barry Coe	1974	Randy Washburn	Mark Miller	1964
Dr. Joel Stratton	Rod McCary	1974	Bill Watson	Richard Caine	1979
Owen Stratton	Joel Marston	1974	Dr. Jeff Webber	Richard Dean Anderson	1976
Dr. Adam Streeter	Brett Halsey	1967	Dr. Lesley Webber	Denise Alexander	1973
Jill Streeter	Karen Purcil	1977	Dr. Monica Webber	Patsy Rahn	1976
Nurse Strickland	Nancy Fish	1991	Dr. Rick Webber	Michael Gregory	1976
Dr. Buzz Stryker	Don Galloway	1985	Dr. Rick Webber	Chris Robinson	1978
Sandy Stryker	Yvette Nipar	1986	Ginny Blake Webber	Judith Chapman	1984
Suki	Dustin Nguyen	1985	Heather Grant Webber	Georganne LaPiere	1976
Kathy Summers	Lisa Lindgren	1980	Heather Grant Webber	Mary O'Brien	1977
Gee Sung	April Hong	1985	Heather Grant Webber	Robin Mattson	1980
Susie	Lisa Capps	1993	Mike Webber	David Mendenhall	1980
Algernon Sutton	Nicolas Hammond	1985	Rick (Jr.) Webber	C. Balme	1986
Charles Sutton	Mark Roberts	1982	Steve Lars Webber	Martin Hewitt	1979
Louise "Lou" Swenson	Danielle von Zerneck	1983	Al Weeks	Tom Brown	1963
Ambassador Tabris	Henry Darrow	1982	Angie Costello Weeks	Jana Taylor	1963
Jennifer Talbot	Martha Scott	1985	Eddie Weeks	Craig Curtis	1963
Tangeneva	Thalamus Rasulala	1989	Eddie Weeks	Doug Lambert	1965
Dominique Taub	Tawny Fere Ellis	1990	Mrs. Weeks	Lenore Kensington	1963
Dominique Taub	Shell Danielson	1991	Nurse Lucille March Weeks	Lucille Wall	1963
Leopold Taub	Charles Lucia	1991	Nurse Lucille March Weeks	Mary Grace Canfield	1973
Diana Maynard Taylor	Valerie Starrett	1969	Dan Weene	Rod Wiley	1995
Diana Maynard Taylor	Brooke Bundy	1973	Samantha Welles	Dawn Merrick	1985
Dr. Peter Taylor	Paul Carr	1969	Birdie Wells	Tricia Donahue	1987
Dr. Peter Taylor	Craig Huebing	1969	Wendy	Marilyn Stoley	1989
Martha Taylor	Brioni Farrel	1977	Karen Wexler	Cari Shayne	1992
Martha Taylor	Jennifer Peters	1978	Rhonda Wexler	Denise Galik-Furey	1992
Mrs. Taylor	Louise Fitch	1992	Agnes Whitaker	Beth Peters	1980
P.J. Taylor	Robert Betzel	1977	Whit Whitaker	Hank Underwood	1980
Jackie Templeton	Demi Moore	1982	Sylvia Whitby	Linda Borgeson	1984
Laura Templeton	Janine Turner	1982	Phillip Wilder	Kevin Bash	1995
Tessie	Elsa Raven	1986	Kate Wilkerson	Shirley Jordan	1994
Randall Thompson	Chuck Wagner	1987	Gina Williams	Nikki Cox	1993
Tim	Ed Beechner	1988	Mitch Williams	Christopher Pennock	1978
Toby	Gary Carpenter	1981	Mr. Williams	Stephen Poletti	1993
Crane Tolliver	Wiley Harker	1983	Mrs. Williams	Jean Pflieger	1993
Hal Tomlinson	Garrison True	1981	Willie	Gregory Croom	1986
Toughie	Kevin Hagen	1986	Dr. Bunny Willis	Beau Kayzer	1983
Constance Townley	Jeanna Michaels	1983	Mel Wilson	Dawson Mays	1982
Dr. Tremaine	William Glover	1984	Denise Wilton	Julie Adams	1968
Trixie	Darlene Conley	1984	Dawn Winthrop	Kim Valentine	1988
Capt. Turner	Bruce Economou	1994	Dawn Winthrop	Sharon Case	1989
Heather Turner	Julie Mannix	1972	Dawn Winthrop	Lisa Fuller	1990
Val	Tuesday Knight	1987	Dawn Winthrop	Jennifer Guthrie	1990
Vanessa	Donna Leavy	1991	Prunella Witherspoon	Chantal Contouri	1988
Baron Varony	Ralph Drischell	1987	Bill Woods	George Nejame	1981
Veronica	Robyn Millan	1987	Fran Woods	Udana Power	1988
Vince	Michael Savage	1986	Kim Wu	Steven Leigh	1985
Amy Vining	Cari Ann Warder	1975	Mr. Wu	Ali Keong	1985
Amy Vining	Shell Kepler	1979	Dr. Wyatt	Al Micacchio	1995
Barbara Vining	Judy Lewis	1975	Judge Young	John Pettlock	1995
Jason Vining	Richard Rust	1975	Judge Young	John Frederick-Jones	1995
Jason Vining	Jonathan Carter	1975	Yves	Garrick Dowhen	1986
Laura Vining	Stacey Baldwin	1975	George Z	Brian Donovan	1995
Vito	Joe Taggart	1988	Danny Zacharowitz	David Gianopoulos	1995
Dusty Walker	Shaun Cassidy	1987	Zack	Michaelangelo Kowalski	1987

GENERAL HOSPITAL

Show Credits

Created by: Frank & Doris Hursley

Executive Producer: Wendy Riche

Supervising Producer: Francesca James

Producer: Julie Carruthers

Consulting Producer: Shelley Curtis

Directed by: Joseph Behar, Shelley Curtis, William Ludel, Scott McKinsey, Alan Pultz

Headwriter: Claire Labine

Written by: Claire Labine, Matthew Labine, Eleanor Mancusi, Ralph Ellis, Meg Bennett, Michele Val Jean, Lewis Arlt, Stephanie Braxton, Karen Harris, Judith Pinsker

Coordinating Producer: Jerry Balme

Associate Producer: Marty Vagts

Associate Directors: Ron Cates, Carol Scott, Christine T. Magarian

Casting Director: Mark Teschner, C.S.A.

Production Designer: Matthew C. Jacobs

Art Director: Mercer B. Barrows

Assistant Art Directors: Jim Jones, Daniel Proett

Production Continuity: Jeffrey Rabin

Production Associates: Brooke Eaton, Christopher Mullen

Production Office Coordinator: Deborah A. Genovese

Script Continuity: Elizabeth Korte

Associate Casting Director: Lisa Snedeker Booth

Casting Assistant: Gwen Hillier

Assistant to the Head Writer: Jane Greenstein

Writers' Assistants: Davis Goldschmid, Marc Alan Dabrusin, George Doty IV

Assistant to the Executive Producer: Susan Brandes

Assistant to the Producers: Kathy Wetherell

Production Assistant: Dania L. Guthrie

Production Managers: John H. McElveney, Bob Piatak

Business Manager: Hilda Recio

Technical Manager: Randy Hooper

Technical Directors: John Cochran, Jim Ralston, Geri Bucci

Lighting Directors: Mark Buxbaum, Roger Dalton, Tom Markle

Audio: Jan Hoag

Sound Effects: Sandy Masone

Music Mixer: Gary Bressler

Senior Video: Leonard Price, Chuck Pharis

Cameras: Dale Carlson, Dale Walsh, Harlie Outler, Ralph Alcocer, D.J. Diomedes, Al DeLaGarza, Ron Brooks, Blair White

Boom Operators: Willie Earl, Fred Fryrear, Sylvia Almstadt, Chris Tyson, Pauletter Croknit

Videotape Editors: Donald Smith, Stephen Burch, Jack Moody, Fritz Curtis

Videotape Recording: John Fernandez, Frank Corricello, Eddie Joseph, Miguel Cancino, Daniel Viveros

Electronic Maintenance: Albert O. Peck Jr., Cas Anchette, Nelson Dearborn

Stage Managers: Dick Amos, Craig McManus, Douglas Hayden

Costume Designers: Bob Miller, C.D.G., Steve Howard

Assistant Costume Designer: Nancy L. Konardy

Costume Supervisors: Jackie Eifert, Phil Wayne

Make-up: Donna Messina Armogida, Rose Davison, Cyndilee Rice

Hair Stylists: Robin Rollins, Catherine Marcotte, Kimber Lee Anderson

Original Music: Marty Davich

Music Directors: R.C. Cates, Paul F. Antonelli

Publicity: Scott Barton

Theme Music: "Faces of the Heart" By Dave Koz, Jeff Koz, Jack Urbont

Videotaped at ABC Television Hollywood

INDEX

Monty, Gloria, 260, 287
Moore, Demi, 252
Morris, Gary, 256

N

Nimoy, Leonard (Bernie), 253

P

Phillips, Joseph (Justus Ward), 270

R

Reilly, John (Sean Donely), 260, 269, 280
Richardson, Cheryl (Jenny Eckert), 276-277
Riche, Wendy, 196, 198, 254, 264, 289
Robinson, Chris (Dr. Rick Webber), 281
Rogers, Tristan (Robert Scorpio), 273, 279
Rollins, Robin, 267
Roseanne (Jennifer), 254

S

Sabato, Antonio, Jr. (John "Jagger" Cates), 262, 276, 284
Samms, Emma (Holly Scorpio), 260, 285
Satterfield, Paul, Jr. (Paul Hornsby), 277, 281
Savior, Paul (Dr. Tom Baldwin), 275, 283
Shayne, Cari (Karen Wexler), 262, 269-270
Sheehan, Doug (Joe Kelly), 271, 281
Simmons, Richard (Richard Simmons), 257, 271, 276, 283, 284, 288
Social relevance, stories with, 124, 172, 185
Springfield, Rick, 255
Stamos, John, 257

T

Taylor, Elizabeth (Helena Cassadine), 212, 252, 255
Teschner, Mark, 266
Thinnes, Roy (Dr. Phil Brewer), 270
Travanti, Daniel J. (Spence Andrews), 255
Turner, Janine, 252

V

Vagts, Marty, 264

W

Wagner, Kristina (Felicia Jones), 265, 273, 278, 281
Weddings
  Ned "Eddie Maine" Ashton and Lois Cerullo, 241, 242, 243
    Ned Ashton and Jenny Eckert, 241
  Lee Baldwin and Caroline Chandler, 235
  Scotty Baldwin and Laura Webber, 236
  D. L. Brock and Bobbie Spencer, 238
  John "Jagger" Cates and Karen Wexler, 242
  Sean Donely and Tiffany Hill, 240
  Cameron Faulkner and Dr. Lesley Williams, 235
  Dr. Steve Hardy and Audrey March, 236
  Dr. Tom Hardy and Dr. Simone Ravelle, 240
  Frisco Jones and Felicia Cummings, 239
  Dr. Tony Jones and Bobby Meyer, 240
  Duke Lavery and Anna Devane, 239
  Audrey March and Dr. Steve Hardy, 234
  Jake Meyer and Bobbie Brock, 239

Weddings (cont.)
  Dr. Kevin O'Connor and Terry Brock, 237
  Bryan Phillips and Claudia Johnston, 237
  Grant Putnam and Celia Quartermaine, 238
  Dr. Alan Quartermaine and Lucy Coe, 242
  Robert Scorpio and Anna Lavery, 241
  Robert Scorpio and Holly Sutton, 236
  Colton Shore and Felicia Jones, 240
  Bobbie Spencer, 238
  Luke Spencer and Jennifer Smith, 236
  Luke Spencer and Laura Spencer, 244-245
  Dr. Peter Taylor and Jessie Brewer, 235
  Dr. Rick Webber and Dr. Lesley Faulkner, 237
  Al Weeks and Lucille March, 235
West, Martin (Dr. Phil Brewer), 273, 286
Wyatt, Sharon (Tiffany Hill), 272, 275

Y

York, John J. (Mac Scorpio), 275, 286

Z

Zeman, Jacklyn (Bobbie Jones), 270, 273, 277, 280

PHOTO CREDITS

All photos and video images are copyright © Capital Cities/ABC, Inc. and are provided courtesy Capital Cities/ABC, Inc. Photographer credits as available are as follows:

83	Erik Hein
121	Jerry Fitzgerald
124	Jerry Fitzgerald
142	Craig Sjodin
143	Jerry Fitzgerald
144	Jerry Fitzgerald
146	Jerry Fitzgerald
149	Craig Sjodin
150	Craig Sjodin
153	Craig Sjodin
155	Craig Sjodin
156	Sharon Beard
157	Craig Sjodin
158	Craig Sjodin
159	Daniel Watson
160	Craig Sjodin
162	Daniel Watson
163	Craig Sjodin
166	Craig Sjodin
170	Craig Sjodin
173	Craig Sjodin
174	Craig Sjodin
175	Daniel Watson
176	Craig Sjodin

184	bottom: Cathy Blaivas
186	Craig Sjodin
188	Cathy Blaivas
189	Cathy Blaivas
190	Cathy Blaivas
193	Wren Maloney
196	Craig Sjodin
197	top right, Donna Svennevik bottom left, Donna Svennevik bottom right, Jerry Fitzgerald
198	all photos, Craig Sjodin
199	top left, Craig Sjodin bottom, Erik Hein
200	top, Craig Sjodin
201	all photos, Craig Sjodin
202	right, J. Marshall
203	top left, Bob D'Amico right, Erik Hein
204	all photos, Craig Sjodin
205	all photos, Craig Sjodin
206	D. Hyman
207	top, J. Marshall bottom left, Erik Hein bottom right, Bob D'Amico
208	top, Sharon Beard bottom, Farber
209	left and top right, Craig Sjodin bottom right, Bob D'Amico
210	Erik Hein inset, Craig Sjodin

211   top inset, Jerry Fitzgerald
bottom middle, Donna Svennevik
bottom right, Craig Sjodin

214   top right, Erik Hein

215   top left and bottom, Craig Sjodin

216   top, Bob D'Amico

217   bottom left, Erik Hein
bottom right, J. Marshall

218   top right, Craig Sjodin

219   top and bottom left, Craig Sjodin
right, Erik Hein

220   top left, Jerry Fitzgerald
bottom left and right, Craig Sjodin

221   top left, Bob D'Amico
top right, Rick Rowell
bottom, Steve Granitz

224   bottom right, Cathy Blaivas

225   top left and bottom, Bob D'Amico

226   top, Erik Hein
bottom left, Brigitte Wiltzery
bottom middle, Bob D'Amico

227   left, Steve Granitz
top and bottom right, Craig Sjodin

228   all photos, Bob D'Amico

229   Craig Sjodin

230   left and top right, Craig Sjodin

231   top left and right, Bob D'Amico

232   top, Craig Sjodin
bottom, Erik Hein

233   top left, Erik Hein
bottom left, Bob D'Amico
inset top left, Craig Sjodin
inset top right, Erik Hein
inset bottom left, Jerry Fitzgerald

237   bottom, Steve Fenn

239   left and top right, Craig Sjodin
bottom right, Bob D'Amico

240   top left, Ken Schauer
bottom left, Jerry Fitzgerald
top and bottom right, Craig Sjodin

241   top left, Jerry Fitzgerald
right, Craig Sjodin

242   all photos, Craig Sjodin

243   Donna Svennevik

244   middle, Bob D'Amico
top and bottom right, Erik Hein

245   top and middle left, Erik Hein

246   Erik Hein

247   top left and bottom, Erik Hein

248   top left, Erik Hein
bottom left, Jerry Fitzgerald
bottom right, Craig Sjodin

249   top left and right and bottom right, Craig Sjodin
bottom left, Wren Maloney

250   top and bottom left and bottom right, Craig Sjodin
top right, Cathy Blaivas

251   top left and middle right, Bob Long
bottom right, Cathy Blaivas

252   left, J. Marshall
right, Erik Hein

253   top, Erik Hein

254   bottom, Michael Yoush

255   top right, Bob D'Amico
bottom left, Erik Hein

256   top, Jim Warren
bottom left and right, Wren Maloney

257   top left, Craig Sjodin

258   top, Erik Hein

260   top right, Erik Hein

261   inset top, Bob D'Amico
bottom, Craig Sjodin

262   top, Steve Granitz
bottom left, Cathy Blaivas
bottom right, Craig Sjodin

Photo Credits